APPETITES AND ANXIETIES

CONTEMPORARY APPROACHES TO FILM AND TELEVISION SERIES

A complete listing of the books in this series can be found online at wsupress.wayne.edu

APPETITES AND ANXIETIES

FOOD, FILM, AND THE POLITICS OF REPRESENTATION

CYNTHIA BARON,
DIANE CARSON, MARK BERNARD

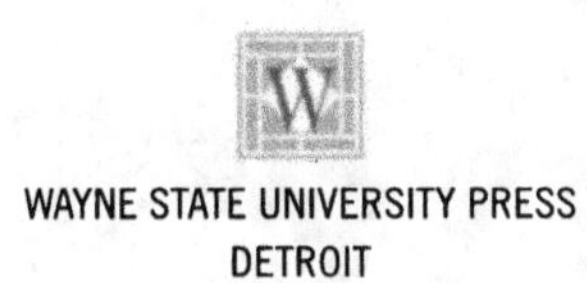

WAYNE STATE UNIVERSITY PRESS
DETROIT

18 17 16 15 14 5 4 3 2 1

Library of Congress Cataloging-in-Publication Data

Baron, Cynthia.
Appetites and anxieties : food, film, and the politics of representation / Cynthia Baron, Diane Carson, Mark Bernard.
pages cm. — (Contemporary approaches to film and media series)
Includes bibliographical references and index.
Includes filmography.
ISBN 978-0-8143-3431-7 (pbk. : alk. paper) — ISBN 978-0-8143-3805-6 (ebook)
1. Food in motion pictures. 2. Motion pictures—Social aspects. 3. Documentary films—History and criticism. I. Carson, Diane, 1954– II. Bernard, Mark.
III. Title.

PN1995.9.F65B38 2013
791.43'6564—dc23

2013018443

Typeset by Newgen North America
Composed in Dante MT

CONTENTS

ACKNOWLEDGMENTS

I first want to thank my colleagues Diane Carson and Mark Bernard for their adventurous spirits and unfailing enthusiasm. Thanks also to the many food scholars who inspired us, in particular Carole Counihan and Warren Belasco. Special thanks to Lucy Long, whose 2001 NEH "Food as a Humanities Subject" seminars suggested ways that food studies could enhance studies of film, and to the Institute for the Study of Culture and Society for the 2011 fellowship that facilitated research. Sincere thanks to family and friends, especially Emily Baron and Donald McQuarie, for their patience, humor, and interest in film and good food.

—CYNTHIA BARON

Throughout this exciting, educational project, I've benefitted enormously from the camaraderie of my hard-working, inspirational co-authors, who have enhanced every aspect of this venture. I thank my best friend and spouse Wil Loy for hours of stimulating conversations about food, film, and life. I also thank my dear friend Ann Schulz for generously sharing her diverse food stylist experiences. Her knowledge about food never ceases to amaze me. I deeply appreciate my friend and fellow film reviewer Martha K. Baker, who scrupulously read early versions of my work. And thanks, finally, to my many associates who offered their keen insights concerning food in film and in their lives.

—DIANE CARSON

I thank my co-authors, Cynthia Baron and Diane Carson, for inviting me along on this amazing journey. Thanks to Sean Moncrieff and all the folks at NewsTalk Ireland for having me on the air to discuss work featured in this volume. Thanks to Dan Charles at NPR and Stephen Rust at the Ecomedia Studies blog for sharing my work on food and film with a larger audience. Thanks to Pamela Robertson Wojcik and everybody at Notre Dame who organized the Food Networks conference in January 2012. Finally, thanks to Fred and Linda Bernard, Bill, Pam, and Brandon Davis, and especially Hope Bernard, who continues to inspire and sustain me.

—MARK BERNARD

We would all like to express our appreciation to filmmaker Daniel E. Williams for doing the frame captures and, finally, to Annie Martin, Barry Keith Grant, and everyone at Wayne State University Press for their faith in this project and for making it a reality.

Earlier versions of sections of this work were previously published as "Food and Gender in *Bagdad Cafe,*" *Food and Foodways* 11:1 (2003) (reprinted by permission of Taylor & Francis); "Dinner and a Movie: Analyzing Food and Film," *Food, Culture & Society* 9:1 (2006) (reprinted by permission of *Food, Culture & Society*); "Cannibalism, Class, and Power," *Food, Culture & Society* 14:3 (2011) (reprinted by permission of *Food, Culture & Society*); and "Transgressing Boundaries: From Sexual Abuse to Eating Disorders in *301/302,*" in *Seoul Searching: Culture and Identity in Contemporary Korean Cinema,* ed. Frances Gateward (Albany: State University of New York Press, 2007) (reprinted by permission of the State University of New York, All Rights Reserved).

Introduction

The Cultural and Material Politics of Food Representations in Film

Films depend on food. Slapstick comedies need pie-throwing scenes that escalate into brawls. To build their resolve, tough guys in westerns and action films down shots of cheap liquor. Gangsters talk with their mouths full. Noir detectives drink alone. Comradeship leads soldiers and officers to share food and drink. Melodramas require disastrous, sometimes heart-warming family dinners. Romantic comedies benefit from chocolates.

Mainstream American cinema is a mosaic of memorable food scenes. In *Citizen Kane* (Welles, 1941), the breakfast scene montage illustrates the deterioration of the marriage between Charles (Orson Welles) and Emily Kane (Ruth Warrick). In *The Godfather* (Coppola, 1972), Don Corleone (Marlon Brando) aims to amuse his grandson but inadvertently shows himself to be the frightening monster he really is when he makes fangs out of orange peels. In *Pulp Fiction* (Tarantino, 1994), hit men Jules (Samuel L. Jackson) and Vincent (John Travolta) reveal their whimsical worldviews as they discuss the European names for American fast-food burgers. Food is important in remarkable but obscure international films. In *Jeanne Dielman* (1975), Belgian director Chantal Akerman highlights the drudgery of cooking by showing meatloaf preparation in real time. In *Bedevil* (1993), Australian Aboriginal filmmaker Tracey Moffatt parodies a cooking show to comment on the troubled legacy of colonial rule. In John Crowley's Irish film *Intermission* (2003), the characters' multipurpose use of brown sauce marks them first as losers and then as inventive extemporizers.

These examples, which likely bring others to mind, are reminders that food regularly functions as a meaningful component of films' mise-en-scène. Filmmakers rely on food to convey characters' personalities, cultural backgrounds, social status, and evolving personal relationships. As cultural anthropologists Carole Counihan and Penny Van Esterik point out: "Food touches everything" (3). People cannot transcend those connections. Instead, food is "the foundation of every economy" (Counihan and Van Esterik 3), and the institutions of power that shape a society's food production and distribution systems impact all aspects of human life. Food is intimately bound up with social power, and thus all interactions involving food are necessarily laden with the implications of social status, cultural difference, ethnicity, sexuality, and other markers of identity. Even in private space, converging and disparate cultural forces shape people's participation in meals and meal systems that reflect "an endlessly evolving enactment of gender, family and community relationships" (Counihan and Van Esterik 3).

Analyzing reasons that food has become an important cultural and research topic, Counihan and Van Esterik note that "feminism and women's studies have contributed to the growth of food studies by legitimating a domain of human behavior so heavily associated with women over time and across cultures" (1–2). They highlight "the politicization of food and the expansion of social movements linked to food" and suggest that studies of food politics have helped to create "an increased awareness of the links between consumption and production" (2). Counihan and Van Esterik find that the "explosion of the field of food studies" since the early 1980s parallels the increase in food journals, the appearance of food films, the rise of food documentaries, and the emergence of "food movements that promote organic, local, fairly traded, and slow food," which together challenge "what fast, processed food has done to our bodies and communities" (2).

Scholars contributing to the rapid growth of the food studies field propose that people in consumer society should think seriously about food. Warren Belasco points out that "Food is important. In fact, nothing is more basic" (*Meals* vii). Echoing that perspective, Sidney Mintz notes, "If you cannot eat, soon enough you will not be able to stay alive" ("Food and Eating" 26). Starvation might be a distant consideration for most people in industrialized countries. Yet today, adequate nutrition, food safety, and basic food security pose local and global crises: "Some eight hundred million people can't afford the food they need and an even greater number—now some one billion people—are obese and suffering from unbalanced diets" (Wilson xi).

These realities are staggering, yet they do not surprise people who have been following health and agricultural debates. On the one hand, food companies and the government agencies that facilitate the industrial food system emphasize individuals' need to eat rationally; they propose that reliance on water, fertilizer, and pesticide-intensive agriculture is the only solution to food security problems. By comparison, middle-scale farmers and agro-ecology researchers argue that industrial food practices must be curtailed before more irreparable damage is done. They find that industrialized food production has produced short-term gains but that the extravagant use of fossil fuels, unlimited water, and an array of chemicals has "led to the specter that peak oil is now linked to peak water [which] is now linked to peak soil and so [also] to peak food" (Wilson xi). In other words, given the interconnected roles that fossil fuel, irrigation, and topsoil resources now play in food production, the point at which petroleum extraction reaches its maximum rate will also be the point when food production reaches its maximum. With water tables falling as irrigation consumes 70 percent of the world's fresh water, with topsoil "eroding faster than new soil forms on perhaps a third of the world's cropland" (Brown "Food Shortages"), and with estimates that conventional crude oil production has peaked or will peak within a decade, lower crop yields now caused by rising surface temperatures and countries' increased reliance on biofuels make declining food supplies one effect of climate change and an important factor for contemporary society.

Existing alongside the studies that underscore the need to address food security problems, work on food and culture emphasizes that "procuring and consuming food is fundamental to our lives, not only for survival but also as it concerns our conceptions of ourselves and our perceptions of the natural and social environments" (Jones et al.,

"Prologue" xii). Thus, while eating is a biological necessity, it is also "an intellectual experience" for people "whose personal and direct impressions occur in varied social settings" (Jones et al., "Prologue" xii). As "an insistent and compelling biological need," eating necessarily "has an immediacy and primacy unique among our concerns and endeavors" (Jones et al., "Resources and Methods" 91). Yet eating also constitutes a decidedly social experience. Food scholars point out that "there is perhaps no more fundamental act than that of sharing food, whether food and drink are distributed to strangers, offered to friends, or used as the basis of, as well as the justification for, interacting with others" (Jones et al., "Resources and Methods" 91). At the same time, eating is personal; as a physiological necessity, sensory experience, and emotional or intellectual experience, eating "is always a singular act" (Jones et al., "Resources and Methods" 91). Food is thus a unique subject because the sensory and social dimensions of eating combine with the primacy of food as necessary to existence.

The multifaceted research on food has already influenced film studies. Volumes like Anne Bower's *Reel Food: Essays on Food and Film* (2004), together with the many articles that examine representations of food in films, have shown that exploring food's dense connotations facilitates new insights into films. Building on the work that has shed light on the food film genre, and on representations of food in various genres, by selected auteurs, and in different national cinemas, our book identifies the value of amending ideological analyses of film to include foodways as a critical lens. Foregrounding the foodways paradigm, which provides a model for analyzing the "behaviors and beliefs surrounding the production, distribution, and consumption of food" (Counihan, *Anthropology* 6), this book does not aim simply to further the study of food in film. Instead, it proposes that the foodways paradigm illuminates distinct and significant factors to consider when doing ideological studies. As with work on race, class, and gender, insights generated by foodways analysis will often intersect with ones arising from the use of other critical lenses. Yet, as the unique discoveries made possible by other approaches to ideological analysis suggest, the foodways paradigm provides a special set of questions when examining films' cultural politics. When looking at films in terms of foodways, the pleasures, dangers, and implications of consumption take center stage.

Scholarship has shown that any film and any aspect of film can be analyzed from an ideological perspective. Thus, in the same way that cinematic representations of race, gender, ethnicity, sexuality, class, and colonial status warrant careful analysis, films' representations of food and food behavior can be examined to better understand their politics. Moreover, as this volume aims to demonstrate, analyzing films through the foodways lens produces readings that illuminate their cultural and material politics—even if food never appears in the film.

Foodways offers a powerful lens for ideological studies of film because food has an ambiguous, unpredictable, contentious, and high-stakes status in consumer society. A dual-edged object of promise and threat, food now has an uncertain character. From everyday life we know that "food can enliven social relations, enrich spiritual affairs, and enhance an individual's sense of well-being" (Jones et al., "The Sensory Domain" 2). At the same time, food can be used to threaten, seduce, "punish and in other ways manipulate behavior" (Jones et al., "The Sensory Domain" 2).

Today, food occupies contentious territory because the transition to consumer and media society that accelerated in the mid-twentieth century has involved an uneven and multifaceted transformation of human subjectivity. On the one hand, consuming has become a way of life; consumer choices denote an individual's identity. In consumer society, purchasing food offers an opportunity to express individuality, while producing food has become largely meaningless. As Mark Bittman notes, "In 1900, 41 percent of American workers were employed in agriculture," whereas in 2008 "that number [was] less than 2 percent" (21). Produced and received like any other consumer product, food tends to be processed, sold, and consumed as quickly as possible. Moreover, the long-term costs of extraction, production, distribution, consumption, and disposal are externalized by food companies; the industry puts responsibility for any of the food system's side effects on individual consumers. In food- and media-saturated society, consumers learn to be satisfied with homogeneity, even to trust it, for corporations design food (and media) to be quickly recognizable, convenient, and the source of easily accessed feelings of pleasure.

At the same time, food's pervasive, personal, and crucial role in human life and human interactions has led to perspectives where food is not just another product in consumer society. Belasco and others document the emergence of a "countercuisine" in the mid-twentieth century (Belasco, *Appetite for Change* 4). Belasco identifies three elements that continue to inform this alternative perspective on food: a "consumerist component" that encourages people to avoid processed food; a "therapeutic component" that invites people to embrace "improvisation, craftsmanship, [and] ethnic and regional cooking"; and a production/distribution component that values organic food production and "a radically decentralized infrastructure consisting of communal farms, cooperative groceries, and hip restaurants" (*Appetite* 4). From this perspective, food is not a commodity but instead a human right; food is not an industrial product but instead an aesthetic and cultural object that necessarily reflects the values of individuals and societies. From this perspective, a person's relationship with food is both personal and political. Whereas the dominant model of food as a consumer product separates personal and political into separate realms, from the countercuisine perspective, personal choices about food are political. For example, Frances Moore Lappé's *Diet for a Small Planet* (1971) illustrates that personal choices counter or contribute to industrialized societies' "cultural pattern of waste" (*Appetite* 58).

The conflicting visions of food that have fueled debates in industrialized societies since the late 1960s make foodways a valuable paradigm for ideological studies of film. The zealous partisanship and deep-seated uncertainties surrounding food in consumer society also help to explain the emergence of food films, which often feature cooking, chefs, restaurants, food shops, kitchens, and family meals, and "consistently depict characters negotiating questions of identity, power, culture, class, spirituality, or relationship through food" (Bower 6). The emergence of food films as a discernible genre in the 1980s and audience interest in these films can be tied to the familiar idea that film genres reflect an era's aspirations and anxieties. Hollywood's profit-based interest in distributing films that might tap into elite consumption trends, and international cinema's calculation that narratives with "exotic" food can attract upscale audiences attuned to culinary tourism, also explains the increased visibility of a genre in which food-related activities are the primary means for conveying character and situation.

Some observers see no connection between the emergence of the food film genre and the rising significance of food in competing perspectives about consumer society. Describing the arrival of food films in the 1980s as a matter of food finally receiving its due, Steve Zimmerman and Ken Weiss write that "a few directors (initially foreign) [eventually] discovered the visual, aesthetic and box office appeal of food" (256). However, other observers have identified food films, along with food documentaries, as responses to consumer society's increasing interest in food as an object of promise and threat. Writing in 2009, Kim Severson, columnist for the *New York Times,* describes the ways that food films and then later food documentaries resonated with audiences: "Movies about food used to make you want to eat. [In the] decade that spanned the mid-1980s to mid-1990s [it] took heroic resolve to walk out of the Japanese spaghetti western 'Tampopo' and not head directly to a ramen bar." Expanding on that point, Severson observes: "Cooks spent entire months trying to recreate 'Babette's Feast' and dreamed of rolling out pasta with Stanley Tucci in 'Big Night.' By the time Ang Lee's 'Eat Drink Man Woman' came out in 1994, moviegoers had come to expect food films filled with glistening dumplings, magical desserts and technically perfect kitchen scenes" (Severson "Eat Drink").

Identifying changes that contributed to food documentaries' increased production and visibility after 2000, Severson explains: "But that was then, before Wal-Mart started selling organic food and Michelle Obama planted a vegetable garden on the White House lawn. Before E. coli was a constant in the food supply, before politicians tried to tax soda and before anyone gave much thought to the living conditions of chickens" (Severson "Eat Drink"). Severson's observations succinctly capture the contrast between the era when mainstream food films reflected budget surpluses and dotcom profits and the more anxious time when audiences became receptive to films like *Food, Inc.* (Kenner, 2008), which critique "the state of the nation's food system [and are] part of a new generation of food films that drip with politics, not sauces" (Severson "Eat Drink"). As Severson notes, *Food, Inc.* does not promote the unquestioned pleasures of lavish and exotic meals that come together by magic but instead presents "eat-your-peas cinema that could make viewers not want to eat anything at all" (Severson "Eat Drink").

Amplifying Severson's insights, we propose that food films and food documentaries have found an audience because they capture the aspirations and the anxieties of people in consumer society who live with the promise and threat of industrialized food production as well as the promise and threat of slow cooking, organic food, and local sources. Weighing the polarized perspectives on food in consumer society, we find that food films—which explore the social politics surrounding gender, race, ethnicity, class, sexuality, cultural background, and community status through characters' interactions with food—exist on a spectrum that features utopian visions of food and society on one end and dystopian visions on the other.

The food film genre has often been identified with movies like *Big Night* (Scott and Tucci, 1996) and *Julie and Julia* (Ephron, 2009). The utopian vision of food and society expressed by these films warrants consideration; as Belasco points out, for Americans, "Food is the first of the essentials of life, our biggest industry, our greatest export, and our most frequently indulged pleasure." However, in a global food system plagued by food insecurity for some and obesity related disease for others, food also epitomizes an "object of considerable concern and dread [because what] we eat and how we eat it together may constitute the single most important cause of disease and death" (Belasco, *Meals to Come* vii). Thus, it is equally important to attend to food films that present ambivalent or even negative feelings toward food and food behaviors. Food films at the dystopian end of the spectrum include *La Grande Bouffe* (*The Big Feast,* Ferreri, 1973) and *The Cook, the Thief, His Wife and Her Lover* (Greenaway, 1989).

With its attention to all the beliefs and activities surrounding food and food behaviors, foodways provides a conceptual framework for analyzing the societal and cultural factors that lead to food films' utopian and dystopian representations of food. Yet the foodways lens not only prompts one to consider the spectrum of experiences depicted in the food film genre, it also leads one to see that food films and food documentaries are best understood together, as responses to conflicting perspectives about food in consumer society. As the food film genre began to emerge in the 1980s, so did food documentaries. While initially not as visible as the fictional food films, documentaries like *Garlic Is as Good as Ten Mothers* (Blank, 1980) and *Fragile Harvest* (Lang, 1986) led to a wave of food documentaries.

Emerging as they do in the 1980s, food films and food documentaries represent identifiable responses to the perception that industrialized countries' escalating reliance on processed, packaged convenience foods was erasing personal, regional, and national identities. Thus, just as food films exist on a spectrum, food documentaries present individuals' interactions with food in ways that range from utopian to dystopian. Food documentaries include productions such as *Good Food* (Dworkin and Young, 2008), which celebrates the work of people contributing to a sustainable food system in the Pacific Northwest, and films such as *The End of the Line* (Murray, 2009), which examines the devastating consequences of overfishing around the globe.

Food documentaries reflect the same cultural understanding as food films, namely, that people's choices of food and drink matter enormously. However, when one considers food films and food documentaries together and through the foodways lens, both lines of work come into sharper focus. In both instances food functions as a window, yet in the fiction films, food behaviors provide a window into individual characters and the social milieu. By comparison, in food documentaries, food mirrors individuals' and societies' relationship with nature. In addition, with the industrial food system presented most often as a threat to health, community stability, and the environment, food documentaries more directly highlight social inequality, resource crises, and systemic institutional problems. By exploring ways in which agriculture is a part of nature and culture, food documentaries also call attention to all aspects of the food cycle, from production to disposal. As a consequence, food documentaries foreground aspects of food that are often elided in food films.

In addition to providing a rubric for analyzing food films and food documentaries together, foodways illuminates the fact that food documentaries supplement food films by showing the unsavory practices the food industry hides. The foodways lens thus provides a logic for seeing films on a continuum marked by what viewers do and do not see of food production, preparation, consumption, cleanup, and disposal. Looking at films from a foodways perspective casts their representations of identity and labor into sharp relief. The approach leads one to see that films often only show the pleasures of food consumption and that they generally ignore the actual labor and the troubled cultural dynamics behind food procurement, preparation, and cleanup. In sum, the foodways lens leads one to consider the identity politics surrounding food in film as well as the economic factors that make certain aspects of the food system untenable subjects for most narrative films.

As with representations of gender, sexuality, and other categories of identity, the political and economic institutions that shape film production, distribution, and exhibition also influence representations of food and food behavior. Mainstream representations of everything that has to do with food and drink are refracted through the vested interests of the food and entertainment industries. Designed to contribute to studies in political economy, this volume examines the intersection between the film and food industries and in particular the consequences of the film industry's self-censorship practices that keep it in good standing with the food industry. Through various mechanisms, the film industry colludes with the food industry by promoting utopian food films and marginalizing food documentaries critical of the food industry. It works to ensure that films like *Ratatouille* (Bird and Pinkava, 2007) reach as wide an audience as possible—its domestic box office was over $200 million and its international theatrical box office topped $400 million—and that films like *McLibel* (Armstrong, 2005) reach as few people as possible—it made $4,000 in its domestic theatrical release. Foodways, with its focus on where food comes from and where food ultimately ends up, cannot help but direct attention to industry practices. The book's examination of industry and economy is one of the most crucial components of our work as we seek to integrate studies of film with work in food studies, a field that has been concerned with personal expression and political economy from its inception.

The Politics of Food's Past, Present, and Future

The polarized views of food that emerged in the mid-twentieth century developed into the "food wars of the 1970s," with food companies and government agencies showing how dominant forces oppose what they perceive as "deviant ideas" (Belasco, *Appetite* 112). However, in the "food-ideological battles of the 1970s, radicals scored points too, forcing adjustments and compromises" (Belasco, *Appetite* 112). In the 1970s, the oil crisis and policies established by Secretary of Agriculture Earl Butz put an end to the "post-war food order" and contributed to the U.S. farm crisis of the 1980s when "world demand slackened, energy and credit costs skyrocketed, and land values plummeted" (Patel 91; Belasco, *Appetite* 133). Throughout the 1970s and 1980s, a steady stream of news reports about problems in the food system eventually created a "lasting perception of technology out of control" (Belasco, *Appetite* 172).

This turbulence led to interest in food films and food documentaries. It also stimulated research in the interdisciplinary field of food studies. From the 1980s forward, analyzing the role of food in human history posed one of the monumental tasks undertaken by food scholars. Their research has shown that food is intimately linked to the foundation of civilization. It has revealed that "the domestication of plants and nonhuman animals for food in the Neolithic era" was a historical event even "more important than the internal combustion engine or nuclear energy" (Mintz, qtd. in Belasco, "Food Matters" 3). Describing the role food plays in human society, Sidney Mintz explains, "The history of our food systems sets us dramatically apart from the rest of the animal world" ("Food and Diaspora" 513).

Food scholarship has shown that food is a troubling, paradoxical subject. On the one hand, the "food quest may be the unrecognized birthplace of the paired concepts of locality and culture" (Mintz, "Food and Diaspora" 515). On the other, "agriculture spawned guns, germs, and steel—the principal material drivers of civilization and conquest" (Diamond, qtd. in Belasco, "Food Matters" 3). Discussing food's primary role in "European exploration and colonization," Belasco concludes: "It is no coincidence that today's billion or so beneficiaries of what might be called the Great Imperial Barbecue suffer from caloric overload, while the ex-colonies that initially supplied those wonder foods now house the poorest fed third of the world's six billion people" ("Food Matters" 3, 4).

Food's place in human history not only shaped the cultures and power structures that exist today; its role in the future of human life is equally significant. As Belasco writes: for an individual or a society, "probably nothing is more frightening or far-reaching than the prospect of running out of food" (*Meals* vii). Yet the specter of scarcity poses only one of the terrifying prospects when it comes to the future of food; the industrialized food industry and the damage it causes to the planet present an equally serious cause for alarm. Mark Bittman begins *Food Matters* (2009) discussing a report by the U.N. Food and Agriculture Organization that finds "global livestock production is responsible for about one-fifth of all greenhouse gases—more than transportation." He then incorporates food's threat-promise dichotomy: while the current "American diet, high in meat, refined carbohydrates, and junk food, is driven by a destructive form of food production . . . by simply changing what we eat we can have an immediate impact on our own health and a very real effect on global warming—*and* the environment, *and* animal cruelty, *and* food prices" (1, 3, 4; emphasis in original).

Opposing constituencies, all with a stake in the future of food, hold polarized views about how to address the looming threats to food security. The United Nations argues for an approach that directly challenges the position of institutions like the World Bank and Monsanto, which persuade the United States and other governments that global food security will only result from more of the "miraculous productivity gains" made possible by "free-market capitalism and biotechnology" (Belasco, *Meals* ix). A 2010 report by the United Nation's Special Rapporteur on the right to food explains that by reorienting "their agriculture systems towards modes of production that are highly productive [and] highly sustainable," countries can respond effectively to the ongoing "ecological, food and energy crises" (De Schutter). In its press release on the report, the United Nations highlights the fact that "small-scale farmers can double food production within 10 years in critical regions using ecological methods" ("Eco-Farming"). It also points out that "extensive review of the recent scientific literature" supports the United Nations's conclusion that agro-ecological methods, which use ecological science in agricultural activities, outperform "chemical fertilizers in boosting food production . . . especially in unfavorable environments" ("Eco-Farming").

Since the 1970s, Monsanto, Nestlé, Vivendi, Archer Daniels Midland, Cargill, ConAgra, and other food industry giants have demonized reports that demonstrate the value of low-input agriculture. Their attacks have swayed public opinion because the food industry is supported by financial institutions, trade associations, and pharmaceutical companies in ways that allow food companies to control global distribution of food and water. Shaping a complex field of activity that includes restaurants, school lunch programs, commodity trading floors, delivery trucks, and garbage dumps, the food industry's reach extends into magazines and blogs where food as an expression of personal identity is not a topic to be analyzed but instead a promise of satisfaction to the person who knows how to consume. Cooking shows and cookbooks support the food industry by offering a menu of lifestyle choices.

Articulating the countercuisine perspective, writers like Marion Nestle, author of *Food Politics: How the Food Industry Influences Nutrition and Health* (2007), have persuasively critiqued the industrialized food system. Reactions against the dominant food system have also "led to nothing less than a social movement" (Nestle ix). Nestle explains that this movement comprises several campaigns that all strive to create a better food future. Consistently opposed to corporate control of food, the campaigns aim to secure a future in which food is plentiful, accessible, healthy, and humanely produced.[1]

While the ongoing battles between the food industry and the countercuisine movements are distinguished by the scope of considerations that impact their agendas, the study of food in popular culture texts such as film has often focused on the moment when food is eaten (or, in some cases, not eaten). That is to be expected. Lucy Long explains that as "the visible focal point of a range of activities," meals are "a starting point for examining [the] extended network of activities surrounding the procurement, preservation, preparation, presentation, performance, and consumption of food" (144). Echoing the idea that meals offer a useful starting point, Belasco outlines ways to examine food in popular culture texts. He observes that films use food as "an enabler of or substitution for sexual relationships" or as "a means by which people communicate" (*Food: The Key Concepts* 37). He notes that "meals are used to advance the plot, enable key conversations, and ground characters in daily rituals" (*Food* 37). A few of Belasco's suggestions point toward analysis of where food comes from and where it ends up. He notes that as "a demographic marker (gender, race, class, region, etc.)," food has great potential to awaken the viewer to the politics of food in film (*Food* 37).

Thus, patterns of study cause meals to be a focal point of analysis. Yet meals are also central to studies because popular culture texts feature food consumption. As Belasco explains, from the beginning of the twentieth century, commercial media has "supported mass consumption, especially of convenience foods" (*Appetite* 156). Tracing developments in magazines, films, and television, Belasco points out that in the studio era "Hollywood's physically splendid performers led such busy, exciting lives that they had no time to cook" (*Appetite* 157). He continues: "As mass entertainment glamorized the convenience-consumption ethic, it mystified—or simply ignored—the details of food production" (*Appetite* 157). Elaborating on that point, Belasco observes: "The classic cowboy drama had about as much to do with cattle raising as soap operas have to do with dishwashing—maybe less. The Hollywood farmer did work hard to get by, but he never suffered from pesticide poisoning. With the exception of an occasional, low-rated documentary or TV movie, entertainment programming shunned the slaughterhouse, industrial bakery, and suburban supermarket" (*Appetite* 157). Given that history, scholars focus on the steak and burger that Vincent Vega (John Travolta) and Mia Wallace (Uma Thurman) consume at the 1950s-retro restaurant Jack Rabbit Slim's in *Pulp Fiction*. But one could ask: Where did the meat come from? From cattle housed at feedlots and fed antibiotic ingredients for months? Who labored to transport and prepare the food? Does the restaurant use undocumented workers to keep costs low? Does the table get cleaned up after Vincent and Mia win the dance contest? What happens to the leftovers? Are they taken to a local landfill?

With commercial media promoting convenience and consumption, and Hollywood's "industry policy" leading films to feature the pleasure of food consumption rather than the various aspects of foodways shown in dystopian and documentary films, what is depicted (consumption) and what is *not* depicted (everything that surrounds consumption) become equally worthy fields of inquiry. In fact, commercial media's focus on food consumption makes analyses of the food activities left out of mainstream representations crucial topics for ideological studies.

Food scholars have looked into the reasons that popular culture ignores certain domains of food. For example, Belasco examines two factors that have caused people to become "so oblivious to food, especially to where it comes from and [so disinterested in] the wider social, political, and psychological implications of our food behaviors" ("Food Matters" 6). The first involves consumer society's belief in a "technological utopianism" that is supposed to eliminate the "unrelenting drudgery" of "farmers, field laborers, butchers, grocers, and so on" ("Food Matters" 8). However, as Belasco points out, technological innovations have not eliminated food workers' drudgery and so the continued need for food laborers constantly challenges the myth that technology is the answer. However, rather than deal with that evidence, consumer society defends its ideological investment in technology as the path to progress by choosing "to 'disappear' food" ("Food Matters" 8). Facts that undermine food companies' claims that food is convenient and labor-free are ignored and discounted.

Consumer society's intransigent impulse to mask out the gritty labor of food production and disposal helps to explain why food labor remains invisible in industrialized societies. However, there is an additional reason that certain domains of food are off-limits and left out of consumer culture's "reality." As Belasco explains: "Even more important in distancing us from nature and tradition have been the efforts of the food industry to obscure and mystify the links between the farm and the dinner table" ("Food Matters" 8). Food companies invest time and resources to keep the public in the dark about the politics of food. As Nestle observes, "Much of what food companies do to create a favorable sales environment for their products—lobbying, marketing, engaging the services of nutrition experts—is conducted out of public view" (xv). Food companies also devote time and resources to keeping certain pieces of the industrial food system out of view. As a consequence, people are generally oblivious to where food comes from and where food waste goes. The food industry has determined that it is profitable to obscure the means by which food gets to markets, restaurants, and dinner tables. Consumers are trained to assume that safe, healthy food magically appears. The steps in between—low-wage labor, intensive use of fossil fuel, factory-line processing—are obscured to the point that even the food industry's efforts to mask food activities outside the bubble of consumption remain invisible.

Nevertheless, recognizing that food provides "a particularly powerful lens on capital, labor, health, and the environment," food scholars have been undaunted in their efforts to bring all aspects of food into the analytical light of scrutiny (Counihan and Van Esterik 7). Despite challenges, "more people are writing about food than ever before" (Belasco, "Food Matters" 9); since the 1980s, food studies has made contributions to "almost every scholarly field" (Counihan and Van Esterik 1). Films' depictions of meals have served as material for the initial wave of interdisciplinary scholarship. The two fields' interest in political economy represents additional opportunities, for that work can shed light on the food and film industries' joint focus on selling an array of enticing consumer products that garner huge market shares by delivering pleasure and hiding the inner workings of industrial practices.

Foodways: A Means for Unlocking the Politics of Food in Film

Research on food and culture has shown that "eating is an ideological as well as physical act" (Counihan and Van Esterik 6). Food consumption expresses "race, class, nation, and personhood" because cuisine "is a medium by which a society establishes its special identity" (Counihan and Van Esterik 5; Belasco, *Appetite* 44). The "foods and seasonings, preparation techniques, and dining etiquette" that characterize a cuisine reflect a selection from a "much wider range of options" and so help "a society's members define themselves" (Belasco, *Appetite* 44). Cuisine choices are thus highly personal and make food a site of communication. Yet food has had an even more profound role throughout human history because it simultaneously creates and transforms cultures. In consumer society, "food commodification is deeply implicated in perpetuating and concealing gender, race, and class inequalities" (Counihan and Van Esterik 6). With mainstream films concealing and often naturalizing cultural inequalities, it takes concerted analysis of food and food behavior to "make unequal power relations visible" and clarify ways in which food "is an index of power" (Counihan and Van Esterik 9, 8).

Foodways is a critical lens that enhances analysis of the personal and political dimensions of food. It offers terms for nuanced description of details within scenes of food consumption and a conceptual model that prompts inquiry into representations that naturalize the dominant values of consumer society. Foodways clarifies the ideological implications of food choices as a marker of identity and makes it possible to develop a broad understanding of food in film that takes into account movies that celebrate fine dining and ethnic traditions as well as those that promote consciousness about food and water resources. Foodways facilitates analysis of films ranging from celebrations of food like *Bagdad Cafe* (Adlon, 1987) to interrogations of the food industry like *Food, Inc.* The foodways lens can show how exploitation pictures like *The Texas Chain Saw Massacre* (Hooper, 1974) and *Cannibal Holocaust* (Deodato, 1980) use food and food behaviors to shed light on inequalities created by structures of power.

Foodways makes a special contribution to studies of food in film because it prompts one to expand analysis beyond the moments of food consumption most commonly depicted in film to consider the whole vista surrounding food, its production, consumption, and disposal. Drawn from the fields of folklore and cultural anthropology, the foodways paradigm throws into relief the fact that the movies designed and promoted to reach wide audiences emphasize the ease, pleasure, and emotional reward of convenient food consumption. The foodways paradigm also sheds light on the fact that this no-consequence consumer-focused vision owes its pervasiveness to mainstream cinema's self-censorship policies that are designed to enhance profits.

Because the meanings and social politics of food in film become visible through the lens of foodways, the paradigm can provide the foundation for a critical approach that illuminates beliefs and practices in a way that is distinct from but comparable to feminist, Marxist, postcolonial, queer, and ethnic studies perspectives. The foodways perspective can also contribute to other critical frameworks; in the same way that issues concerning gender and ethnicity often intersect, inquiries into foodways can be brought to bear in studies that also examine films through the more familiar ideological lenses of race, class, gender, and sexuality.

Like feminist or Marxist studies, which show that mainstream films generally reinforce the status quo in gender or class relations, the foodways lens reveals that films backed by substantial financial investment tend to reinforce dominant views about food practices. However, this predictable conclusion is not a reason to forego foodways analysis. Feminist studies, for example, offers new insights into films and film practice, even with the predictable conclusion that representations tend to reflect the values of patriarchy. In a parallel fashion, studies of film that draw on foodways are important, for despite their recognition that marketable films support the status quo, foodways studies call attention to aspects of film, culture, and personal experience not captured by other critical frameworks.

Foodways' wide vista of analysis—from performance, production, and procurement to preparation, presentation, consumption, cleanup, and disposal—informs the scope and nature of discussions in the book. The paradigm's vision of food's journey from procurement to disposal leads us to examine questions of political economy. It prompts us to examine food's representation (and sometimes its lack of representation) as connected to cultural identity, social settings, power structures, and material relationships that surround it. Making it possible to examine the various degrees to which any film represents or fails to represent these food practices, foodways calls attention to the stages of food's lifecycle that films commonly emphasize and those stages that films most often elide. The contrast between what films do and do not show about food illuminates beliefs and practices in consumer society; what is and is not depicted strikingly reveals a film's politics and its attitude toward labor, industry, and capitalism.

The material dimension of the foodways perspective opens new terrain for writing about film and makes it possible for studies of film to grapple with questions that food scholars have been tackling for decades. The food wars of the 1970s led to a charged environment in which food scholarship, food films, and food documentaries first explored the cultural and economic conflicts surrounding food. Since that time, food scholars have examined the ideological *and* material dimensions of food politics, whereas writing on food in film has devoted more attention to food as personal expression. Using meals as a starting point, scholarship that examines representations of food to show how they convey class, race, gender, ethnicity, and "more subjective conditions, such as obsession, indifference, depression, elation" has focused on food as communication (Keller 1). For example, James R. Keller's look at "the metaphor of the filmmaker as chef and/or artist" leads him to argue that "the preparation and consumption of elaborate meals and dishes signifies the material process of producing a film" (6). Looking at food and film as personal expression, Keller sees the visual appeal of food images as a method that cooks and directors use "to increase the sensory response" of their audience (1). Yet studies of film grounded in foodways can contextualize films' use of food's alluring qualities; the foodways lens prompts one to consider not only questions of personal expression but also consumer society's focus on food's sensory pleasures and its habit of "disappearing" the wide range of food activities that exist outside the frame of food consumption.

The first two chapters in the book examine film practice in light of foodways and aim to supply a foundation for ideological and material analyses of food in film. Chapter 1 provides coherent vocabulary for analyses. The basis for this vocabulary is, of course, foodways, the multifaceted paradigm that considers procurement, preparation, consumption, and cleanup of food. The array of activities that fall under the foodways rubric extends from extraction of consumable resources to the disposal of unused food. Chapter 1 illustrates the various aspects of foodways by looking at a collection of films. The examples suggest that foodways brings a wide range of films into the conversation about food and that it does so in surprising and illuminating ways. The discussion illustrates some aspects of foodways using familiar titles in the food film genre, while other aspects of foodways are explored in unexpected titles such as the cult film *Repo Man* (Cox, 1984).

The second chapter turns the foodways lens on the film industry and examines the way that Hollywood's industry policy has shaped the type of food representations featured in mainstream cinema. Coined by William Hays and Joseph Breen, "industry policy" is the term given to "dealing with those films that, while technically within the moral confines of the code . . . were adjudged 'dangerous' to the well-being of the industry . . . because they dealt with politically sensitive topics" (Black 245). Industry policy discouraged films with overt criticism of the government or free enterprise system; films with realistic treatments of poverty, racism, or unemployment in the United States; and films with positive images of union organizing or collective action by working-class Americans. Chapter 2 identifies a connection between industry policy and the fact that only a handful of widely distributed fiction films have ventured to use food as a sign of character identity, a symbol of larger cultural realities, *and* as the subject of a narrative about production or consumption. Exploring Hollywood's reluctance to distribute films like *The Plow That Broke the Plains* (Lorentz, 1936), the chapter also considers the impetus behind films that challenge the effect industry policy has had on mainstream representations of food.

The similarities and bonds between the film industry and food industry warrant analysis. Both industries shroud their operations in secrecy, and they do so to ensure profit and secure protection from legal action. For example, the deliberately vague term "industry policy" obscures the film industry's standard practice of suppressing representations that might offend powerful constituencies and thus jeopardize film companies' profits. In a parallel fashion, food companies drape actual production practices in secrecy and hide the fact that they sell unhealthy products for immeasurable profit. By analyzing the food industry's response to *Food, Inc.*, Chapter 2 examines ways in which industry policy in the entertainment business dovetails with legislation like state veggie libel laws and the federal Animal Enterprise Terrorist Act, which together reflect the food industry's position that criticism of the commercial food system represents an unacceptable threat to profit.

In addition to facilitating analysis of the ideological and material dimensions of food in film, the next two chapters, which consider food films as they exist on a spectrum of utopian and dystopian visions, show that foodways also offers a productive way to analyze food behaviors in the food film genre. With food preparation and presentation a central focus, food films often take place in dining rooms, kitchens, restaurants, and food shops. Reflecting food's conflicting connotations in consumer society, the depiction of food in these films ranges from utopian to dystopian. Following utopian films such as *Tampopo* (Itami, 1985) and *Babette's Feast* (Axel, 1987), food films' recurring narrative and iconographic elements have been featured in productions like *Eat Drink Man Woman* (Lee, 1994) and *Soul Food* (Tillman, 1997). To contribute to the research on films in which food serves as a vehicle for creating community, Chapter 3 explores the role that food and food interactions play in *Bagdad Cafe*.

Other food films mount social critiques and mobilize the shock value embedded in the nexus of food taboos. Thus, alongside food films that share optimistic, even utopian resolutions, food is central to ironic and sometimes stridently dystopian films like *Delicatessen* (Jeunet and Caro, 1991) and *Scotland, PA* (Morrissette, 2001). Aiming to extend studies of these more difficult narratives, Chapter 4 takes a close look at *301/302* (Park, 1995), a dystopian film that explores connections between sexual abuse and anorexia, and sexual frustration and extravagant cooking. The central characters' opposing but equally troubled relationships to food illustrate the multivalent connotations surrounding food in contemporary consumer society.

The next two chapters suggest additional ways that foodways analysis can contribute to studies of food in film. Chapter 5, which focuses on cannibal films, shows how the foodways paradigm unlocks the implications of films that seem to have little to do with food, but in fact dramatize one of society's greatest food taboos. The chapter's analyses of *How Tasty Was My Little Frenchman* (dos Santos, 1971), *The Texas Chain Saw Massacre,* and *Cannibal Holocaust* propose that these films depict aspects of human interaction with food that mainstream cinema ignores, not simply because they feature cannibalism but because they give screen time to the often overlooked labor involved in food procurement, preparation, and cleanup. The films' explicit use of humans as the food product, sometimes even as the centerpiece of the holiday meal, not only illustrates the characters' socioeconomic situations; it also provides the basis for their commentaries on social and cultural inequalities.[2]

Chapter 6 demonstrates ways that insights generated by the foodways lens can enrich genre and auteur studies. Food figures into films in genre specific ways. The chapter offers a sample of that process by examining the way food functions as promise and threat in various gangster films. With ethnic food playing a central role in the narratives, food choices and behaviors in gangster films illuminate the illusory goal of achieving upper-class WASP status. To illustrate ways that foodways analysis can contribute to auteur studies, the chapter briefly explores ways that food and food behavior create meaning in films by Steven Spielberg, John Ford, Alfred Hitchcock, and Luis Buñuel. As the discussion reveals, representations of food in films by recognized directors exist on a spectrum that ranges from utopian to dystopian visions.

Turning from directors of fiction films to those working in nonfiction, the next two chapters focus on directors' use of documentary forms to examine food as a part of nature and society. The chapters illustrate a distinction between food films' emphasis on characters in consumer society and food documentaries' attention to the natural world. They show that food documentaries provide additional ideological insights because they place consumer society in a larger frame. Chapter 7 considers documentaries about food and water resources as belonging to documentary traditions where film is "a medium of education and persuasion" (Barsam 80). Today's food documentaries are cut from the same cloth as landmark works like John Grierson's documentary about herring fishermen *Drifters* (1929), which broke new ground by emphasizing the dignity of everyday labor, and Pare Lorentz's *The Plow That Broke the Plains,* the study of the Dust Bowl that argued for "the conservation of human and natural resources" (Barsam 153). Today's food documentaries reveal the filmmakers' belief that cinema can "be used to further social progress" (Barsam 80); they belong to the social movements that aim to foster sustainable agriculture, environmentally responsible use of land and water resources, fair labor practices, and the right to healthful food and clean water. Contemporary food documentaries continue the work of various documentary traditions and show how documentaries reflect periods of agricultural crisis, such as the Great Depression and the contemporary era when the gains offered by industrial farming and fishing have become unsustainable.

In fictional films, characters' cuisine reveals their beliefs and values. Food behavior makes characters' relationships visible. By comparison, in documentaries food production and cleanup scenes shed light on larger social values; scenes of food processing and food disposal reveal power relations in consumer society. By showing foodways activities that lie outside the frame of consumption, food documentaries tacitly highlight the food and film industries' power to control representations in consumer society. Chapter 8 uses the foodways lens to examine the effects of the food and film industries' overlapping and intersecting activities. Focusing on the industrial context that determines the type of representations that will have wide circulation in consumer society, the chapter looks at food documentaries that slip through the cracks of film censorship by going into exhibition without an MPAA rating. It examines the exhibition and reception context for films such as *The Corporation* (Achbar and Abbott, 2003), *The Future of Food* (Koons, 2004), *King Corn* (Woolf, 2007), *We Feed the World* (Wagenhofer, 2005), *FLOW: For*

Love of Water (Salina, 2008), and *The End of the Line* (Murray, 2009). The chapter proposes that food documentaries have limited circulation because they offer evidence that challenges the vision of food promoted by commercial media and the food industry.

Analyzing the material factors that create the limited exhibition opportunities for food documentaries illuminates certain aspects of American national cinema. Considering films through the foodways lens can also facilitate insights into patterns in other national cinemas. To conclude our exploration of ways that the foodways paradigm can enrich ideological and cultural studies of film, Chapter 9 employs foodways analysis in brief studies of films from several national cinemas. It also explores the intersection of food, gender, and ethnicity in *Mr. Saturday Night* (Crystal, 1992) to illustrate the contrast between corporate and traditional food cultures, and considers the complex way *Mysterious Skin* (Araki, 2004) critiques fast-food society and uses characters' interaction with consumer culture food products as windows into the promise and anxiety surrounding desire, seduction, and sexuality. The chapter concludes with a final look at the contrast between mainstream and countercuisine visions of food that is clearly etched in two essay films, Agnes Varda's *The Gleaners and I* (2000) and Dorris Dörrie's *How to Cook Your Life* (2007). Giving expression to the countercuisine perspective, the filmmakers explore the personal and political dimensions of food practices. By featuring subjects who think carefully about food and its connection to people, society, and nature, the films document and validate human behavior that lies outside the picture offered by commercial cinema.

From its inception, cinema has presented audiences with narratives that depend on viewers apprehending and interpreting character through passages that show characters sharing meals. Lumière actualities such as *Baby's Breakfast* (*Repas de bébé* 1895) represent one of the first instances, for it established a connection with audiences of the French Third Republic by showing Auguste Lumière with his wife and infant child sharing a meal in a simple but private bourgeois garden. Films' multifaceted use of food means that today, whether looking at genre films, art cinema, independent documentaries or commercial blockbusters, films from silent cinema, the studio period, or the contemporary era, foodways facilitates analysis of individual films, cultural politics, and material factors of production and reception. Characters can be analyzed by looking at their eating protocols and food preferences, their use of food as a gesture of hospitality, their substitutes for food nourishment, their use or misuse of food preparation tools, and their relationship to settings such as markets, picnic areas, kitchens, diners, cafes, and restaurants. As discussions throughout the book illustrate, exploring the connotations suggested by characters' food and drink preferences, and tracing the meanings that emerge from their interactions during scenes with farming, cooking or eating, it is possible to locate evidence for interpretations that address issues of national and ethnic identity, gender and sexuality, regional and age differences, and power and class relations. Especially when considering food films and food documentaries together, the foodways paradigm facilitates unique insights into consumer culture. Foodways also provides a basis for studies in political economy, for by using it as a critical lens through which to consider any and all films, it becomes possible to identify the influence of the food and film industries more specifically.

1

Foodways as an Ideological Approach

"Foodways" refers to "the entire complex of ideas and behaviors associated with food" (Lockwood 11). It concerns "the beliefs and behaviors surrounding the production, distribution, and consumption of food" (Counihan, *Anthropology* 2). This multidimensional concept provides a framework for investigating the cultural, aesthetic, and material dimensions of food. As an ideological approach that involves "structural analysis of eating patterns" (Kittler and Sucher 14), it prompts inquiry into the complex relationships between individual meals and meal systems. Foodways offers a unique perspective on personal desires and social hierarchies by focusing attention on what constitutes a meal, who prepares it, and who eats it. Grounded in a materialist orientation, foodways analysis also examines labor-intensive food activities that extend from the extraction of food resources to the disposal of food products. Thus, the critical lens denaturalizes a culture's norms, values, and beliefs about food products, meal systems, and the procurement, preservation, preparation, presentation, consumption, and cleanup of food.

The concept entered academic discourse in the early 1970s when folklorist Don Yoder used the term "foodways" in his article "Folk Cookery" (Thursby 121). The chapter gained visibility through inclusion in

Richard Dorson's *Folklore and Folklife: An Introduction* (1972). In that influential chapter, Yoder discusses the value of exploring what he calls "the meal system—every phase of the relation of food to folk culture" (Yoder 326). Addressing his argument to cultural anthropology's interest in folk traditions, he calls for a "study of folk cookery" that includes not only "the study of the foods themselves" (Yoder 325), but also research into foods' "morphology, their preparation, their preservation, their social and psychological functions, and their ramifications into all other aspects of folk-culture" (325). Yoder thus envisioned food as a pathway to understanding a culture and society and, borrowing a term from cultural anthropologist John J. Honigman, contributed to the emergence of inquiry into "foodways" (325).

Yoder argued that close attention to a culture's food system and food behaviors leads to a better understanding of its "environment and climate; [its] settlement history and ethnic demography; [its] changes due to urbanization and innovations in technology; [its] economic history; [its] sociological factors; and [its] religion" (328). A look at food and food behaviors illuminates all of these aspects of culture, as long as the analysis includes not only the more visible food product and meal choices, but also food's entire material cycle, how it travels through the culture, and what it signifies in the various stops along its journey.

By crystallizing the insight that the way a society eats reveals its cultural beliefs and attitudes, Yoder prompted other scholars to explore foodways. For example, identifying food behavior as a way to ascertain the degree of community coherence in a culture, Carole Counihan has analyzed ways in which "manners and habits of eating are crucial to the very definition of community, the relationships between people, interactions between humans and their gods, and communications between the living and the dead" (13). Examining food and culture, Counihan has considered that while "communal feasts involve a periodic reaffirmation of the social group," the opposite also applies, for "the collapse of food sharing is often linked to the breakdown of social solidarity" (13, 14).

Films reflect that reality. In some instances, representations of food and food behaviors convey a move toward community solidarity. At other times, they depict an evolving communal dissolution. Films use food to convey both utopian and dystopian visions of community.

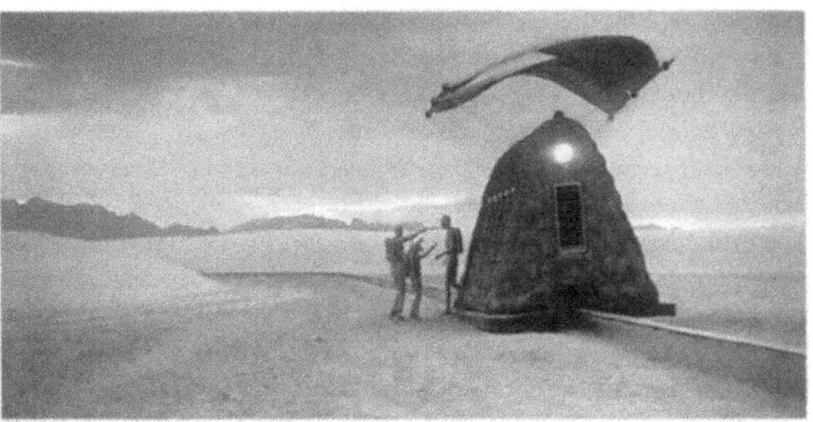

Cultural anxieties surrounding the food wars of the 1970s found allegorical expression in The Man Who Fell to Earth *(British Lion Film Company, Cinema 5).*

Utopian films envision a world where food brings a community together into a harmonious whole. Conversely, dystopian films depict worlds where no one eats together or where they use food to kill themselves. Making food a site of conflict, dystopian films show people being starved, forced to eat, or being transformed into the food product. In apocalyptic worlds without food, water, or meaning, characters do terrible things to obtain food, water, and community. Reflecting its era's anxieties about global resources, *Soylent Green* (Fleisher, 1973) offers an allegorical look at food politics in its sci-fi narrative about a future where fruit, vegetables, and animals have become extinct. In Marco Ferreri's *La Grande Bouffe* four wealthy men, bored and alienated by years of unfettered modern consumption, join together to end their empty existences by eating themselves to death. Nicolas Roeg's *The Man Who Fell to Earth* (1976) suggests a prescient allegory about the world's looming water crisis and explores the addictive nature of modern consumption.

Food can become a battleground because it is necessary for survival and because it plays such a crucial role in social interactions. Food scholars have shown that cuisine, etiquette, and taboos illuminate the complex interplay between individuals and cultures. As Counihan notes, food and food behaviors function as "a language accessible to all" (19) because eating is both a universal experience and something that is shaped by specific cultures. Highlighting crucial terms in the "language" of food and food behavior, Counihan calls attention to "*cuisine,* the food elements used and rules for their combination and preparation; *etiquette and food rules,* the customs governing what, with whom, when, and where one eats" (19, emphasis in original). Writing about food behaviors, Counihan highlights the important role of food taboos, "the prohibitions and restrictions on the consumption of certain foods by certain people under certain conditions" (19–20). Foodways thus illuminates the norms, values, and functions of eating.

Individual food choices are fraught with ideological implications. Representations of eating and drinking are charged with dense connotations that arise from culturally and socially determined meal systems that identify "correct" versus "incorrect" food behaviors. Food choices in films not only reveal character but also also illuminate cultural beliefs. For example, horror and action films will sometimes include a character, usually male, that eats with gusto even when handling dead bodies in a morgue. John Sayles's uncredited cameo in *The Howling* (Dante, 1981) sparked a series of medical examiner characters that appall and unnerve their colleagues. Appearing briefly in the werewolf thriller he cowrote, Sayles's cheeseburger-munching morgue attendant makes reporter Terry Fisher (Belinda Balaski) shrink away in revulsion from the attendant's half-eaten burger lying next to a pan of blood and brains. Disgusted, Fisher says, "I don't know how you can stand it." Yet Sayles's character shrugs it off: "It doesn't bother me." The character's food consumption and failure to clean up after eating show that he is a crude, unscrupulous slob. However, from a foodways perspective—with its emphasis on the cultural norms and values surrounding food—the moment reveals even more: it highlights food taboos, in particular squeamishness when it comes to the sanctity of life and the human body. To blur the boundaries between food and the human body is tantamount to cannibalism, one of society's greatest food taboos.

Food Performance and Product: Meals and Meal Systems

Even in mundane moments, *food performance,* narrowly defined as the way "people interact with each other through food, using it for conversation, for bonding, for competition" (Long 146), reveals a great deal about characters, their relationships, and their cultural values. For instance, in the spy movie spoof *Burn after Reading* (Coen and Coen, 2008), the animosity between boorish CIA agent Harry Pfarrer (George Clooney) and high-strung agency analyst Osborne Cox (John Malkovich) is quickly but clearly established by their bickering about hors d'oeuvres at a party. More broadly, the concept of food performance highlights the fact that the meaning and significance of food and food behaviors arise from their context.

Intensely intricate meal systems determine when, where, and why people share food with other people. These cultural constructs lead to expectations dense with ideological implications. Noting that we have "different expectations of breakfast and lunch," Lucy Long points out that people's expectations about meals in general are multifaceted (146). Those expectations are about "what foods will be offered and at what times" (Long 146). More strikingly, acculturated expectations determine "who may dine with whom in each eating situation" (Kittler and Sucher 2); coffee with a coworker is different from having a lover share a holiday dinner with relatives. These factors make questions about food performance, which concerns the place of food products within "the usual meal system and cuisine," a primary concern (Long 146). As Long explains, food scholars have shown that "a meal must be understood within the larger framework of the overall daily, weekly, annual, and celebratory meal cycles" (146).

In studies of films, exploring food performance—that is, how a scene involving food or drink compares with the characters' usual choices—can illuminate the meaning of a particular moment and a film's underlying ideological position. Recognizing the complex nature of food performance prompts inquiry into "the kinds of interactions that might occur" at filmic meals; it invites and requires a look at the tone and "formality of the event" (Long 146). The foodways concept of food performance can illuminate even fleeting representations of food in film; it provides an especially powerful lens for analyzing scenes where the food product conveys the emotional weight of the narrative moment.

For example, in the Chinese film *Red Sorghum* (Zhang, 1987) the story is set at a simple, almost primitive sorghum winery in rural China in the 1930s, just before the Second Sino-Japanese War (1937–45), when conflicts involving warlords, the Chinese Nationalist Party led by Chiang Kai-shek, and the Communist Party of China created a period of civil war in the Republic of China. The central characters, peasants who work at the winery, rarely if ever drink the wine they produce from the fields of sorghum grass that surround the winery. However, in a clear break from daily routines, the laborers at the winery drink a special batch of sorghum wine to honor their former coworker Luohan (Rujun Ten), who had refused to cooperate with the invading Japanese army and so was flayed (skinned alive) in public.

The toast to Luohan not only shows their respect and personal affection. It is also a utopian moment in which commensality strengthens community. This singular instance of the workers sharing wine that is the result of their labor reflects and contributes to the transformation of their identities. No longer disenfranchised individuals, they now have a community identity that joins nation, locality, and personhood. The deep, lusty sound of their united voices as they sing the toast reflects the group's newfound identity. The food product, the dark red wine that seems supple when it splashes into the ceramic bowls that serve as cups, gives visual expression to the vibrancy of their feeling. The rich earth tones of drinking bowls and their simple but elegant design convey the point that this is a heartfelt experience and that their cause, the defense of their homeland, is just and honorable.

This moment in *Red Sorghum* also shows that while culturally defined meal systems determine the meaning and significance of food and food behaviors, the *food product,* "the food itself [including] the actual recipes and ingredients used," is "the most visible aspect of foodways and the one most readily accessible" for analysis (Long 145). In films, a great deal of attention is paid to the food product as food stylists labor to make food a meaningful element of the mise-en-scène (see Appendix 1). Representations of food in film are designed with the awareness that characters' food product choices are "expressive of their culture, their values, their food aesthetics and [food's] symbolic connotations" (Long 145). Thus, characters' choices about food product reveal a great deal about their cultural identities. Moreover, those choices disclose dominant and sometimes alternative cultural beliefs concerning cuisine, etiquette, and taboos. The absence of food product in a film is also significant. That absence can suggest the characters' hunger, frustration, and discontentment. It can also point to ideological perspectives embedded in the narrative; with food and cooking "a domain of human behavior so heavily associated with women over time and across cultures" (Counihan and Van Esterik 1–2), one might expect that food would be elided in representations that reflect the values of patriarchy.

A food product's symbolic potential and connotations come most clearly into view when there is something unnatural, irregular, or especially significant. Not surprisingly, food product figures into the notorious *Salò, or the 120 Days of Sodom* (Pasolini, 1975). Harrowing scenes abound in the film's depiction of the kidnapping and subsequent mental, sexual, and physical torture of a group of young people during the last days of Italian fascism. Among the most indelible of the film's horrors is a banquet scene in which the fascist leaders force the young people to join them in the consumption of feces. The fecal matter is elaborately presented on elegant silverware and delicate china. With shit smeared across their faces and dripping from their mouths, the fascists revel in this debauchery while the young captives gag as they fight to not regurgitate their meal. In this instance, food product and the taboos the fascists transgress provide a potent and unforgettable metaphor for the twisted dystopia created by the fascist state.

Characters' relation to the food product (the raw ingredients and recipe elements) takes on special ideological importance when humans are placed in the food product category. Jean-Luc Godard's *Weekend* (1967) offers a strident critique of capitalism in its conclusion, which features a morally bankrupt Parisian woman casually gnawing on a limb of her husband's body that has been cooked by the oddball band of "revolutionaries" that are her current companions. In Jonathan Demme's *The Silence of the Lambs* (1991), Hannibal Lecter need do nothing more than brag about his cannibalistic behavior to confirm his sociopathic nature. As our discussion of cannibal films (Chapter 5) illustrates, films use cannibalism to highlight the ills of a corrupt society or to confirm the monstrosity of villainous individuals.

Films make statements about society by referencing recognizable commercial food products like Coca-Cola. For example, in *Masculin Féminin* (1966), Godard inserts a title card that describes the central characters as "the children of Marx and Coca-Cola" to highlight the superficiality of the young people, who select their "radical" tastes and politics from a ready-made menu of fashionable objects and ideas. In a sharply contrasting vein, films such as *One, Two, Three* (Wilder, 1961)

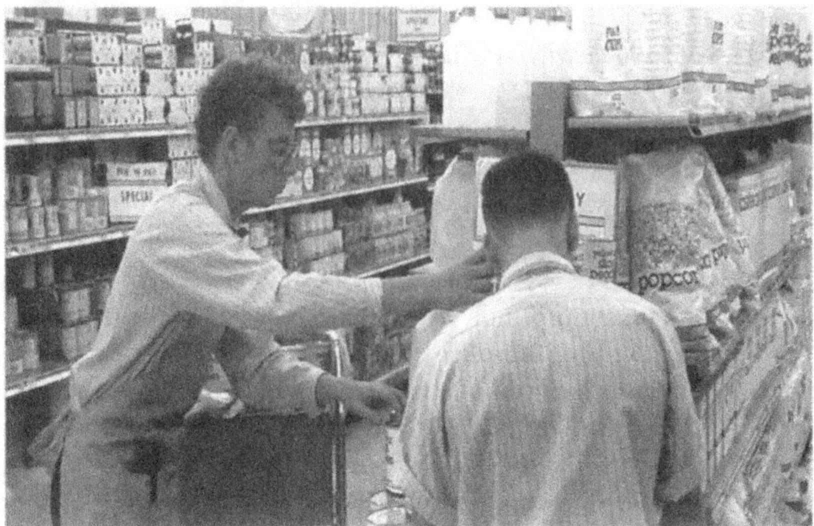

Generic labels mock food companies' efforts to differentiate their industrial products in Repo Man *(Edge City).*

and *The Gods Must be Crazy* (Uys, 1981) incorporate Coke products in lighthearted commentaries and so are featured on the company's official website ("Coke Lore"). Coca-Cola's endorsement of films that place its products in a positive light is a reminder that films' use of food is inextricably tied to product placement; Morgan Spurlock's 2011 documentary *The Greatest Movie Ever Sold* denaturalizes product placement but at the same time gives exposure to various food and drink products.

Alex Cox's 1984 film *Repo Man* offers a more coherent and strident commentary on films' use of food products. It suggests that food in film has less to do with revealing character and more to do with product placement. Its punk, do-it-yourself aesthetic opts out of conventional realism. Instead, the film features "generic" food and drink products in uniform blue and white packaging. Mocking companies' shameless campaigns to enforce brand loyalty, the characters sing advertising jingles written to promote Seven-Up and sitcoms; they stock supermarket shelves crammed with "generic" popcorn, canned fruit, and other processed food; they eat food from cans labeled "Food," drink beer from cans labeled "Beer," and rob convenience and liquor stores filled with popcorn and drinks in the film's blue and white "generic" packaging.

Preparation, Presentation, and Consumption: Individual Expression in Consumer Society

Repo Man's attack on "processed 'plastic' food" represents one counterculture response to "mainstream foodways" and the way "mass entertainment [has consistently] glamorized the convenience-consumption ethic" (Belasco, *Appetite* 3, 157). The emergence of food films that celebrate "improvisation, craftsmanship, ethnic and regional cooking" represents another, more pervasive response by people aligned with "countercuisine" (Belasco, *Appetite* 3). These films will often feature scenes of *food preparation,* which includes communal or individual activities that begin "in advance of the consumption of the meal" (Long 145). With the counterculture successfully transforming food preparation into a field for personal expression, mainstream cinema has found ways to include scenes of polished and personally fulfilling cooking experiences. In a glossy Hollywood production such as *No Reservations* (Hicks, 2007), food preparation scenes are characteristically efficient and attractive; chefs do not hunt for ingredients, use the wrong utensils, or misremember recipes. Skill in food preparation is so taken for granted that dramatic conflict arises in fact from the contrast between the central character's mastery of cooking and the many things she needs to learn about the rest of life. In *Julie and Julia,* food preparation is also central, and here again the characters' mastery of cooking belongs to a larger narrative about their mastery of skills for leading a happy life.

The counterculture's embrace of ethnic and regional cuisines created a niche audience for films with elaborate scenes of food preparation. In films like *Tampopo, Eat Drink Man Woman,* and its remake *Tortilla Soup* (Ripoll, 2001), ethnic cooking provides a vehicle for personal expression and offers an alternative to commercially produced and promoted convenience food. *What's Cooking* (Chadha, 2000) shows four families in Los Angeles as they prepare dishes for their Thanksgiving Day meals. The families belong to different ethnic groups (African American, Jewish, Mexican, and Vietnamese), and the scenes of food preparation reveal characters' embrace of their cultural traditions. The scenes of food preparation also illustrate the sensual delight of meal ingredients and the intensely social dimension of food preparation.

Scenes of food preparation in films like *What's Cooking* and *No Reservations* have a very different tone and message from ones produced by Third Cinema filmmakers. Whereas shiny upscale kitchens and stories of personal fulfillment are the stylistic and thematic center of mainstream food films, earthen colors and the pragmatic demands of subsistence living are integral to the understated scenes of food preparation in Haile Gerima's *Harvest: 3,000 Years* (1976). The cooking show segment in Tracey Moffatt's *Bedevil* (1993) takes place outdoors in hot, dry, insect-filled brush. A world away from temperature controlled television studio kitchens, the scene's crystal wine glasses, white porcelain plates, silver sauceboat, and flowing tablecloth on a large table next to a simple grill make cooking show conventions seem absurd. The sound design ensures that cooking show conventions, not Aboriginal cuisine, seem odd. Whereas cooking shows elide the fact that they are recorded performances, here the sound of film running through the camera calls attention to the scene's artifice. In addition, whereas cooking show hosts are distinguished by their fluid, melodic, well-modulated, sometimes "sophisticated" vocal delivery, here the host's Australian outback twang varies from staccato to languid. The scene concludes its critique of cooking shows' naturalized signs of "civilized" food preparation with the host's ironic comment that the woman who has prepared the traditional Aboriginal dish fancies herself to be the "Queen Victoria of bush cuisine."

Contrasts between food preparation scenes provide useful material for cross-cultural analyses. Characters' debates about recipes and their idiosyncratic cooking methods provide telling material for ideological analyses. Food preparation scenes will sometimes reflect counterculture values (craft versus convenience, natural versus plastic, and so on). They always create opportunities for character development; having characters bond over the preparation of a meal is an economical and unequivocal way to show they are becoming close. Moreover, for ideological analyses, questions about representations of food preparation lead to insights that extend beyond cultural identity and character dynamics. That films rarely show the tedious, demeaning, and dangerous aspects of industrial food preparation is a telling indicator of the food and film industries' successful efforts to mask the labor involved in food production; it also indirectly illuminates the way class and oftentimes race figure into consumer society.

Charles Burnett's *Killer of Sheep* (1979) is an exception that proves the rule, for the film depicts the labor and drudgery of the food preparation that takes place long before cuts of meat appear in the kitchen. Burnett explores the personal toll of low-wage, labor-intensive "modern" industrial slaughterhouse work. The gritty, isolating, and repetitious demands of his job leave Stan (Henry Gayle Sanders) physically exhausted and emotionally numb. For this laborer, food preparation is not a matter of self-expression but instead is the only job available to him; it is not an opportunity to embrace his ethnicity but instead is labor that reflects his place in America's racial hierarchy. For Stan, the labor of food preparation is followed by more work around the house and the desire to get some decent sleep.

By comparison, when films frame food preparation as personal expression and authentic experience, they will also often dwell on the manner in which food is arranged and served and so include scenes of *food presentation,* which "refers to how [food] is physically displayed, brought to the table, served to consumers" (Long 146). Food presentation scenes are often dramatically significant. For example, in *What's Cooking* the family's emotional harmony and the hours of food preparation are put in jeopardy when the Williams's dining room table suddenly collapses under the weight of the Thanksgiving turkey just brought out from the kitchen. Food presentation can figure into narrative closure; the presentation of the sumptuous meal signals the culmination of *Babette's Feast* and the penance Babette has undertaken to absolve herself of her affiliation with the French elite during the revolution. Food presentation illustrates narrative developments and can communicate nationalist sentiments. In *A Chef in Love* (Dzhordzhadze, 1996), food presentation scenes show the negative impact the Soviet revolution has on Pascal (Pierre Richard), a French chef living in the southeastern European country of Georgia in the 1920s. In the pre-Soviet era, the meals Pascal prepares are given ostentatious display, but after the Soviets arrive, his cooking falls from favor and his meals are eliminated from public space.

In *The Last Laugh* (Murnau, 1924), food presentation scenes highlight class difference and critique class privilege. The modest income of the hotel doorman (Emil Jannings) is made plain by the humble display of food at his niece's wedding celebration. By comparison, in the film's postscript, when the doorman goes from washroom attendant to

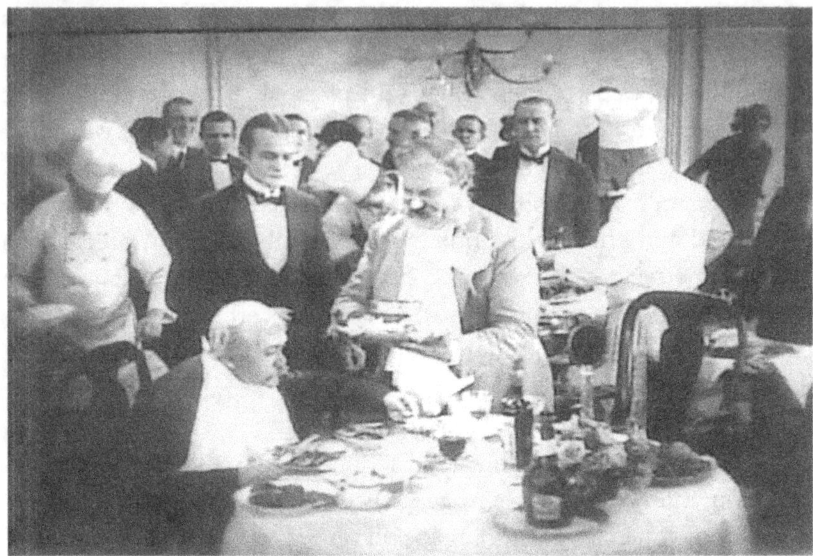

A moment of opulent food presentation discloses unspoken upper-class privilege in The Last Laugh *(Universum Film).*

wealthy man of leisure, the excessive display at the meal staged by the hotel is in keeping with the scene's fantasy status. Given the doorman's usual cuisine, the opulent food presentation scene signals that this is a special occasion. The food presentation scene also conveys the film's attack on upper-class values. While Jannings's enthusiastic gusto reveals that the doorman fails to understand elite rules of etiquette, the film suggests that the real problem is the distain for lowbrow behavior that the wait staff and the elite hotel clients at surrounding tables express. Highlighting their devotion to artificial decorum, it suggests that "refined" choices about food presentation serve to keep elite conspicuous consumption inconspicuous.

The scene in *The Last Laugh* also illustrates that depictions of *food consumption* (rules about how to eat) convey characters' place in social hierarchies. Food consumption "refers to how people eat the meal: what utensils they use, what mixtures they create, and the order in which items are consumed" (Long 146). It is the foodways stage most commonly presented in film. Food films and other productions commonly linger over scenes of consumption, whether it involves immaculately costumed dinner guests at a sumptuous feast in a period drama or cops on a stakeout wolfing down doughnuts in an action movie. Characters' table manners, eating styles, and food etiquette choices are a clear indication of their personalities, culture, and social status.

In a memorable scene from *The Bicycle Thieves* (De Sica, 1948), the contrasting table manners of Bruno (Enzo Staiola) and the rich kid in the restaurant (Massimo Randisi) embody a succinct comment on social and political injustice in Italy following World War II. The contrast captures the cultural tensions of a time when wealthy Italians who had supported Italy's fascist regime during the war continued to lead privileged lives while the partisans who had contributed to the Allied victory in Italy were among the many Italians suffering the consequences of Italy's ill-advised partnership with Axis nations Germany and Japan.

Prior to the scene, Antonio (Lamberto Maggiorani) has for a time feared for Bruno's life. Relieved to learn that Bruno is alive and in an effort to make amends for being irritable with him as they searched for the stolen bicycle, Antonio suggests that they get a bite to eat. However, unable to afford anything on the menu, father and son order only bread with melted cheese. As Bruno and his father wait quietly for their food, Bruno notices a group of wealthy people at a table nearby. They talk loudly, wear garish, expensive looking clothes, and their table is filled with plates, glasses, silverware, and bottles of champagne. Bruno studies the noisy group even after he and his father get their simple plates of bread and melted cheese.

As Bruno continues to watch, the effete, pampered looking boy around his age turns and looks over at him with a sneer. Tellingly, the rich boy's pinky finger sticks out as he holds his fork. As if his curiosity is finally satisfied, Bruno turns his attention to his bread with melted cheese. Happy to be having a meal that reestablishes the bond with his father, Bruno eats with gusto; each time he takes a bite, he pulls the open-faced sandwich away from his mouth so that strings of cheese stretch from the sandwich to his mouth. The scene illustrates Italy's continuing class divisions and national disunity by setting the anemic quality of the rich boy's affected etiquette in opposition to the hearty quality of Bruno's enjoyment. By presenting the rich boy's table manners in a decidedly negative light, the scene also seems to suggest that Italy's postwar economic crises were tied to the moral weakness of Italy's fascist-affiliated upper classes.

Table manners and characters' interactions with food in Frank Capra's *It Happened One Night* (1934) convey a very different ideological position. Here, they are a means for creating community and overcoming class difference. Capra's film does not critique the upper class, but instead envisions adjustments the wealthy could make to contribute to American society. In sharp contrast to *The Bicycle Thieves,* the wealthy are not presented as anemic or excessive, and they are not placed in the background. Instead, Ellie Andrews (Claudette Colbert), the spoiled daughter of a Wall Street banker, is a lively young woman who takes center stage. Whereas etiquette and cuisine mark insurmountable class differences in *The Bicycle Thieves,* Capra's film uses scenes of food consumption to give expression to the melting pot ideal.

Traveling on her own for the first time, Ellie meets Peter Warne (Clark Gable), the out-of-work newspaper reporter who decides to help the runaway heiress reach New York so that he'll have material for an exclusive story. Along the way, Ellie's food choices and food behaviors take on significance because they reveal a fundamental change in her cuisine. For example, early on, Ellie refuses to eat the raw carrots Peter

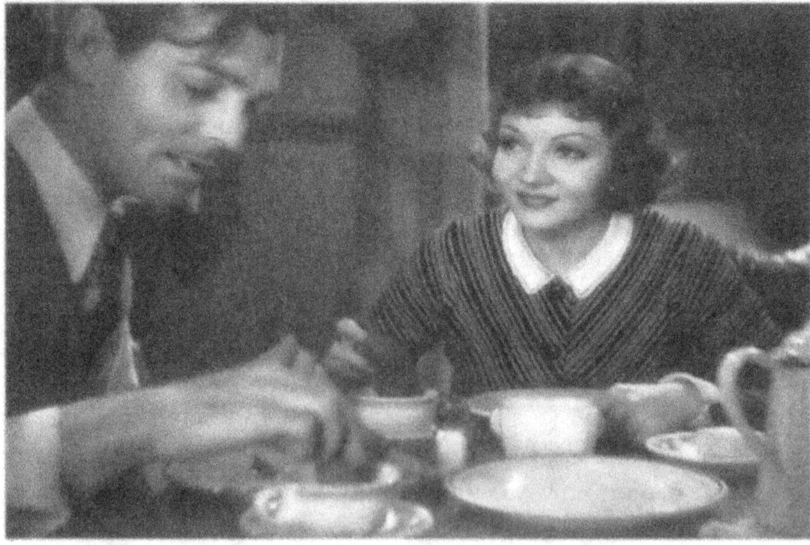

Shared table manners are the basis for a classless, utopian vision of American society in It Happened One Night *(Columbia Pictures Corporation).*

offers because she has eaten only cooked carrots all her life. Later, raw carrots communicate the moment Ellie becomes a "real" American, for she finally surrenders to her hunger, takes a raw carrot, and starts munching on it.

In another scene, unglazed doughnuts (a far cry from French pastries) and evolving table manners convey another milestone in Ellie's move toward the melting pot ideal. She discovers that her upper-class eating protocols are useless when compared to the pragmatic practices of an ordinary American. Peter dunks his doughnut and gives Ellie a lesson in how best to do so. Her rebellious streak—she started the dunking—and the promise that Ellie has an innate goodness are communicated by her enthusiasm about dunking doughnuts. The scene suggests that wealthy Americans are really like working people; they just need a chance to find themselves.

Procurement, Preservation, Cleanup: Deconstructing the Material Food System

From a foodways perspective, the meal is only a starting point for analysis of beliefs and behaviors that surround the meal. For ideological studies of food in film, representations of activities surrounding meals are also only a starting point. A great deal can be gleaned by examining the nuanced relationships between characters' specific meals and their meal cycles. Scenes of cooking, food presentation, and meal consumption provide extremely useful material for ideological analyses of race, gender, and other markers of social identity. At the same time, examining meal-centered scenes in light of the material system that goes from food procurement to food disposal deepens analysis of the more familiar and more visible food scenes. Put another way, analyzing films' food scenes in relation to the complete range of food activities contextualizes and denaturalizes mainstream representations of food. Attention to the full spectrum of food-related behavior illuminates the fact that films' representations of food sustain or sometimes trouble consumer society's norms, values, and beliefs. However, reckoning with food procurement, preservation, and cleanup, activities that fall outside the frame of meal-centered activities, makes clear how little consumer-society audiences see of the food system.

As Belasco notes: "Mass entertainment [has] glamorized the convenience-consumption ethic [and] mystified—or simply ignored—the details of food production" (*Appetite* 157). After decades of commercial media, the realities of food extraction and procurement, of preservation processes and distribution systems, and of food cleanup and disposal simply do not fit into the narratives and "reality" of consumer society. The fact that human survival depends on sustainable food production falls outside the frame of representation in consumer society. For subjectivities shaped by consumer society, production itself does not exist. Foodways analyses of film representations can make that dominant cultural belief visible.

Some would argue that foodways studies have a limited value. Writing in the late 1980s, Robin Wood bemoaned the use of "later Barthes, Lacan, and 'deconstruction'" in film studies because the conceptual frameworks led to political inefficacy (*Hitchcock's Films Revisited* 27). Recognizing the political dimension of Derrida's use of deconstruction, Wood still found that appropriating deconstruction for political purposes violated "its basic premise [that] language itself is slippery and unstable, [and that] every text can be deconstructed" (28). He imagined that "when the next cultural upheaval produces the next wave of popular radicalism" (28), deconstruction would keep academics sequestered "in a back room deconstructing one another's texts" (29).

To highlight deconstruction's political inefficacy, Wood cites an interview with director Arthur Penn. Echoing Wood's disdain for deconstruction, Penn explains he had been reading about "a big movement" of scholars and critics "called deconstructionists," but that he had also just seen "a woman pick a carrot out of the gutter on Columbus Avenue where now the rents for a store are twelve, fifteen thousand dollars a month" (qtd. in Wood 27). The experience led Penn to conclude: "You know, money is flowing on that street, and here is this woman picking a filthy carrot out of the gutter in front of a Korean vegetable store" (qtd. in Wood 27). Wood uses Penn's observation to make the point that deconstruction has no purpose in a world where millions go hungry. Asking how questions about the nature of language put food on the table, Wood attacks deconstructionists who go about their work while "old women are still bending down to retrieve carrots from gutters all over the world" (28). For Wood, deconstruction is worthless when it comes to matters of food, hunger, and starvation.

Our book takes the opposite position; it proposes that representations must be deconstructed to parse out the naturalized ideological perspectives of consumer culture. Deconstructing films' representations calls attention to the appearances—and absences—of food in consumer culture. It is true that deconstructive readings of food in film do not put food on the table. However, foodways analysis calls attention to food activities outside the "consumption-convenience ethic" (Belasco, *Appetite* 157); the work necessarily involves a deconstructive approach that makes the politics of food and the politics of food in film visible. A foodways approach proposes that the cultural and material aspects of food and food behaviors remain unseen in film until they have been deconstructed.

Food procurement, the process of "obtaining the ingredients and items needed for a meal" (Long 145), is one of the most labor intensive aspects of the foodways system; and long before it also became one of the most industrialized aspects of the food system, the production of food had been a site of intense social strife. Slaves, serfs, and undocumented workers are integral elements of the multifaceted agricultural institutions that for centuries have ensured that the people who labor to produce food occupy a very different social and economic place from the people who control the conditions of production. Not surprisingly, consumer society's drive to "disappear" or erase the drudgery of (food) labor, and the intertwined efforts of the food and film industry to mask the liabilities and costs consumers incur because of their profit-focused production practices, make it unusual for film narratives to explore the politics of food procurement. Gillo Pontecorvo's 1969 film *Burn!* (*Queimada*), starring Evaristo Márquez as the charismatic leader of a Caribbean island slave revolt and Marlon Brando as the mercenary sent to ensure uninterrupted delivery of sugar to the British empire, is an exception that proves the rule. Interestingly, D. W. Griffith's *A Corner in Wheat* (1909) is another. Editing, framing, set design, and performance style all contribute to the film's contrast between wealth and poverty; these cinematic elements establish a causal relationship between the actions of the wealthy and the experience of those in poverty. Using a simple but efficient design, the film intercuts more tightly framed scenes of animated, wealthy stock brokers—plotting to control the wheat market, enjoying a bountiful meal, and outbidding competitors on the stock exchange floor—with wider opening and closing shots of

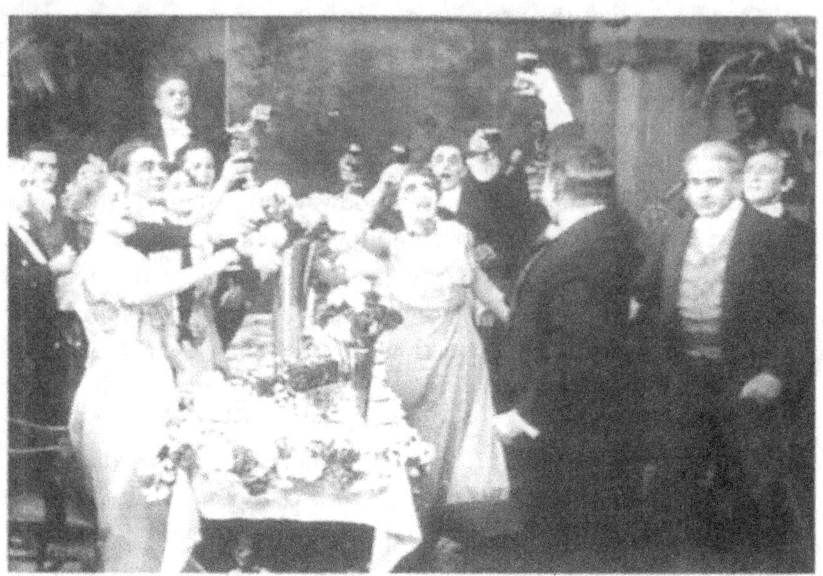

Supporters toast to the Wheat King who "corners" the market in A Corner in Wheat *(Biograph Company).*

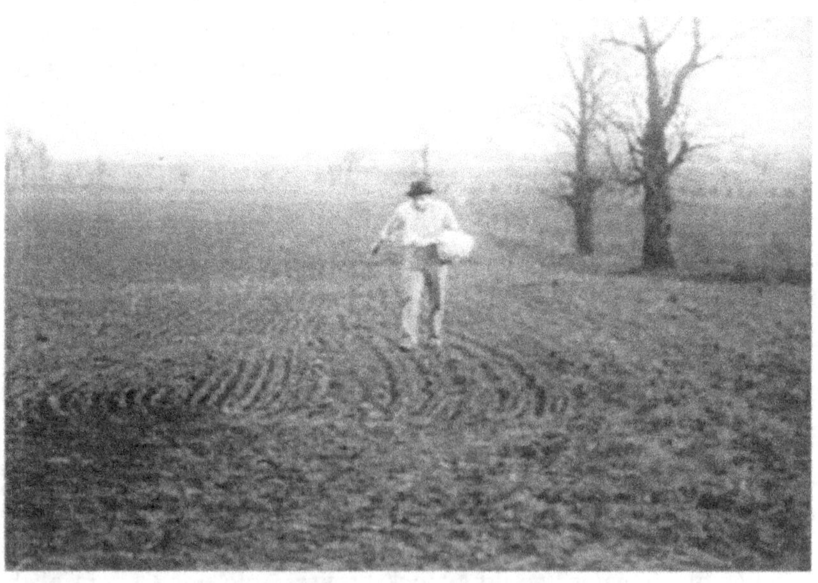

A farmer endures hardships created by upper-class control of the market in A Corner in Wheat *(Biograph Company).*

a slow moving, almost static wheat farmer sowing the corner of a barren field, unable to pay the grocer's price for bread.

The activities related to food procurement vary and have changed over time. Food procurement can thus refer to a multitude of actions, from hunting and slaughtering animals to planting, nurturing, and harvesting fruits and vegetables. In consumer society, procurement is consistently presented as consisting of buying groceries at the market. Some films throw the uncertain and shifting definition of food procurement into relief. For example, Nicolas Roeg's *Walkabout* (1971) teases out the often overlooked link between "civilized" and "primitive" food procurement by intercutting shots of a white Australian butcher, chopping apart a rack of lamb ribs, with shots of an Aboriginal youth chopping off the leg of a kangaroo he has just speared.

A look at Depression-era films also suggests ways that conceptions of food procurement have changed over time. As if anticipating the food documentary *Our Daily Bread* (Geyrhalter, 2005), King Vidor's feature film *Our Daily Bread* (1934) shows how characters are impacted by production-distribution problems in America's increasingly industrialized food system. Vidor's film, a precursor to *The Grapes of Wrath* (Ford, 1940), celebrates the value of communal farming in ways that make it similar to the documentary *The New Frontier* (McClure, 1934). The 1934 documentary was used to publicize a U.S. Federal Emergency Relief Administration program at "Woodlake, an experimental community in east Texas, [that was] one of a number of FERA projects to resettle farmers and residents in rural areas and introduce them to cooperative ways of work and life" (Kahana 108).

In these films, the hard work needed to produce food, especially in the face of drought conditions, figures prominently and so contrasts sharply with representations in contemporary Hollywood films. Ultimately quite idealistic about the salvation offered by collective action, Vidor's *Our Daily Bread* nevertheless depicts the complex circumstances involved in food production, including the severe agricultural destruction of the 1930s Dust Bowl. Realizing that the crop crucial for their survival will wither and die without irrigation, the farm collective mounts a massive effort to dig a trench that will deliver the needed water. In an exciting, culminating scene, the hard work of the group succeeds. Exceptional for its emphasis on the group rather than the individual, *Our Daily Bread* finds drama in food production, an area that later Hollywood films seldom address.

While not confined to the Depression period, the films of Charlie Chaplin and Buster Keaton belong to a time in American film history when depictions of food often conveyed the challenges of modern industrial society. Scholars have noted that in Chaplin's films, the lower-class character is consistently the one that is hungry and in pursuit of food (Orgeron and Orgeron 88). Taking a different approach, Keaton's films reflect anxieties of modern consumer culture in that they "depict their main character . . . as a consumable product" (Orgeron and Orgeron 85). While Keaton's films "use food production and consumption" to comment on class differences in modern society, depictions of food in Chaplin's films often reveal "his nostalgia for an earlier, less technologically driven era" (Reinholtz 269). For example, Chaplin's film *Modern Times* (1936) features a daydream sequence in which an urban modern home is just like a rural cottage, only better. The Tramp reaches through his living room window to pluck an orange from a tree; he calls a Holstein to the kitchen door and has her milk fill a pitcher to the level he requires. He picks a handful of grapes on a vine outside the kitchen door, and he is accompanied by a beautiful young woman who serves him a huge steak.

The impact of this idyllic interlude is intensified because of an earlier scene in which Charlie is subjected to a feeding machine that goes haywire, an experiment undertaken by the factory owner so that assembly line workers can continue to work through their lunch hour. Even the burglars, who break into the department store where Charlie works as a night watchman, just want food. Ironically, *Modern Times* concludes with Charlie as a waiter struggling valiantly to deliver food to a customer as a crowd of revelers repeatedly sweep him into their midst and away from the customer's table. Though played for laughs, the centrality of food—desire for it, its elusiveness, its divine accessibility—subsumes important issues about hunger, control of food, commercial transactions regarding food, and the usual erasure and exploitation of labor.

The 1980s farm crisis in the United States led to a series of Hollywood films that dramatized the problems surrounding food procurement in ways not seen since *The Grapes of Wrath*. The hardships of

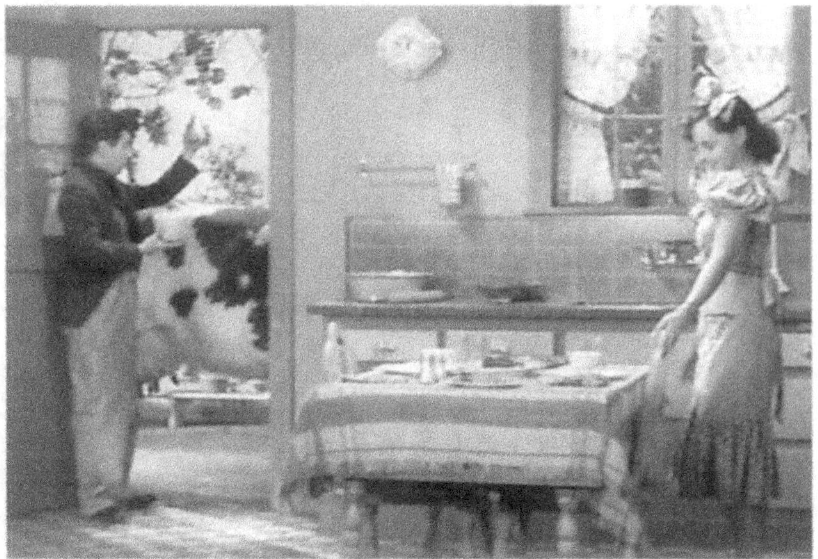

Modern Times *(Charles Chaplin Productions) presents a fantasy of food procurement for Depression-era American audiences.*

farming and the threats the "modern" agricultural system posed to family farms were explored to varying degrees in a series of films that included *Places in the Heart* (Benton, 1984), with Sally Field, Danny Glover, and John Malkovich; *Country* (Pearce, 1984), with Jessica Lange, Sam Shepard, and Wilford Brimley; and *The River* (Rydell, 1984), with Mel Gibson, Sissy Spacek, and Scott Glenn. To varying degrees, these films show the actual procurement of necessities, from fruit and vegetables to meat and potatoes.

However, contemporary mainstream cinema rarely considers farm work (soil preparation, planting, weeding, harvesting, and delivery to market). Even when stories are set on farms or ranches, dramatic human relationships dominate, and the hard work of food production and the tragedy of natural disasters are relegated to the background. In Terrence Malick's *Days of Heaven* (1978), breathtaking scenes in golden light create an idyllic backdrop for the film's romantic conflicts, which take precedence over devastating events like the plague of grasshoppers that destroys the farmers' wheat crop. Similarly designed to reach a wide (urban) audience, Martin Ritt's *Hud* (1963) does not explore the

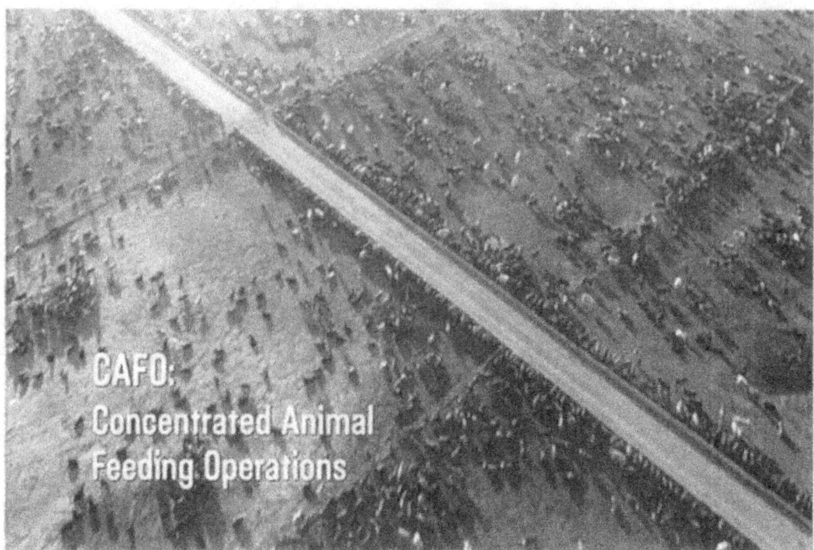

Food, Inc. *(Magnolia Pictures, Participant Media, River Road Entertainment): Documentaries explore the connection between burgers and CAFOs elided by fiction films.*

rich potential of its ranch setting. Instead, the hoof-and-mouth disease that leads to the destruction of the cattle herd is a passing tragedy in a plot that focuses on the sexual escapades of Hud Bannon (Paul Newman) and his rebellion against his father, Homer (Melvyn Douglas). With scenes of food procurement missing from or tacitly ignored in fiction films, filmmakers of food documentaries have taken it upon themselves to show components of the industrial food system, such as CAFOs, the Concentrated Animal Feeding Operations that "congregate animals, feed, manure and urine, dead animals, and production operations on a small land area [where feed] is brought to the animals rather than the animals grazing or otherwise seeking feed in pastures, fields, or on rangeland" ("Region 7"). An integral part of food production since the 1970s, CAFOs now make up 15 percent of animal feeding operations in the United States, with large CAFOs housing more than 1,000 cattle, 55,000 turkeys, 125,000 chickens, and so on.

Food preservation, which concerns "strategies used for keeping food frozen or fresh and storing them until needed" (Long 145), also receives little attention in mainstream cinema because this stage of food's journey to the dinner table reveals the degree to which the food system has become industrialized. Images of food preservation run counter to consumer society's fantasy that food makes its way magically, without human labor or industrial intervention, from family farm to family kitchen. However, as Frederick Wiseman's 1976 documentary *Meat* reveals, food preservation is a part of the food business that effectively delivers inexpensive consumer products. Going into a modern slaughterhouse to show what consumer society and the food and film industries have deemed unimportant and in bad taste, Wiseman invites audiences to consider its ghostly image of cattle carcasses that have been tanned and then covered in white sheets to protect them from cold, and that stretch from ceiling to floor, suspended from the hook and rail system that moves them slowly from the kill floor to the storage unit where they will be held until butchering.

Food preservation's noticeable absence in fiction films makes the isolated scenes that touch on food preservation stand out. Clara Law's *Autumn Moon* (*Qiu Yue,* 1992) provides an especially remarkable scene in which food preservation carries resoundingly positive connotations and in fact leads to an expanded and enriched cross-cultural community. The film's turning point is the moment that Tokio (Masatoshi Nagase), a young Japanese man who has come to Hong Kong in search of a good meal, opens the refrigerator in the apartment where the teenager he has befriended (Pui-Wai Li) lives with her grandmother (Choi Siu Wan). Having enjoyed several of the grandmother's modest but uniquely satisfying meals, when the young man sees the collection of ingredients she has preserved in the family refrigerator, he realizes that care and years of experience have made the grandmother a great cook. That insight provides the life lesson he sought when he set out for Hong Kong. It also illustrates the way food can serve as a vehicle that allows characters to transcend traditional cultural boundaries.

However, the utopian vision of food preservation that emerges from *Autumn Moon*'s attention to its role in personal expression and cross-cultural understanding is quite unusual. The delimited depictions of food preservation tend to reveal consumer society's anxieties about food, the industrial nature of today's food system, and the underlying fear that, in this system, humans can easily become the food product. Concerns that humans can become preserved food product are given vivid expression in Tobe Hooper's *The Texas Chain Saw Massacre* when one of the victims almost lurches out of the kitchen freezer. In Martin Scorsese's *Goodfellas* (1990), gangster Frankie Carbone (Frank Sivero) is executed and hung from a hook in a meat freezer. In David Cronenberg's *Eastern Promises* (2007), the Chechen gangster who has been spreading rumors about troubled but well-born Russian gangster Kirill (Vincent Cassel) is preserved in a freezer after he is executed; and as if echoing Sayles's cameo in *The Howling*, Cassel conveys Kirill's lug-headed inability to respect social norms as he casually munches on snack nuts while his inferior Nikolai (Viggo Mortensen) is charged with properly disposing of the frozen corpse.

The realities surrounding food procurement and food preservation are not the only areas of the food system that are too troubling for consumer society and the food and film industries. Not surprisingly, *food cleanup* is also rarely seen in films. As with food preservation, the general absence of cleanup scenes not only makes instances of food cleanup stand out but also serves to highlight the alignment, on the one hand, between personal expression and food as vehicle for the creation of utopian community, and between material realities and dystopian visions of food cleanup and disposal.

For example, in *Bagdad Cafe* scenes of cleanup suggest connections between characters that might otherwise be overlooked. Decades earlier, the Max Linder comedy *Troubles of a Grass Widower* (1912) establishes a connection with "modern" urban audiences by depicting scenes of daily life's duties gone awry. In the short, Linder plays a self-centered middle-class fellow whose unhappy wife has left him. The film centers on the man's difficulties with the distaff duties of cooking, cleaning, and shopping. He cannot figure out how to make the bed or get food home from the market. He leaves the feathers on the chicken he tries to cook and gets shoe polish in the food. To top this off, Linder's solution to doing the dinner dishes is to take them outside and spray them down with a hose. A gag too amusing and accessible to be left to silent cinema, the same garden hose approach reappears in *Overboard* (Marshall, 1987) when heiress Joanna Stayton (Goldie Hawn) is required to do the dishes for Dean Proffitt (Kurt Russell) and his young sons. Echoing Ellie's evolution in Capra's *It Happened One Night*, Joanna's food-related behaviors mark her transformation from snob to regular person and disclose the film's utopian vision of a classless American society where wealthy people are good natured and really not all that different from ordinary Americans.

By comparison, the labor, economic, and environmental problems surrounding cleanup and food disposal are some of the most elided aspects of the food system. Food films often avoid the unglamorous task of tidying up after the meal, and most films avoid cleanup scenes with a disgust comparable to that held by Joe Buck (Jon Voight) in *Midnight Cowboy* (Schlesinger, 1969), the big dreamer who excitedly ditches his dishwashing job at the local diner in hopes of becoming a New York gigolo. Hollywood films present a consumer-friendly vision of activities directly related to meals; there are movies about chefs, but very few about characters that go home from work every day to cook dinner; superheroes might eat but they do not bother with mundane details like shopping, cooking, and doing dishes. Mainstream cinema's glamorization of "the convenience-consumption ethic" ensures that there are no scenes of food disposal (Belasco, *Appetite* 157). The documentary *We Feed the World* begins by showing truckloads of uneaten bread being hauled to and dumped in landfills, but those scenes will never appear in Hollywood movies. In sharp contrast to Agnes Varda's *The Gleaners and I,* entertainment films will not represent the standard industrial practice of dumping millions of potatoes because they are too big or too small to sell to supermarkets or fast-food franchises. A documentary like *Dive!* (Seifert, 2010) will cover the practice of grocery store dumpster diving, but given Hollywood's longstanding practice of mystifying or ignoring the realities of the food system, it would be surprising if mainstream cinema ever explores the waste of the industrial food system.

Consumer Society: Devoid of Class, Labor, or the Natural World

Mainstream cinema creates a world where meals reflect personal choices and even belong to culturally specific meal systems. It does not, however, present food as something that belongs to a material food system that is anchored on either end by the natural world and that depends on often low-wage labor to move food through the various stages of the system. In the high-tech, air-conditioned bubble of consumer society, the natural world exists in the remote past; ironically, that reality is succinctly conveyed by a high-tech CGI film like *WALL-E* (Stanton, 2008). For modern society, food is a disposable consumer item. Labor and class division do not exist. Realistic depictions of poverty and labor have been unspoken taboos in Hollywood cinema since the early twentieth century, and this practice has profoundly informed its representations of food; scenes of consumption might entice, but scenes of cleanup threaten to highlight the drudgery of food labor.

However, the labor surrounding food is important, and foodways analysis can be used to "read against the grain" to open up questions concerning the politics of food and film. Foodways analyses can inform deconstructive readings that shed new light on films' ideological meanings. If one is willing to analyze food in film in a deconstructive manner—that is, to consider how food signifies within a larger network of possible significations that are evoked by food's appearance—generally ignored or mystified aspects of food system practices can be drawn out.

A film's representation of food discloses its politics. Representations of food in mainstream American films reveal a great deal about dominant attitudes about class and labor in the United States. Historically, Hollywood cinema has been reluctant to feature realistic depictions of class and labor. No doubt, this hesitation results from Hollywood's well-established "industry policy," which has disallowed depictions of systemic inequality or interrogations of free-market capitalism (more on this in Chapter 2). Attending to Hollywood's representations (and non-representation) of food and food behaviors generates insights into the workings of political censorship in Hollywood cinema. Foodways prompts one to ask: Why does food magically appear in most mainstream films? Why do audiences not see where food comes from? Why is food disposal off limits? Inquiries along these lines reveal that mainstream films mask out or hide a great deal about food. They highlight the fact that representations that focus on food consumption and ignore procurement and disposal sustain dominant capitalist ideology.

However, the labor and industrial interventions required for modern food procurement, preservation, preparation, cleanup, and disposal are not the only aspects of the food system that mainstream films elide. Utopian food-focused films are often the only films that show characters actually taking the time to enjoy what they eat. A film like *Antonia's Line* (Gorris, 1995) might feature scenes where characters enjoy others' company during relaxed meals in a bucolic setting. Yet films rarely show characters bonding with the larger community via food. Just as the absence of the food labor speaks volumes about a culture's views on labor and class, the relative absence of pleasure in mainstream representations of food consumption indirectly illuminates contradictions surrounding consumption in consumer society. Consumers are enticed, cajoled, and shamed into consuming. However, they are encouraged not to take pleasure in one item or experience. Instead, consumer society drives individuals to constantly search for objects to consume because products are touted as the same but different, new and improved, more advanced, more esoteric, more exciting. Driven by anxieties about the physical pleasure of eating and drinking, and the feelings of boredom and isolation that abound in consumer society, food consumption can bear little resemblance to the vision of shared food as a means for creating comfort and a sense of belonging. Films reflect the dystopian reality that, in contemporary consumer society, more people eat solitary meals made up of fast foods; fewer people watch movies in the communal setting of the movie theater; and being isolated consumers is now a way of life for many people.

Conclusion

Analysis of food in films by different directors, in different genres, and from production contexts shaped by different national cinema traditions, political regimes, and time periods reveals that close attention to films' use of food and drink can contribute greatly to ideological studies of film. Analyzing characters' seemingly natural food behaviors reveals a great deal about a film's representational politics. An ideological approach that uses food as a touchstone to explore subjectivity and material culture, the foodways perspective illuminates the drive to "disappear" labor, class, and the effects of capitalism in consumer society. As a starting point for ideological analyses, the foodways paradigm denaturalizes commercial media's well-established support of mass-produced convenience foods. Foodways provides a comprehensive taxonomy for analyzing how representations sustain or sometimes challenge the prevailing picture of food as a consumer product designed for fleeting personal satisfaction. It illuminates ways in which films conceal or sometimes disclose the food and film industry practices that mask both the labor of food workers and the profits amassed by today's food corporations.

Foodways is a conceptual lens that facilitates analyses of films' representational politics. For studies of race, class, gender, sexuality, ethnicity, and colonial legacy, it provides terms for nuanced descriptions of food-focused scenes and a coherent way to examine the personal and political dimensions of films' representations of food and food-related behavior. While consumer society minimizes demographic distinctions to generate the image of the consumer, it makes some identity markers the basis for niche marketing, as conventional notions of race, gender, and sexuality underlie marketing of everything from steaks and salads to action films and chick films. Budweiser might be marketed to America's white rustbelt while microbreweries cater to upscale multiethnic urbanites, but the foodways lens highlights the fact that consumer society ignores the reality of class division that places laborers and owners in very different positions as consumers. When subjectivities are shaped by consumer society, no one aspires to produce food or any other product, for consuming, rather than producing or renewing resources, is the only acceptable behavior.

Research on people's food behaviors in daily life can be easily adapted to analysis of filmic representations because food scholars' inquiries go beyond simple oppositions between personal expression and norm-based behavior in mass culture. Ethnographic studies show how recipe designs embody people's deep-seated beliefs; political economy research demonstrates the way marketing promotions get consumers to buy specific brands of ingredients. The attention scholars have paid to the aesthetic, cultural, economic, and political aspects of food choices and practices in daily life parallels interest in the socioeconomic forces underlying film production and reception. Chapter 2 examines a crucial bond between food and film: ways that the food and film industries reflect and shape consumer culture as they work to create a highly circumscribed picture that obscures the practices that make it possible for their products to generate profit by flowing unfettered through the marketplace.

2

Food and Film Industries

A Filter for the Food We See in Films

Representations of food seen by large audiences reflect the influence of commercial media's century-long support of "mass consumption, especially of convenience foods" (Belasco, *Appetite* 156). Today, the vision of food as a consumer product and vehicle for self-expression is continually reactivated by "advertising's big four," Omnicom, WPP Group, Interpublic Group, and Publicis Groupe (Elliott 1). These "megacompanies" coordinate the co-promotions food and other companies use as they turn away from television and print advertising and toward product placement and brand integration in response to audiences' increasing use of instant streaming, digital download, and digital video recorders (DVRs) (Elliott 1). Synergistic commercial partnerships fuel the $500 billion a year advertising and marketing industry. Films with global appeal are ideal brand integration partners (Sauer). As a consequence, co-promotion of products sold by film and other consumer product companies are orchestrated by companies like Norm Marshall Associates, which has been described as "the leading entertainment industry marketing agency representing the world's top brands to the entertainment media through product placement, promotions, entertainment media outreach and celebrity seeding" ("Corbis Acquires Norm Marshall Group").

With co-promotions bringing disparate companies together in synergistic production and marketing ventures, films more obviously exist as a node in a larger network of corporate media and communications conglomerates (Wasko 13). Perhaps even more significant, they also exist in marketing networks that include companies like Ford, Apple, Red Bull, Coke, and BMW ("Leading Brand Appearances This Year"). Representations of food are thus one of many filmic elements impacted by co-promotion arrangements. For example, co-promotions involving *Avatar* (Cameron, 2009) included partnerships with companies ranging from McDonald's to Panasonic. *The Amazing Spider-Man* (Webb, 2012) was produced and marketed in partnership with Activision, Carl's Jr., Gameloft, Hardee's, Kellogg's cereals, Keebler cookies, Cheez-It crackers, Schick, Twizzlers, Visa, D-Box, Vuforia, and Standup2cancer.org ("The Amazing Spider-Man—Partners").

These partnerships not only provide film studios and food companies with nearly unlimited opportunities for advertising and cross-promotion, but are also ideologically charged and provide a platform for Western corporate supremacy. An example of this type of food/film partnership is apparent in the blockbuster film *Iron Man* (Favreau, 2008), which reflects the film's financial connections to Burger King, Dr. Pepper, and a dozen other brand partners, including the U.S. Armed Forces. In the film, the first thing arms developer-cum-nascent superhero Tony Stark (Robert Downey Jr.) wants after escaping captivity in Afghanistan—an escape he engineers by constructing a suit of armor from weapon scraps—is to stop by Burger King for an American cheeseburger. Later in the film, after the Afghan terrorists unsuccessfully attempt to reconstruct Stark's Iron Man suit and technology, the film makes the point that when it comes to weapons technology, nobody beats the United States military, a message well suited to a film sponsored by the U.S. Air Force. In addition to the geo-political imaginary the film creates, it also emphasizes that the United States makes the best cheeseburgers—Stark wolfs down Burger King burgers while holding a press conference upon his return. Thus, the film promotes U.S. weapons and Whoppers and underscores American superiority in both arenas.

Iron Man provides only one example of how representations of food play a central role in films' co-promotion operations. As Morgan

Spurlock notes in *The Greatest Movie Ever Sold*, "All the big blockbusters have tie-ins with fast-food restaurants, cups, toys, you name it." Brand integration with fast food and other consumer products has been central to the *Star Wars* and *Star Trek* franchises since the 1970s. *E.T.: The Extraterrestrial* (Spielberg, 1982) partnered with Reese's Pieces. *Night at the Museum: Battle of the Smithsonian* (Levy, 2009) partnered with Hershey. Coca-Cola works with the *Tron* franchise; Burger King and *Twilight* films co-promote. *The Green Hornet* (Gondry, 2011) partnered with Carl's Jr. The synergy between the food and film industries is seamless when brand integration involves soda, sweets, and snacks paired with films featuring familiar, formulaic narratives filled with vampires, space travelers, and costumed superheroes.

The food industry's size and capital advantage over the film industry colors the dynamic between food companies and Hollywood. The differing power of the two industries comes to light in an anecdote from the late 1960s, when the synergistic horizontal entertainment-marketing system was starting to replace the vertically integrated studio system. As head of corporate giant Gulf + Western, Charles Bluhdorn had led the corporate takeover of Hollywood by acquiring Paramount Pictures in 1966. Insiders report that the boisterous Austrian-born magnate would, at the conclusion of Paramount business meetings, "pound the table" and exclaim in his thick accent, "Vile ve've been zidding here, I made more money on sugar dan Paramount made all year" (Biskind, *Easy Riders* 144). In other words, for someone accustomed to the profits global food companies made on sugar holdings in places like the Dominican Republic, movies generated paltry returns.

Not much has changed since Bluhdorn's reign at Paramount. Disney, Paramount, Sony (Columbia), Twentieth Century Fox, Universal, and Warner Bros. are still the principal members of the Motion Picture Association of America (MPAA), and the studios continue to move in and out of larger corporate conglomerates. The Disney film and theme-park empire now includes ABC assets. Paramount belongs to (National Amusement's) Viacom; in 2006, a new media conglomerate (with no film studio) emerged when the companies surrounding CBS left Viacom to become the CBS Corporation. Sony (Columbia) remains an MPAA member but is relegated to a second-tier status (Meehan 115–16).

News Corp. owns Twentieth Century Fox; Warner Bros. is part of TimeWarner's holdings.

Moreover, as in Bluhdorn's day, as massive as the holdings of the six major media conglomerates are, one could say that these corporate giants are small fries when compared to food and beverage companies. A few key figures reveal the food industry's profit advantage. Taken on its own, Disney's $4.8 billion net income for 2011 is staggering (Garcia). However, this number pales in comparison to McDonald's $27 billion revenues in 2011 ("McDonald's Corp"). Similarly, in contrast to the evolving legal and economic challenges Sony has faced (Toor), Kellogg's continues to sail along, making a $13 billion profit in 2011 ("2011 Kellogg Company"). Thus, while co-promotion with *The Amazing Spider-Man* enhances Kellogg's appeal in a crowded breakfast-cereal market, Sony's superhero needs the Rice Krispies mascots Snap, Crackle, and Pop more than they need him.

Co-promotions between the film industry and various types of companies looking to sell consumer products provide a useful way to understand the synergies between the food and film industries. Not surprisingly, these mutually beneficial relationships lead to films' focus on the convenience and personal pleasures of consumption. In addition, films' highly circumscribed depiction of foodways tacitly illustrates developments in media history and the mechanics of inter-industry relations. These developments have contributed to a consumer society where corporate partnerships that were once well-kept secrets are now highly touted status symbols. One can identify points in that transformation. While Clark Gable without an undershirt could start a clothing fad in *It Happened One Night*, dunking generic doughnuts was a sign that class divisions could be overcome. By comparison, advertisers' decision to pair *Captain America: The First Avenger* (Johnston, 2011) with Dunkin' Donuts instead of McDonald's, for example, is a sign that even during production the film had been assigned to second-tier status.

There are many ways to analyze and illustrate the powerful role mainstream cinema's corporate partners have played over time. Contemporary business case studies are very illuminating. At the same time, there is value in looking back at the origins and early operation of "industry policy" in American cinema. Representations of food (and other) products in films that have wide circulation today reflect a century of "institutional constraints" that have been woven into movies so seamlessly and so insistently that by now they appear to be little more than "filmic conventions" (Jacobs 87). To get a better sense of the forces shaping representations of food in film, there is also value in examining the often bullish intimidation tactics the food industry uses when it interacts with other corporations, the media, and activist groups (Nestle 159). The promise of astronomical profits leads food and film companies to co-promotion ventures. The threat posed by the food industry's size and capital advantage over the film industry leads the film industry to produce and distribute films that portray food products in ways that conform to the expectations and desires of the food industry.

Food and Beverage Giants

Marketable representations of food focus on the ease and pleasure of food consumption. They facilitate the food industry's efforts to eliminate any representation, report, or action that might jeopardize food companies' profits. To enhance profits, food companies "obscure and mystify the links between the farm and the dinner table" (Belasco, "Food Matters" 8). Following suit, big-budget film productions will do the same because film companies' profits depend on good relations with partners that control food and drink product placement and high-profile marketing at fast-food chains, convenience stores, and supermarkets.

Over time, there have been a handful of fiction films that do not represent the industrial food system in a positive light. As noted earlier, Griffith's *A Corner in Wheat* (1909) contrasts farmers' subsistence living with the opulent lives of commodity traders who make vast sums by manipulating the market. However, whereas a film like Griffith's *The Birth of a Nation* (1915) has had lasting influence, *A Corner in Wheat* had little or no impact; commodities market manipulation still contributes to the global food crises that have become increasingly dire since 2008. *Chinatown* (Polanski, 1974), *The Man Who Fell to Earth, The Milagro Beanfield War* (Redford, 1988), *Erin Brockovich* (Soderbergh, 2000), and *Rango* (Verbinski, 2011) explore conflicts surrounding water resources.[1] Yet the challenge posed by these films is often defused by marketing and publicity that directs audience attention to more familiar topics such as the work of the directors, the film's stars, or the inventive use of genre conventions.

Richard Linklater's *Fast Food Nation* (2006) translates Eric Schlosser's well-known exposé *Fast Food Nation: The Dark Side of the All-American Meal* (2000) into a series of interwoven stories. One story focuses on illegal immigrants who find work in a meat processing plant; another features disgruntled youths interested in animal rights; and a third is about a fast-food executive who has to find out how manure is getting into the chain's best-selling hamburgers.[2] Rated R for what the industry's rating board described as "disturbing images, strong sexuality, language and drug content," *Fast Food Nation* made $1 million in theaters. That figure is extremely low, of course, when compared to blockbusters' box-office figures. *Fast Food Nation*'s depiction of food safety problems at fast-food restaurants and of the dangerous working conditions at food-processing plants made the film an unappealing co-promotion partner.[3]

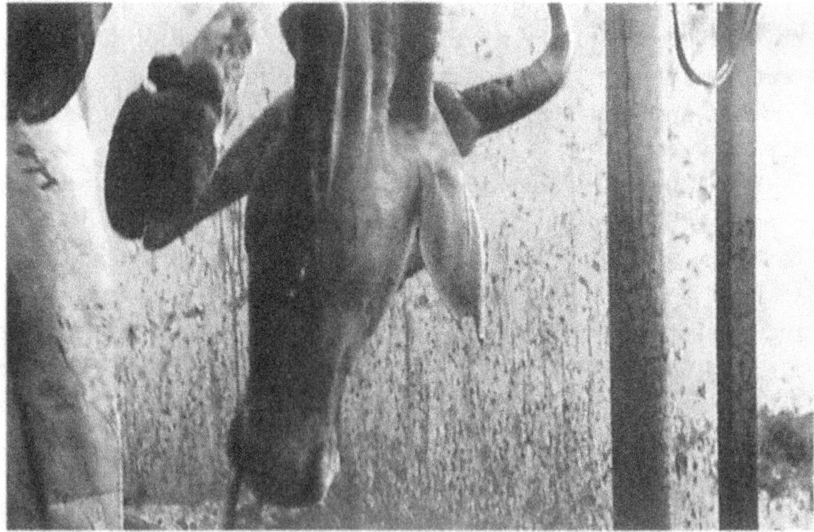

Fast Food Nation *(Recorded Picture Company, Participant Productions, Fuzzy Bunny Films, BBC Films) includes a reminder that depictions of industrial food procurement do not suit co-promotion.*

Hollywood's synergistic relationship with other commercial industries makes a film like *Fast Food Nation* the exception that proves the rule. In a national cinema shaped by studios' well-publicized focus on supplying entertainment, films that include realistic depictions of industrial food procurement, preservation, preparation, cleanup, and disposal tend to be documentaries with small budgets and limited theatrical releases. Before food films caught on in the 1980s, fiction films used food to reveal character, but food's aesthetic appeal and cultural significance were largely "ignored or hidden from view" (Zimmerman and Weiss 1).

That point can be taken another step: while utopian films explore food's aesthetic appeal and its role in creating community, topics that disrupt the pleasure of film entertainment, such as the toxicity of diets infused with corn syrup, the economic downside of "cheap food," and the problem of food insecurity even in leading food exporting countries like the United States and Brazil, have been consistently "ignored or hidden from view." The power of food and beverage giants helps to explain this practice. For example, in 2010 PepsiCo, the world's second-largest food and beverage company, made $60 billion. If it were a country with a $60 billion economy, PepsiCo would rank "sixty-sixth in gross national product, between Ecuador and Croatia" (Seabrook 54). The company's financial status has cultural implications. With its longtime control of the market, PepsiCo food and drink products are now "deeply embedded in our social rituals and national institutions" (Seabrook 54). That status will be reflected in films.

While fast-food chains and convenience food and drink products vie for visibility, other segments of the food industry work behind the scenes with the government and other key agencies to assure that their products can move unimpeded through the marketplace (Nestle 1). As in other industries, food companies have increasingly consolidated their assets. Fewer and larger companies now control the narrow passage that connects the world's food producers and consumers, who are now isolated from one another in the two spheres of the food system's hourglass. CEOs in the food industry include Hugh Grant (Monsanto), Ellen Kullman (DuPont), Patricia A. Woertz (Archer Daniels Midland), Greg M. Page (Cargill), Gary Rodkin (ConAgra), Paul Bulcke (Nestlé), Irene Rosenfeld (Kraft Foods), Martin Baggs (Thames Water), and Joe

Jimenez (Novartis). Other people such as Larry Pope (Smithfield), Donnie Smith (Tyson), Jim Perdue (Perdue), and Jose Concepcion (Swift Foods) also play key roles in today's food industry. Nestlé and Kraft Foods are the largest food companies in the world. Monsanto controls the world's seed supply; other companies profit by delivering bottled water and public water supplies. Archer Daniels Midland, "supermarket to the world," runs the world's largest soy extraction facility in Decatur, Illinois. Cargill, a grain and financing company twice the size of ADM, has controlling interests in Brazilian soy production and is the largest privately owned corporation in America. Cargill often works with Monsanto to control the marketplace, just as ConAgra, based in Colorado, home to the nation's largest CAFOs (Concentrated Animal Feeding Operations), works with ADM and Novartis, one of the largest pharmaceutical companies in the world (Patel 199).

With commercial media's co-promotion strategies molding the representations of food that receive wide circulation, very few consumers realize that the food industry will push any product that they believe will sell, even if the product is unhealthy or unsafe (Nestle xiv). Thus, the food industry is similar to big tobacco. They pressure public officials to eliminate and overlook regulations, seek out "experts" to vouch for their products, and have no qualms about marketing unhealthy food to vulnerable populations like "children, members of minority groups, and people in developing countries" (Nestle xiv).

These practices stem from industrialized countries' abundance of food. In the United States, there is "enough to feed everyone in the country nearly twice over" (Nestle 1), so food companies are not only trying to outsell their competitors, but are also trying to convince people to consume their products in amounts that vastly exceed actual nutritional needs. Companies use various strategies to attract customers and increase consumption. Sometimes they play on consumers' "sentimental attachment" to the "idealized image of the family farm" by presenting themselves as a service that links farm and kitchen (Manning 2). At other times, they market their high profit commodities as enticing, exotic new taste sensations.

In food-saturated consumer society, to be profitable, food companies are required to attract consumers to products in which the companies have invested resources. Government subsidies ensure that costs for physical food production and processing are kept in check. Food companies thus focus their expenditures on "advertising and public relations" that assure governmental agencies and everyday consumers that food product are healthy or, at least, safe (Nestle 1). Most of these mechanisms work in ways unseen by a majority of the general public, while marketing and image control are now integral components of commercial food production (Nestle 1). The disparity between cultural beliefs (family farms supply food) and the facts of food production (food companies market food for profit) make it necessary to "disappear" the role of advertisers, lobbyists, and any other aspect of the industrial food system that does not lend itself to co-promotion. Thus, as with other consumer products, films' representations of food are not direct reflections of personal or cultural values. Instead, they are designed to sustain and enhance the market share of the consumer product companies themselves.

Industry Policy: Self-Regulation to Secure Relations with Food and Other Industries

Representations of food and food-related behavior circulate in an industrial system controlled by well-established institutions that determine what is and is not widely distributed. That system reflects the interests of interrelated businesses that benefit from a government-supported free market system. The film industry maintains sizable profit margins through control of its labor force and the wide circulation of its products. To ensure unhindered circulation, the film industry remains sensitive to the interests of other capital-intensive industries. Thus, while sex and violence have been the most visible areas of the film industry's censorship activities, the elimination of content that might offend other industries has played an equally if not more important role in shaping film content, audience expectations, and subjectivity in consumer society. With self-censorship "routinely sanctioned by the 'profit principle'" (Jansen 15), films have been molded to elide the negative effects of modern industrial practices. In film products designed for wide circulation, "the process of self-regulation" reflects "the existence of previous texts, which [have] exerted their own pressures on the production [and distribution] process" (Jacobs 94).

In the case of film's representations of foodways, films' narrow focus on food consumption depends on cinematic conventions that have developed over the years in response to industry policy mandates; the directives themselves emerged over time to facilitate financially beneficial relationships with powerful constituencies like food and beverage giants.

The film industry's decision to direct consumers' attention to foodway activities that make food companies comfortable and encourages them to co-promote goes back to the early years of cinema, when people first realized films' power to shape public perception. The practice of molding any and all aspects of widely distributed film content started in the first decade of the twentieth century. Powerful constituencies determined, for example, that films dealing with class struggle were "more threatening than cinematic displays of sex and violence" (Ross 87–88). Long before the transition to sound, filmmakers "hesitated to make labor-capital films" because censorship boards in 100 cities had shown they would act with hostility toward any films critical of free-market capitalism (Ross 196; see Gianos 2).

As many recall, the American film industry sought to protect its investments by making political censorship a regular part of the production-distribution-exhibition system. Joseph Breen, the head of Hollywood's Production Code Administration from 1934 to 1954, "coined the term 'industry policy' for dealing with those films that, while technically within the moral confines of the code . . . were adjudged 'dangerous' to the well-being of the industry . . . because they dealt with politically sensitive topics" (Black 245). Marshaling his era's most damning invective, Breen labeled screenplays about racism, poverty, unemployment, or labor-management conflicts in America as violations of industry policy, and these screenplays were altered because Breen believed that any look at these subjects constituted "communistic" criticism (Black 246). Today, the film industry calls attention to the way it categorizes representations of sex and violence, but it avoids the topic of industry policy because executives recognize there is no "public relations advantage to be gained by advertising the industry's accommodating attitude toward big business," powerful lobbies, foreign governments, and U.S. administrations' interest in the wide circulation of films that depict "class harmony" (Vasey, *World* 6; Ross 125).

Two events in December 1908 illuminate the forces that have molded representations of food and other consumer products. The MPPC, the Motion Picture Patents Company, was established on 18 December 1908. As David Cook explains: "To ensure their continued dominance of the market, Edison [and other well-placed companies] pooled the sixteen most significant U.S. patents for motion-picture technology and entered into an exclusive contract with Eastman-Kodak" (32). On 24 December 1908, powerful constituencies made certain that the newly consolidated film business would recognize its responsibility to other commercial interests. To address business leaders' worry that films were appealing to working-class concerns, the mayor of New York closed the city's movie theaters for a brief time. In response, the MPPC struck a deal in March 1909 with the newly formed New York Board of Motion Picture Censorship, later known as the National Board of Review (Black 14; Vasey, *World* 48). The 1909 deal secured unfettered circulation for films that presented other industries in a favorable light.[4] In subsequent years, films that depicted food and other consumer products in ways that might hurt sales would not fare well in the marketplace.

The MPPC was dissolved in 1915 as a result of a federal antitrust suit. Yet that same year, film producers, distributors, and exhibitors formed the Motion Picture Board of Trade of America to handle negotiations with local censors and the National Board of Review. In 1916, that public relations trade association was replaced with NAMPI, the National Association of the Motion Picture Industry. NAMPI was a prototype of the MPPDA, the Motion Picture Producers and Distributors Association, in that it handled "trade relations, export conditions, and technical and logistical matters as well as censorship" (Vasey, *World* 27). A far less visible entity, MPPA, the Motion Picture Producers' Association, was also created in 1916. This group, comprising "twenty-five of the largest film companies," was an open-shop (anti-union) trade association formed in response to "the creation of Actors' Equity and the more radical Photoplayers' Union in 1916" and the efforts of the American Federation of Labor to organize "the studio crafts (stage hands, electricians, cameramen, and laboratory workers) into a single union" in 1916 (Ross 61).[5] Operating beyond public view, MPPA members subsequently "locked out all disgruntled workers and refused to meet with federal mediators or negotiate with AFL [American Federation of Labor] representatives" (Ross 132). Striking workers responded with a nationwide boycott of Hollywood films. However, by 1922 workers belonging to the International Alliance of Theatrical Stage Employees, Moving Picture Technicians, Artists and Allied Crafts of the United States had returned to work without winning concessions, and "by the end of 1922, the new era of labor militancy had come to an end" (Ross 133).

At the time of its widely publicized creation in March 1922, the MPPDA, the Motion Picture Producers and Distributors Association, was presented to the public as a response to Hollywood scandals involving sex and drugs (Cook 185–86). However, establishment of the MPPDA actually reveals a streamlining of existing institutional activities.[6] The public relations duties of NAMPI were assigned to the new MPPDA.[7] The hardball industrial relations work of the MPPA was taken over by the newly established AMPP, the Association of Motion Picture Producers. Throughout the 1920s, the MPPDA held public meetings with various constituencies to polish the film industry's public image. Yet when studio executives decided to undertake a coherent approach to controlling film content, they handled the process internally. In 1927, AMPP members privately adopted a resolution "listing eleven subjects that the producers would not, in the future, represent in their motion pictures and twenty-five subjects that would only be represented with the exercise of 'special care'" (Vasey, *World* 47; see 30–31). This internal industry agreement, which escaped public attention, indicates that the studios' self-censorship policies would protect the companies and officials who might be represented in films. Moreover, it was also designed and adopted to enhance film industry profits, for representations that might offend influential figures or other industries could have a negative impact on film sales.

A "set of constraints that gradually took shape throughout the 1920s and 1930s" formed the industry policy component of the Production Code formally established in 1934 (Vasey, "Beyond" 102). Industry policy represented a response to the demands of foreign governments, state and local censorship bodies, individuals and organizations with the power to generate negative publicity, and, most especially, proponents of free market capitalism (Vasey, "Beyond" 103). Ruth Vasey explains: "Industry policy not only covered the depiction of foreigners and foreign locales. . . . It ensured the general probity of onscreen public officials, as well as the benevolence of cinematic bankers, lawyers, doctors, teachers, social workers, newspapermen, and police. . . . It was in these little-publicized areas of the MPPDA's activities that its effects were, in practice, most censorious" (*World* 194, 195).

Public pronouncements about the Production Code Administration and later the Code and Rating Administration (renamed the Classification and Rating Administration in 1977) suggest that the film industry has been concerned with protecting audiences from representations of sex and violence. However, since 1909, the film industry has distributed fewer and fewer films that criticize powerful figures or expose problems in other industries. The 1968 rating system's focus on sex and violence provided a space for films that challenge cultural taboos, but it left problems in the commercial industrial system for films released without support from Hollywood or its corporate sponsors. The investment required for producing and marketing mainstream films makes industry policy's attention to the priorities of other industries a factor for any film production that hopes to secure co-promotion partners and wide audiences.

The Industrial Food System: A Test Case for Industry Policy

Hollywood's prudent disinterest in films that illustrate problems in the food system goes back at least as far as *The Plow That Broke the Plains.* The film posed a problem for American distributors because it conformed to the industry's strictures on sex and violence, but ran afoul of its policy to maintain good relations with other industries.[8] The film offered what Pare Lorentz termed a "picturization" of findings in a 1936 government report that blamed the agricultural, economic, and social crisis in the Great Plains on the "mistaken homesteading policy" of previous administrations and on a system of agriculture that served the interests of government and business but not individual Americans (Clement 4). Its examination of the drought-affected areas of the Great Plains not only made food procurement the central issue. It also outlined problems in the industrial food system, illustrating government and business policies that had promoted "over-cropping and over-grazing" in an approach to agriculture that offered quick profits but could not be sustained (Clement 4).[9]

The Plow That Broke the Plains was a film with unparalleled credentials. It was the first film produced "by the United States Government for commercial release and distribution," the first film "placed in the Congressional archives," and it "would have become the first film screened at a joint session of Congress had the capitol chambers been equipped to show a sound film" (Clement 2). However, it was denounced by opponents as New Deal propaganda (Clement 2; Barnouw 117). In addition, even after a series of successful previews, Hollywood refused to distribute it. Rather than expose its policy of working closely with other industries, Hollywood claimed that it would not distribute Lorentz's film because as a government-funded production it represented unfair competition. The charge of unfair competition was a ruse, of course, for the majors distributed (self-censored) films funded by United Artists, Poverty Row companies, and prestige producers like Selznick and Goldwyn on a regular basis (Tzioumakis 19–62).

However, *The Plow*'s representation of food as a business was reason enough for the studios to see it as a risky distribution venture. Moreover, it was not a safe entertainment product because Lorentz had been a vocal critic of Hollywood's industry policy. Hired by Roosevelt's Resettlement Administration to make films, Lorentz was known to be concerned with "the social role of cinema" (Barnouw 114). An outspoken journalist, Lorentz made no secret of his contempt for what he saw as the film industry's acceptance of censorship for profit (Lorentz, *Lorentz on Film* xii, 51).[10] Lorentz described the corporate control of American film, discussed the industry's monopolistic practices, and identified Bethlehem Steel's influence as the reason for the highly visible presence of the U.S. Navy in American newsreels (Lorentz, *Lorentz on Film* 20; see 82–83). Lorentz's observations about the "soporific effect" of love stories, banal music scores, and comfortable theater seats made the point that Hollywood movies were the opiate of the people (Lorentz, *Lorentz on Film* 23).

Censored: The Private Life of the Movies (1930), co-authored by Lorentz and civil-libertarian lawyer Morris L. Ernst, proposed that self-appointed or politically appointed state, national, and corporate censors secretly controlled the movies and that their arbitrary decisions had made American films nothing more than a commodity, with censorship leading to more corporate income and infantile films (Ernst xiv, 175).[11] Ernst and Lorentz cataloged censors' arbitrary and self-interested decisions on representations of crime, sex, and vulgarity. Examining instances of political censorship, they found that censors required American films to whitewash the "breakdown of our courts," shield "the *dominant* religious groups and the leading national minorities from criticism," and follow the "tyrant's creed" that public officials could not be ridiculed (Ernst 95, 96, 142; emphasis in original).

Identifying the Republican Party as shaping Hollywood's industry policy, Ernst and Lorentz argue that Will Hays, Republican Party chair and later head of the MPPDA, became interested in movies after *Civilization* (Barker and Ince, 1916) seemed to aid President Woodrow Wilson's narrow reelection victory over Republican Charles Evans Hughes; Hays resolved "that nothing of that kind should happen again" (Ernst 122). Discussing the 1920 presidential campaign that is remembered for the advertising techniques used to promote Republican candidate Warren G. Harding, Ernst and Lorentz identify meetings between Hays, Adolph Zukor, William Fox, and other movie moguls as the reason "Harding got in the newsreels, in the White House, and Hays was made Postmaster General" (Ernst 122). Turning to Hays's work after leaving the largely symbolic postmaster general position to become head of the MPPDA, they describe Hays as a "super-press agent" whose skillful management of censorship had increased corporate profits (Ernst 123).[12]

In other publications about film and the Depression era's economic challenges, Lorentz outlined his view that "citizens should ask the government for explanation, information, and direction to help them solve their problems" (Barsam 152). In Lorentz's view, since Hollywood was uninterested in producing films that informed the public about social problems, the government should fill this gap (Barsam 152). Lorentz's position as a Hollywood outsider was confirmed when he was fired (a second time) by William Randolph Hearst after he praised Henry A. Wallace and the New Deal farm program in a column he had been hired to write for the Hearst papers (Barnouw 114; Lorentz, *FDR's Moviemaker* 36).[13]

With Lorentz directing, Hollywood could be certain that *The Plow* would offend powerful constituencies. The film violated industry policy because it described systemic, not isolated problems. It identified government and business practices, rather than the isolated actions of a few bad apples, as the source of the agricultural, social, and economic crisis in the Dust Bowl. It exposed the dire consequences of land speculation that allowed the wealthy to control food procurement. The film highlighted the way war profiteering could shape not just American manufacturing but also American agriculture. It showed that promise of profits from the wartime sale of wheat had led to the bellicose refrain of the U.S. government and its allies in agribusiness that "wheat will win the war!"

To counter that jingoistic rhetoric, *The Plow That Broke the Plains* employs irony to make the case that highly capitalized agribusiness *broke* the Great Plains. It shows that land speculation and war profiteering all but destroyed the land and the families who tried to farm the prairie between the Rockies and the Mississippi. In the visual and musical design created by Lorentz and composer Virgil Thomson, music and sound do not simply echo connotations conveyed by the images. Instead, the film uses visual and aural counterpoint to link, for example, dust rising from a wheat field and smoke rising from a battlefield. Creating links between tanks and tractors, the film points out Americans' naïve belief in the justice of war. Combining a cheerful marching song with images of tank battles and farmers tilling the soil, the film suggests that American farmers have inadvertently become "part of [the] war machine" by engaging in food production (Barnouw 116–17).

The major film distributors refused to handle *The Plow.* But Arthur Mayer, Hollywood insider and a former executive at Paramount who had moved on to manage the Rialto Theater in New York City, decided to use this controversy to sell the film (Barnouw 118). When he opened the film on 28 May 1936, Mayer publicized it as "The Picture They Dared Us to Show!" and in advertisements that included positive reviews, Mayer added: "Yet Hollywood has turned its manicured thumb down!" (Barnouw 118). Lorentz's film, which informed the American public about the connection between war profiteering and the hardships of food procurement experienced by Dust Bowl farmers, was subsequently shown in as many as 3,000 independent theaters; its critical acclaim led to a series of new developments (Barsam 157). The U.S. Film Service was established, "critics began to pay more serious attention to the development" of nonfiction film, *The March of Time*

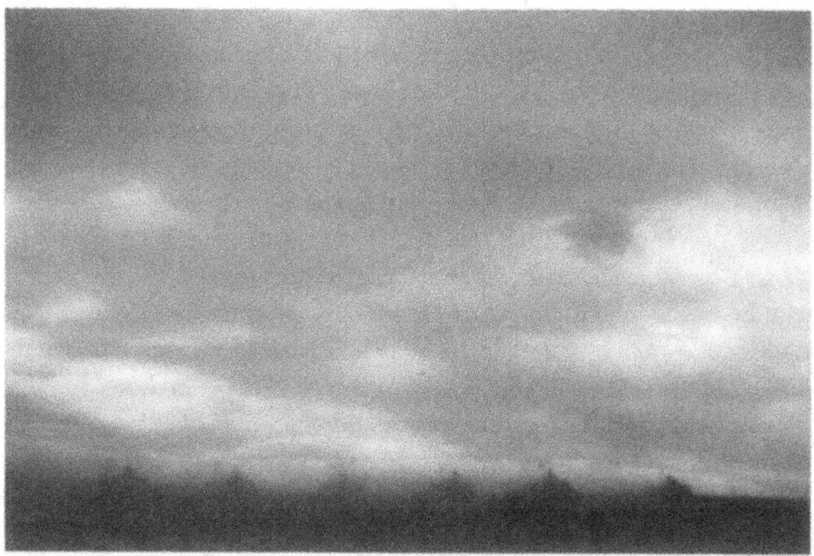

The Plow That Broke the Plains *(Resettlement Administration): Exposing problems caused by the American government and industries made this film unfit for distribution by Hollywood.*

newsreels "received an Academy Award in 1937 for having 'revolutionized' newsreels," and Lorentz's next film, *The River* (1937), was picked up for distribution by Paramount (Barnouw 157, 122).[14]

At the same time, very little else changed. Paramount's decision to distribute *The River* came only after the film had done well in cities along the Mississippi River and in Chicago and New York metropolitan theaters (Lorentz, *FDR's Moviemaker* 110; see 59, 111). Moreover, when the Academy debated whether or not to nominate the film for an Oscar, Walt Disney led the campaign against it on the grounds that nominating *The River* "would create an unhealthy precedent for competition between government and private enterprise" (156).[15] Given Hollywood's vocal opposition to government-produced films, Paramount's belated decision to distribute *The River* might have been an effort to placate the U.S. Justice Department as it was compiling the antitrust suit *United States v. Paramount Pictures* that was officially filed in July 1938. Paramount's decision might also reflect its interest in acquiring product that could be as popular as *The March of Time* newsreels.[16]

Today, the MPAA, the Motion Picture Association of America, the trade organization that protects the intellectual property rights of Disney, Paramount, Sony, Twentieth Century Fox, Universal, and Warner Bros., plays an important role in the American film industry. Its rating system, managed by the Classification and Ratings Administration, is what assures the free and unfettered circulation of the products sold by the film industry.[17] Like the food business, the film industry's final packaging stage facilitates the illusion that film consumers have a great deal of freedom and individual choice. The MPAA's rating system, established in 1968 by MPAA president Jack Valenti, not only offers audiences a sense of comfort by providing a seal of approval but also gives audiences the impression they have a wide menu of options to choose from, and gives studios a more precise way to market films to specific audiences (Bernard 59). The new rating system allowed Hollywood to update their product lines, with R-rated films guaranteeing a certain level of sex and violence—and with the rating board's seal of approval ensuring that these films would screen in movie theaters without interference from local or state censorship boards (Bernard 61).

Valenti's salesmanship, grounded in his ability to make each segment of the audience hear what it wanted to hear (parents were protected, teenagers could see exciting films), made him a public figure during his tenure as MPAA president, from 1966 to 2004. His successor, Dan Glickman, who ran the group from 2004 to 2010, while never as visible, illuminates the parallels and integral connections between the food and film industries. A U.S. congressman from Kansas beginning in 1977, Glickman served as the nation's secretary of agriculture from 1995 to 2001. From there he became a lobbyist at Akin, Gump, Strauss, Hauer & Feld, LLP, one of the country's largest lobbying firms and a lobbyist for biotech companies.[18] In its search for a lobbyist and industry representative whose Washington connections were as extensive as those of Will Hays, Eric Johnston, and Jack Valenti, all three with high-profile political careers, the MPAA determined that Glickman was a good person for the position because of his "international experience" as agriculture secretary and "his membership on the House Judiciary Committee, which handles copyright matters" (Birnbaum). Glickman himself outlined the links between the food and film industries in 2004, when he was asked what his experience as secretary of agriculture had to do with being head of the MPAA: "Granted, soybeans are not movies, but there are a lot of parallels in the international world of trade and market opening" (Boliek). Emphasizing the food and film industries' shared need for "the developed and developing world to respect copyrights . . . eliminate piracy and permit market access," Glickman told reporters that "agriculture and the creative rights of the movie and music industry are the great export assets in this country" (Boliek).

To locate Glickman's successor, the MPAA again turned to Washington. Christopher Dodd, a former U.S. senator from Connecticut, became MPAA president on 17 March 2011. The studios were reportedly attracted to Dodd because of his experience running the Democratic National Convention (Barnes and Cieply). In announcing Dodd's appointment, the *New York Times* noted: "Mr. Dodd is familiar with at least some of the industry's problems. Jackie M. Clegg, a former Export-Import Bank executive whom he married in 1999," had been a director at Blockbuster Entertainment (Barnes and Cieply). Highlighting the significance, the article continues: "Blockbuster, once a major contributor to studio income, filed for Chapter 11 protection in September after piracy took a toll on home entertainment revenue and competitors like Netflix moved in with low-cost alternatives to store-based sales and rentals" (Barnes and Cieply).

The MPAA's appointment of Dan Glickman and then Christopher Dodd is a reminder that film companies mount highly visible campaigns against piracy. However, the film business calls less attention to the constituencies it accommodates to increase profits and secure unhindered sale of its products. For decades, industry policy has molded film content so that wide releases promote rather than impede profits in other industries. For an industry that distributes representations of food, that policy has been prudent, because when advertising, marketing, and other efforts fail to achieve food companies' desired results, they have and will use the threat of lawsuits to manage and control representations of foodways.

Incentives to Focus on the Pleasures of Food Consumption

Food disparagement laws, sometimes known as veggie libel laws, give food and beverage giants a way to recover damages they believe have resulted from reports or representations that for them constitutes "disparaging statements or dissemination of false information about the safety of the consumption of food products" (Bederman). Food disparagement laws affect and are comparable to Hollywood's industry policy because their power resides in their chilling effect. Litigation stemming from veggie libel laws has not resulted in food company victories. However, these laws and others provide ground for the food industry's extra-legal responses. Veggie libel laws continue to be a factor shaping representations of food in film because they remain on the books of the thirteen states that passed them between 1991 and 1997.

For instance, in 1997 attorneys representing the United Fresh Fruit and Vegetable Association sent a letter to a Vermont environmental group called Food and Water that stated: "As you are no doubt aware, nearly 30 state legislatures have passed or are considering legislation which codifies a cause of action against persons who disseminate false statements regarding agricultural products" (Petersen). Marshaling that inflated count in its threat and declining to mention that the legislation had never been the basis for recovery of damages, the letter continued: "We must advise you that Food and Water's actions will be closely scrutinized'" (Petersen). More than a decade later, in 2009 the Nebraska Farm Bureau elected not to file a suit against the producers of *CSI: Miami,* the Fox dramatic series *Bones,* or the Warner Bros. talk show hosted by Ellen DeGeneres, but that option was the backdrop for members' protests against what they perceived as agriculture disparagement (Flynn).[19]

The food disparagement bills appeared after a 26 February 1989 story on CBS's *60 Minutes* discussing the carcinogenic properties of Alar, a substance produced by Uniroyal Chemical Company to improve apples' appearance and increase their shelf life. The story aired after the Environmental Protection Agency banned the use of Alar on 1 February 1989 but noted "that the test results showed no immediate health threat," allowing growers to "use the chemical for 18 more months" (Egan). From the early 1970s to the late 1980s, the number of apples produced and consumed had doubled as the fruit was pushed by the food industry as a healthy snack (Egan); when consumers learned that apples were sometimes sprayed with Alar, sales took a significant drop, and apple growers lost an estimated $75 million dollars (Turano 5). In response, the Washington State Fruit Commission withdrew "$71,300 worth of television advertising . . . from three CBS affiliates," and in 1990 Washington State apple growers filed the class action suit *Auvil v. CBS "60 Minutes"* ("Fruit Growers"; Egan). In the 1993 decision, the federal district court found that the apple growers failed to prove that CBS had disparaged apples per se or that *60 Minutes* had dispersed any untrue information (Turano 7). Apple growers appealed the decision but lost again in the Ninth Circuit Court of Appeals in 1995 (Turano 7).

In the years following that decision, proponents of food disparagement laws argue that they represent states' attempt "to protect their economies by guarding their agricultural industries" from consumer groups' grabs for publicity and television programs' use of the "opinions and conclusions of 'investigative' news reporters" to boost ratings (Cochran 1). Critics of the food disparagement laws make the case that they violate the right to free speech because they do not follow "common law torts of defamation and product disparagement," which require the plaintiffs, in this case food producers, to prove that defendants have made false statements (Turano 1). Instead, all but two of the state food disparagement laws "place the burden on the defendant . . . to prove the veracity of the disparaging statements" (Turano 21; see 22). It is not difficult to see why views about food disparagement laws are polarized: some people believe they are necessary to keep media outlets from producing sensationalistic and unverified reports about food products in order to drum up ratings, while others feel the laws discourage and make impossible vital and crucial criticism of a food industry that has proven in the past to be disingenuous at best and, at worst, willing to expose consumers to potential danger just to make a profit (Turano 3).

Even though there have been only five recorded cases invoking agricultural disparagement against media, food disparagement laws remain looming and intimidating factors for the film industry to consider (Turano 24–25). In 1995 the groups Action for a Clean Environment and Parents for Pesticide Alternatives filed a suit against the state of Georgia to determine the constitutionality of its food disparagement law; the case was dismissed (Turano 30). The high-profile *Texas Beef Group et al v. Oprah Winfrey* case also left the status of food disparagement laws uncertain, for while the 1998 decision found in favor of

Winfrey and rejected the plaintiffs' argument that she had engaged in food disparagement, the court did not rule on the constitutionality of such laws.

The plaintiffs, led by Texas rancher Paul Engler, initiated the suit against Winfrey during the height of the mad cow disease panic in the United Kingdom, a period of decreasing revenues for cattlemen in the United States (Rampton and Stauber "One Hundred"). Engler, "the world's largest cattle feedlot operator," had been a key player in "the formula pricing system" in which cattle owned by meatpackers and closely allied sources were used as "captive supplies . . . to force down the market price of cattle" owned by non-affiliated ranchers (Rampton and Stauber "One Hundred"). The cattlemen's $10.3 million dollar lawsuit alleged that "false, disparaging statements about their products" made during the 16 April 1996 *Oprah Winfrey Show* were responsible for the cattlemen's loss of revenue (Turano 25). The Northern District Court of Texas ruled against the cattlemen, determining that "cattle were not 'perishable' within the meaning of the [1995 Texas food disparagement law] and that the plaintiffs failed to meet their burden of proving that the defendants knowingly made false statements" (Turano 27). The cattlemen appealed the ruling; on 10 February 2000 the Fifth U.S. Circuit Court of Appeals upheld the verdict that rejected their claims against Winfrey, her company, and activist Harold Lyman ("Appeals Court").

While food disparagement laws have not enabled food companies to recover losses they attribute to public statements made by consumer groups and others, the laws have silenced critics of the food industry and kept films focused on the pleasures of food consumption. Journalist Melody Petersen explains that while "some publishers and broadcasters continue to put out new reports on food, other media companies, especially smaller ones [have] worried about the high cost of defending a lawsuit, have stricken information from manuscripts, avoided certain food issues, or, in one case, dropped a book project that was already at the printer" (Petersen). *The Corporation* follows one of the extra-legal uses of food disparagement laws. In 1997, Monsanto threatened to sue the Fox affiliate in Tampa Bay if it aired a story on Prosilac, the Monsanto bovine growth hormone linked to cancer and already banned in the United Kingdom (Casten 164). The threat led the station to kill the story and eventually fire reporters Jane Akre and Steve Wilson. In a 2010 survey of legal cases involving food disparagement laws, Rebecca Turano sums up their chilling effect: while "no case has been filed in over a decade, there have been numerous instances in which individuals have been compelled to restrict free speech with the threat of a lawsuit" (33). Those instances include actor Alec Baldwin being unable to find an outlet for a four-part TV documentary entitled "The History of Food" that would have examined the use of "pesticides, herbicides and some disputed practices used in beef" (Petersen).

For the film industry, the chilling effect created by food disparagement laws has been amplified by legislation sponsored by the food and biotech industries in their efforts to respond to what they see as "eco-terrorists" and "animal rights terrorists." In 2006, food and biotech companies, with assistance from lobbyists at the Center for Consumer Freedom, persuaded Congress to expand the 1992 Animal Enterprise Protection Act. The more sweeping 2006 Animal Enterprise Terrorism Act makes it illegal to picket, boycott, or engage in any investigation that might negatively impact the profits of a factory farm or research facility that conducts experiments on animals. As of 2010, thirty-nine states have laws designed to protect animal and environmental "enterprises" and that require "special penalties for activists" (Potter 130).[20]

The 1992 federal law reflected legislation passed in twenty-three states between 1988 and 1991 in response to vandalism by the Animal Liberation Front (ALF). The term "eco-terrorism" dates back to 1983, when Ron Arnold of the Center for the Defense of Free Enterprise coined it to describe sabotage perpetrated by radical environmentalists (fictionalized in Edward Abbey's 1975 novel *The Monkey Wrench Gang*) (Potter 53). Whereas animal activists in the United Kingdom had used arson for years, it was "a watershed moment" when ALF members adopted the tactic on 16 April 1987 at an animal laboratory being built at the University of California, Davis (Potter 119). After that, actions by animal-rights activists were classified differently and treated with much more severity. For the first time, the FBI classified animal-rights crimes as "domestic terrorism" (Potter 119).

Even with that change, it was not until 1998 that law enforcement became more focused on the activities of animal-rights and environmental activists. In 1998, members of the Earth Liberation Front (ELF) caused $26 million worth of damage at a Vail, Colorado, ski resort to protest the resort's expansion into the Rocky Mountains (Potter 57). That same year, Justin Samuel and Peter Young were indicted under the 1992 Animal Enterprise Protection Act for freeing mink from their cages; Samuel was arrested in 1999, Young in 2005. The stakes were raised again in 2001. ELF member Jeff Luers was sentenced to almost twenty-three years in prison for an arson attack in 2000 (Potter 89). More visibly, the 9/11 attacks increased opposition to ELF actions; for example, on 12 September 2001, Rep. Greg Walden (R-Oregon) told reporters that the ELF "posed a threat 'no less heinous than what we saw yesterday here in Washington and New York'" (Potter 58).

This position was supported by a 2003 report from the American Legislative Exchange Council (ALEC), which conservative activist Paul Weyrich, who coined the term "moral majority," founded in 1973 and which counts among its sponsors corporations such as Philip Morris, R. J. Reynolds, Amoco, Chevron, Shell, and Texaco. In 2004 FBI officers called for expansion of terrorism laws and explained that "investigation of animal rights extremists and eco-terrorism matters [was the agency's] highest domestic terrorism investigation priority" (Potter 25; see Potter 125, 127).

In 2004, members of Stop Huntingdon Animal Cruelty (SHAC) were arrested for openly supporting the actions of animal activists; they were tried in 2005 under an expanded interpretation of the 1992 Animal Enterprise Protection Act and sentenced in 2006. After the sentencing, David Martosko at the Center for Consumer Freedom told reporters that the government should "build on the victory against SHAC and take aggressive action against mainstream organizations like PETA [People for the Ethical Treatment of Animals] and the Humane Society of the United States," which he called "farm teams for the eco-terror problem" (Potter 113). An FBI investigation begun in 2004 led to the 2006 indictment of eleven activists for actions committed "in the name of the ELF and ALF" from 1995 to 2001 (Potter 63). Here again, defendants were charged under the 1992 law that established "the crime of animal enterprise terrorism" to cover the actions of a person who "'intentionally causes physical disruption to the functioning of an animal enterprise by intentionally stealing, damaging, or causing the loss of, any property'" (Potter 122). For Daniel McGowan, an ELF member arrested in 1995 for arson and domestic terrorism related to several incidents, and SHAC member Andy Stepanian, the enhanced terrorism charge meant that their incarceration included time at a Communication Management Unit (CMU) designed to "isolate prisoners with 'inspirational significance,' to use the government's language, from the communities and social movements of which they are a part" (Potter 216; see Malek).[21]

Consequences for Representations of Food in Film

With food disparagement and animal enterprise laws in place, the film industry and individual filmmakers have to weigh their legal risks before undertaking a project. Even mainstream films have been charged with promoting "eco-terrorism." *Hoot* (Shriner, 2006), a PG movie about teenagers who fight a construction project that threatens endangered owls, essentially trains "a generation to look cute while burning homes and cars and stores," in the words of Ron Arnold (Potter 136). The Center for Consumer Freedom, a vocal advocate of enhanced sentences for animal-rights and environmental activists, sees the 2006 version of *Charlotte's Web* (Winick) as a film that "promotes animal rights extremism" (Potter 136). *Avatar* has been criticized for fostering "eco-terrorism." Summarizing the responses of "political conservatives," journalist Patrick Goldstein notes that the films' critics believe that conclusions about climate change are open to debate, that Hollywood "disrespects religion," and that the U.S. military should never be presented in an "unflattering light" (Goldstein).

In 2006, filmmaker Adam Durand was tried and sentenced for criminal trespass after obtaining footage of industrial egg production facilities at Wegmans Egg Farm. Upon appeal in 2009, however, the Appellate Division of the New York Supreme Court overturned Durand's six-month sentence (*People v. Durand*), and he enjoyed a moderate success when his documentary *Fowl Play* was screened at festivals and animal-rights events (Durand and Runkle). While of a decidedly different nature than the sentence and CMU imprisonment of an activist such as Daniel McGowan, Durand's sentence nevertheless reflects the contentious environment for representations of the industrial food system.

Drawing as it does on Eric Schlosser's book *Fast Food Nation* and Michael Pollan's books *An Omnivore's Dilemma: A Natural History of Four Meals* (2007) and *In Defense of Food: An Eater's Manifesto* (2009), *Food, Inc.*, as David Denby noted in the *New Yorker*, is "an angry blast of disgust aimed at the American food industry" (85). Yet the film "steers clear of animal liberation arguments while pushing for a return to grass-fed, hormone-free meat production" (Golding). It also carefully avoids support for environmental activists while relying on information provided by mainstream journalists and established policy makers. Having discovered the power of the food industry and the complications of making such a documentary, director Robert Kenner noted that "he and his crew were denied interviews by agribusiness, and [that] they encountered numerous people who were afraid to talk for fear of being sued" (Golding). The food system "is a much more frightening subject than [he] ever imagined, [and] a much more litigious subject" (Golding). As for food companies' lack of transparency, Kenner observed: "I think you could be making a film about nuclear terrorism and have easier access" (Golding). And with food disparagement laws and federal legislation that makes any action perceived as a threat to corporate profits a crime of domestic terrorism, the food industry has "a lot of clout and they use lawyers very freely to intimidate," noted Kenner: "I spent more on legal fees for this film than all my past 15 films combined" (Golding).

The food industry's campaign against *Food, Inc.* is just the sort of response Hollywood usually aims to avoid. Monsanto still maintains a link on its corporate website with material designed to discredit points from *Food, Inc.* ("Food, Inc. Movie"; "Spoiling"). The website reiterates Monsanto's position that criticism of the company's practices constitutes criticism of America's hard-working farmers. It also emphasizes that biotechnology and high-input agriculture are the only solutions to global demands for food. Monsanto's online "response to Food, Inc." is also linked to the website for the industry-funded Center for Consumer Freedom headed by Washington lobbyist David Berman. With the American Meat Institute in the lead, the food industry also created a website called SafefoodInc.com (see Kearney). The website features a "Myths and Facts" page that discredits *Food, Inc.* and a "Take Action Now" page that recommends as follows: "If you are concerned about your school system's use of the film in the classroom, tell your State Department of Education and your local school district that equal time is needed from university experts or industry representatives." This multi-prong offensive against *Food, Inc.* exemplifies the industry's retaliation against representations of food that distract consumers from the pleasures of consumption.

The film industry's failure to control such representations in this case was especially problematic because Kenner's documentary calls attention to the veggie libel laws that food companies want to hide from the general public. In its account of *Texas Beef Group v. Oprah Winfrey,* the film suggests that the laws pose a threat to whistleblowers even though the court found that Winfrey was not guilty of food disparagement. The film lets the public know that the U.S. government has limited oversight of food processing. It explains that after the Meat and Poultry Association pursued legal action against the U.S. Department of Agriculture, the courts decided that the USDA does not have the authority to shut down private processing plants even if its food products have been linked to illness and death. In transgressing industry policy and representations actively promoted by the food industry, *Food, Inc.* "connects the dots between factory farming and E. coli

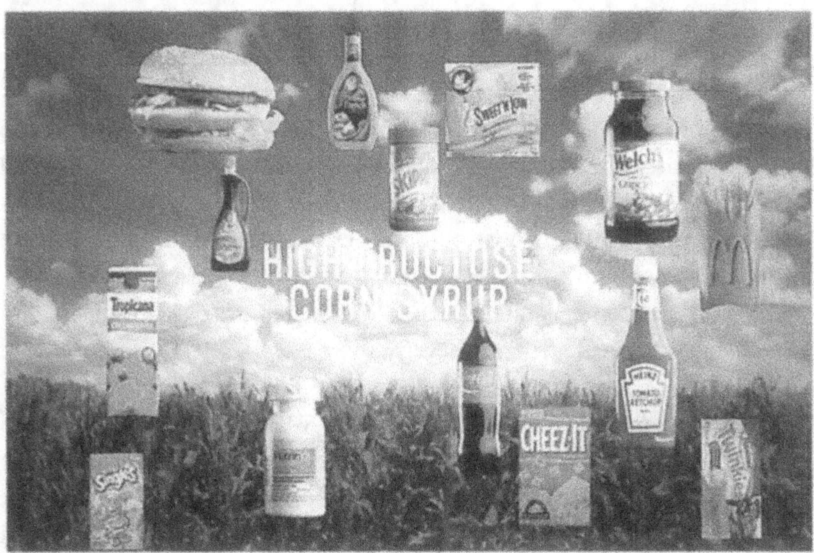

Food, Inc. *(Magnolia Pictures, Participant Media, River Road Entertainment): The food industry had to step in and discredit the documentary after Hollywood failed to control its representation.*

outbreaks, government subsidies and the diabetes epidemic—even slaughterhouses and illegal immigration" (Friedman). It "reveals the vast gulf between how our food is produced and how its production is represented to us" (Friedman).

Food, Inc. is a problem for the food industry because it suggests that consumer society's inexpensive food has "a 'hidden' price tag that takes an enormous toll on our environment, our health, and our society" (Harrington). Rather than focus attention on the ease and pleasure of consumption, the film examines food as "a health issue, an environmental issue [and as] a human rights issue" (Straus). With its view of the industrial food system stretching from procurement to disposal, the film shows that the rising costs in health care and disaster relief are related to "the way Americans produce and consume food" ("'Food, Inc.' Offers"). Even people who "avoid junk food, with many sighs of relief and self-approval," notes David Denby, discussing the film's look at industrial food procurement, "may still be eating junk a good deal of the time" (85).

The basic premise of *Food, Inc.* is that consumers have "the right to know what's in our food" (Amato and Hamid), contrary to the food and film industries' modus operandi. As journalist Luke Harrington observes: "Discovering and enacting solutions must begin with fact-finding and debate—and these are the very things that the food industry wants to silence" (3). Reactivating the food wars of the 1970s, the film articulates the counterculture's objections to the industrial food system and its interest in alternative methods of food production, distribution, preparation, consumption, and disposal. The film's release in 2009 also coincided with First Lady Michelle Obama's "organic vegetable garden on the White House grounds and articles about sustainable, local, and pesticide-free food [that were appearing] every week in newspapers and magazines, not just in the lifestyle pages but in business sections as well" (Amato and Hamid). With like-minded films also slipping through the cracks in Hollywood, it is not entirely surprising that Dan Glickman was asked to step down before completing his first term as MPAA president. While Glickman recognized the food and film industries' parallel desire to "eliminate piracy and permit market access" (Boliek), the former secretary of agriculture proved unable to eliminate representations of food in film that were inconsistent with food companies' marketing and image-control campaigns.

Conclusion

Cinema's aesthetic conventions and distribution practices that shield consumers from viewing the grim realities of the food system in their entertainment options have evolved over time, influenced by Hollywood's longtime industry policy that complex political subjects, thorny social problems, and the destructive commercial practices of other industries are not suitable movie topics. The food and film industries create their own synergies by foregrounding the pleasures and benefits of consumption. After decades of film production and distribution choices, industry policy has made dinner and a movie an icon of consumer society, and co-promotions between fast-food chains and movie blockbusters a basic fact of modern life. Industry policy keeps consumers focused on food as a convenient object of pleasure and distracted from food companies' profit-driven practices. For more than a century, industry policy has, for the most part, effectively masked the reality that "food companies—just like companies that sell cigarettes, pharmaceuticals, or any other commodity—routinely place the needs of stockholders over considerations of public health" (Nestle xiv).

Assessing Hollywood films in a 1939 essay entitled "Movies with Blinders," Pare Lorentz observed that decisions made by the Hollywood studios, "the richest group of manufacturers in the country," necessarily reflect their desire to increase profit and avoid lost income (*Lorentz on Film* 167). To achieve that objective, they eliminated material from films that might offend other governments, including those controlled by dictators (*Lorentz on Film* 167). To avoid lost income, film industry executives dodged any "manuscript that dealt with unemployment, relief, labor, agriculture, or politics," since depictions of health or economic problems might offend the judges, church leaders, government officials, corporate executives, and other individuals who enjoyed the dividends of social inequality (*Lorentz on Film* 167). That assessment applies equally well today, as *Fast Food Nation* and other films that shed light on problems in the food system reveal what the food and film industries work so hard to keep consumers from seeing.

Film companies' multifaceted relationship with food and beverage giants warrants study, for, as Janet Wasko points out, "economic and political analysis" provides an important "grounding for ideological readings and cultural analysis" (9). Political economy studies of the film industry itself have yielded illuminating insights; additional information emerges when one examines film companies' working relationships with industries led by Monsanto, Coca-Cola, and Cargill. Lorentz anticipated this line of inquiry when he examined newsreels' habit of featuring the U.S. Navy in light of Hollywood's ties with the steel industry (*Lorentz on Film* 82–83).

Almost from its inception, the film industry established working relations with other industries. Ignoring or mystifying the unseemly aspects of other industries has allowed film companies to avoid conflict with powerful constituencies. Maintaining good relations with them has enhanced profits and minimized lost revenue. As the links between blockbusters and fast-food chains reveal, synergy continues to characterize relationships between the food and film industries. Advertisers and lobbyists work overtime to keep food and film consumers focused on the pleasures of the FMCGs, the "fast-moving-consumer-goods" sold by the linked industries ("Glossary").

As a longtime contributor to food companies' marketing and image-control ventures, the film industry has effectively kept food companies' secrets. With the food industry in a dominant position, it has been prudent for mainstream film companies to elide the messy and troubling stages of foodways. The film industry is, rightly, nervous about upsetting the juggernauts of an industry that pumps money into film companies via product placement and fast-food tie-ins. Over time, the wide circulation of films that facilitate food companies' marketing and image-control measures has helped to shape familiar filmic conventions. Food-focused films illustrate ways that these conventions are mobilized to depict utopian and dystopian experiences.

3

Foodways Syntax

Utopian Films' Use of Food to Create Community

The influence of food companies such as Kraft, ConAgra, and Burger King and film companies such as Paramount (Viacom), Twentieth Century Fox (News Corp.), and Universal (NBC) has long shaped depictions of food and food behavior in mainstream cinema. In recent decades, the film industry's escalating involvement in co-promotions has increasingly made food a consumer item that movies use to convey character and promote excessive consumption. With food one of many products that could signify sophisticated consumption, films such as *Tampopo, Babette's Feast, Eat Drink Man Woman,* and *Big Night* contributed to the expectation that "food films [would be] filled with glistening dumplings, magical desserts and technically perfect kitchen scenes" (Severson "Eat Drink").

The production-reception context for representations of food necessitates ideological studies that draw on foodways analysis. As Anne Bower points out: "Food is part of the way that, for a century now, movies have been telling us who we are, constructing our economic and political aspirations; our sense of sexual, national, and ethnic identity; filling our minds with ideas about love and romance, innocence and depravity, adventure, bravery, cruelty, hope, and despair" (3). Food has functioned seamlessly as an integral part of cinema because the deep-seated personal and cultural dimensions of eating and drinking mean that the choices of filmic characters about what to eat and drink, where and when to eat, whom to eat with, how to prepare food, and so on can have tangible meaning for audiences. To paraphrase a point Rick Altman makes about successful genres, a film's representation of food or food behavior will owe "its success not alone to its reflection of an audience ideal, nor solely to its status as apology for the Hollywood enterprise, but to its ability to carry out both functions simultaneously" (37).

Some studies of food's potential to convey meaning in film have followed the lines of genre studies that examine "conventions, iconography, settings, narratives, characters, and actors" (Grant, *Film Genre* 2). The work has located "recurring semantic elements" in a collection of American and international films (Altman 39). For example, James Keller explores the rich and varied meaning generated by "culinary imagery" in a dizzying array of films (1). Writing about films "in which food production, preparation, service and or consumption play an operative and memorable role in the development of character, structure, or theme," Keller discusses films such as *A Thousand Acres* (Moorhouse, 1997), *Chocolat* (Hallström, 2000), and *Dinner Rush* (Giraldi, 2000) (1). Amplifying those studies by considering "the broader uses of food imagery in cinema," Keller also touches on scores of additional films ranging from *Mildred Pierce* (Curtiz, 1945) to *Harold and Kumar Go to White Castle* (Leiner, 2004).

Other work on "recurring semantic elements" has identified "a list of common traits, attitudes, characters, shots, locations, sets, and the like" in films' use of food (Altman 39, 31). To limit the genre to a handful of canonical films, some studies argue that certain semantic elements must be present in sufficient degree for something to qualify as a food film. Steve Zimmerman and Ken Weiss propose that food films must have five elements: "Food has to be an essential part of the plot"; it "must be seen on screen, in close-up, at times throughout the film"; "preparation and cooking of food must be featured"; "serving of food . . . must be shown"; and "Food must be influential in the lives of at least one of the featured characters" (212).

Their emphasis on semantic elements leads Zimmerman and Weiss to see *La Grande Bouffe* as comparable to *Tampopo*. However, while one needs "to recognize that not all genre films related to their genre in the same way or to the same extent," a useful description of the genre would need to explain why the "syntax" in these two films is entirely different (Altman 34, 31). In *La Grande Bouffe,* "the structures into which" food preparation, presentation, and consumption "are arranged" are decidedly dystopian, for they create a narrative in which "four middle-aged, financially successful but very bored men . . . decide to end their lives by eating themselves to death" (Altman 31; Zimmerman and Weiss 212). By comparison, in the quirky utopian world of *Tampopo,* a truck driver with a keen interest in cuisine helps a recently widowed woman "turn her restaurant into a huge success," become "a confident entrepreneur," and locate a new husband (Zimmerman and Weiss 219).

As Bower notes, studies concerned with semantic elements have called attention to domestic or professional cooks as leading characters in food films (5). Cook- or chef-centered films will logically focus on food preparation and presentation. In addition, "the restaurant kitchen, the dining room and/or kitchen of a home, tables within a restaurant, a shop in which food is made and/or sold, will usually be central settings" (Bower 6). However, grouping films based on these recurring characters draws together a diverse body of work that includes *Dona Flora and Her Two Husbands* (Barreto, 1976), *The Chinese Feast* (Hark, 1995), *The God of Cookery* (Chow and Lee, 1996), *A Chef in Love, Big Night, Felicia's Journey* (Egoyan, 1999), *Simply Irresistible* (Tarlov, 1999), *The Magic Kitchen* (Lee, 2004), and *Julie and Julia* (Ephron, 2009).

The casting of Stanley Tucci in both *Big Night* and *Julie and Julia* echoes the familiar practice in which "stars and genres reinforce each other" (Grant, *Film Genre* 19). Yet the distinct contrast between *Big Night* and *Felicia's Journey,* for example, complicates the films' shared semantic elements of iconography, setting, and character. In *Big Night,* the drive that Primo (Tony Shalhoub) has for creating exquisite meals is a sign that he is an "artist who refuses to compromise his work in order to appeal to the philistine tastes of Americans who want quantity rather than quality in their food" (Keller 126). By comparison, *Felicia's Journey* features a series of scenes in which serial killer Joseph Hilditch (Bob Hoskins) prepares "dinners large enough for an extended family's holiday feast and then [eats] alone in his formal dining room" (Keller

83). It suggests that by recreating the elaborate dishes his mother had once prepared on her cooking show, he "can symbolically consume the mother's body through the emulation and consumption of her recipes" (Keller 81).

Altman proposes that "the interplay between syntax and semantics" explains thematic differences in films that have shared iconography, settings, and characters (36). For instance, films with science fiction semantics sometimes borrow from "the syntax of the western" and at other times from "syntactical relationships previously established by the horror film" (Altman 36). In a parallel fashion, food film semantics will be combined with the syntax of romantic comedies in films like *No Reservations,* while *Superstar: The Karen Carpenter Story* (Haynes, 1988) employs horror film syntax. Contrasts between films like *La Grande Bouffe, Felicia's Journey,* and *Superstar* on the one side and films like *Tampopo, Big Night,* and *No Reservations* on the other might suggest that food films have "recurring semantic elements [but] never develop a stable syntax" (Altman 39). The contrasts between the dystopian and utopian films might be taken as evidence that the genre will "develop slowly, change constantly, and surge recognizably before settling into a familiar pattern" (Altman 29). The films' shared semantics but contrasting syntax might lead one to see food films as a genre that will "go through an extended series of paradigms, none of which may be claimed as dominant" (Altman 29).

The sharp but consistent contrast in food films' syntax suggests that they reflect the profoundly ambiguous place of food in contemporary society. Touching on the films' ambivalent representations of food, Bower notes that food films "depict characters negotiating questions of identity, power, culture, class, spirituality, or relationship through food" (6). Some of those negotiations will lead to community, unity, harmony, and fulfillment. In other films, those negotiations will mark stages of decline, dissolution, imbalance, and social fragmentation. Highlighting food's dual-edged character, Bower points out that representations of food preparation and consumption can be "reassuring signifiers of cultural continuity," while in other films "cannibalism, food fights, or food disorders" give expression to cultural anxieties (4). Articulating a position central to our book, Bower places greater emphasis on syntactical relationships when discussing the genre's "specific meaning-bearing structures" (Altman 33). Describing a related view that informs our work as well, Bower concludes that food's paradoxical status is mobilized in narratives when "films fall into the food film genre or simply make effective use of food as a communicative element" (6).

The contrasting syntactical relationships represent differing responses to food politics in consumer society. Some films structure representations of foodways to depict the joys of cooking and eating, whereas others explore the contradictions and traumas surrounding individual and societal food experiences. Importantly, those structured, thematic differences cannot be boiled down to a contrast between films that sustain or critique the status quo. Some films embody dominant ideology and celebrate conspicuous consumption; others call attention to food-related problems. However, utopian films do not always support the status quo; while *No Reservations* reinforces the ideals of consumer society by identifying happiness and individual worth with conventional beauty and upscale consumption, *Bagdad Cafe* offers a more folkloristic view of community and harmonious relations as the source of personal and social happiness.

Thematic contrasts created by films' utopian and dystopian depictions of foodways reflect the paradoxical status of food as promise and threat. That view of food films parallels the position that Jim Kitses and others have proposed in describing the western as a genre that "grows out of a dialectic between the West as garden and as desert (between culture and nature, community and individual, future and past)" (Altman 32). Arguably, food films reflect the conflicting visions of food that have fueled cultural debates in industrialized societies since the food wars of the 1970s.

Films and film genres reflect an era's social anxieties; deep-seated uncertainties about food in consumer society provide one explanation for the rise of food films. Food films may have begun with *La Grande Bouffe* and *Who's Killing the Great Chefs of Europe?* (Kotcheff, 1978) (Zimmerman and Weiss 212–17), the genre serving as a response to the perception that escalating reliance in industrialized countries on processed convenience foods designed by the food industry for use by modern consumers was erasing personal, regional, and national identities. *La Grande Bouffe* is a stridently dystopian attack on over-consumption in food-saturated consumer society. *Who's Killing the Great Chefs of Europe?*

sets food critic Max Vanderveere (Robert Morley) in opposition to fast-food entrepreneur Robby Ross (George Segal) and so captures the counterculture's "consumerist component" that strongly encouraged people to avoid processed food (Belasco, *Appetite* 4).

The food film genre has sometimes been identified with films like *Babette's Feast* that give expression to the fact that "food can enliven social relations, enrich spiritual affairs, and enhance an individual's sense of well-being" (Jones et al., "Sensory" 2). However, food films are more complex because they capture the aspirations and the anxieties of people in consumer society who are living not only with the promise and threat of industrialized food production but also the promise and threat of the countercuisine's emphasis on slow cooking, organic food production, and local sources. In the same way that polarized perspectives on food in consumer society exist on a spectrum, one finds utopian as well as dystopian representations of food and society. Food films present people's hopes and concerns about food; in utopian films like *Chocolat* and *Soul Food* (Tillman, 1997), food brings people together; in dystopian films like *Delicatessen* and *Scotland, PA,* food is an element in a devolving world.

Bagdad Cafe as a Utopian Food Film

In *Bagdad Cafe,* German director Percy Adlon uses food products and food behaviors to show how characters' evolving relationships transform a rundown diner on an old highway that crosses the vast Mojave Desert into a bountiful oasis that nourishes relationships and sustains families, laborers, and wanderers without a home. In *Bagdad Cafe,* cuisine choices and food etiquette are integral to the utopian narrative; characters' ideas about recipe design, often about the way to make coffee, illustrate their steps toward harmony. Food products eventually connect members of the community. The utopian diner community that finally emerges depends on the characters' mundane interactions involving coffee, crackers, hard-boiled eggs, melons, squash, serving trays, and wash buckets.[1]

The film's food-centered narrative makes food products and an evolving food performance or meal system keys to understanding the characters. In addition, their interactions surrounding other aspects of foodways—procurement, preparation, preservation, presentation, consumption, and cleanup—illuminate characters' temperaments, cultural identities, economic status, power dynamics, and changing personal relationships. Scenes of food consumption are important, but rather than focus on the sensory pleasure of exquisitely prepared meals, *Bagdad Cafe* directs attention to meaning conveyed by changes in the eating environment and characters' ideas about who should eat together and what food should be eaten on different occasions. The story world—with a diner at its center, a multi-ethnic collection of characters, and a setting largely isolated from external influences—foregrounds characters' food behaviors. Their relationships change when they share or exchange traditional food items, when their food interactions cross ethnic or national divisions, and when eating or drinking figures into the evolving group identity of the diner community (see Brown and Mussell).

Full-figured German actress Marianne Sägebrecht plays the film's central character, Jasmin Münchgstettner, the matronly German tourist who transforms the Bagdad Cafe community and is herself transformed by the diner community. Guyana-born actress CCH Pounder plays Jasmin's initial antagonist, Brenda. Pounder conveys the steps by which Brenda, the proprietor of Bagdad's desolate truck stop, becomes the welcoming host of the bountiful diner as well as Jasmin's closest friend and trusted advisor. The film opens with parallel scenes of Jasmin and Brenda arguing with and then being left by their husbands. The two women eventually recognize their shared sense of loss and isolation. Moving forward from that shared experience, their eccentric experiments nourishing themselves and the people around them secure a bond between them that circumvents differences in race, nationality, and personal experience.[2]

While Brenda's husband stays close by, interestedly monitoring developments at the diner to determine when he might return, Jasmin's husband is content to go it alone and the couple end up living on different continents. In his absence, Jasmin gains a smitten admirer, the aging bachelor Rudi Cox (Jack Palance). Rudi, an eccentric retired Hollywood set painter who lives in a dated Airstream trailer parked near the Bagdad Cafe, is the diner's most regular customer. To Brenda, he is both Mr. Cox and like a member of the family. When he is not silently drinking coffee in the dim light of the diner with Cahuenga (George Aguilar), the diner's Native American cook, Rudi paints mystical landscapes of the local desert and primitive still life illustrations of squash, melons, and other fruit native to desert climates. His paintings call attention to the symbolism carried by food because they feature items rarely if ever found in traditional European still-life paintings.

Foodways: Signs of Impoverished Lives

In *Bagdad Cafe,* food products and food behaviors provide a window into the characters' evolving identities and sometimes difficult steps toward community. In the opening scenes, the diner's broken coffee machine and the German tourists' abandoned Rosenheim coffee thermos are vivid indices of the characters' initial dystopian existence. With the thermos and coffee machine out of commission, the absence of tools for food preparation and preservation makes nourishing relationships difficult if not impossible. That situation is confirmed by other aspects of the characters' foodways. Coffee as an essential food product is missing from the characters' lives. There is no meal cycle (food performance system) that gives meaning and structure to individual meals. The characters have trouble securing provisions (food procurement) and customer service (presentation) is not a priority. There is no space set aside for the family's food consumption; even customers do not receive full meals.

Cleanup of other people's meals is the most constructive activity available. The pre-credit sequence shows Jasmin and her husband in the midst of a marital battle at a desolate rest stop up the highway from the Bagdad Cafe. The scene suggests that the couple has just finished a decidedly unpleasant meal stop. Short, disconnected shots, each one at a canted angle, convey the idea that their meal had not been a cheerful picnic lunch. Jasmin, having derived little joy from consuming food with her husband, tries to get satisfaction through food cleanup. Determined to find some sort of fulfillment in the windblown rest area, Jasmin delays their departure by taking time to pick up aluminum cans that are littering the ground. Frustrated with her interest in food cleanup, Jasmin's husband decides to leave. However, he inadvertently backs their oversized car into the rusted remains of the rest stop's outhouse. Its ruined condition and scatological connotations underscore the sorry state of the couple's marriage.

Seeing her husband's predicament, Jasmin becomes fed up with his cigar-smoking incompetence. She collects her things and storms off with her plane ticket and one of the couple's overstuffed suitcases. To counter her flamboyant gesture of anger, Jasmin's husband drives off alone with polka music blaring on the car radio. He pauses to leave their huge, bright yellow Rosenheim coffee thermos at the rest stop entrance, but Jasmin does not see it because she has already started down the highway. His ostensibly thoughtful gesture gives him the final word in their argument. The abandoned thermos, something they had likely brought with them from Germany, no longer binds them together but instead marks the dissolution of their relationship.

Food preparation and preservation tools communicate the emotionally malnourished condition of the Bagdad Cafe community. With the diner's coffee machine broken, the diner cannot provide even the most basic comfort for the family members and customers who often count on a cup of coffee to get conversations started. Cahuenga, Brenda, and her husband Sal (G. Smokey Campbell) all understand they have failed their community. Cahuenga has stopped cooking. Sal cannot procure food. Brenda, who has decided to take her frustration out on everyone, cannot nourish her son Sal Junior (Darron Flagg), her daughter Phyllis (Monica Calhoun), or Sal Junior's infant son. She is in an impoverished state, overwhelmed because she cannot provide for her family and customers. Her male counterparts are in an equally wretched condition. Cahuenga spends most of his time sleeping; Sal cannot remember to bring home the new coffee maker they have purchased in town.

The film presents the diner community as a poor one by symbolizing its social disarray through the absence of coffee. As fictional embodiments of America's disenfranchised lower class, the characters' failure to provide coffee, and thus their inability to extend even a basic "gesture of hospitality" to their guests, points to the dehumanizing consequences of economic structures that trap some members of American society in perpetual impoverishment (Fitchen 395).[3] The diner family's "perpetual condition of limited financial resources" also deeply affects when, where, and with whom the characters eat (Fitchen

392). There are no chairs, tables, plates, cups, glasses, or utensils that belong to the family; there is no special or separate place for them to eat. While in the end this situation facilitates a more inclusive community than is possible when private property is central, at the beginning of the film the family members act as if they are homeless. Their emotionally impoverished condition carries over into the diner's customers as well, for at first none of the characters eat or even sit together. The group's lack of commensality, of sharing a table, is significant, for, as Carole Counihan notes, in everyday life "the collapse of food sharing is often linked to the breakdown of social solidarity" (14). In the absence of familial or community support, Brenda's children fall back on survival strategies. Sal Junior copes by withdrawing into classical music and, rather than holding and nurturing his infant son, he straps the baby into a high chair next to his keyboard or leaves him outside on a baby blanket. Phyllis uses pop music and a steady stream of boyfriends to sustain herself. The group's disrupted condition causes Sal Junior to see existence as a solitary experience. It prompts Phyllis to forget about home-cooked meals and to work instead on getting "bread" for concerts.

Food Preparation: A Vehicle for Creating Relationships

However, in this ultimately utopian film, the food preparation and preservation tools that mark divisions between people also bring the characters together. Thus, even in the garbage-littered dystopian world presented in the film's opening moments, there is a promise that the characters will find their way out of isolation and social discord. Sal might not remember to pick up the diner's new coffee machine, but he prudently recovers the thermos that Jasmin's husband left at the rest stop. Soon after, with the thermos in the back of his truck, he stops to ask Jasmin if she needs a ride. Sal's acts of good sense (retrieving the thermos) and kindness (offering Jasmin a ride) begin to replenish the diner community. A portable food preparation and food preservation tool, the thermos is a talisman; there is something magical and recuperative about Sal recovering it. The film emphasizes that point. In a tracking shot, Sal's truck moves slowly past Jasmin. The framing focuses attention on the huge yellow thermos in the back of his truck.

Then, as if to add a blinking neon arrow pointing to the thermos, the scene's realistic desert tones shift to a surreal purple-blue color eight times in rapid succession.

From the start, the cheerful thermos functions as a yardstick for measuring the grace, wisdom, and compassion of the characters. Brenda reveals her impoverished emotional state when she condemns Sal's attempt to use the thermos to restart the diner community's ritual of drinking coffee together. In slightly better shape, Cahuenga and Rudi can be friendly as they examine the thermos and experiment with its strong coffee. Cahuenga shows that he is the most in touch with important food matters: working quietly and without fanfare, he starts using the Rosenheim thermos as a coffee maker and thus makes it the means by which the group makes its first tentative steps toward the bonds that arise from sharing food and drink.

Initially focused on himself rather than the diner community, Rudi tries to use the Rosenheim thermos coffee in a failed attempt at flirtation that leaves him looking like a silly dandy in snakeskin boots. When Jasmin first enters the diner and squeezes herself into a chair close to the door, Rudi takes it upon himself to offer her coffee from the newly discovered thermos. Assuming that this shy, uncomfortable woman could not drink the strongly brewed coffee he had choked on a few minutes earlier, Rudi offers to add hot water to her cup. But Jasmin, accustomed to drinking espresso, declines. So, rather than complete his gracious gesture with the gallant flourish of adding the water, Rudi has to retreat to his table in the corner. The characters' exchange about coffee illustrates the cultural divide that initially separates the two, for food preparation and individuals' choices about food product are indices of cultural identity. As Belasco notes, "A cuisine helps a society's members define themselves" (*Appetite* 440). The "foods and seasonings, preparation techniques, and dining etiquette" that characters choose thus carries a great deal of meaning (*Appetite* 44).[4]

A remarkable force from the moment it arrives, the thermos' cheerful presence disturbs the patterns that have kept members of the diner community isolated from one another. Early in the film Rudi, Cahuenga, and Sal are still bound to conventional ideas of masculinity and so express their fondness for the thermos by saying it is practical. However, through framing, performance style, and choreography of performance, the film shows that the men's explanation masks their actual interest in the thermos as a means for communicating with one another. In a comical shot that features the three men pleading with Brenda to keep the thermos, the men look like three big kids, particularly because G. Smokey Campbell (Sal) stretches out his neck as he moves his head into the frame. Treading a precarious line between racist imagery and a whimsical lampooning of conventional masculinity, Sal becomes a comic figure not unlike the character of the Kalahari bushman who finds the Coca-Cola bottle in the South African film *The Gods Must Be Crazy.* Despite or due to that lapse of taste, what is clear is that the arrival of the Rosenheim thermos signals the beginning of changes in the diner community.

Bagdad Cafe uses characters' interactions with the bright plastic Rosenheim thermos to mark stages in the characters' progress toward a more compassionate view of each other. Rudi's inability to drink thermos coffee unless it is diluted is paired with Jasmin's insistence that adding water makes it taste like brown water. Their opposing choices

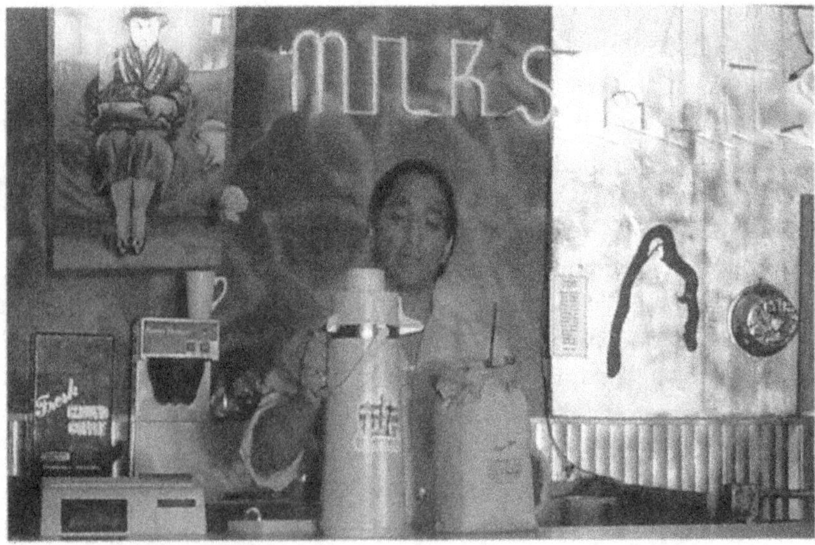

Food preparation is a way for the characters to transcend their cultural boundaries in Bagdad Cafe *(Bayerischer Rundfunk, Hessischer Rundfunk, Pelemele Film, Pro-ject Filmproduktion).*

not only establish the characters' initial culinary provincialism; they also exemplify the isolation the characters experience at the beginning of the narrative. Eventually, however, character interactions with the thermos and its coffee confirm the group's substantial progress toward community. In a quiet scene just before Jasmin returns to make the diner her permanent home, Cahuenga shows his affection for Jasmin by brewing a thermos of coffee using portions that would please her. Cahuenga's embrace of Jasmin's coffee preference is a sign that the Bagdad Cafe has, over time, become a place where everyone has a place at the table.

Moving from Cannibalism to Shared Food Cleanup and Food Procurement

Scenes in which the Rosenheim thermos marks the characters' steps toward community are joined by others that illustrate the characters' evolution from isolation to inclusion. The film contrasts scenes that allude to cannibalism, which signals uncivilized choices about food product, with scenes of cleanup and food procurement that reveal the possibility of building community. As in other films, in *Bagdad Cafe,* even characters' passing thoughts about cannibalism are a sign of social distress and disarray, for the most remote possibility of cannibalism activates the global taboo against placing people in the food product category.

The film references stereotypical images of cannibalism to quickly convey the initial cultural divide between the diner family and the German tourist. Early on, Jasmin has a brief, nightmarish hallucination of being boiled alive; Brenda also succeeds in unnerving this racist woman by ordering Cahuenga to cook Sal Junior's infant son for supper. These scenes are vivid indications of the incomplete socialization that initially troubles the group (see Counihan 21).

Jasmin's hallucination is a response to Brenda's demand that Jasmin explain how she intends to pay for her motel room. The hallucination sequence features images of plump, perspiring, and pink-cheeked Jasmin wearing a small green pheasant-feathered Bavarian hat. In the comedic, surreal scene, Jasmin is being cooked in a huge pot as black "natives" with spears and painted bodies circle the cauldron chanting.

Although Adlon's inclusion of this scene has been criticized (see Smelik 128), it is possible that the scene's over-the-top racist imagery conveys Jasmin's irrational fear of Brenda and shows that her racism is one of the reasons the diner community is in a dystopian state.

As if to clarify that its racist reference to cannibalism is conscious parody, the film follows Jasmin's paranoid nightmare of being cannibalized with a second reference to cannibalism. Here, Brenda gets the prejudices of the bigoted German tourist out in the open. Starting with their first encounters, Brenda has sensed that Jasmin sees her as an uncivilized native. With that prejudice present, Brenda is quickly angered when Jasmin picks up Sal Junior's infant son. To reestablish the boundary Jasmin has just crossed, Brenda yanks the infant out of Jasmin's arms and hands him over to Cahuenga. Then, glaring at Jasmin, Brenda tells Cahuenga that he should cook the baby in a pot. Brenda's reference to cannibalism lets Jasmin know that she is painfully aware of the prejudices in a racially divided world. Required to stay on her side of that divide, Brenda's initial inclination is to maintain the separation between privileged individuals like Jasmin and outcasts like herself.

In counterpoint to the cannibalism references that highlight the racial divide that initially troubles the diner community, scenes of cleanup, housework, and food procurement illustrate steps in the community's increasing harmony. While the cannibalism scenes show what separates Brenda and Jasmin, scenes of cleanup establish their shared experiences. Opening scenes show both women cleaning up garbage; Jasmin picks up aluminum cans at the rest stop, and Brenda collects empty oil cans in front of the diner.

After Jasmin checks into the motel, she recognizes that Brenda is overwhelmed with women's work. To help out, Jasmin cleans her motel room and from there takes on the task of cleaning Brenda's junk-filled office. Though Jasmin is ostensibly well intended, her efforts to help create more friction with Brenda. Soon, however, they contribute to the diner community's improved health; with the office no longer burdened with junk, Brenda takes a step toward getting the respect she desires from her children when she insists that her daughter get her feet off the desk.

Food procurement succinctly illustrates the community's halting steps toward well-being. Jasmin helps Cahuenga with the grocery list Brenda will need when she goes into town. A sign of the community's still disconnected state, the grocery list consists of potentially unrelated food items such as bread, bacon, pickles, oil, tomatoes, peanuts, and salad. At the same time, just as their experiments with the thermos coffee gave Cahuenga and Rudi a reason to communicate, the task of contributing to the community's food procurement by preparing the shopping list offers an occasion for Cahuenga and Jasmin to work together. At this middle stage of evolution, Brenda still sees Jasmin as intruding into the family realm without invitation. Suspicious of someone who seems foreign, Brenda refuses to accept Jasmin's help with the grocery list, just as she had rejected Sal's attempt to solve the diner's coffee dilemma with the Rosenheim thermos.

Brenda's eventual realization that she and Jasmin have a great deal in common takes place during another scene of women's work, this time the duty of childcare. Discovering Sal Junior, Phyllis, and Sal Junior's infant son comfortable and relaxed as they spend time with Jasmin in her motel room, Brenda becomes enraged: she bursts into the room and shouts, "Play with your own children." Jasmin's subdued but pained response takes Brenda by surprise; Jasmin explains that she has no children. Brenda suddenly sees that Jasmin feels isolated, and so makes an indirect admission that she too feels alone. With that their magical partnership begins and the community makes a giant step toward harmony; throughout the rest of the story Brenda and Jasmin counsel one another, as when Jasmin decides that before agreeing to Rudi's proposal of marriage she should "talk it over with Brenda."[5]

Food Products Reveal Jasmin's Evolving Subjectivity

While Jasmin begins as the stereotype of a German tourist, her surprising contributions to the diner eventually make the foreigner a beloved member of the community. Incremental changes in visual details illustrate her evolving subjectivity and role in the community. Slight but continual shifts in Jasmin's demeanor, costumes, and props convey her transformation from uptight German hausfrau to a woman whose warmth, grace, and sensuality are a reflection of her inner beauty and the community's blossoming harmony.[6]

Foodstuffs mark the stages of Jasmin's personal growth and emerging closeness with Rudi and Brenda. From the start, food products are woven into a network of allusions that conveys developments in

Jasmin's and Rudi's relationship. In an early scene, Rudi lounges in his trailer, admiring an ornamental gourd that he holds in his hand. Above him there is a banner with images of gourds, grapes, sausages, cherries, bananas, beans, and a pitcher. Next to him there is a table with melons, squash, and ornamental gourds. Later, Rudi asks Jasmin if he may paint her portrait. Her assent leads to a series of quirky paintings that use food items to convey Rudi's evolving perception of Jasmin.

Food products are the key to the painting sequence. In each portrait, a different foodstuff symbolizes Jasmin's state of being, not as an objectified female nude, but as a woman the artist admires and adores (Berger 57). Moving from an image of Jasmin rigidly holding an egg, then an ornamental gourd, then a winter squash, then different types of melons, then a flower, and finally of her lounging with a strawberry held to her lips, the sequence blocks Jasmin's objectification, each portrait a reminder that there is a profound distinction between the food objects and the human subject. The sequence begins with a moderately realistic portrait of Jasmin in her very proper Bavarian outfit and ends with Rudi's folk art rendition of Jasmin as a fertility goddess. The paintings suggest that while Rudi might have seen Jasmin as a hard-boiled egg when she arrived, over time he has discovered that her grace, good humor, and openness to wonder warranted the affection and respect reserved for earth goddesses, symbolic of Jasmin's development from embryonic state to full flower.

The paintings borrow from Western traditions in portraiture, still life, depictions of the female nude, and historical or mythological paintings. However, with food products providing commentary in each portrait, fine art traditions are used to create representations that differ from conventional scenes of men gazing at and producing images of women. Like some exceptional nudes in Western art, Rudi's paintings do not provide stimulating images but express his personal vision of a complex woman who is caring, adventurous, and gifted with a mischievous sense of humor (Berger 57–61). For example, Jasmin's portraits contrast with Rubens's painting *Venus at the Mirror* (1613–14) by leaving out the nude's doting female black slave.[7] They give screen time to Sägebrecht's soft, large body rather than one that conforms to normative notions of the ideal woman (Smelik 137). The sequence also presents Rudi as an artist absorbed in the process of making the paintings, rather than someone interested in staring at Jasmin as if she were an object (Alpers 140). There is a mirror placed above and behind Rudi; here, the mirror does not symbolize the female nude's vanity but instead draws attention to the artisan's efforts to represent the woman he loves (Berger 50–51). Rudi's quirky but respectful study of Jasmin is comparable to Sal watching Brenda with engaged concern throughout the film. After Sal moves out, he takes a position on a nearby hill and watches events at the diner through binoculars, not as a voyeur, but like a friend who stays nearby though out of the way.

The gourd, squash, and melons that are symbols of Jasmin's evolving identity belong to Jasmin's and Rudi's immediate environment. They are all fruits that thrive in hot, dry climates like the Mojave Desert. They also help to transform Rudi's Airstream trailer, which is shaped like a cucumber, another member of the gourd family, into an environment that fosters growth and nourishment. Jasmin discards the role of the preyed upon woman who must hold tight to her belongings; Rudi lets go of the idea that men are predators who should take what they can get.

The food items themselves are symbolic. In the first portrait, there is an egg that suggests Jasmin's real identity has not yet emerged. The egg's hard but thin shell captures Jasmin's defensive but vulnerable demeanor when she first arrived at the diner. In the second portrait, Jasmin holds an ornamental yellow-flowered gourd that seems to be a gherkin. The inedible warted gourd seems to be a suitable emblem of Jasmin as the comical German tourist. The funny little yellow gourd is the first of several foodstuffs from the gourd family (cucurbitaceae) that convey Jasmin's multifaceted identity. In the third portrait, a small green winter squash, perhaps a butter squash, less weird than the gherkin but still odd looking, fits with the awkwardness of Jasmin posing in increasingly revealing clothing.[8]

The foodstuffs featured in Jasmin's fourth and sixth portraits (the fifth is implied rather than shown) make playful reference to ideas first suggested by the squash. In the fourth and sixth paintings, Jasmin holds a melon, a fruit that is also in the gourd family. In the fourth, she cradles a Crenshaw melon that has been sliced in half; she holds it so that we see the round inner seed core surrounded by soft fruit. In the sixth painting, she holds up a muskmelon that has a small vertical slice cut

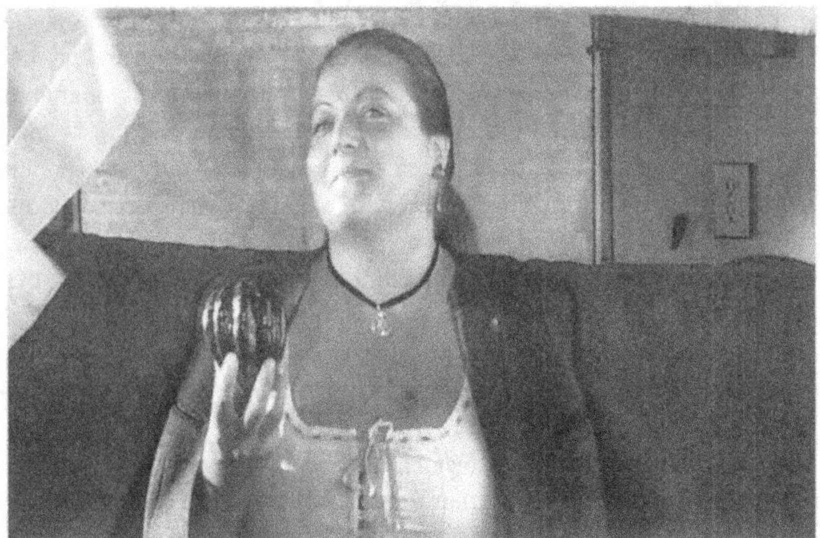

Comical, symbolic food products convey Jasmin's lively imagination in Bagdad Cafe *(Bayerischer Rundfunk, Hessischer Rundfunk, Pelemele Film, Pro-ject Filmproduktion).*

in it. Sharing the frame with Jasmin, the melons serve as lowbrow puns about her huge breasts. Cut and displayed as they are, the melons are also juvenile jokes about vaginas. The melons' earthy symbolism suggests that the food products communicate Jasmin's emerging comfort with herself and her sexuality.

In the seventh painting, Jasmin appears to be growing more confident and so poses with bare breasts. The flower Jasmin holds, which she makes appear by magic, suggests that Jasmin herself is blossoming. Linked to connotations suggested by the egg in the first portrait, the flower is a sign that Jasmin's effort to realize her worth is coming to fruition. In the final portrait, Jasmin is pictured as a goddess. Its primitive folk art style shows Jasmin, her face surrounded by beams of light, holding a strawberry to her lips as she rests on her stomach wearing only pink-feathered slippers. A pink diaphanous veil enters the frame just as the camera begins to pan up Jasmin's legs, and there is a quick cut to the portrait Rudi has painted. The scene thus draws attention to connotations surrounding the luscious strawberry and ensures that Jasmin is seen as she appears in Rudi's adoring eyes.

By using food products to transform conventional representations of women, *Bagdad Cafe* highlights "the criteria and conventions by which women have been seen and judged as sights" (Berger 47). Rather than presenting the foodstuffs as still life objects arranged in a pleasing way for the viewer, the artist's arch use of food symbolism allows the film to convey, rather than deny, the subjectivity and inner life of the woman pictured.[9]

Food Presentation and Food Performance as Signs of Unity in the Diner Community

The film amplifies its irreverent use of food products in the painting sequence by intercutting the portrait scenes with humorous moments of food presentation in the diner. The food presentation scenes illustrate stages in Jasmin's friendship with Brenda and show that her entertaining contributions nourish the diner community. Jasmin's gift for magic and sleight of hand reveals that in her case there is more than meets the eye. As the film cuts between scenes in Rudi's trailer and the magic scenes in the diner, jolly calliope music and warm, diffused lighting convey the community's emerging sense of harmony. The magic tricks involving crackers, eggs, serving trays, and other mundane items suggest that Jasmin's emerging relationships with Rudi and Brenda are replenishing the diner community. They also highlight the role food presentation can play in creating community. Instead of seeing food presentation as a matter of serving food to others, Jasmin transforms the experience into a magical act of connection.

After sitting for her first portrait, Jasmin astonishes everyone at the diner when she unexpectedly takes it on herself to serve two customers their bowls of chili. She surprises them even more when she makes the customers' crackers magically appear. Food becomes another point of contact when Jasmin makes eggs appear from behind Cahuenga's head. As if to recognize Brenda's role as the diner's hostess, Jasmin gives her a magic red rose. With Jasmin now in the role of Brenda's assistant, Sal Junior is finally welcomed into the (family) diner space when he gets a flower from the bouquet that appears in Brenda's hands by magic. In later food presentation scenes, Jasmin continues to transform food serving into a magical opportunity to create harmony and unity with others. In one instance, she makes gold coins appear from behind customers' ears. On another occasion, Jasmin and Brenda entertain a crowd of customers by hiding their wallets, hunting knives, and toupees under a cloth on the serving tray Brenda carries as she passes through the diner. Laughter abounds as Jasmin returns the customers' belongings; the easy circulation of goods created by this last trick shows the abundance that has emerged from characters' use of food to establish connection.

The series of food presentation scenes also shows that a meal system has finally developed in the Bagdad Cafe community. The packed diner and truck-filled parking lot show that the community has made a profound transition from the time when its grocery list included a few disparate items and the diner had one or two customers who dropped in on random occasions. Once Jasmin returns to make Bagdad Cafe her permanent home, the meal system becomes completely stabilized. With an increasingly wider circle of regular customers, the diner's expanded menu features banana pies, chili sides, and desserts known as the garden of delight. The diner community eats together and even sings together about their joy in being "home on a gas range." In a nod to musical genre conventions, the film's closing magic show and musical number illustrate the community's newfound harmony as Jasmin, Brenda, Rudi, and the other members of the extended family celebrate the diner as a space for commensality.

Foodways activities are integral to *Bagdad Cafe*'s portrait of a community that prospers as relationships between characters become more connected and reciprocal. Jasmin's decision to leave her husband at the desolate picnic area and Sal's decision to pick up the Rosenheim coffee thermos are the first steps in a process that leads to a utopian community sustained by affection and mutual respect. Food products illustrate Jasmin's blossoming as a person, just as increasing structure in the meal system suggests the other characters' growing grace and maturity. *Bagdad Cafe* creates empathy for characters that work and eat with one another, who see each other as subjects to paint and not as objects to consume. In the utopian world of the Bagdad Cafe, the characters' idiosyncratic but sincere engagement with one another provides Jasmin, Brenda, Rudi, and the entire Bagdad Cafe community with the emotional nourishment for which they have been searching.

The evolving diner community is fundamentally different from fast-food or haute cuisine society. The steps by which characters come together are awkward as each one slowly learns how to contribute. However, through that process, the characters become like elements of a satisfying meal, for the group's well-being depends on the harmony that exists between its individual constituents. At the Bagdad Cafe, community is quite different from the customer satisfaction promised by fast-food franchises and the personal happiness promised to consumers able to afford items on the menu of ideal identities sold by entrepreneurs like Martha Stewart. The character relationships that eventually transcend racial and national divisions show that women with unconventional beauty and unconventional friendships warrant screen time, as do the unconventional men who see them as subjects rather than objects. A distinctly utopian film, *Bagdad Cafe* shows that food products and meal cycles (food performance) matter and that the mundane details of food procurement, preparation, preservation, presentation, consumption, and cleanup enrich portraits of fictional worlds where stranded tourists, small-time laborers, lonely truckers, and families struggling to keep roadside diners in business find their oasis.

Bagdad Cafe: Placing This Utopian Film in Context

Bagdad Cafe's unconventional vision of food and relationships is markedly different from representations of food in male bonding films like *Diner* (Levinson, 1982), social problem films like *Do the Right Thing* (Lee, 1989), campy spoofs like *Eating Raoul* (Bartel, 1982), and exploitation fare like *Blood Diner* (Kong, 1987) and its model *Blood Feast* (Lewis, 1963). The film's vision of women, food, and community also contrasts with the meaning conveyed by some more familiar food scenes. *Bagdad Cafe*'s use of food to illustrate a female character's inner life contrasts with *Women in Love* (Russell, 1969); Rupert's sexually explicit description of the correct way to eat a fig gives him a clever way to inflict pain on Hermione, the wealthy woman he no longer desires. *Bagdad Cafe,* which uses food to reveal the subjective experiences of a female character, differs from *Tess* (Polanski, 1979); here, young women's bodies are equated with ripe fruit, and picking strawberries is a metaphor for the thoughtless but entirely "acceptable" way Alec forces himself on Tess.

However, Adlon's film has parallels with *Tampopo.* Both films give ample screen time to their female characters and convey character development through interactions that involve recipe design, choices about meals for everyday and social occasions, and questions about tools and environments for sharing food and drink. In *Tampopo,* the title character is the one who takes us through the story; she is the voice of the film, the character that provides the film's literal point of view. The intensive regime of mental, physical, and spiritual training that she undergoes creates the film's overarching structure, and it carries the overt message of the film. Other characters complicate the links between cooking, rational progression, and self-improvement suggested by Tampopo's story. The meaning conveyed by the scenes with the crime boss and his girlfriend provide a countervailing connection between eating, personal desire, and the search for contentment.

Distinguished by its folk art aesthetic, *Bagdad Cafe* offers a more progressive vision than the more commercial *Mystic Pizza* (Petrie, 1988). Despite the films' shared use of magic tricks to suggest women's unrecognized power, Adlon's film ends with the characters in a harmonious community, whereas Petrie's closes with the characters still isolated individuals. In *Bagdad Cafe,* the women's magic acts establish connections between the characters. By comparison, in *Mystic Pizza,* publicity about the magical pizza sauce recipe is a surprise happy ending for the disparate narrative threads. In *Bagdad Cafe,* food symbolizes Jasmin's evolving subjectivity, whereas *Mystic Pizza* uses food to objectify women; at the pizza parlor the young women wear tight T-shirts with "a slice of heaven" printed on them so that the words stretch across their breasts. In *Mystic Pizza,* the women's lives are determined by defining romantic experiences in which the woman becomes a sexual object or piece of property. In *Bagdad Cafe,* community depends on the reciprocal relations male and female characters create.

The vision of food conveyed by *Bagdad Cafe* is entirely different from a dystopian food film like *The Cook, the Thief, His Wife, and Her Lover.* Both films use fine art allusions to generate meaning. However, whereas Adlon's utopian film about the magic of people sharing food and drink uses allegorical elements to delight and inform, Greenaway's dystopian film damns consumer society and uses allegory to instruct and cajole (see Johnston). Greenaway's film references Masaccio's masterpiece *The Expulsion of Adam and Eve* (c. 1425), while Adlon features amateurish portraits and brightly colored folk art renditions of gourds, grapes, bananas, cherries, and beans. The films' contrast in logic and tone is especially visible in their depiction of food practices that violate social norms. Whereas Greenaway's grueling study of human depravity culminates in cannibalism, Adlon's look at the healing power of human relatedness takes audiences on a journey from a dystopian world marked by imagined or rhetorical threats of cannibalism to a happily crowded environment that offers food, entertainment, and emotional nourishment. As the next chapter illustrates, the contrast between utopian and dystopian visions of food becomes especially vivid when one considers *Bagdad Cafe* alongside a film such as *301/302* (Park, 1995).

4

Foodways Structured to Convey Disorder and Dysfunction

Sharing a collection of semantic elements, food films tend to be set in diners, kitchens, and restaurants. Stories focus on cooking, eating, and drinking. Interactions surrounding food products, recipe design, and food consumption convey characters' changing relationships. However, food films also employ strikingly divergent syntax. They structure and arrange their mutual semantic elements in contrasting ways. Food films' differing syntactical uses of foodway elements generate observably different visions of food and society. In some cases, interactions surrounding food lead to harmony, unity, and balance. In other films, foodways communicates characters' pain and isolation, and food behaviors signify a disordered, toxic society.

In *Bagdad Cafe*, the foodways syntax leads to the film's ultimately utopian vision. However, South Korean producer/director Chul-Soo Park's *301/302* (1995) structures its representation of foodways to dramatize a profoundly dystopian scenario. *301/302* focuses on two isolated individuals mired in a circumscribed, destructive relationship. Placing their constrained interaction at the center of *301/302*, Park shows food procurement, preparation, presentation, consumption, and cleanup, but he makes the unconventional choice to present these foodways components as having negative, even repulsive, connotations.

While food films often feature scenes of characters enjoying savory meals, Park shows that women who have suffered sexual victimization sometimes find little if any pleasure in food consumption, because the idea of anything entering their bodies has become terrifying. Similarly, whereas food films frequently celebrate gourmet cooking and depict meal preparation as a fulfilling vehicle for self-expression, Park shows that for women, especially modern Korean women trying to keep pace with global consumer culture, the requirement that women be skilled in the kitchen is yet another way male-dominated society causes women to feel unfulfilled and, in extreme circumstances, to exhibit neurotic behavior to the point they become "a singularly frightening spectacle" (Kee 454).

Several noteworthy films about dystopian, even post-apocalyptic societies have made food and water central to their plots. In these films, food does not nourish or heal. It does not establish beneficial communities or encourage supportive individual relationship. Science fiction syntax sometimes underlies the narratives that structure foodways representations to explore the problem of increasingly scarce resources. Films that employ science fiction syntax include *Soylent Green, The Man Who Fell to Earth, The Road* (Hillcoat, 2009), and *The Hunger Games* (Ross, 2012). At the heart of each of these dystopian worlds is a critical food or water shortage. The title character in *The Man Who Fell to Earth* seeks water for his family on a dying planet. *Soylent Green* involves eating rations made from human beings. *The Road* mixes threats of starvation with marauding gangs that resort to cannibalism. In *The Hunger Games,* survivors are threatened with starvation inside and outside the games. Environmentalists repeatedly warn of reckless indifference to use of diminishing resources. With human existence in varying degrees of crisis (a growing problem for developed countries and an immediate reality for developing ones), films alleviate pervasive anxieties through utopian narratives and confront them through representations of challenging dystopian worlds.

With eating disorders a prevalent form of food crisis in consumer society, *301/302* concentrates on foodways to dramatize the experiences of two traumatized young women. Despite the distinguishing details of this culturally specific narrative, the centrality of food gives this South Korean story a global resonance, for women's eating disorders as a response to sexual and emotional trauma crosses borders and cultures. Resonant with pan-national metaphors and tropes of Korean national cinema, *301/302* focuses on personal food worlds gone awry. The film thus explores a revealing study of women's resistance and eventual collapse without ignoring the complex implications of a national identity in crisis.[1]

In its narrative, *301/302* highlights the divergent but equally dysfunctional responses of two women living in adjoining apartments in a Seoul high-rise housing complex.[2] The title characters Song-Hee Kang (Eun-jin Bang) and Yun-Hee Kim (Sin-Hye Hwang) are known by their respective apartment numbers, 301 and 302, a detail that points to the powerfully dehumanizing experiences that shape these two characters whose lives provide a glimpse of the ordeals some contemporary women confront. Myopically preoccupied with their own pas de deux, the two show how troubled food behavior can reflect personal trauma: infidelity in the case of 301 and rape in the case of 302. In its syntactical arrangement of foodways, *301/302* foregrounds Song-Hee's and Yun-Hee's diametrically opposed, but equally troubled, relationship to food. The foodways syntax illustrates the contentious encounters of the two principals. The visceral and emotional impact of the collision between these two women and their different ways of dealing with food and trauma has personal and cultural resonance.

As they react to their significantly different but equally traumatizing experiences, both women reveal emotional damage that prompts self-destructive behavior expressed through food choices: 302 becomes a woman who cannot eat anything without gagging and vomiting, while 301 obsesses over cooking and eating until it defines her life. 302 remains passively incapable of defense; 301 vents her rage through transgressive food behavior. *301/302* presents a culturally specific narrative that foregrounds the powerlessness of two socially and sexually victimized women who displace their neuroses into food disorders: eating disorders for 301 and 302, and an obsessive-compulsive cooking disorder in the case of 301.

Overall, the film uses the characters' interactions with food to comment on the devastating consequences of a victimization legacy. 302, thoroughly complicit, literally becomes 301's meal. A male detective is sent to investigate 302's disappearance. The detective's attempt to determine the cause for each woman's behavior gives director Park the opportunity to carry his dystopian vision to its ultimate conclusion: unwittingly, the detective will eat portions of 302. The detective suspects nothing. After all, given gender and societal norms, it's not unusual for a friendly, polite young woman to prepare food for a man who occupies a position of power. The characters play their traditional gender roles, albeit with a stinging twist, because 301 implicates the detective in her act of cannibalism. With foodways arranged to generate a dystopian vision, all of the characters' relationships to food can create intense responses. With cannibalism a fundamental cultural taboo, and consumer society marked by fixations on dieting and food fads, and uncertainties about matters as basic as nutritional requirements, it is difficult to remain indifferent to the film's disquieting representation of food and food behavior.

To amplify viewer unease, Park uses a disjointed narrative to present the troubling story. As Joan Kee writes, "The first fifteen minutes of . . . *301/302* is a veritable mélange of stylized poses, lush surroundings, and glances ranging from coy to sullen" (449). The nonlinear sequence requires the viewer, like the investigating detective who serves as the catalyst for unraveling the story, to gradually piece together the causes and effects of the central characters' behavior. Signaling its dystopian focus, from the start *301/302* portrays food preparation and presentation in confrontational ways. Adding to the discomfort that creates, 301 works with food and 302 reacts to food in visceral ways. Their strange food behaviors undermine the visual appeal of food films' customary colorful, attractive, high-end cuisine. There is a hint early on that the characters have serious problems with food when cooking-obsessed 301 begins asking anorexic 302 about her food choices. The exchange intimates that representations of food preparation, presentation, and consumption (or refusal to consume) will be important to the dystopian vision of society that the film creates. It suggests that whereas utopian films use meals to illustrate the building of community, this dystopian film will probe neuroses and show that the inability to accept food and the drive to force others to eat are signs of severe dysfunction.

As the momentum builds to the final act of 301 (Song-Hee) killing, cutting up, cooking, and serving 302 (Yun-Hee), the art direction intensifies the film's impact. Throughout the film, both women are confined to sterile apartments: 301 is squeezed into a small apartment when she is with her husband; the barren adjoining apartments of 301 and 302 underscore the women's isolation. Moreover, as Barry Walters points out, "nearly every shot is some kind of close-up, and the tight focus on the women gives the film an intense sense of claustrophobia" (Walters). Within this restricted and restrictive environment, snippets of the characters' memories occasionally intrude, immersing viewers in the women's stream of consciousness. Combined with the claustrophobic settings, the memories and the women's contrasting obsessions with food generate apprehension.

One of the most basic of all human needs—nutritional sustenance—becomes *the* vehicle for the characters' self-destructive behavior. The film uses food and food preparation to communicate the characters' distress and disorder. As the *Los Angeles Times'* Kevin Thomas observes, "301 is constantly preparing food, but her actions—most often photographed in claustrophobic close-up—are so repetitive, the parade of luscious-looking dishes so unending, that Park is able to evoke attraction-repulsion reactions in the viewer that suggest the depths of desperation in both women" (Thomas). Walters adds, "The more we learn about the women, the less we can laugh at them or enjoy the torture they exact on one another. Even the food stops looking good" (Walters).

By contrast, the foodways syntax in films as diverse as *Tom Jones* (Richardson, 1963), *Tampopo, Babette's Feast, Like Water for Chocolate* (Arau, 1992), and *Eat Drink Man Woman* creates visually appetizing and aesthetically pleasing food. Moreover, *Tom Jones, Tampopo,* and *Like Water for Chocolate* specifically link food and food consumption to sexual pleasure. For example, in the seduction scene between Tom (Albert Finney) and Mrs. Waters/Jenny Jones (Joyce Redman), *Tom Jones* exploits the pleasurable food-sex association with titillating indulgence and riotous joyfulness. In a shot reverse-shot series between Tom and Mrs. Waters, the dinner escalates lasciviously over three and a half minutes from a course of soup and then lobster to chicken and oysters on the half-shell followed by pears, a two-shot of their drinking wine, and their immediate rush to the bedroom. As films that employ foodways syntax to create utopian visions of the world, none of these films use food to examine sexual dysfunction. The contrast places *301/302* on the dystopian end of the spectrum with other films that remind consumers that positive food images tell only the sugarcoated part of the story. Just as individuals' relationship with food is marked by constructive as well as destructive urges, utopian films disregard the negative aspects of food while *301/302* chooses not to look away.

The Film and Its Foodways Content

In the opening moments of *301/302,* food products and food preparation establish an attraction-repulsion dichotomy. The credit sequence arranges foodways elements so that food that would be savory in other circumstances becomes unappetizing. Ostensibly tantalizing food images, which begin before and then interrupt the opening titles, suggest meanings that become clear in the characters' succeeding, confessional encounters. The brief flashbacks anticipate scenes in which the characters' memories intrude to reveal the experiences that precipitate their food-centered neuroses. From the start, Park lays out ingredients of the characters' psychological problems with the measured care of a gourmet chef as he probes the underlying cause of 302's anorexia and the reasons behind 301's bingeing and obsessive cooking.

The challenge to unravel the characters' back-stories begins with the fragmented credit sequence. Disjointed close-ups of food being vigorously prepared and discarded identify food as the film's unifying theme. On an initial viewing of *301/302,* viewers might realize that the tone and content of the opening foreshadow the film's major theme—the intense emotional connections between sex and food, food and control. However, the connections among the abrupt shots, separated from one another by shots of white credits on a black background, are so obtuse that only on later viewings does it become apparent that the first few minutes present a virtual synopsis of the film's dystopian portrayal of foodways.

The first words spoken are "In our refrigerator, we have a lot of food. But I don't ever eat anything that is cold." Accompanying these words, the camera tilts down from a blue wall that fills the screen to a young girl saying the lines, looking toward but just off-camera, knees pulled up to her chest in a protective way. (Later shots clarify that this girl is cooking-obsessed 301.) Since the shot of the girl lasts about twelve seconds, there is barely enough time to grasp the context. However, as proof of her words, the next shot of a refrigerator shows food crammed into the door with a variety of drinks (Gatorade, grape juice) and other items, including "Slice cheese" (one label reads), an egg, a lemon, and several tins. The girl's voice continues, bragging about eating a warm, home-cooked meal once her mother returns. Subsequent shots again show the refrigerator jammed with food. The girl's singsong voice continues, as a tilt up from the floor shows this girl from the back, standing on books to reach the counter, intoning, "But she did not come home even in the very late hour." A reverse shot from the front shows the girl using a large knife to slice a cucumber, an action echoed later in the film when she is an adult. Several slices of what looks like Spam already lie on the counter in the right-front portion of the frame.

This thirty-five second, five-shot sequence confirms the girl's peril, her intense connection to food, and her mother's irresponsibility. Preparation, preservation, and the appearance of food dominate the emotionally worrisome scene. Apparently alone, the young girl, wielding a knife, fixes her own food, and the palpable sense of danger is signaled by her discordant voice and disquieting lyrics. The mother's neglect is conveyed by the food product, for instead of offering her young daughter a nutritious hot dinner, the mother has forced the girl to prepare her own cold food. The film communicates the mother's disregard for her daughter through the cold food 301 prepares and the mother's physical absence from this scene of food preparation. It thus uses food product and food preparation to convey the mother's complete lack of involvement in her young daughter's life.

Reinforcing the ominous mood, a jolting cut moves from silence and a composition dominated by muted colors to the glaring sight and sound of a buzz saw shearing through bright red meat. The scenes' jarring linkage augments the disconcerting sensations created by the new environment and the appearance of a second young girl. (Later shots establish that she is anorexic 302.) After two shots of the meat being cut, a young girl's lips, in an extreme close-up suffused with red light, fill the screen. She explains, again in singsong fashion, "We always have red meat. My mommy knows how to cut the meat off the bone." In another close-up bathed in red light, raw red meat is cut authoritatively with a sharp knife. Then in medium long shot, a girl with glasses and braids, squatted down but turned forty-five degrees from the camera, finishes, "But I think I would prefer to have orange juice or green apples in the refrigerator." In addition to her gender and age connecting her with the previous girl, she's also squatting against a wall. A woman shown from the waist down walks past the girl and into a freezer; she grabs a slab of meat and returns as the titles continue. The girl walks off-camera in the direction of the meat locker. A fade to black ends these brief introductions to the two girls and their telling monologues about food.

Neither girl receives the emotional or physical nourishment she craves. Young 301 prepares a cold meal where the meat product is Spam, a precooked, canned combination of varied meat ingredients preserved with a gelatinous coating. However, what she really wants is a warm, home-cooked dinner. By contrast, young 302 is surrounded by raw, red meat, but she longs for fresh fruit or fruit juice. The characters' problems revealed in the course of the story connect directly to the missing emotional nourishment indicated in the opening seconds of the film. Physical and psychological well-being stem from supportive home environments. As the film illustrates, lack of physical and emotional sustenance expresses itself through dysfunctional relationships with other individuals and the food essential for survival.

This opening sequence ominously introduces the characters' relationship to food. Distressing verbal and nonverbal details foreshadow more dire associations to come. Even at this early stage, little of the food product looks appealing. Before the titles end after approximately three and a quarter minutes, twenty more images of food or food-related items telegraph the tragic tale. The insistent music that accompanies the first title and the next shot of a broken egg that falls onto a knife and a cleaver deepen the troubling mood that has been quickly created. Viewer curiosity and a growing tension are sustained through shots of a boiling pot, prepared food, sterile shelves of dishes, leftovers tossed into the garbage, a knife thrown into a sink, and other close-up shots, including one of fingers dripping blood and another of a knife with blood on the blade. These images establish that the two girls will become the women whose lives have food as their problematic anchor. In their dystopian world, food does not nourish, food products are unappealing, and the food products on offer are not those desired by the young girls.

Physiological needs, including food, must be met before people can achieve love, esteem, and self-actualization. The film thus uses food to communicate the dystopian environment of 301's and 302's childhoods. With the characters' foundational problems set up, the credits conclude and the story proper begins. A police detective arrives at Song-Hee Kang's apartment 301 to announce his investigation of the disappearance of Yun-Hee Kim, the resident of apartment 302. Through a series of dialogues with 301, the detective elicits details of the relationship between 301 and 302. Brief flashbacks and flashbacks within flashbacks reveal the reasons for the women's current situation. 301 keeps a food diary, cooks gourmet meals and evening snacks, chats about recipes, and obsesses over her weight gain from 100 to 158 pounds. Recently divorced, she had struggled to keep her husband emotionally attentive and sexually interested through elaborate meals.

However, for 301 food can be used as a weapon. When her intensive, inventive food preparation and its seductive presentation fail as an invitation to sex and as a bonding element in their marriage, food becomes her means for vengeful retaliation. Typical of dystopian films, the food product becomes a site of conflict and a means of conveying the family rupture. 301's displacement of pain and resentment into sadistic action finds an unusual vehicle—the family dog.[3] 301 discovers her husband had been having an affair. Feeling angry and trapped, she kills, cooks, and serves her husband's Maltese pet.[4] Consistent with its straightforward representation of disturbing behavior, the film shows the results of 301's heartless action. The scene parallels the moment in *The War of the Roses* (DeVito, 1989) when Barbara Rose (Kathleen Turner) serves paté made from the family dog to punish her husband, Oliver (Michael Douglas), as they engage in an antagonistic divorce. However, whereas *The War of the Roses* mixes its dystopian vision with dark, outrageous comedy, *301/302* provides no hint of comic relief.

301/302 suggests reasons that 301 cooked the dog, but it does not excuse what is for many people an inconceivable choice. As in other food-focused dystopian films, Park's narrative uses characters' food choices to explore the intense emotion surrounding cultural taboos. Like other dystopian films, it proposes that sadistic drives lie just beneath the patina of civilized food behavior. It shows viewers 301's rationale for her decision that emerges gradually through interactions with her husband. Over the course of their marriage, he shows increasing affection for the dog and mounting irritation with 301. On several occasions, he treats the dog as a substitute child, and in one instance directs his wife to bathe the dog since she has "nothing else to do all day."

By cooking the dog, 301 transforms the object of her husband's attention into a food product, and the rival for his affection into a meal that shows her food preparation expertise. Like many other filmic cooks, for 301 the very act of food preparation takes on pronounced fetishistic importance. The activity becomes divorced from anything but its own intrinsic and symbolic meaning. Killing the dog, making him part of her culinary creations, is 301's way of mounting her retaliation to personal and social structures that together make her largely powerless. Cooking becomes her voice, killing and preparing a taboo dish her protest.

Knowing nothing about 301's ability to transgress cultural food boundaries, the detective begins his investigation in 301's kitchen, where he drinks her wine and eats the best "chicken" he's ever had. Responding to his question about any male guests anorexic 302 might have had, 301 highlights a dystopian food/sex parallel: "Yun-Hee refused sex as well as food." As the detective searches 302's apartment, Yun-Hee appears or, more accurately, since the detective does not actually see her, 302's presence is visualized in several shots. He discovers a bottle of pills while searching apartment 302. Subsequently, a male voiceover explains that the pills are for an eating disorder, that 302 connects love and sex with food, and that food is a tool for controlling love. The dystopian sex/food connection permeates the densely layered information: a detective investigates, Yun-Hee appears in apartment 302, and an unidentified male expert (perhaps a psychiatrist) relates a conventional interpretation of sex/love and food. Sex, illness, and food become conflated into dysfunctional behavior that experts cure with pharmaceutical prescriptions. Lamentably, the expert interpretations do not address the myriad social factors that affect 302 or the recognition that the "level at which individuals consumed with the love of food and consumed with a hatred of it are very much the same, imprisoned by inexorable, implacable needs" (Thomas).

That love-hate dichotomy describes the characters' yin-yang personalities while the unwavering depiction of unsavory food associations makes *301/302* noteworthy in its single-mindedness. With its concentrated focus, *301/302* excludes diversions that would relieve its dystopian vision. For some viewers made uncomfortable by the unfolding story, *301/302* may suffer from its steadfast refusal to show the titillating aspects of sex or the sensory appeal of food. The context and arrangement of the food preparation and presentation scenes rob the gourmet dishes of their attraction. In contrast with the more familiar filmic treatment of food as an enticement to and enhancement of sexual pleasure, *301/302* follows an uncommon agenda. Whereas films as different as the American *9½ Weeks* (Lyne, 1986), the Mexican *Like Water for Chocolate,* and the Cuban *Strawberry and Chocolate* (Alea and Tabío, 1993) exploit the sexually seductive aspects of food, *301/302* dramatizes behavior that channels the effect of sexual abuse into dysfunctional eating habits. While films such as *Life Is Sweet* (Leigh, 1990) and *Years of Hunger* (Brückner, 1980) integrate troubling food use into their characters' actions, utopian films tend to avoid this rich, politically charged area.

Stylistic Choices Reinforce Dystopian Foodways Syntax

The troubling material Park explores through the dynamic clashes of 301 and 302 is powerfully conveyed by the film's formally rigorous staging. *301/302*'s cumulative effect gains force from technical choices that support its representation of foodway elements. In a precise and careful translation of content to style, with camera moves as controlled and calculated as the women's behavior, Park mixes extreme close-ups with high-angle long shots, direct address to the camera, and disembodied voiceover commentary. Summarizing the film's style, Marjorie Baumgarten explains that *301/302* is "visually arresting to look at, creating a hyper-real canvas of vivid images and fully exposed ciphers. Using crisp cinematography and extreme close-ups, saturated colors, compelling set decoration, the overall production design is, in large measure, responsible for creating the movie's lingering sense of disturbance and disquiet" (Baumgarten). For example, when Song-Hee moves in to apartment 301, Park signals and heightens the unconventional friction between 301 and 302 by using offbeat angles, overhead shots, camera tilts and arcs, and fish-eye shots through 302's keyhole.[5] In the next sequence, Yun-Hee (302) and Song-Hee (301) pass one another as they walk in opposite directions outside the apartment building. The viewer hears their internal monologue as voiceover. Song-Hee (301) notes 302's excessive thinness and says, "She's like a mannequin," while 302 thinks that 301's breasts could "feed a hundred men. Such a pig." In other words, anorexic 302 is perceived as a lifeless body; cooking-obsessed 301 is accused of mammary excess. The characters' neuroses make their respective perceptions informative. The characters' dichotomy extends to minor details as well. Yun-Hee (302) wears glasses, prefers dark-colored clothing, and wears her always neat hair straight. Song-Hee (301) wears light colors, no glasses, and has disheveled, curly hair. Her loose, relaxed nonverbal mannerisms contrast with Yun-Hee's more controlled body movements.

Like images in a picture that slowly become clear, 301's and 302's contrasting appearances and different associations with food and sex crystallize but change little from the characters' memories that are revealed in the first fifteen minutes of the film. What does change is the cat and mouse interaction between 301 and 302, which becomes marked by anorexic 302's attempts to avoid and resist 301's increasingly aggressive intrusions. Ever more assertive, 301 presses her food on 302 because her self-perceived value depends on how much control she exerts through her food. However, the more aggressively 301 intrudes into 302's life, the more 302 recoils and resists, finally undercutting all of 301's efforts.

Park's art direction also structures the dystopian food scenario through a thematically nuanced color design. For example, in the flashback sequences the sterile white in the office of 301's husband mirrors his unresponsiveness. The blood red glow of 302's parents' butcher shop and the raw meat roughly handled express the elemental animal action taking place there. Red meat in particular is photographed and presented with violent literal action (chopping, sawing, quartering) and grotesque symbolic suggestions. 302 is, after all, little more than "meat" to her rapist father. By comparison, 301 feasts on meat and serves it proudly to her husband. The film further reinforces the contrasts between the two characters in a sequence that begins with 302 working at her computer and then remembering a sexual attack; the images are bathed in a suffused red light. Next, in a realistically illuminated composition, 301 neatly arranges her dishes, and then looks off-camera; a subsequent shot cuts to a thematically motivated flashback. In it, 301 packs her plates and cups, this time in preparation for leaving her husband. Calmly telling her that he will miss her cooking he adds, "I even ate a dog."

The apartments each woman inhabits complement their contrasting food behaviors. Cooking obsessed 301's exceedingly organized and westernized kitchen conveys her control fixation; anorexic 302's stark office signals her sexual sterility. 301 bustles about in an industrial cooking and eating space; 302 has no space for food preservation, preparation, consumption, or disposal. During the detective's first visit to 301's apartment, he comments on the extreme neatness of her kitchen. Registering surprise and his first inkling that 301 is involved in 302's disappearance, he says, "I hadn't noticed it before, but this place looks like a restaurant." His remark suggests that he sees something strange about 301 because there are no signs of personal expression in her kitchen.

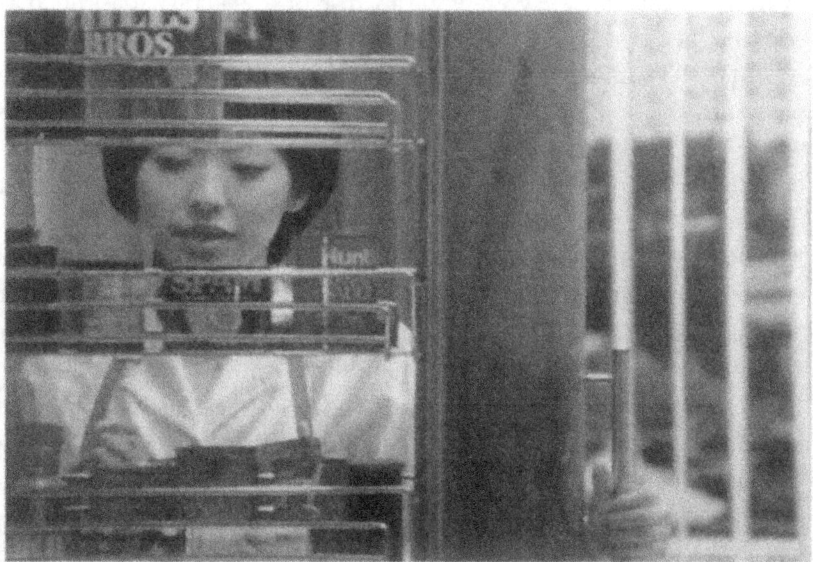

301 is trapped in her exceedingly organized kitchen filled with American products in 301 / 302 *(Park Chul-Soo Films Ltd.).*

Instead, it is apparent that for 301 food preparation is work, something one does to control people like her husband and 302.

The fact that 301's kitchen looks like a restaurant differentiates *301/302* from mainstream fare. The increasingly distressing food prepared there and the domestic kitchen's institutional look block any comforting associations with a space that utopian films use as a stage for friends and family to gather on festive and casual occasions. By subverting the syntax of utopian films, the film intensifies the negative emotional effect of its dystopian microcosm. The art direction in *301/302* contributes to that effect; in 301's kitchen, the vertical and horizontal bars of the food racks show that food preparation can be imprisoning rather than personally liberating.

Consuming and Disposing of Food in a Dystopian World

For her part, 301 is completely aware of the food-sex interdependency and explicitly identifies it early in her interaction with 302. In one of her early attempts to entice 302 to eat, she offers her sausage mignon. When 302 says, "No, thank you. Especially not sausage," 301 replies, "You must not like sex. Were you raped? Not me. I crave it as much as cooking. I enjoyed having sex with my ex-husband even without love." As 301 speaks off-camera, 302 gags and convulses onscreen. Walking back into the scene, 301 eats the sausage she had cooked; 302 looks at her and, choking, hurries out of the room. In the next shot, 301 is back in her apartment as she addresses the camera and says, "Sex isn't disgusting, love is." Inverting the usual idealization of love over sex, 301 claims a surprising preference for physical rather than emotional contact. Such an endorsement is as provocative as it is consistent, for 301 had tried to seduce her husband through the sensory appeal of her cooking rather than through commensality.

Fixating on the physical pleasure of food and sex, 301 persists with her modus operandi, using food as her method of attack. She soon prepares a particularly disgusting looking meal of organ meats, but the nature of the food is completely irrelevant to 302. Already traumatized, 302 seeks recourse in her rejection of all external offerings. Despite some dishes' delectable appearance, they cause nausea in 302, who runs to the toilet and gags even when she has not eaten a morsel. She avoids confrontation with 301 by accepting and then surreptitiously throwing all of the carefully prepared meals into the garbage. Attempting to use food to control other people, 301 epitomizes the individual who tries to gain favor by preparing tempting meals. Unable to stop 301 from cooking and forcing food on her, 302 focuses on food disposal as a way to avert contamination by this intrusive victimizer.

The point-counterpoint between the main characters continues. Stunned when she discovers 302 has not eaten a bite of her food, 301 increases the pressure. Echoing the disproportionate reaction she had when her husband resisted her attempts to run their lives, 301 will not take no for an answer because 302's refusal to eat her meals challenges 301's identity. Grabbing 302's garbage bag full of uneaten food, 301 arranges the food on plates, voraciously eats several bites herself, and tries to coerce 302 to do the same. Instead, the red sauce on the food prompts another of 302's painful flashbacks to her repeated rape, the butcher shop, and her predatory stepfather. The scenes are suffused with red light. Once again, the color red—red meat, red sauce, blood on knives, red illumination—triggers 302's agonizing memories and negative food

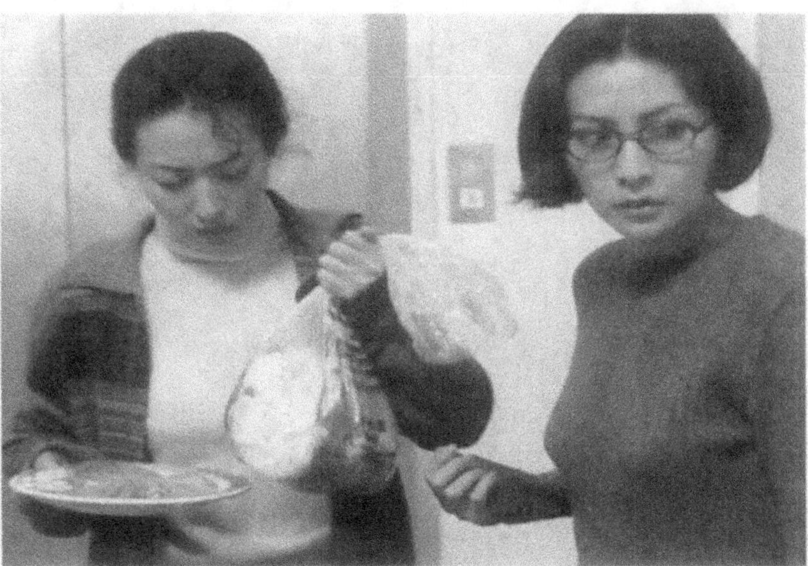

302 is caught throwing away food that she cannot force herself to eat in 301/302 (Park Chul-Soo Films Ltd.).

associations. In this instance, her recollection of the painful sexual assault leads 302 to imagine herself slashing her stepfather. Her daydream appears in shots that alternate 302's face with her as a girl. The sequence suggests that, like 301, 302 entertains brutal fantasies.

To convey 302's fragile, fragmented reality, Park edits together a jigsaw puzzle series of shots that reveal significant moments in 302's past. By comparison, he discloses 301's full story in an extended interlude about one hour into the film. The scenes with 301 and her husband trace the deterioration of their relationship. After a sexually satisfying period, the husband grows disaffected; 301 then uses food in a desperate attempt to win him back. The marriage continues to fail, and food becomes 301's substitute for the sex that her meals had once instigated. Events culminate in her killing the husband's dog. While the killing takes place offscreen, the subsequent scene leads to a shocking realization. After unwittingly eating the dish prepared with the dog, the husband discovers its head boiling in a pot. Violating food product decorum, this haunting shot pushes the dystopian vision to an unnerving extreme. Knowing 301 has killed and served the pet dog as food is

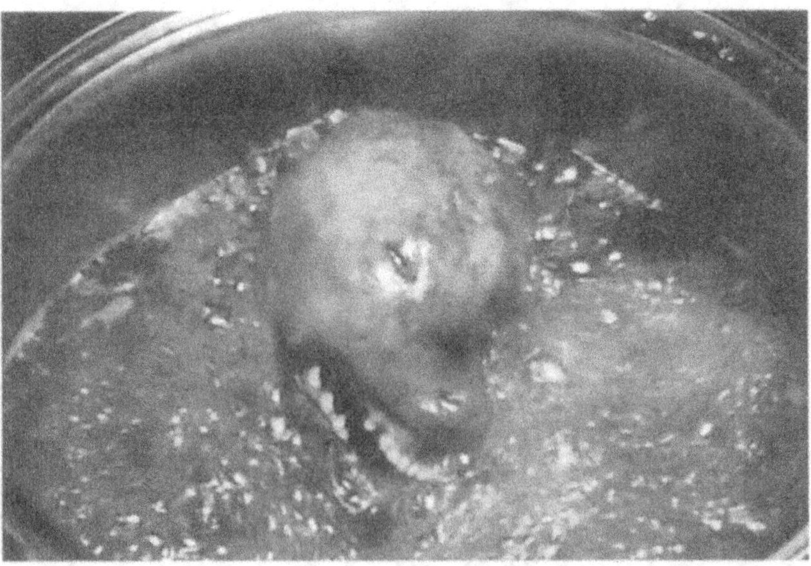

Food behavior in a dystopian world: 301 cooks her husband's beloved pet as revenge for his emotional and physical neglect in 301/302 (Park Chul-Soo Films Ltd.).

a distasteful, repulsive idea to process. The ugliness of the head with its teeth bared, eyes grotesquely closed, and hairless skin glistening prompts visceral revulsion and underscores the film's dystopian vision of food and society.

The extended flashback creates an increasing disgust with the food 301 cooks and a growing irritation over 301's inability to cope. However objectionable the husband's behavior may be, the retaliation through the dog confirms beyond a doubt 301's mental instability. However, when 302 learns about 301's execution of the dog, she does not react with horror. Instead, she obliquely suggests her own murder. "Wouldn't I taste good?" she asks. Since 301 has once again failed to control another person through the food she cooks, she obliges. The extreme measure 301 takes causes visceral feelings of revulsion even though 301's murder and cooking of 302 are conveyed only by suggestive details.

Metaphoric and Sociocultural Contexts for Dystopian Food Behavior

Parallels in the characters' traumatic childhoods do not create a sense of community for the characters. Instead, as anorexic 302 gradually reveals, she responds to her trauma in an entirely different way from 301. As a young girl whose family ran a butcher shop, a victim for years of incestuous rape by her stepfather, 302 literally cannot stomach eating. It follows that when 301 thrusts food at her, 302 repeatedly flees to the bathroom to vomit. Rather than finding that, as 301 says, "Eating is everything," 302 explains that "I just can't eat things. My body rejects everything." It is not unusual for victims of sexual abuse to feel dirty because of the violation; 302 articulates a sentiment common for sexually abused women when she says, "It's not that I'm dieting. I just can't eat. My body is filled with dirtiness. So how am I supposed to have a man in me or put food in my stomach? I just want to disappear." 302 connects anything she takes into her body with phallic violation. She'd rather have no body at all. As she explains, "My body can't digest anything. No matter how much I try, it's no use."

301's odd, unsympathetic reaction to 302's statement of feeling dirty is to place a light blue drinking glass between the camera and

302. With the glass blocking out 302's face, 301 fills it with water. She thus covers 302's pained facial expression with a life-sustaining liquid. While water can purify and clean, here the water obstructs the view. It obscures viewers' ability to see clearly, to grasp 302's struggle, and to identify with her food behavior. The obstructed view also transfers 301's and 302's obstructed perspectives about food to audiences' spectatorial position.

Even after 302 has been pressed to explain the revulsion she feels when she attempts to eat, 301 continues her attempts to reach and control her through food. In 301's mind, forcing 302 to eat is an act of compassion. Initially 301 believes 302 needs her encouragement, perhaps even assistance, to gain or regain her appetite. Just as 301 used food to insinuate herself into her husband's affection, she resorts to using food as her way to reach 302. Yet 301 is unable to repair 302 because the traumas 302 has experienced extend beyond sexual molestation. Attempts to hide from her stepfather had resulted in another tragedy when a young neighbor girl who wanted to play hide-and-seek with 302 ended up frozen to death in the meat locker. Unable to save the girl on her own, 302 had directed a plaintive cry for help to her mother. However, just as her mother had turned a blind eye to her daughter's sexual abuse, here again she ignores her daughter's troubles, choosing instead to count and recount the money in her cash register.

Having been doubly betrayed and abandoned, 302 explains to 301 that it is not only food that her body refuses, "but everything that has to do with this world." With 302's slowly building, inexorable pull toward death channeled into sinuous camera moves, Park communicates but never actually shows 301 killing and cooking 302. In the scenes with the husband's Maltese dog, Park does not hold back from showing the grotesque head, though he elides the actual killing of the dog. However, since 301's cannibalism completely violates food product protocols, the film more delicately suggests, while also making clear, 302's fate. Watching the detective consume what we know to be 302 concludes this dystopian food-obsessed story with the ultimate transgression for human society.

However symbolic the cannibalism might be, it invites strong emotional and physical responses. As reviewers have noted, audience reactions could approximate those of 302, that is, food may look decidedly unappetizing after seeing the film. For example, Walters writes that several scenes "will make you wish you hadn't just polished off a large popcorn with a side of Milk Duds" (Walters). Baumgarten opines that "you probably won't feel like going out to eat afterwards" (Baumgarten), and John Hartl notes that in *301/302* "eating does almost seem a form of punishment. . . . This movie will cure you of any temptation" (Hartl). With consumption of popcorn, candy, and soda an integral indulgence at film screenings, those reactions highlight the dissonant chord that the film generates.

The pronounced discomfort elicited by 302 being killed and consumed may be matched by nervous reactions to the food-sex neuroses on display. Given the primacy of the food-sex connection and the centrality of the two women, female viewers, in particular, may respond more personally and powerfully to the characters' dysfunctional behavior. Women's eating disorders have received attention over the past several years. In the United States, studies about eating disorders and sexual abuse have been done, but their statistical components remain unreliable. Moreover, it is difficult to determine the degree to which studies of women in the United States reflect the experiences of women in Korea. Yet the story's explanation of 302's avoidance of food is confirmed by studies in the United States, for, as Arthur Crisp has found, "about 30% of female anorexics seem to have been subjected" to childhood sexual victimization (252). In another extensive study, for women "a perceived negative interpersonal response to the disclosure of their childhood sexual abuse predicted higher levels of vomiting" (Fallon and Wonderlich 398). That data suggests behavior consonant with 302's and, however qualified the application of these studies, the film presents that behavior as a plausible response to sexual victimization.[6]

What is the viewer to make of this yin/yang of sex and food, mind and body, so directly confronted? Since 301's extreme measures—killing and cooking her dog and then her neighbor—exceed civilized behavior, to what extent should the viewer interpret this film on a symbolic level? That food functions as a means of opening communication channels and as a weapon for destroying them comes as no surprise. The complex psychological dimensions of food continue to astonish and fascinate. Long a vehicle for ritualization and manipulation, foodways behaviors and activities provide an accessible and powerful means for symbolic and cultural commentary. Dystopian scenarios capitalize on food's multivalent connotations in ways that hit cultural nerves and offer a counterpoint to utopian reassurances.

Public debates surrounding food have confirmed food's central role in human experience, and academic interest has led to the establishment of food-oriented publications.[7] As utopian films suggest, food is often an enjoyable part of daily life. Yet in consumer society where food lays bare psychological neuroses on a daily basis, a wide range of fears and anxieties promoted by news reports and individual experiences are captured by 302's phobia of food. In consumer society, food and water contamination, shortages, and mismanagement have garnered notice; droughts, genetic modification, and nutritionally deficient products have prompted alarm. Thus, just as horror films permit confrontation with nightmarish situations, dystopian food films may serve a therapeutic function by allowing audiences to work through troubling scenarios.

Conflating social and personal anxieties, 301's and 302's self-destructive food behavior provides a conduit for examining cultural and individual concerns. At opposite ends of the spectrum in their irrational conduct, 301 overindulges; 302 abstains. With food as the vehicle, each character symbolizes and particularizes very specific problems. 301 gravitates to obsessive control through her cooking; 302 shares characteristics of anorexic patients who struggle to maintain control through their refusal to eat. However, 302's behavior has the more alarming origins. Her gagging in response to any food comes from repeated sexual trauma, not a loathing of her body provoked by the negative self-image shared by many anorexic and bulimic individuals lured by popular media to subscribe to the thin ideal, to which few can measure up.[8] As Park's film makes plain, 302's hatred of her body comes, as explicitly revealed in flashbacks, as a result of her repeated rape by her stepfather. To underscore that sexual trauma is the source of 302's eating disorder, the character writes an advice column and books on the subject of love. The work or vocation highlights the characters' mind-body split and peculiar interest in helping others when she cannot repair her own psyche.

The film's unconventional presentation of foodways prompts thoughtful and meditative responses to its dystopian vision of food and interpersonal relations. The relatively subdued, reserved acting style of Eun-Jin Bang (301) and Sin-Hye Hwang (302) and the film's omniscient point of view block strong identification with either character. Although the inhumane treatment 302 endures as a child makes her a sympathetic character, her passivity and inaction keep her from being an engaging one. 301's unthinkable and truly nauseating food behavior make her emblematic of a dystopian world where food does not nourish or heal, where food activities do not establish beneficial communities or encourage supportive individual relationships. Yet by presenting this troubling vision of food and allowing audiences to observe these distraught characters, the film may well prompt one to think seriously about food. The foodways lens, inclusive in its survey of food issues, encourages this step as *301/302* joins the collection of films dramatizing the myriad of responses to, and problems concerning, food.

5

When Humans Are the Food Product

An Ideological Look at Cannibal Films

Cannibal films have a complex and unsettled relationship to food films. Discussing the food film genre that emerged in the 1980s, Anne Bower highlights the genre's use of restaurants, kitchens, and food shops, and its focus on food as a means for conveying characters' identities, social situations, and personal relations. Having identified food films' semantic patterns and central thematic concerns, which can be structured to emphasize utopian or dystopian visions of food and society, Bower tests the boundaries of the genre by considering the question: do cannibal films belong to the food film genre? The inquiry leads her to conclude that an "overreliance on strict genre definitions may be limiting" and that the "semiotic uses of food are even more multivalent and powerful than a concentration on 'food films' alone would allow us to understand" (6, 7).

Cannibal films confirm and illustrate Bower's point, for their "semiotic uses of food" provide a clear view of the characters' values, beliefs, and social status. Their depictions of cuisine choices, procurement policies, and eating protocols take on heightened significance precisely because human beings are placed in the food category. In this circumstance, characters' interaction with the food product becomes the most salient marker of individual and cultural identities: engaging in cannibalism places characters squarely on one side of the divide between civilized and uncivilized behavior. Like dystopian food films, cannibal films often use characters' food behaviors to signal personal and social disorder. In addition, whereas some cannibal films do little more than exploit cultural taboos to generate sensation, other films use troubling representations of foodways to comment on class, colonial, and cultural injustice. By examining the larger implications of consumption, cannibal films delve into dimensions of food rarely featured in commercial cinema.

Films in which humans are the food product often comment on the symbolic but systemic cannibalism of imperial and economic ventures. They reflect the fact that empires have framed their military campaigns as righteous efforts to consume and cleanup "uncivilized" behavior. The films mirror the reality that corporations tout their ability to devour the competition; executives flaunt their ability to "eat that guy for lunch." With flesh-eating metaphors part of everyday life, cannibal films go on to complicate the simple opposition between civilized and uncivilized people. They tap into people's awareness that, historically, accounts of cannibalism have been unreliable, designed to serve the interests of "civilized" people in search of profit or lasting fame. Thus, today, cannibal films rely on people's knowledge that cannibalism can function as a sign of primitive savages *and* as a marker of savage empires and corporations.

Variations in the films that deal with cannibalism confound efforts to map out a set of shared semantic elements that extend beyond their common use of humans as the food product. Films also use cannibalism in different syntactical structures. For example, in a utopian film like *Bagdad Cafe,* the early references to cannibalism show that the isolated individuals need to create community. By comparison, *301/302* wraps up its deeply dystopian vision of food and society with the characters in power (the detective and the cooking-obsessed woman) engaging in cannibalism. Other representations of cannibalism reflect the utopian-dystopian spectrum. Cannibal films include comedies like Abbott and Costello's *Africa Screams* (Barton, 1949), Herschel Gordon Lewis's gore favorite *Blood Feast,* campy satires like *Eating Raoul,* psychological thrillers such as *The Silence of the Lambs,* and its sequel from 2001 and prequels from 2002 and 2007. Cannibalism is central to the various comedy, horror, and musical versions of the pulp fiction and stage melodrama *Sweeney Todd* (1926, 1928, 1936, 2007), along with *The Hills Have Eyes* (Craven, 1977), which led to Wes Craven's 1984 direct-to-video sequel as well as Alexandre Aja's 2006 remake of the original and the 2007 sequel to this remake directed by Martin Weiss.

The consumption of humans by flesh-eating zombies features prominently in several horror films, perhaps most notably in writer/director George Romero's numerous "living dead" films: *Night of the Living Dead* (1968), *Dawn of the Dead* (1978), *Day of the Dead* (1985), *Land of the Dead* (2005), *Diary of the Dead* (2007), and *Survival of the Dead* (2009). Although one could argue that zombie films do not feature actual cannibalism because zombies technically eat outside of their species—most zombies consume only humans or animals, not other zombies—these films are often lumped in with cannibal films due to their obvious similarities. Without a doubt, zombie films do contain some of the most striking instances of humans as food product, as these films regularly depict the human body being graphically torn apart and consumed by the ravenous undead in apocalyptic scenarios.

Cannibalism is a significant feature in the post-apocalyptic narratives *Tooth and Nail* (Young, 2007) and *The Road*. It anchors the troubling survival narratives of *Ravenous* (Bird, 1999), *Van Diemen's Land* (auf der Heide, 2009), *The Last Confession of Alexander Pearce* (Rowland, 2008), and even *The Life of Pi* (Lee, 2012). Cannibalism figures into films based on Jack Ketchum's misogynistic novels *Offspring* (van den Houten, 2007) and *The Woman* (McKee, 2011), which venture into increasingly problematic conventions of torture porn. In contrast, cannibalism plays a role in sentient comedies like *Fresh Meat* (Mulheron, 2013) and inventive dramas like *We Are What We Are* (Glau, 2010). Audience response confirms that cannibalism remains a hot topic for film lovers. Some of the most important and infamous cannibal films still belong to the cycle of Italian horror films released in the 1970s and 1980s, which includes *Deep River Savages* (Lenzi, 1972), *The Last Cannibal World* (Deodato, 1977), *Mountain of the Cannibal God* (Martino, 1978), *Cannibal Holocaust, Eaten Alive!* (Lenzi, 1980), *Cannibal Ferox* (Lenzi, 1981), and *Cannibal Holocaust II* (Climati, 1988).[1]

Despite their variations, cannibal films reflect the fact that food consumption in consumer society is fraught with uncertainties; people do not know what they are eating; they do not know where their food comes from or where their disposed food will go. The films capture and hold audience attention because their shared focus on humans as the food product implicates all the other foodways elements. If a film presents humans as a food product, how does that figure into the characters' food performance system? Is cannibalism part of a rare, celebratory feast as in *How Tasty Was My Little Frenchman,* or is it a regular part of the meal cycle of impoverished Americans as in *The Texas Chain Saw Massacre*? If humans are presented as a food product, could representation of food procurement, preservation, preparation, presentation, consumption, and cleanup be anything but troubling? The question highlights the ramifications of narratives that present humans as the food product. Horror films like *Cannibal Holocaust* reveal that films explore those ramifications in sensationalized but potentially insightful ways.

Cannibal Narratives

A range of sources continually reactivate interest in films that make humans the food product. For instance, although accounts of the routine or ritualized cannibalistic practices of "primitive" people have been called into doubt, anthropologists continue to offer new evidence of cannibal customs in remote places of the globe (the Wari in Brazil), in non-Anglo societies in North America (the Anasazi in Colorado), and in Europe's distant past, with marks on Neanderthal bones found in France providing the basis for claims that the cannibalism of Homo Sapiens led or contributed to Neanderthals' extinction (see Conklin; Turner and Turner; Rozzi et al.). Tellingly, these accounts are not confined to academic journals, but instead spice up headline news ("Scientist"). There are also intermittent reminders that humans do serve as food in extreme circumstances, as in the case of the people who turned to cannibalism to survive after their plane crashed in the Andes in 1972. The practices of serial killers such as Albert Fish and Jeffrey Dahmer are reminders that cannibalism occurs close to home. The news even carries stories about consensual cannibalism, as when Bernd-Jurgen Brandes answered Armin Meiwes's personal ad in 2001 for "Well-built men, 18–30, who like to be eaten by me" (Clark 1).

Less spectacularly, folk tales in various parts of the world make reference to cannibalism. The cannibalism in stories like "Hansel and Gretel" and "Jack and the Beanstalk" is so familiar one almost fails to notice it. Moreover, symbolic or sacred cannibalism is part of Christian culture. Some believers consider the Eucharist a symbolic act, whereas others adhere to the doctrine that transubstantiation transforms the bread and wine into the actual body and blood of Christ. The Christian idea of communion as an act that creates connection with the spiritual domain accords with both ecclesiastical and secular theory. Both perspectives envision a process of evolution in which people first killed and ate humans for food; then killed and ate humans only in ritual situations; then replaced humans with animals in ritual sacrifice; and eventually reached the point where "anthropophagy [the eating of human flesh by human beings was] replaced by a symbolic sacrifice and the consumption of a spiritual essence" (Arens 16).

The view that "primitive" people remain in the first two stages of spiritual and social evolution is often a corollary of the position that the Christian Eucharist is a sign of advanced civilization. However, as cultural theorist and anthropologist William Arens points out: "The most certain thing to be said is that all cultures, subcultures, religions, sects, secret societies and every other possible human association have been labeled anthropophagic by someone" (139). In other words, the "idea of 'others' as cannibals, rather than the act" is the central point in cannibal narratives (Arens 139). Noting that stories about cannibalism go back as far as Herodotus, who referred to the human flesh eating habit of very distant, unnamed nomads, Arens finds that accounts follow clear patterns. People locate cannibalism in "neighboring societies" (as Herodotus did). They "employ the idea as a mythic marker in the progress of their own cultural development" (as in the Christian scenario) (Arens 159). They also attribute cannibalism to members of their own society as part of explanations for the existence of misfortune (as in the Inquisition when witches, heretics, and sometimes Jews were accused of cannibalism) (Arens 10, 95).

The limited evidence of flesh-eating customs—as distinct from isolated incidents of survival or pathological cannibalism, customs of ritual killing, or sacred practices that involve ingesting literal or symbolic vestiges of a person—lead Arens to argue that the "significant question is not why people eat human flesh, but why one group invariably assumes [and charges] that others do" (139). His position has stirred debate since the publication of his book *The Man-Eating Myth* (1979). Some anthropologists reject Arens's position that there is insufficient evidence to substantiate claims that established customs lead people to consume human flesh; others recognize the value of circumspect inquiry into the logic behind accounts of cannibalism (Osborne; Hulme).[2]

Rather than concerning themselves with researching the veracity of recorded accounts of cannibalism, scholars persuaded by Arens's views instead examine the rhetorical function of cannibal narratives and focus on who benefits from the circulation of these narratives. For example, analyzing depictions of cannibalism in missionary documents, in P. T. Barnum's display of "Fiji cannibals," and in various pieces of nineteenth- and twentieth-century literature, Jeff Berglund identifies patterns in the way cannibalism is used in narratives about "an alien Other" (22). Echoing Arens's position, Berglund finds that "cannibalism is often a verbally created reality predicated on false evidence, fanciful imaginings, or ideologically inflected logic" (3). He proposes that accounts and representations of cannibalism are best understood as establishing—rather than describing—the existence of cannibalistic practices (21).

Postcolonial scholarship amplifies Arens's view that cannibal narratives serve the interests of the people who formulate them. Official accounts that concern "cannibalism," rather than anthropophagy, reflect Europeans' New World colonial exploits, with their "intertwined projects of Christianizing, capitalism, and imperialism" (Berglund 22). As Arens and others point out, the term "cannibal" did not exist until Columbus published a summary of "his journey to the land of the 'Great Khan,'" in which he claimed that man-eating Carib Indians inhabited islands that he passed (Arens 46). Once established, the concept was put to use. As early as 1503, even though "official royal policy initially prohibited enslavement of the inhabitants of the [Caribbean] islands . . . the monarchs adhered to this policy except in the case of 'a certain people called Cannibals'" (Arens 49–50). The Caribs' continued resistance to pacification and colonization caused "resistance to foreign invasion" to become "the operational definition of cannibalism" and the pretext for "being sold into slavery" (Arens 51).

What is striking is that cannibalism is not only a "political fiction that Europeans employed to justify exploitation of indigenous people" (Cheyfitz 143), it is also "indelibly linked to notions of Americanness" because the concept "coincides with the founding moment of 'the Americas'" (Berglund 3). Given that legacy, cannibalism has continually disturbed visions of food in powerful industrialized societies. The anxieties that privileged consumers have about unhealthy food and their gnawing awareness that food labor is generally "disappeared" translate rather easily into sensationalized narratives about cannibalism. Concerns about personal food choices and the experience of being cut off from food production gives resonance to disturbing stories about humans as the food product. With foodways' many stages shrouded in mystery, cannibal narratives reflect consumers' enduring unease about the methods that have long been used to make delicacies easily available to those in power.

Cannibals from New York City

Ruggero Deodato's *Cannibal Holocaust* is one of many films that critique first-world exploitation of "primitive" people and "civilized" experts' attribution of cannibalism to indigenous people.[3] Pointed commentary about the "cannibalism" that goes along with the first world's exercise of military, economic, and cultural power can be found in other Italian cannibal films produced in the 1970s and 1980s. These notoriously graphic films have their antecedents in adventure movies like *The Most Dangerous Game* (Pichel and Schoedsack, 1932) and *The Naked Prey* (Wilde, 1966). They compare to Romero's *Night of the Living Dead,* its sequel *Dawn of the Dead,* and a cycle of Italian zombie films with splashy, over-the-top gore effects that followed in the wake of Romero's bloody *Dawn.* They also parallel the ultraviolent spaghetti westerns of directors like Sergio Leone and Sergio Corbucci, the sado-voyeuristic *giallo* horror films of Mario Bava, Dario Argento, and Lucio Fulci, and the Italian shockumentary series initiated by *Mondo Cane* (Prosperi, 1962). Reflecting on Italy's cannibal films, David Cook observes that while they are "arguably obscene, the apocalyptic carnality of several cannibal films [lends] them a perverse lyricism, attracting many steadfast and serious admirers as well as armies of outraged critics" (554–55).

The "apocalyptic carnality" of the Italian cannibal films also makes them useful material for ideological studies of food in film. With humans as the food product, all other foodways aspects become disturbed, and unusual depictions of foodways take center stage. Designed to get international attention in a global market dominated by big-budget Hollywood movies, Italian cannibal films feature gore, pornography, and the sacrilege of literal cannibalism. Surrounded by sensational stories at the time of its release and sometimes seen as the most infamous cannibal film of all time, *Cannibal Holocaust* has become an icon of cult cinema, with its continuing appeal illustrating how the cult and camp criticism of writers such as Manny Farber, Parker Tyler, and Jonas Mekas not only influenced viewers' taste in film, but also "transformed the way we think about art" (Taylor 153). *Cannibal Holocaust* has a reputation for its visceral impact, yet the film comments on accepted truths of science, commerce, and global politics, in part because the film is about a North American news crew that fabricates eyewitness accounts of cannibalism in South America. With scenes in the Amazon jungle intercut with ones set in the concrete jungle of New York skyscrapers, and with depictions of the news crew raping and killing the people they characterize as threatening savages, *Cannibal Holocaust* makes a clear statement about the media's misrepresentation of people in the third world.

The news crew fabricates stories about cannibalism to secure celebrity status. The film links their self-interested misrepresentations to academics' exploitation of indigenous people. It takes direct aim at the North American anthropologists who made their careers circulating now suspect accounts of cannibalism in South America. American anthropologist Napoleon A. Chagnon provides the model for the film's fictional New York University anthropologist who is sent on the mission to find the news crew that has gone missing in South America. Chagnon "made his reputation on his work with the Yanomami" and "had a virtual monopoly on the interpretation of Yanomami culture" (Rabben 13, 40).

Chagnon's book *Yanomamö: The Fierce People* came out in 1968 and since that time has sold millions of copies. In addition, beginning in the late 1960s, the "Yanomami, like the Bushmen, became the most filmed non-Western, non-industrialized society in the world" (Ruby 22).

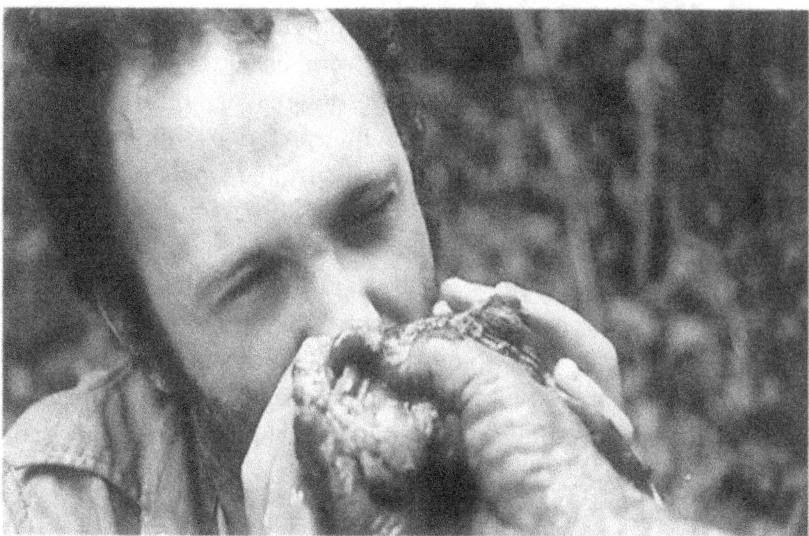

Cannibal Holocaust *(F. D. Cinematografica) is an exploitation film with a social critique that features porn star Robert Kerman as the New York anthropologist with expertise in cannibalism.*

While acts of cannibalism were never filmed, Chagnon's book created a sensation by alleging that there were cannibals living in northwest Brazil. Researchers have subsequently debunked Chagnon's "findings" and documented the destructive effects of the anthropologists' intrusions into Yanomami society (Rabben; Tierney 3–122). Deodato's 1980 film represents an early challenge to Chagnon's work. In the same way that *How Tasty Was My Little Frenchman* deconstructs "official" colonial reports of cannibals on Brazil's east coast, *Cannibal Holocaust* undercuts "expert" accounts of cannibalism among the Yanomami in northwest Brazil.

Deodato's film builds on skepticism first generated by *The Ax Fight* (Asch, 1975). This short film, which Tim Asch and Chagnon started in 1971, eventually discredited Chagnon's view that anthropology could offer "an accurate representation" of what researchers encounter in field work (Ruby 28). Asch's four-part film first shows unedited footage that Asch shot in a Yanomami village; then the screen goes black and audiences hear a conversation between Asch, Chagnon, and soundman Craig Johnson. The film's second segment returns to the footage using "narration, slow-motion and arrows identifying the principals" (Ruby 26). This is followed by "a third section with kinship charts" (Ruby 26). The fourth segment shows an edited version that demonstrates the degree to which editing frames viewers' interpretations (Ruby 26).

The contrast between the edited and unedited footage is troubling. However, the off-screen comments by the anthropologist and the filmmakers are what completely undercut "the 'scientific' certainty of anthropological explanations" (Ruby 25). Audiences hear the anthropologist and the filmmakers describe what they are watching as "wife-beating" and then as "a club fight" (Ruby 25). Audiences then hear contradictory statements about when the event began, what was involved, and why the incident took place (Ruby 25). Asch's film never shows any scenes of a wife-beating or a club fight.

Deodato uses the unconfirmed comments and contradictory statements as a model for several scenes of the North American news crew recording false verbal descriptions of events. For example, audiences see the news crew set fire to a village. Then, in the aftermath, the journalists record a news segment that describes the destruction as the result of tribal warfare. Audiences see the men in the news crew gang rape a young woman. The film implies that they kill her and then impale her on a pole. Here again, the news crew prepares its report after the incident. With their news camera now rolling, journalist Alan Yates (Gabriel Yorke) attributes the girl's fate to natives' ritual killing. Anchored by scenes that point to the unreliability of authoritative accounts, Deodato's film presents an angry challenge to "information" offered by social scientists and corporate media. *Cannibal Holocaust* reflects its era's rethinking of anthropology and imperialism, expressing points made in volumes such as Talal Asad's *Anthropology and the Colonial Encounter* (1973) and Edward Said's *Orientalism* (1978), which proposed that "anthropologists have, sometimes unwittingly, contributed to maintaining the hierarchy of power of the colonial system" (López 30).

Cannibal Holocaust makes the unseemly and unethical aspects of "civilization" explicit. To highlight the savagery of modern corporations, the film's final scene leads viewers to see that the sacred scar of the Atari tattoo, which had served to identify the film's cannibals, is none other than the logo for Boise Cascade, the North American lumber company that has cleared acres of Brazilian rainforest. *Canni-*

bal Holocaust's closing scene also draws attention to the "Avenue of the Americas" street sign and so suggests that the modern commerce represented by the busy city street depends, at least in part, on the kind of unethical behavior that marks the American "experts" in the film. *Cannibal Holocaust* employs these references in its narrative, mobilizing a ripple effect in which humans are the food product. Food procurement, preparation, and presentation all become tainted. Food consumption by the journalists and the anthropologist becomes a metaphor for first-world abuse of indigenous people. The North's consumption is framed as isolated personal gain that is anathema to community and survival in the South.

A Frenchman: A Tasty Centerpiece for a Holiday Meal

Given its critique of first-world institutions, Deodato's horror film shares common ground with Third Cinema, which takes a path that differs from Hollywood (first cinema) and European art film (second cinema) by being accessible and socially conscious. For example, *How Tasty Was My Little Frenchman,* directed by Brazilian filmmaker Nelson Pereira dos Santos, has a whimsical tone that invites, rather than forces, audiences to reflect on the consequences of cultural imperialism. The film's fanciful depiction of Tupi Indian foodways allows audiences to consider colonial contact from the perspective of the indigenous people. Employing a method akin to de Antonio, where documentary evidence undercuts official accounts, dos Santos deconstructs one of the first purported eyewitness accounts of New World cannibalism, *Brazil: The True History of the Wild, Naked, Fierce, Man-Eating People.* The book, published in German in 1557, was based on the stories of German sailor Hans Staden, "who describes his capture by the cannibalistic Tupinambá when he was living among the Portuguese in the area now known as Rio de Janeiro" (Sadlier 58).[4] Staden's account may have led Chagnon to add the sensationalized subtitle "the fierce people" to his "scientific" study of the Yanomami.

However, rather than build on Staden's account, dos Santos makes the German sailor a Frenchman. The change reflects dos Santos's disinterest in sensationalized accounts and his concern with the often-overlooked influence French culture has had on Brazil. Dos Santos's film also resists "the romanticizing and/or valorization of a victim identity" by showing the Tupi Indians as belonging to a complex society that could be as brutal, shortsighted, and capable as the Portuguese and French adventurers who came to the New World to make their fortunes (Berglund 24). The film reveals the shortcomings of the European imperialists and the New World inhabitants. It shows the greed of the Europeans as they devour New World riches (gold, pepper, wood). However, *How Tasty Was My Little Frenchman* also proposes that New World people made a mistake by ingesting foreign influences. It thus illuminates the twofold problem of imperialism that stretches back to the sixteenth century: global powers destroy local cultures throughout the world, and people attracted to the toxic but tasty morsels offered by powerful institutions contribute to their own demise.

The film's overt subject is the cannibalism of the Tupinambá Indians, "who have come down to us today as man-eaters *par excellence*" (Arens 22). This group of Tupi Indians came to be seen as the "quintessential cannibals" due to various classics of the early colonial period, "including the works of Hans Staden, André Thévet, Jean de Léry, and Michel Montaigne" (Watson 8). Whereas noble savages had been popular figures in nineteenth-century Brazilian literature, the Tupi Indians provided the inspiration for Oswald de Andrade's 1928 "Manifesto antropófago." Aiming to redefine Brazil's national identity, the manifesto inverted the stigma of New World cannibalism to make it a metaphor for Brazil's mosaic society that had been created by "internalizing pieces of other cultures" (Young 82).

Dos Santos uses Oswald de Andrade's manifesto as a point of departure. His film more closely resembles Joaquim Pedro de Andrade's *Macunaíma* (1969), which turned "the theme of cannibalism into the springboard for a critique of repressive military rule and of the predatory capitalist model of the short-lived Brazilian 'economic miracle'" (Stam 239). Both films suggest that the "civilized" world has been and continues to be far more cannibalistic than any "primitive" culture. Both films are emblematic of the "cannibal-tropicalist" phase of Brazil's Cinema Novo. This new wave film movement sought to create an "esthetic of hunger" to oppose "digestive cinema" (Stam 239), which for the filmmakers consisted of local and international "films about rich people with pretty houses riding in luxurious automobiles; [and]

cheerful, fast-paced, empty films with purely industrial objectives" (Johnson and Stam 68).

Even though *How Tasty Was My Little Frenchman* is set in the late sixteenth century, dos Santos presents the story as if it were a contemporary subject, using natural light, hand-held camera, and other visible "techniques of cinéma vérité" (Peña 192). Tentatively comparing the film to a verité "portrait film" such as *Dont Look Back* (Pennebaker, 1967) about Bob Dylan, Richard Peña notes that in the absence of interviews and voice-of-god narration, and with the presence of contradictory information, "we are forced to come to our own conclusions about the subjects of the portrait [by] considering the pattern and larger implications of their actions" (192–93). However, although there are points of contact between vérité and the approach used in *How Tasty Was My Little Frenchman,* for dos Santos Euro-American cinéma vérité was not a recipe for authentic Brazilian cinema. Instead, as fellow Brazilian filmmaker Glauber Rocha made clear in a manifesto published the year *How Tasty My Little Frenchman* went into production, Third Cinema filmmakers in Asia, Africa, and Latin America must set aside a host of influences: "the commercial-popular esthetics of Hollywood, the populist-demagogic esthetics of Moscow . . . the bourgeois-artistic esthetics of Europe," and "neocolonialist left" work like cinéma vérité (Rocha 89).

Dos Santos's depiction of the Tupi Indians aims to "faithfully replicate the lifestyle and language of a civilization that had suffered foreign invasion and extermination" (Sadlier 72). This approach presents events from the Tupi's perspective and explores aspects of their lived experience omitted from official accounts. Darlene Sadlier notes that the film's "documentary-like or 'anthropological' style directly participates in an effort of reinterpretation" (74). The film provides "the viewer with a simulation of what has been lost, not just in time but also through [a] selective cultural process [that has been shaped by] the interests and values of the dominant class in Brazil, which has always identified with Europeans, especially the French" (Sadlier 74).

The film's almost commonplace "depiction of the Indians, who live a rather docile, mundane existence while trying to cope with foreign armies," distinguishes *How Tasty Was My Little Frenchman* from both romanticized nineteenth-century Brazilian novels modeled on

European fiction and from Brazilian manifestos filled with polemical, French-influenced rhetoric (Sadlier 72). Breaking with French models is especially significant; as Sadlier points out, although "Brazil was a Portuguese colony until the early nineteenth century, its cultural and intellectual life after [it became an independent empire in] 1822 was far more profoundly influenced by France" (63). Like other former colonies, even after Brazil became a republic in 1889, it has been colonized by French aesthetic and cultural theory.[5]

Dos Santos's consciously "Brazilian" depiction of Tupi daily life allows audiences to look at New World encounters from the perspective of the people who were there before tasty Frenchmen came to shore. The film does not dispute the idea that the Tupi were cannibals. Instead, it casts the activity in a new light. Dos Santos's film suggests that the Tupi were not determined to destroy the Europeans invaders, but instead were willing to consume the foreign products that seemed tasty. It was not apparent to the Tupi that trading with and fighting alongside the French would lead to the Tupi's destruction. Dos Santos's film suggests that Europeans conquered Brazil's indigenous people because the Europeans refused to consume New World culture in any meaningful way. By comparison, the pattern of seeing foreign products as more tasty than indigenous ones has made it possible for Brazil's inhabitants to be conquered in military, financial, and cultural terms.

The film's representation of Tupi foodways conveys those ideas in lucid terms. Its various scenes of Tupi women tending healthy fields of cultivated crops make the point that these "quintessential cannibals" were capable farmers who lived primarily on a plant-based diet. The Tupi's interactions with the Frenchman throughout the film make it plain that he is a special dish for a holiday celebration. The Tupi do not eat him because they are starving, angry, greedy, or "primitive." Instead, the Tupi make the Frenchman the centerpiece of their feast to celebrate the tribe's victory over their rivals, the Tupiniquins, who fight alongside the Portuguese.

How Tasty Was My Little Frenchman takes audiences through all the steps that lead up to the holiday meal. Early on, there is the procurement process, with the Frenchman (Arduíno Colassanti) taken by the Tupi chief as a spoil of war. Shown as a special but straightforward act, undertaken simply but deliberately, in much the same way someone would order a Thanksgiving turkey at a butcher shop, the Tupi chief, Cunhambebe (Eduardo Imbassahy Filho), makes his selection from the choices available, opting for the blond-haired prisoner, the Frenchman, over the dark-haired (Portuguese) prisoners. Double-checking his decision, the Tupi chief sizes up the Frenchman's build the way someone would inspect a cut of meat. As he starts home, he remarks that he wants to show this unusual "Portuguese" prisoner to the women of the village. It is soon clear that he made the right food product choice; when the warriors return to the village, the women show that they are delighted about the tasty treat the chief has brought home.

In preparation for their holiday meal, the Tupi set out on an eight-month period of food preservation and preparation. The Frenchman is fed well; the Tupi keep him in good condition by making him help with hunting and warfare. Following food protocols, a beautiful young woman, Seboipepe (Ana Maria Magalhães), whose husband has been recently killed in battle, is assigned to be his companion. Although this aspect of the holiday meal preparation conforms to colonial fantasies, the film presents it as a prudent food preservation choice on the part of the Tupi, for only someone like this circumspect young woman could have kept the Frenchman from escaping. From the beginning to the end of the long preservation and preparation process, there is a heavy emphasis on following food protocols. Cunhambebe and Seboipepe provide detailed explanations of why the Frenchman should be eaten, how he should act at the ceremony in which he will be killed, and which body parts will be eaten by various members of the tribe.

As with many holiday meals, the social aspects of preparing their feast are paramount for the Tupi community. In a final ceremony, the Frenchman is presented to the village in elaborate bird feathers and body paint. Cunhambebe and Seboipepe again lead the proceedings and carefully follow Tupi rules of decorum by reiterating the reasons the Frenchman can and should be eaten. Given the event's symbolic focus, the practical dimensions of food preparation and consumption are secondary at best. Shown in an extreme wide shot, the Frenchman falls to the ground after a single blow to the head, and a few villagers carry his body to a funeral pyre. Celebrations unrelated to eating begin immediately. Racing through the village with two small cannons on his shoulders, Cunhambebe asserts his control of the weapons that

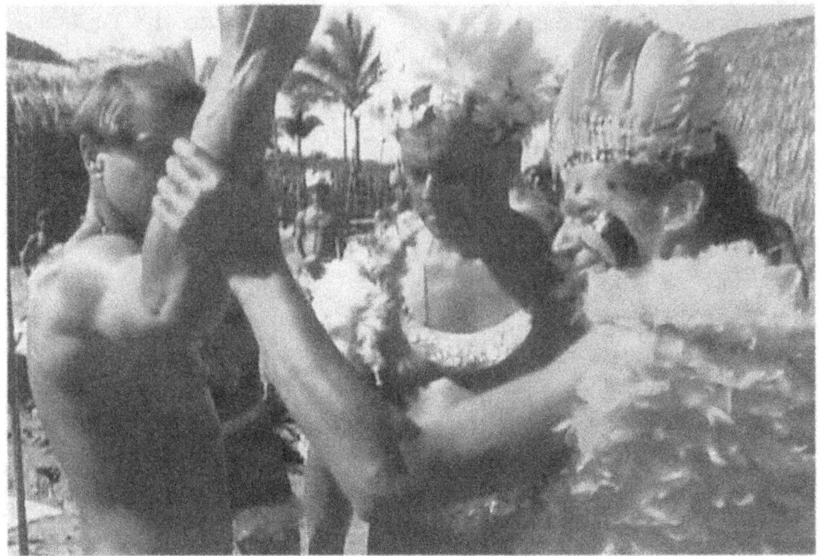

The best parts of the holiday meal go to key members of society in How Tasty Was My Little Frenchman *(Condor Filmes, Luiz Carlos Barreto Produções Cinematográficas, Regina Filmes).*

had once been the Frenchman's source of mystical power. Equally significant, the audience's only glimpse of cannibalism is a quick shot of Seboipepe, who for a moment looks directly at the camera as she takes a small bite from what appears to be the piece of the Frenchman she was promised. The brief, private, and singular moment of consumption suggests that eating human flesh is incidental to the Tupi meal system, whereas cannibalism, or symbolic cannibalism, belongs to Tupi sacred belief systems and is thus comparable to Christian norms. The shot's rupture of the conventional fourth wall, which normally allows viewers to gaze unseen into fictional worlds, is also a reminder that outsiders' belief that other people are cannibals is the salient factor in cannibal narratives.

By presenting the Frenchman as a highly symbolic aspect of a holiday meal, *How Tasty Was My Little Frenchman* puts the cannibalism of the Tupi in an entirely new light. With the Frenchman falling into a category that is quite different from the food the Tupi raise or catch to eat during regular meals to sustain themselves, the film suggests that consuming the Frenchman at a special holiday feast is an activity designed to nourish the spiritual needs of the Tupi. It is a sacred and private act, not unlike the Christian Eucharist, in which people partake of the body and blood of Christ. With extensive screen time allotted to the steps leading up to the feast and only seconds given to what passes as flesh eating, the film makes the point that for the Tupi and their enemies, it is the idea of cannibalism that is important.

Concluding with what might be a wry allusion to cleanup, *How Tasty Was My Little Frenchman* tacitly reminds viewers that the Tupi's resistance to European incursions caused them to be wiped out in the same way other New World "cannibals" were. This final scene also highlights the distance between facts and European accounts of the New World. In doing so, the conclusion brings viewers back to the film's opening. There, the narration, which is based on an official Portuguese report from 1557, bears little relation to what is shown onscreen. The voiceover narration does not match the film's visual depiction of the Europeans' actions. The official Portuguese report also fails to match the images of the Tupi, for whereas the voiceover describes the godlessness of the "natives," the images show smiling Tupi women offering baskets of fruits and vegetables to the sailors. Dos Santos's film thus anticipates the critiques of official accounts in *The Ax Fight* and *Cannibal Holocaust*. The film also highlights that depictions of food behavior, such as the Tupi women's generous sharing of food with strangers, offer insights into "the beliefs, aesthetics, economics, and politics" of a social group (Long 144).

"Laboring" the Food Film

Films like *Cannibal Holocaust* and *How Tasty Was My Little Frenchman* reveal that cannibal films sometimes use food and food behavior to show that "civilized" people might be the real cannibals. Cannibal films also use foodways to convey and comment on social problems caused by uneven distribution of wealth. Characters' food choices illuminate their class, ethnic, regional, and national identities. The dynamics of identity, class, and power central to food films are at the heart of Tobe Hooper's *The Texas Chain Saw Massacre,* which established the franchise active from 1974 to 2013. Here the cannibals are not found in the

Amazon, but instead in the "uncivilized" world of rural America and its working class.

That vision of cannibalism has a venerable history that goes back to the writings of Herman Melville. Berglund points out that as early as the mid-nineteenth century, American writers "were interested in the subject of cannibalism as a way to meditate on perceived differences, even if readers, fans, or consumers were aware of the fabrication of such cannibal tendencies" (10). Cannibalism "became a way to critique not only systems enforcing racial inequality but also those enforcing inequalities of gender, sexuality, and class" (Berglund 10). When set within the United States, "the cannibal presence in cultural and literary fictions estranges familiar, homey national narratives" of a united country "by highlighting divisive historical and contemporary practices that preclude the many from becoming the one" (Berglund 24). That point is especially pertinent when one considers the role played by food in Hooper's film, for "the figure of the cannibal disrupts the notion of a mythic national unity, highlighting the disunity that emerged with the nation's founding and remains today as much a part of the fabric of U.S. identity as any sense of collective harmony" (Berglund 4).

Cannibal narratives consistently focus on questions surrounding identity. Berglund writes: "Defining the Other as a barbaric cannibal, one who may extinguish your life, clearly distinguishes the boundaries between good and evil, between me and you" (8). The historical usage of the term "cannibal" to demarcate lines between "civilized" people (who eat animals) and "uncivilized" people (who eat other people) was used to justify conquest of the New World; asserting that indigenous peoples "violated natural law by practicing such barbarous outrages as idolatry and cannibalism" allowed any act of European savagery to seem legitimate (Lepore 110).

However, despite cannibal narratives' division between "civilized" and "uncivilized" peoples, they do not present stable identities. Instead, stories about cannibalism suggest that identities are actually quite fluid. Berglund proposes that "consumption by another collapses identity boundaries: in being consumed, You become Me, I become You-Me. Figuratively, cannibalism threatens one's sense of integrity" (8). Cannibal narratives are thus paradoxical; they demonize a group and justify its subordination by labeling it as "cannibal," but, at the same time, call into question the identity of those making the accusations. With foodways as the narrative's foundation, the dilemmas of cannibalism, identity, and power are all at play in *The Texas Chain Saw Massacre.*

There is already an excellent body of scholarship that examines issues of class in Hooper's 1974 film. A look at the film's depiction of foodways contributes to that work. Foodways analysis reveals that the film conveys class differences through characters' food behavior. It shows how the film foregrounds the procurement and preparation of food. That approach reveals that Hooper's film carefully examines the food labor that commercial films and even other food films do not show. Looking at Hooper's film through the foodways lens also draws attention to the behavior and presentation that surround consumption of the human food product. Analysis of food consumption in this film indicates that *The Texas Chain Saw Massacre* problematizes the boundaries between "normal" (the middle-class young people) and "abnormal" (the working class cannibal family), largely through its depiction of Franklin (Paul A. Partain), whose tastes run the gamut from acceptable to unacceptable.

Robin Wood has proposed that the 1970s were "the Golden Age of the American horror film" (*Hollywood* 63). For Wood, *The Texas Chain Saw Massacre* helped create that golden age and is a film that warrants thoughtful analysis because it "achieves the force of authentic art" (84). Wood is impressed by the film because it shows ways that the "proletariat" is "exploited and degraded" under capitalism (82). For Wood, the cannibal family members are not mere monsters but "victims, too—of the slaughter-house environment, of capitalism" (83). Hence, when the cannibal family kills and consumes the "affluent young" people, the film calls attention to class difference and problems of scarcity in America's capitalist society, even if it does not offer any solutions to these problems (Wood 82).

Others have continued Wood's analysis of class in *The Texas Chain Saw Massacre* and the horror film in general (see Hutchings; Newitz). However, they have not explored ways that Hooper's film employs food to examine class issues, despite the fact that food activities and characters' food choices are central to the narrative. Early in the film, when the unsuspecting victims pick up the Hitchhiker (Edwin Neal), he informs the teenagers that several members of his (cannibal) family used to work at the slaughterhouse. He explains, however, that with the "new way" of killing cattle (a mechanized bolt gun), "people got put out of jobs." The film thus suggests at the outset that the cannibal family is in dire straits—overworked, living in a dilapidated house—because the food industry's increased mechanization cost them their good middle-class jobs.

As the film continues, its articulation of class difference emerges from its depiction of the food labor elided by most films. Hooper's film focuses on the labor behind food, explicitly exposing stages of food procurement, preparation, and preservation normally left out of film representations. That concern begins even before the appearance of the cannibal family. Driving along before they pick up the Hitchhiker, the teenagers notice a terrible stench. As they complain about the smell and roll up the windows, Franklin informs them that the smell is coming from "the old slaughterhouse" where his grandfather "used to sell his cattle." As Franklin explains how cows used to be dispatched there, Hooper cuts away to a close-up shot of a panting, exhausted cow in a feedlot. The image disrupts Franklin's description and the film's narrative, for it makes visible the unseemly aspects of the food system.

People writing about food in film have noted that movies use food primarily in three ways: as a piece of the setting that allows characters to interact, as a transition device (to show the passing of time), and as a way to "symbolically or metaphorically" reveal information about characters (Zimmerman and Weiss 2). Thus, even dystopian food films will elide the decidedly unglamorous labor required to procure food, preserve food, and prepare daily meals. Moreover, with commercial cinema emphasizing the convenient consumption of food, films consistently leave out the slaughterhouse labor required to transform living creatures into "food." They also mask out the questionable ingredients used in food preparation (to cut costs and increase profits) and the questionable practices that may take place during the food-making process (exploitation of laborers, faulty cleanup procedures, and so on).

By contrast, the laborious steps in the food-making process are brought to the forefront in *The Texas Chain Saw Massacre.* In fact, a good deal of the film's narrative is concerned with procurement, preservation, and preparation. For most middle-class audiences, even at holiday time the procurement of food ingredients is limited to "placing a special order at a butcher shop or turkey farm, shopping at the local grocery, or perhaps visiting a pumpkin patch or apple orchard" (Long

145). However, for the impoverished cannibal clan, these luxuries are not available, so it is up to Leatherface (Gunnar Hansen) to procure the family's food by killing Kirk (William Vail), Pam (Terri McMinn), Jerry (Allen Danziger), and Franklin when they wander close to the house.

In addition to procurement, the film makes other stages of food preparation visible as the teenagers are picked off one by one. Leatherface kills Kirk and takes him to the kitchen. He then captures Pam, carries her into the kitchen, and hangs her live, fresh body on a meat hook. As she hangs on the hook screaming, Leatherface turns to the task of chopping up Kirk's body, which has been laid out on the kitchen table. In this scene, the preparation stage, which includes "chopping, marinating, and otherwise readying food to be cooked," becomes visible in ways rarely seen outside of food films (Long 145). Later, when Jerry enters the kitchen looking for Kirk and Pam, he hears a noise coming from a large food freezer. He opens it and Pam's partially frozen body jumps from the freezer. In this harrowing moment, the preservation stage, which includes the "strategies used for keeping foods frozen or fresh and storing them until needed," is made visible (Long 145).

Borrowing a term coined by Michael Denning, one could say that Hooper's use of foodways to highlight class difference involves a "laboring" of the food film genre. As Denning notes when he discusses the "laboring of American culture," during the 1930s, members of the Popular Front, with their attention to class and labor issues, were able to transform mass and popular culture into a "contested terrain" in which issues of labor and class were visible (50, 47). In a similar way, *The Texas Chain Saw Massacre* "labors" the food film by focusing on food procurement and the early stages of food preparation and by making visible the labor involved in obtaining and preparing food. With the film industry's self-regulatory practices generally curtailing representations of labor and class difference, it makes sense that these issues would reappear, in an allegorical form, in Hooper's horror film.

The Texas Chain Saw Massacre provides a glimpse into unacceptable topics. It makes the labor that must be expended before a meal is consumed horrifically visible. The film also illuminates the starvation of America's working class. Fittingly, given the cannibal family's tough economic situation, very little consumption takes place onscreen. During its climatic dinner scene, Sally (Marilyn Burns), the sole survivor, is tied to a chair at the dinner table and forced to endure the howls and taunts of her captors. Audiences see the Hitchhiker take a bite of the food. Yet like Leatherface and the Cook (Jim Siedow), he remains far more interested in the meal as an opportunity to bond with family members. For poor people, food consumption is not a time for relaxed enjoyment. Instead, as the scene illustrates, even during the meal the cannibal family is working, for once again they are engaged in food preparation. In this case, the process involves tormenting Sally, the fresh food product, until she is suitable for eating. Thus, as a component of the characters' meal system, human meat might sustain them physically, but work is what nourishes their family ties and defines their social identities.

Prior to the Hitchhiker eating during the "dinner" scene, Franklin is the only character shown eating. When the hapless teens stop by the gas station and barbeque stand operated by the Cook, affluent young Jerry, oblivious to its human ingredients, picks up some barbeque for the group. Franklin is the only one to eat it, and he tears into the meat with gusto. While his consumption of human flesh might seem incidental (he has no idea what he is eating), it becomes more

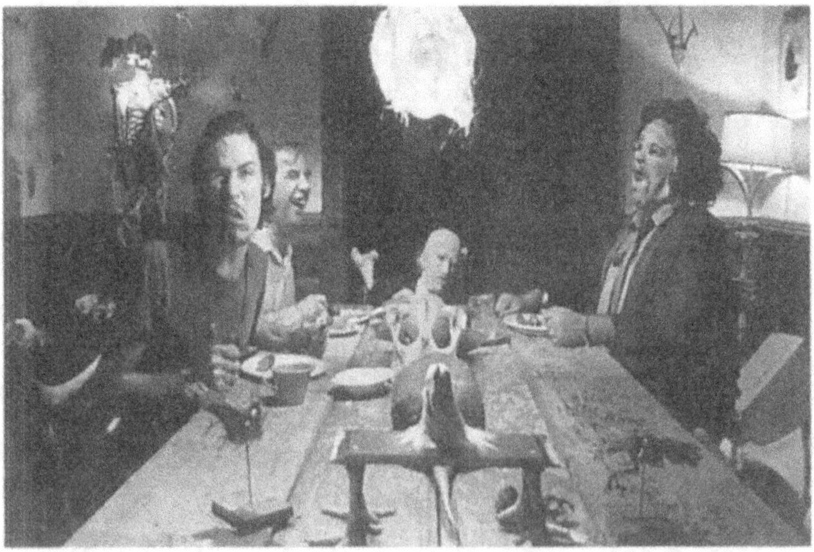

During a snack at dawn, the family continues its exhaustive food preparation labor in Tobe Hooper's allegorical horror film The Texas Chain Saw Massacre *(Vortex).*

significant when considered alongside Franklin's other distinguishing traits. For Wood, Franklin is a key figure in *The Texas Chain Saw Massacre* because he disrupts the clear boundaries between "normal" and "monstrous" (83). Wood proposes that Franklin is "as grotesque, and almost as psychotic, as his nemesis Leatherface" (83). Because of his food choices, Franklin also disrupts the boundaries between middle-class animal-meat consumer and working-class cannibal.

The insensitive way the other teenagers treat Franklin also suggests that the "monstrous cruelties of the slaughterhouse family have their more pallid reflection within normality" (Wood 83). Franklin, disabled and in a wheelchair, is physically distinct from the middle-class teens. He is also overweight, especially when compared to his slender, good-looking companions. While the "burden" that Franklin's disability creates for his friends might be the reason they are cruel to him, other incidents suggest that his body size is the cause. Kirk and Pam come across the dried-up ditch that had been the swimming hole that Franklin and his sister Sally had enjoyed as kids. Kirk asks, "How did Franklin ever get down here?" Pam answers, "Someone must have carried him when he was little." But Kirk scoffs and replies, "Franklin never was little." Later, when Franklin suggests that he and Sally go look for their missing friends, she replies in exasperation, "Franklin, I can't push you!" The implication is that he simply weighs too much.

Franklin's size sets him apart from the middle-class teenagers, but his food preferences put him in league with the working-class cannibals. A key example of that connection occurs early in the film when the teenagers pick up the Hitchhiker. Franklin and the Hitchhiker talk about the slaughterhouse, and the Hitchhiker describes, in gory detail, how headcheese is made. He concludes his story by asking Franklin, "You like it?" Franklin answers, "Oh yeah, sure I like it. It's good!" By comparison, the Hitchhiker's graphic description has made the others feel sick. When Pam asks, "Can't we talk about something else?" Franklin replies, "You'd probably like it if you didn't know what was in it." That remark prompts Kirk to yell at him for "makin' everybody sick." Thus, Franklin is "grotesque" at least in part because of his cannibalistic, underclass tastes. Here again, Hooper's film conveys class difference through food choice.

Franklin's character also reveals the slippage or collapse of identities that can take place in cannibal narratives. Even though cannibal fictions construct an opposition between "civilized" and "uncivilized" people, the nature of cannibalism leads some stories to erase that "difference through the collapse of boundaries" (Berglund 9). Hooper's film suggests that it is possible for almost anyone to slip into cannibalism. All it takes is a certain set of circumstances. Job loss and difficult economic times turn the Hitchhiker, the Cook, and Leatherface into cannibals. In Franklin's case, an innocent bite of food from a roadside diner transforms him into a cannibal. However, the transformation may not be entirely negative: being willing to try the local food is just one more thing that sets Franklin apart from the other middle-class teenagers. Without figures like Franklin, who reveal the uncertain boundary between "civilized" and "uncivilized" behavior, the middle class remains cut off from the realities of the food system, which includes diners where meat comes from suspect sources and workers' low wages make it impossible to buy normal, healthy food.

Like *Cannibal Holocaust* and *How Tasty Was My Little Frenchman, The Texas Chain Saw Massacre* presents audiences with images that do not conform to conventional scenes of "civilized" dining. All three films suggest the need to reflect on "civilized" behavior and the larger implications of food consumption. There are, of course, salient differences between the three films. The sensationalized violence in *Cannibal Holocaust* and *The Texas Chain Saw Massacre* makes those films popular with contemporary audiences. Emblematic of cult cinema, the films move easily through the marketplace because they can sustain prejudice and channel lower-class anger. However, as films that prompt uncomfortable responses, the horror films can also offer insights into deep and generally unquestioned beliefs about food and food behavior.

Ideological analysis of cannibal films highlights that the films draw attention to social and cultural inequalities. Moreover, with cannibal films exploring the various ways that people devour one another, they make clear that food choices are "a key to the identities" of fictional characters, so that what they consume, literally and figuratively, is "expressive of their culture [and] their values" (Long 145). Looking at cannibal films—the limit case—from a foodways perspective shows what is at stake in food consumption and amplifies ideological readings of identity, class, and culture in other films' representations of food. Analysis of cannibal films thus expands understanding of food in film and contributes to studies that examine cultural values and beliefs.

6

Food as Threat and Promise

Genre and Auteur Analysis

Cannibal films use violations of food taboos to explore the figurative consumption of individuals and cultures whose livelihoods and traditions are destroyed by "progress." The films reveal that food behaviors are often fraught with contradiction. Even less sensational narratives reflect people's conflicting associations with what they eat and drink. For example, food films and food documentaries communicate the anxieties and hopes that people in consumer society have about food consumption and its emotional and material implications.

Cannibal films' unique representation of food choice and food behavior also points to the idea that genres, cycles, and groups of films deploy foodway elements in specific ways. Films' representations of food can illuminate contrasts between directors' thematic preoccupations, and just as performance manifests itself "differently in different genres" (de Cordova 116), depictions of food mirror and manifest a genre's stylistic and thematic conventions. As Rebecca Epstein notes, analysis of a "film's food enriches our reception of the film and its generic codes" (196).

Meals as Connection and Conflict in Gangster Films

Food can be integral to "the structure, themes, and characters typical of traditional Hollywood genre films, such as the western, musical, or screwball comedy" (Epstein 195). One could argue that "filmmakers in *all* film genres turn to food to communicate important aspects of characters' emotions, along with their personal and cultural identities" (Bower 1, emphasis in original). Genre films create contrasts between characters and convey narrative progression by including some scenes that highlight food's soothing associations and others that draw out the frightening connotations of food behavior. Yet each genre opens up different aspects of food's contradictory status. Some genres tend to emphasize ways that "food can enliven social relations, enrich spiritual affairs, and enhance an individual's sense of well-being" (Jones et al., "Sensory" 2). Others stress ways that food can be used to threaten, seduce, "punish and in other ways manipulate behavior" (Jones et al., "Sensory" 2). Still others explore food's role as a dual-edged object of promise and threat.

Genre films use the semantic elements featured in food films. In genre films, scenes are set in kitchens, dining rooms, and restaurants. There are scenes of food preparation, presentation, and consumption, and rarely scenes of food procurement, preservation, or cleanup. Audiences understand the significance of a food choice or meal by comparing it to the meal system (food performance) established in the narrative. At times, genre films "depict characters negotiating questions of identity, power, culture, class, spirituality, or relationship through food" (Bower 6). Genre films also convey visions of food that range from utopian to dystopian. In some instances, sharing food becomes a means for creating community. At other times, food behaviors are a sign of characters' and societies' disorder; for example, in gangster films, characters' food behaviors can illustrate personal problems that result from disparities of cultural and economic power.

Gangster films consistently mobilize food's opposing connotations. As Epstein explains, in gangster films "Dining with others typically facilitates communication, problem solving, and social comfort" (197); at the same time, meals can be "rife with social conflict" and the site where "the threat of social difference" emerges (197). In gangster films, food is a source of comfort and community. It is also a weapon, and meals can be pivotal moments when scores are settled and characters' weaknesses and misconceptions are put on full display.

Epstein points out that the gangster film's "subtext of (failed) class mobility" is often expressed through characters' food behaviors (198).

As the genre's many food scenes reveal, some films link the gangster's failed class mobility to his uncivilized nature. Other films suggest that class and ethnic divisions are simply insurmountable. The etiquette and cuisine requirements of the Protestant upper class make it impossible for even "civilized" gangsters to transcend their ethnic, lower-class origins. As a consequence, gangsters' only sustaining option is to reside with their families in a separate realm where conventional upper-class (food) protocols are set aside. A gangster might achieve financial success, but his inability to master upper-class (food) behavior shows that he can never belong to elite society. Moreover, by embracing non-ethnic upper-class cuisine, the gangster separates himself from everything that has sustained him and his family.

Since the 1930s, food has played a critical, albeit circumscribed, role in gangster films. Foodways analysis illuminates when, where, and how foodways communicates character and ideological perspective in these films. As products of commercial cinema, within the gangster genre, food's narrative function directs attention to characters' relationships and so elides food labor and the material implications of food consumption. The films also tend to feature traditional food choices and so further defuse challenge to the status quo. However, despite the films' limited range of food activities depicted, gangster films give vivid expression to the shared experience that meals are a conduit for connection and a site of conflict.

Some gangster films make food's threatening connotations explicit. In these instances, food becomes a literal weapon and a means for presenting a gangster as uncivilized and inhuman. In an iconic film moment from *The Public Enemy* (Wellman, 1931), Tom Powers (James Cagney) exposes his volatility and heartlessness when he squashes a half-grapefruit into Kitty's (Mae Clarke) face. The gangster's antisocial food behavior solidifies his questionable moral status, suggested by the unmarried couple sharing breakfast with Kitty still wearing frilly pajamas and Tom in pajamas that make him look like he is already in prison. In contrast to the gangster's moll who drinks, smokes, and consumes store-bought food, Ma Powers (Beryl Mercer) cooks good old-fashioned meals to bring her "boys" together. However, home cooking cannot mend the rift between Tom and his straight-laced brother Mike (Donald Cook) because Tom has violated so many of the protocols that make community possible.[1]

In *White Heat* (Walsh, 1949), behavior that breaches essential norms and beliefs about meal systems (food performance) underscores the gangster's inhumanity. Rather than abide by longstanding conventions that determine when to eat and when not to eat, a clearly deranged Cody Jarrett (James Cagney) casually bites on a chicken leg as he callously shoots bullets into the trunk of his car to give Roy Parker (Paul Guilfoyle), who is trapped inside, "some air." As this and scenes in films such as *Eastern Promises* demonstrate, characters who eat in the presence of dead bodies display their profound failure to follow "correct" food behavior. By rejecting even the most basic principles of meal systems, gangsters show that they are uncivilized barbarians.

In *White Heat,* the familiar, positive associations with mealtime also contrast with Cody's behavior and thus suggest that he is even more uncivilized than other criminals. When Cody is incarcerated and he learns that his beloved "Ma" has died, he goes berserk in the prison mess hall. The location adds an uncomfortable intensity to his unhinged outburst because it contrasts so greatly with the other inmates' orderly behavior during mealtime, which offers them a rare opportunity for simple social interaction and so is one of the more pleasant experiences of their day.

In *The Big Heat* (Lang, 1953), the gangster's violation of food protocols illustrates his inhumanity; an everyday food once again serves as a literal weapon. The sadistic Vince Stone (Lee Marvin) suspects gangster moll Debby Marsh (Gloria Grahame) of slipping Detective Sergeant Dave Bannion (Glenn Ford) information. As Vince argues with Debby about her lack of loyalty, he impulsively picks up and throws a scalding pot of coffee into her face, scarring her for life. By using coffee as a weapon, the gangster shows that he is so uncivilized that he is unfit even for life in the lower class that has long depended on sharing coffee to create community.

Gangsters' transgressions of basic food protocols confirm that they are not suited to the upper-class status they desire. These moments also highlight a dystopian vision of food, for the characters' behaviors are a sign of their disorder and dysfunction. Marlisa Santos points out that in the gangster film, food is often a metaphor "for the consuming nature of [the gangster] lifestyle, with its rapacious devouring of territory and money" (210). The scenes of antisocial food behavior in *The Public*

Enemy, White Heat, and *The Big Heat* illustrate the inhumanity of men who are consumed by their desire for power. Like cannibals, gangsters show that they belong on the uncivilized side of the divide that separates civilized people from barbarians. Gangsters violate fundamental food protocols when they use food as a weapon and refuse to follow meal system conventions that determine when to eat and when not to eat. A gangster like Cody becomes inhuman simply by munching on a chicken leg as he shoots bullets into the trunk of the car.

Scenes in restaurants, kitchens, and dining rooms help to create the separate world of the gangster in *The Godfather.* Meals provide life-sustaining community and an opportunity to settle scores. Thus, food "is the glue that binds together the often contradictory elements of the American Mafia way of life" (Santos 209). Accordingly, food is ever-present in the lives of the Corleone family. It serves as a means for utopian moments of shared experience and as a sign of family distress. The film uses selected food products as motifs. For instance, the presence of oranges signals a shift from calm to calamitous moments. Don Corleone (Marlon Brando) handles oranges at an outdoor street market before being shot. He toys with orange peels in his playful interaction with his grandson moments before dying in his garden.

Characters' food choices communicate the family's shared emotional experiences. In most instances, family members enjoy Italian cuisine. However, when Sonny (James Caan), his brother Michael (Al Pacino), and their colleagues wait for word about Michael's meeting with Sollozzo (Al Lettieri), who had ordered the hit on Don Corleone, the men eat Chinese takeout from cartons. The Chinese takeout food is a far cry from the glorious wedding banquet featured in the opening scene. The men's food choice reveals that the family's daily routines have been disturbed; the women are not cooking because they are trying to care for the Don at the hospital. The Chinese takeout also shows that the Corleone men are in repose but still working; from their perspective, this type of food can be set aside at a moment's notice without offense to the family members who have labored to prepare the meal.

Other scenes in *The Godfather* present meals as a paradoxical site of connection and conflict in a world that is separate from conventional society. For instance, Michael eventually commits to the criminal life of his family during a meal scene set in an Italian restaurant. To settle scores and thus reestablish order in the separate world, Michael shoots Sollozzo and his police body guard McCluskey (Sterling Hayden). McCluskey does not appreciate how meals function in Mafia society; unafraid, he eats heartily. Sollozzo picks at his food carefully; he knows that meals are integral to Mafia business transactions and that they bring together the separate society's contradictory elements of safety and danger. Michael cannot bring himself to eat; he recognizes that for the sake of his family, he must violate basic meal system protocols by mixing food and death. By breaching food etiquette, Michael leaves behind the wider world for the separate realm of the gangster family that operates according to its own primitive codes.

In *Goodfellas,* violations of food consumption practices once again establish that the gangsters are uncivilized. Tommy (Joe Pesci), Jimmy (Robert De Niro), and Henry (Ray Liotta) do not know when to eat and when not to eat. In the middle of the night, they sit down and enjoy a home-cooked meal at Tommy's house even though they have a body locked in the trunk of their car parked outside. The men's illicit meal implicates other family members; when the men arrive, Tommy's mother (Catherine Scorsese) greets them warmly and insists on feeding them. The scene shows that meals provide an opportunity for connection among the gangsters; the sacrilegious middle-of-the-night meal also suggests the degree to which gangsters and their families exist in a realm cut off from conventional social norms.

Despite the community that the characters experience in their separate realm, meals can be a time of danger for gangsters. In *Goodfellas,* even at events that are ostensibly about familial bonding, meals are sites of conflict. They provide the occasion for the pointed inquiries Mafia boss Paulie (Paul Sorvino) makes about Henry's involvement in drug trafficking and the disappearance of Billy Batts (Frank Vincent), a man Tommy has murdered in a fit of rage. Another meal provides the occasion for confrontation when Jimmy meets Henry in a cold, sterile, impersonal diner. Jimmy selects a location separate from the world of family kitchens and dining rooms because he suspects Henry of "ratting out" his friends and family. For Jimmy, this is a business meeting and so he gets to the restaurant first. Henry knows he is in trouble the moment he arrives because he sees that Jimmy "hasn't touched a thing." Both gangsters recognize that there are basic food protocols, and Henry recognizes that death is imminent because Jimmy has put off eating.

Describing the way food functions as threat and promise in gangster films, Marlisa Santos notes that in this genre "food [is] integral to the duality of violence and familial bonds" (210). In *Goodfellas,* the dinner scene in the prison illustrates the way commensality creates community in the separate realm that the gangsters inhabit. Henry's voiceover explains: "In prison, dinner was a big thing. We had a pasta course and then we had a meat or a fish." Henry praises Paulie's "prep work" of slicing the garlic so thin it liquefied in the pan; he notes that "Vinnie was in charge of the tomato sauce." As Henry's description makes clear, the contrast between the Italians' meals and standard prison fare shows that they "owned the joint." The gangsters' earnest attention to food product, preparation, presentation, and consumption reveals that for these men, food "signified bonds of trust and loyalty" (Santos 218). The gangster's obsession with fine cuisine also discloses their vigorous efforts to maintain their elite status. As Santos points out, while food scenes in *Goodfellas* reflect the gangsters' adherence to "codes of tradition, honor, and loyalty," they are "more about opulence, power, and what it means to be 'civilized'" (215).

The gangsters' food choices and attention to food preparation illuminate their drive to be seen as wise, sophisticated, and highly civilized men. Scenes with food also reveal their failure to achieve that goal. Late in the film, the FBI busts Henry for dealing drugs, a business activity that Paulie had warned Henry not to do. As Paulie more deeply understands, for Italian gangsters who rely on their continually reaffirmed family connections, the consequences of getting caught are too high, the sentences handed down for narcotics charges are too severe. Tempted by the money to be made dealing drugs, Henry does it behind Paulie's back. After Henry is busted, he must go to Paulie to beg for forgiveness and, even more humiliating, for money.

When Henry and Paulie meet, it is not in a restaurant, where gangsters can break food protocols for the sake of family stability. Instead, they meet in Paulie's kitchen; the domestic setting signals that death will not be part of this confrontation. However, the men do not even sit down; standing, they converse in the kitchen while Paulie fries sausages in a pan. Paulie dismisses Henry with a small amount of money and instructions never to contact him again. While Paulie's focus on the food preparation might suggest that Paulie wants Henry to know that the young man no longer matters to him, Paulie's attention to cooking conveys the significance of Henry's betrayal. Henry's duplicity has reduced Paulie's sphere of influence so radically that it extends no farther than the kitchen.

Epstein notes that gangster films are often concerned with "power relations between those eating and those preparing and serving food" (197). With Paulie returning to his "civilized" prison-stint activity of preparing food, the film suggests that Henry's betrayal has put Paulie in a vulnerable position. Henry will betray his Mafia connections and consign the once-mighty Paulie to life in prison. At the same time, Paulie's food choices and food activities ensure that he maintains "a link to the past and tradition" (Santos 218). Paulie might spend his life in prison. However, in contrast to Henry, who will be consigned to life in the white-bread suburbs, Paulie is the civilized man who has chosen family over fortune. *Goodfellas* thus uses food's opposing connotations of promise and threat to explore different visions of "civilized" food behavior.

Gangster films such as *The Godfather* and *Goodfellas* complicate the division between civilized and uncivilized (food) behavior. In contrast to films from the 1930s and 1940s where the gangster's food behaviors clearly place him on the uncivilized side of an insurmountable divide, gangster films from the 1970s forward have often presented food as "the glue that binds together the often contradictory elements of the American Mafia way of life—the seeming incongruities of family, tradition, and religion joined with murder, bloodshed, and brutality" (Santos 209). *Bugsy* (Levinson, 1991) provides another illustration of that point, for the film's use of food suggests that gangsters are not monstrous or glamorous. Instead, gangsters fail to achieve conventional upper-class status because the drive for class mobility cuts gangsters off from tradition and nourishing community.[2]

Barry Levinson's film looks at the life of brash and sometimes brutal 1940s gangster Benjamin "Bugsy" Siegel (Warren Beatty), who moves between New York, where his Jewish family lives in Scarsdale, and Los Angeles, where he becomes enamored of movies in general and actress Virginia Hill (Annette Bening) in particular. Bugsy's nemesis is his boyhood friend and fellow Mafia operative Meyer Lansky (Ben Kingsley), who challenges Bugsy's dream to build a gambling oasis in the desert town of Las Vegas. Bugsy's confidant is hit man Mickey Cohen (Harvey Keitel). Bugsy falls in and out of the Mafia's good favor until he eventually becomes too great a liability for them and so is eliminated.

Food choices, preparation, presentation, and consumption show that while the gangster is uncivilized, the more fundamental problem is that he believes that the cuisine and etiquette requirements of the WASP upper class will sustain him. The first time Virginia cooks dinner for Bugsy, it becomes clear that Bugsy possesses neither upscale table manners nor a sound appreciation of ethnic food traditions. "I hope you like scampi served on a bed of soft brown rice rimmed by carrots and peas," Virginia says as she serves attractive plates of food. Virginia eats; Bugsy focuses on his newspaper, jealous and resentful of Virginia's experiences with other men. After a couple of bites, she objects to Bugsy letting his food get cold. She puts down her knife and fork, lights a cigarette, gets up from the table, and throws an ashtray at Bugsy. Suddenly, Jack Dragna (Richard Sarafian) arrives. After Jack leaves, Bugsy spits out, "We gonna eat?" He heads to the dining room where he shovels food into his mouth, one forkful after another, stuffing in bites of bread as well. Bugsy's primitive food behavior and manic confrontation with Jack have left Virginia stunned and amorous. She drapes herself over him, smothers him with kisses, and the couple and the plate of food fall to the floor. Virginia's "proper" meal served in a lovely house clashes with the characters' crass manners. The conventional, upscale food and setting contrast with the characters' "uncivilized" behavior. Decorous presentation of appetizing food yields to coarse consumption. The scene thus conveys the characters' emotional disorder and disconnection from nourishing traditions.

Underscoring that point, the expensive, non-ethnic food delivered to Bugsy in jail asserts that "for Bugsy the rules are being bent and he expects a different form of treatment from regular prisoners. When the cart rolls in, the silver dome implies an upscale selection of food, and the cart the waiter brings in has white linen and lovely silverware. He's serving time but is also being served in an elaborate way with the waiter in a tux" (Schulz). The elaborate meal shows that Bugsy has powerful connections. It also reveals Bugsy's vision of "opulence, power, and what it means to be 'civilized'" (Santos 215).

That conception, which separates Bugsy from family and tradition, will eventually fail him. Later, still in prison, during another meal with Virginia, Bugsy becomes increasingly exasperated as she tells him about problems in the construction of his prized Las Vegas casino resort. To convey his frustration, Bugsy picks up a carrot stick and bites it angrily while still talking. Food stylist Ann Schulz explains, "His biting for emphasis is a subconscious gesture; parts of the carrot fly off his lip as the food defines and expresses his emotion at the moment" (Schulz). Shortly after, Bugsy concludes that discussion by placing the silver warming dome over his plate. A moment later, his anger spent, Bugsy tells Virginia, "I just wish the two us of could be alone on Coney Island eatin' a couple of fucking hot dogs at Nathan's." Bugsy realizes that elegant WASP food might signify upper-class status, but it will never nourish him the way ethnic comfort food does.

Cut off from family and tradition, the gangster life often makes Bugsy feel isolated and vulnerable. Thus, the gangster at times tries to use food to secure some comfort. As they sort things out, Bugsy and Mickey Cohen share a snack at L.A.'s Union Station. Dwarfed by the scale of this huge public space, the men look ordinary and unremarkable. Mickey eats a hot fudge sundae; his food choice suggests a desire to return to a less complicated time. Bugsy eats scrambled eggs; his selection also reveals a need for simple food. Bugsy's agitated eating style conveys his frustration that he has little agency in the wider world. Aggravated with a newspaper account of his confrontation at a club the night before, Bugsy says, "First of all, it wasn't a .45, it was a .38. I was not brandishing it. I was concealing it softly to make a point." To emphasize his statements, Bugsy jabs at his plate and shoves two and then three forkfuls of eggs into his mouth. His forceful gestures make him look foolish. Unable to control the world around him, Bugsy is reduced to stabbing at a plate of soft scrambled eggs.

In the next scene, Bugsy again attempts to secure comfort through food, and again his failure to achieve power and control is communicated by his interaction with food. Bugsy has baked a birthday cake for his daughter Millicent (Stefanie Mason). Through this food preparation effort, Bugsy hopes to repair his relationship with his daughter and his wife, Esta (Wendy Phillips). However, the increasingly powerful Meyer Lansky and five of his thugs arrive unexpectedly just before the birthday celebration begins. Their intrusion into his home illustrates that for Bugsy, being a gangster fails to provide the power he desires. The gangster life also makes him lose the support of his family and costs him his role as man of the house.

Lansky's arrival leads to farcical action reminiscent of slapstick comedy. Bugsy wears a toque on his head and a white apron with a stain that resembles a smear of blood. He rushes through the swinging kitchen door and in and out of rooms in his home. Increasingly impatient, Millicent waits in the dining room. Esta, perturbed, fusses about in the kitchen. Meanwhile, in the study, an aggravated Lanksy attempts to maintain a businesslike deportment. As the scene unfolds, Esta completes writing "Happy Birthday" in icing on her daughter's cake; Lansky cannot get a straight answer; Bugsy is twice interrupted by phone calls from Mickey, whom he has directed to find Virginia. After a long wait, Millicent runs up to her room in disgust. Lansky and his gang eventually leave to get something to eat. Bugsy then walks slowly to the empty dining room and sits down. A close-up of the cake

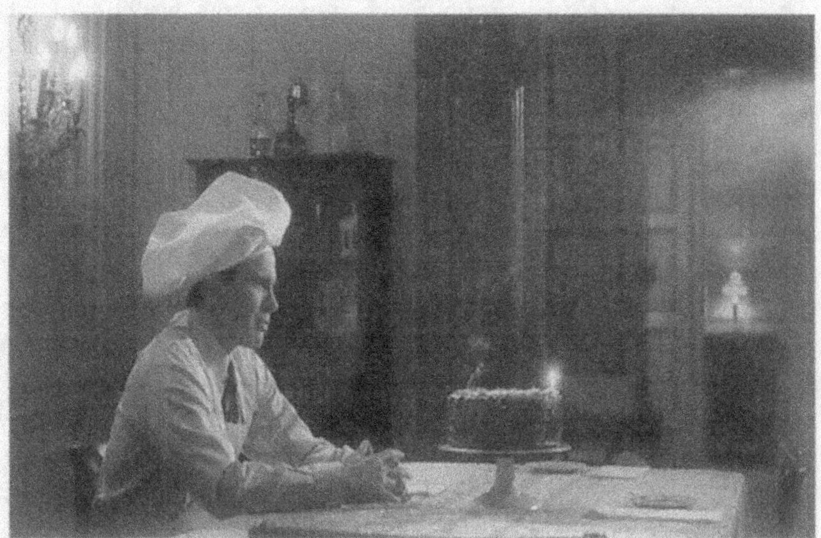

A gangster cut off from his family and ethnic community is as lifeless and pathetic as the uneaten birthday cake in Bugsy *(TriStar Pictures, Mulholland Productions, Baltimore Pictures).*

shows that essentially all the candles have burned out; one small, weak flame barely flickers.

Sharing the birthday cake was supposed to bring the family together. However, rather than confirm family bonds, the food becomes a sign of the gangster's dystopian world. The uneaten cake symbolizes the distress and disorder that Bugsy's reckless life has brought into his family. Thus, as in other gangster films, in *Bugsy* meals provide an occasion for connection or conflict. Like other gangsters, Bugsy's failure to master conventional etiquette shows that he is not suited to upper-class life. At the same time, upscale WASP cuisine fails to provide the sustenance he requires. The clash between ethnic and non-ethnic food, between lower-class and elite-society meals, illuminates a core dilemma for gangsters who desire class mobility. These men find that they can only feel truly nourished by food that connects them to their lower-class origins.

Directors' Use of Foodways to Reinforce, Question, and Challenge the Status Quo

The foodways lens can contribute to auteur studies by illuminating thematic and iconographic constants across a director's body of work. Recognition of the director's role in shaping representations of food is implicit in discussions throughout the book. For example, Chapter 1 notes that Chaplin uses characters' hunger to convey their beleaguered condition, whereas Keaton will take it another step and present his main character as "a consumable product" in modern society (Orgeron and Orgeron 85). This chapter's analysis of gangster films suggests, for example, ways to consider depictions of food in various films by Francis Ford Coppola and Martin Scorsese. A productive area for mise-en-scène analysis, food-centered scenes in films by Frank Capra, Alfred Hitchcock, Stanley Kubrick, Woody Allen, and other canonical directors often catch the attention of food and film scholars. Analyzing directors' bodies of work illuminates their uniquely inventive uses of food imagery and food behavior. It also reveals that directors' representations reflect the fact that food signifies both promise and threat. Films by Steven Spielberg, John Ford, Alfred Hitchcock, and Luis Buñuel succinctly illustrate the spectrum of utopian to dystopian visions of food.

Steven Spielberg's films have often had box office success insofar as they reactivate familiar narratives in ways that appeal to and fulfill audiences' expectations. In his commercially successful films, representations of foodways will tend to reinforce values and beliefs central to consumer society. To use a culinary metaphor, films like the Indiana Jones series (1982–2008) operate within conventional boundaries and could be described as audiovisual comfort food. When Spielberg works in the more comfortable utopian vein, characters' interactions with food often emphasize the potential of imagination and the power of mind over matter. Yet given people's paradoxical relationship with food, Spielberg films also present characters' food choices and food behaviors in dystopian ways to convey breakdown, distress, and social dissolution.

An anecdote from early in Spielberg's career evinces his views on food and how it connects to cultural attitudes. In 1973, Spielberg was collaborating with screenwriter/director Paul Schrader on a screenplay that would eventually become *Close Encounters of the Third Kind* (Spielberg, 1977). The two had a serious disagreement about the lead character, a man who grows obsessed with UFOs and eventually leaves the planet on a spaceship with benevolent aliens to explore the galaxy. Spielberg pushed for the character to be a person "from the suburbs, just like the people [he] grew up with." Schrader argued: "If somebody's going to represent me and the human race to get on a spaceship, I don't want my representative to be a guy who eats all his meals at McDonald's." Spielberg's reply was emphatic: "That's exactly what I *do* want!" (qtd. in Biskind, *Easy Riders* 262, 263). The anecdote reveals Spielberg's ideological focus: films should emphasize familiarity and comfort; films' depictions of food should convey that. In his view, successful film and food products are appealing commodities that satisfy predictable tastes. Thus, when appealing food is unavailable or when food becomes unfamiliar or inadequate in Spielberg's films, the audience immediately knows something is dreadfully wrong.

Accordingly, Spielberg seamlessly integrates food into film narratives. In *E.T.: The Extra-Terrestrial* (1982), dinner scenes bind the family together while the trail of Reese's Pieces entice E.T. from hiding. In *Close Encounters of the Third Kind,* Roy Neary (Richard Dreyfuss) sculpts mashed potatoes served at family dinner into the shape of Devils

Tower. In other films, fantasy food inventions bear little resemblance to conventional cuisine, yet Spielberg's use of the food remains the same; food provides a window into the characters but not the larger issues in consumer society.

In *Hook* (1991), Spielberg's adaptation of the iconic 1904 James M. Barrie play *Peter Pan,* the food evokes a "fanciful and imaginative fantasy" consonant with the Neverland world of the Lost Boys led by Rufio (Dante Basco) (Schulz). The film begins with middle-aged, financially successful, but emotionally stunted lawyer Peter Banning (Robin Williams) returning to the London of his youth to visit ninety-year-old Granny Wendy (Maggie Smith). When Captain Hook (Dustin Hoffman) kidnaps Peter's two children, Peter must journey to Neverland to face his nemesis, who is aided by sidekick Smee (Bob Hoskins.) In Neverland, Peter encounters the Lost Boys from whom he learns about imagination and survival. Peter and the Lost Boys engage in an animated food fight; the confrontation expresses Peter's emotional transformation in physical terms as he takes the first step to recovering his heretofore-suppressed humanity.

Aiming to transport viewers from the real world to an imaginative one, Spielberg relied to a large extent on food. For the food fight, food stylist Ann Schulz created an edible tree, a chocolate statue of Pan, and a replica of Hook's boat made of mashed potatoes. Schulz also prepared watermelons carved with the names and the faces of the Lost Boys. She sculpted baked turkeys and cheddar cheese blocks; she carved the boys' names on ears of corn so that if the husks were pulled back, the name would appear. To create a childlike world, Schulz used primary colors for the food thrown in the fight (see Appendix 1).

Characters' use of food (who has it, when and how they eat or use it) defines their role in the food fight. The scene's composition and editing choices focus attention on who controls the food (who presents it, gives it, takes it, and first bites into it). Describing the way food choices and behaviors function in the first food fight, Schulz explains that "food became a form of leverage because whoever imagined the food had power, and who first threw the food wielded literal as well as figurative authority" (Schulz). When the Lost Boys and Peter sit down to eat, Peter does not know that the boys pantomime eating, and that they never have real food. After astonishment registers on Peter's face, he and the

Lost Boys' leader Rufio hurl insults at each other in an escalating war of words. Peter dominates through the more innovative insults, concluding, "Don't mess with me, man. I'm a lawyer."

In the feat that confirms his power, Peter imagines food and it appears. The imagined food provides the basis for community as Peter and the Lost Boys joyously grab, throw, and get plastered with the brightly colored food that materializes thanks to Peter's and then their own inventiveness. Softly at first, one boy says, "You're doing it." Peter asks, "Doing what?" to which the boy replies, "Using your imagination, Peter." As the scene builds, the boys shout, "You're doing it!!" This initial food fight scene sets up the film's final fight when the Lost Boys employ food as their fanciful weapons. In that confrontation, the Lost Boys' ability to create food out of their imaginations proves that they have the ability to defeat Captain Hook's tyranny if they believe in themselves enough to secure their liberation.[3]

When characters in Spielberg films lack the power to create appealing meals that can satisfy or sustain their culinary appetites or are confronted with unfamiliar food, the films move into dystopian territory. These dystopian moments occur even in Spielberg's most conventional films. For instance, one of the most memorable scenes in Spielberg's *Indiana Jones and the Temple of Doom* (1984) takes place when the iconic hero (Harrison Ford), his love interest (Kate Capshaw), and kid sidekick

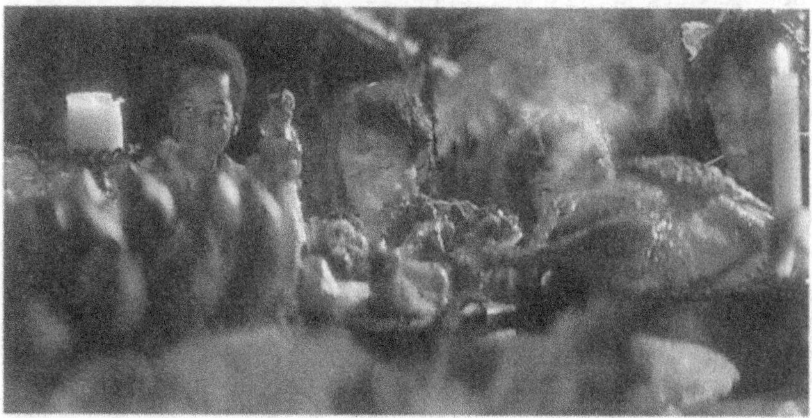

The feast that appears when Peter's imagination takes hold creates community for the Lost Boys in Hook *(Amblin Entertainment, TriStar Pictures).*

(Jonathan Ke Quan) sit down to dine at the palace of Hindu Indians, who turn out to be members of a villainous cult that worships the Hindu goddess Kali and practices human sacrifice and child slavery. The bizarre cuisine served by their hosts emphasizes the danger that the film's protagonists are in; the dinner includes snakes, beetles, eyeball soup, and, for dessert, chilled monkey brains served in monkey skulls. While the scene and the protagonists' reactions to this bizarre foreign fare are played mostly for laughs, the scene has an undercurrent of danger. It also foreshadows the villainy of their hosts, which is problematically linked to the antagonists' ethnicity, with the non-Western cuisine serving as evidence linking "disgusting" eating habits and blasphemous beliefs.

Another example of dystopian food in one of Spielberg's more conventional narratives is in *War of the Worlds* (2005), with the dystopian moments arising due to a divorced father, Ray (Tom Cruise), being unable to provide adequate and satisfactory food for his son, Robbie (Justin Chatwin), and daughter, Rachel (Dakota Fanning), in the face of an alien invasion. Early in the film, before the Martian invasion begins, Ray's emotional distance and estrangement from his children is conveyed in terms of food. When Ray's ex-wife (Miranda Otto) drops off their kids to spend the weekend with Ray, she inspects the refrigerator and disappointedly notes that Ray is "out of milk . . . and everything else." The point is underscored by the mise-en-scène: the kitchen is not overrun with food and cooking utensils, but is littered, rather ridiculously, with a car engine resting on the table and other automotive parts scattered about. In these scenes, food—or the lack thereof—and Ray's inability to properly keep a kitchen communicate that Ray is not fit to take care of the children, a dystopian situation that is anathema in Spielberg's primary worldview because it signifies an environment devoid of comfort and family unity.

Food is used to further emphasize the disunity between Ray and his children in a scene showing how his culinary tastes greatly contrast with his daughter's. When Rachel asks him what they have to eat, Ray blows her off, instructs her to order out, and selfishly goes to bed. He wakes up to discover that she has ordered from a health food store, and he is grossed out when he tries a bite of hummus. Rachel angrily replies to Ray's disgusted reaction: "You said order!"—to which Ray snidely responds, "I meant order *food*."

Just as the gulf between Ray and his children is established by food interactions, so the emotional turmoil brought on by the devastation of the Martian attack is dramatized through food. After Martians level Ray's neighborhood, he and his children barely escape (with very little food due to Ray's poorly stocked refrigerator), and Ray drives them to their mother's house, which they find has already been abandoned in the wake of the attacks. To keep the kids from panicking when they discover that the house is empty, Ray pathetically attempts to calm them by taking them into the kitchen and preparing a meal for them. Obviously at a loss when it comes to food procurement and preparation, Ray finds a jar of peanut butter and a loaf of bread and announces that he will make peanut butter sandwiches for the group. Rachel angrily informs him that she is allergic to peanut butter, and she is indignant that her father does not know this basic fact about her. When Robbie also refuses to eat and dejectedly tells Ray that he is not hungry, Ray explodes in frustration, angrily throwing a piece of bread covered with peanut butter against the kitchen window. Spielberg cuts to a medium shot of Ray's reflection in the window, as the bread with peanut butter plastered against the window slowly slides down. Looking out the window, away from his children, Ray fights to keep his composure as he murmurs, "Ever . . . everybody just relax, okay? Because we're here now. We're safe, and we're gonna stay. And in the morning, your mom and Tim [her boyfriend] are gonna be here, and everything's gonna be fine, okay?" At this moment, Ray admits his failure as a parent. The peanut butter sandwich slowly sliding down the window is a potent metaphor for this failure and a reminder that Ray's inability to be an adequate parent is directly tied to his inability to master food behaviors. It is from this potent dystopian food moment that Ray's redemption as a parent begins.

As Spielberg navigates between family-oriented fare to more adult-focused, historical dramas, his depictions of food grow ever more complex, challenging, and, very often, dystopian. A striking example of extremely dystopian food representation can be found in Spielberg's *Munich* (2005), a film released the same year as *War of the Worlds*. *Munich* follows a secret task force of Israeli assassins sent to track and kill the people responsible for the murder of eleven Israeli Olympic team members by the Palestinian group Black September at the 1972 Munich Olympics. Led by Avner (Eric Bana), an Israeli intelligence officer, the group of assassins tracks its first victim, Wael Zwaiter (Makram Khoury), to Rome, confronting him as he returns to his apartment with a bag full of food he has just purchased at the grocer. They shoot Zwaiter in the chest, and a bottle of milk in his bag of groceries explodes. As Zwaiter bleeds onto the ground, his blood mixes in a swirl with the milk. Stephanie Zacharek speculates that this image is "possibly a visual metaphor for the commingling of purity and guilt" (Zacharek "*Munich*"). While this reading is valid, a familiarity with the way Spielberg positions food as either the gateway to happiness and contentment when it is good and plentiful or a sign that things are very wrong when it is disgusting, unfamiliar, or absent suggests a more specific reading. In this scene, the mix of blood and milk can be read as a deadly dystopian moment that suggests that the assassins have, with this inaugural murder, left behind the comforts and reassurances of "normal" life and are entering into treacherous, uncertain territory. Spielberg thus depicts food in powerful ways ranging from utopian to dystopian—yet his representations of food return to the idea that food should be comforting and that it is threatening when it is not present or familiar.

By representing food in varying ways, Spielberg continues traditions established by classical Hollywood directors such as John Ford, whose depictions of food exemplify different points along the utopian-dystopian spectrum. As filmmaker and historian Michael White notes, "The concept of 'the meal' is a prominent and crucial aspect of the John Ford universe. Scenes set around dining room tables are more important in Ford than almost any other director I know" (White). Indeed, meals are tremendously significant in Ford's films, as they reveal either communities coming together in unity or falling apart in disunity. For instance, the meal scenes that appear early in Ford's iconic western *The Searchers* (1956) present a utopian vision of family life on the frontier held together by relationships around the dinner table. Of particular interest is the introduction of Martin Pawley (Jeffrey Hunter), an individual of mixed ethnic heritage who has been adopted by the Edwards family. While it is clear that their visiting, racist uncle Ethan (John Wayne) is leery of Martin, the rest of the Edwards family accepts Martin as one of their own, and their emotions are made clear through their food behaviors. When Martin sits down, the eldest Edwards daughter, Lucy (Pippa Scott), automatically hands him a plate of bread, only pausing when Ethan insultingly remarks, "Fella could mistake you for a half-breed." Ironically, it will be the racist and antiquated Ethan who is shut out of the community at the end of the film (and Martin who is welcomed in), and Ethan's eventual exile is prefigured by his exclusionary behavior at the dinner table, a place where, for Ford, "a community [should come] together over a meal" (White).

The utopian unity conveyed through commensality is often a crucial achievement for characters in Ford's films. However, this achievement is often hard won, as characters frequently use food and drink the way Ethan Edwards does in *The Searchers,* as a way to divide people according to social hierarchies. For example, disunity is on display in another canonical Ford western, *Stagecoach* (1939). As Barry Keith Grant explains, a simple drink of water illustrates how food and drink reinforces prejudicial bounds between people ("Introduction" 12–13). In the film, Hatfield (John Carradine), the aristocratic Southern gambler, has committed himself to protecting delicate and pregnant Lucy Mallory (Louise Platt), a social "insider, a married woman, and defender of custom" (Browne 31), who is traveling west to be with her cavalry officer husband. Hatfield fetches Lucy a drink of water, but rather than have her drink from the "communal canteen," he pours the water into "a silver cup he produces from his breast pocket" (Grant, "Introduction" 12). By comparison, when the Ringo Kid (John Wayne), the "more egalitarian Western hero," offers a drink of water to Dallas (Claire Trevor), the prostitute who has been exiled from town, "Hatfield repockets the silver cup, an obvious social snub to Dallas" (Grant, "Introduction" 13).

The social hierarchy that Lucy and Dallas represent is emphasized in another scene that involves food and drink. When the stagecoach makes a stop at a small town, its disparate passengers settle in for a meal. For Nick Browne, this dinner scene is extremely important because it shows that the film's narrative point of view does not reside with one particular character or with an ideal spectator external to the film (26). Instead, shot selection and editing reveal "a state of affairs within the group, a relationship among the parties [and] the interplay of social positions in a group" (Browne 30–31). The social interplay is epitomized by the women: Lucy, whose revered position of cavalry wife officer's and mother-to-be makes her the ultimate insider in the film's social world, whereas Dallas is the absolute outsider in this society. This dynamic is cast into relief by food etiquette, which dictates that the two women be treated differently. Lucy occupies the head of the table, while Dallas does not approach the table until Ringo, the epitome of the Westerner who does not care for society and its rules, offers her a place. This scene represents a dystopian food moment because the group should come together over food, but cannot due to lingering prejudice.

Some of society's prejudices begin to dissolve, however, as many of the stagecoach passengers begin to work together. Here again, food plays a crucial role in fostering moments of social connection. One such moment occurs when Lucy begins to give birth. Not only is Dallas able to play a greater role in their small community due to the birth of Lucy's baby, but Doc Boone (Thomas Mitchell), another passenger on the stage who has been exiled, also finds a path to redemption that is paved with food and drink. Indeed, it is drink that initially exiles Doc Boone from the community as it is revealed, in one of the film's most prevalent dystopian depictions of food and drink, that he is an alcoholic. However, drink also provides Doc Boone a pathway back to respectable, responsible society. As the birth of Lucy's baby looms and hope seems lost, Boone resolvedly puts aside his bottle, dramatically removes his coat and hat, and commands, "Coffee. Gimme coffee. *Black* coffee. Lots of it." The next scene depicts the sheriff, Curley (George Bancroft), forcing hot coffee down Boone's throat, and sure enough the doctor is able to pull himself together and successfully deliver Lucy's baby, a moment of communal triumph made possible by the strategic use of drink. As the brief discussion of these two iconic films suggests, food exists on the utopian/dystopian spectrum in Ford's universe and serves as a powerful metaphor for community building or for times of community disarray.

While Ford links utopian and dystopian representations of food to larger communal concerns, Alfred Hitchcock, another canonical Hollywood director who represents food as a profoundly ambivalent object of promise and threat, conceives of food in a more insular, personal manner that foregrounds conflicts of pleasure and guilt. Donald Spoto explains that Hitchcock's "pictures often suggest an attraction and repulsion about food and eating . . . that reflect his own life" (516). David

Greven proposes that throughout Hitchcock's films, "eating symbolizes the wrenching struggles for gendered power" (309). The importance of food in the fictional worlds of his films *and* in the director's personal life has led to unique publications. There is a French cookbook with recipes for dishes featured in Hitchcock films (Martinetti and Rivière). In addition, Hitchcock's daughter, Patricia Hitchcock O'Connell, includes several of her mother's recipes in a book (cowritten with Laurent Bouzereau) about her mother, *Alma Hitchcock: The Woman Behind the Man*. As in most mainstream films, Hitchcock focuses on the presentation and consumption of food rather than procurement, preparation, and cleanup. However, the ways in which Hitchcock depicts food ranges from comforting to horrifying.

In Hitchcock, food can signify the promise of sexual fulfillment. For example, there is Dr. Constance Petersen's (Ingrid Bergman) "romantically vocalized choice of a 'liverwurst' sandwich while on a picnic" with protagonist John Ballantyne (Gregory Peck) in *Spellbound* (1945), or Frances Stevens (Grace Kelly) asking cat burglar John Robie (Cary Grant) if he would prefer a "leg or breast" while on a picnic in *To Catch a Thief* (1955) (Holm). *Psycho* (1960) opens with Marion Crane (Janet Leigh) and Sam Loomis (John Gavin) after they have just finished having sex during Marion's lunch hour.

However, food and food utensils are more often ominous in Hitchcock's world as they threaten characters with guilt feelings or, even worse, psychical violence or death. As early as his first sound film, *Blackmail* (1929), an innocent breakfast scene between Alice (Anny Ondra) and her father (Charles Paton) becomes nightmarish when Alice's father asks her to pass him the bread knife. In an earlier scene, to defend herself Alice has killed a man with a knife. Thus, for her, the commonplace knife lying next to the loaf of bread quickly becomes an ominous object. Hitchcock conveys the anxiety Alice experiences by framing the knife in a point-of-view close-up that features light bouncing off the knife's sharp edge, while on the film's sound track the word "knife" seems to jump out of the surrounding conversations to heighten Alice's guilt.

The scene prefigures an almost equally famous moment in *Sabotage* (1936), when long-suffering wife Mrs. Verloc (Sylvia Sidney) murders her terrorist husband (Oskar Homolka) with a knife after he sends her brother (Desmond Tester) to his death by having the young boy deliver a bomb to a specific location in London. In contrast to the scene in *Blackmail* which builds dread with the word "knife" seemingly repeated over and over, the dread in *Sabotage* builds when the scene grows silent as Mrs. Verloc begins serving her husband supper. After he mutters callous remarks about the boy's death and starts to order her around, Mrs. Verloc's hand grips a knife. Her silence alerts her husband that something is wrong, but it is too late to save his life; after he stands up and approaches her, she plunges the knife into his chest, bringing the meal to an unexpected end before the routine can begin.

In *Shadow of a Doubt* (1943), family dinner scenes become increasingly uncomfortable when Uncle Charlie (Joseph Cotten) airs his misogynistic attitudes. Over time, his heinous actions as the "Merry Widow" murderer become clear to young Charlie (Teresa Wright). By exposing Uncle Charlie's evil nature during these sacred family meals, Hitchcock intensifies the contrast between Uncle Charlie's nihilism and the traditions that have made sharing food the basis for harmony, unity, and community. Exploring the way meals are occasions for connection and conflict, Hitchcock contrasts the family's utopian ideal (meals provide physical and emotional nourishment for a family) with the dystopian condition Uncle Charlie introduces (the rupture of familial affection takes place during meals).

Hitchcock continues to explore food's dual-edged nature in a scene of food preparation. Emma (Patricia Collinge), Uncle Charlie's sister and young Charlie's mother, has a brief exchange with Saunders (Wallace Ford), a detective on the "Merry Widow" murders case who gains access to the family home by posing as a magazine photographer. Emma insists there is a proper way to make a cake, and she refuses to deviate from the correct sequence for combining ingredients, chastising Saunders for thinking one could alter it. There is a correct way to prepare food, as the tradition-bound Emma knows, and it cannot, must not, be changed. Emma recognizes that order keeps anarchy at bay, especially when it is becoming increasingly clear that the threat to safety and social order lurks within her own idyllic home. Hitchcock thus positions the siblings, Emma and Uncle Charlie, at opposite ends of the moral spectrum, with their respective behaviors around food embodying its promise of security and the threat it can pose.

In *Notorious* (1946), Alicia Huberman (Ingrid Bergman) proves she cannot cook, the familiar insult to non-traditional women, when she tries to seduce Devlin (Cary Grant) with a dinner at her apartment. Later, she is pressed into service as a spy, marrying a suspected Nazi sympathizer, Alexander Sebastian (Claude Rains). However, he discovers her subterfuge. In a subsequent scene, Alexander and his mother (Leopoldine Konstantin) offer Alicia a cup of tea. The image of a teacup takes over visually as Alicia realizes that it is poisoned and that she must drink it to avoid a direct confrontation. Earlier, innocuous instances of drinking tea make its later sinister presence eerie and unsettling. Here again, Hitchcock mobilizes the range of associations attached to food. By presenting familiar food products and food behaviors in troubling contexts, Hitchcock intimates that assumptions about the everyday world are open to question.

In *Psycho,* Norman Bates (Anthony Perkins) serves ordinary sandwiches to Marion Crane who, in Norman's words, "eats like a bird." The sandwiches function initially as a nondescript prop that sustains character interaction. They seem to embody a gesture of care and concern. However, the sandwiches become more ominous as Marion picks at them absent-mindedly. Marion's meal does not nourish or sustain her. Instead, it provides an occasion for Norman to observe her. The discomfort Marion experiences leads her to reconsider her act of theft earlier in the film. For Marion, eating alone with a stranger watching her confirms and even heightens her anxiety that she will be isolated and afraid as long as she has the stolen money.

Here again, Hitchcock uses innocuous food experiences and unexceptional food products and then alters their connotations. Hitchcock elicits apprehension by first incorporating ordinary food activities into the story worlds and then overturning the warm atmosphere of the meal or the soothing qualities of the food. This strategy is exemplified by the simple glass of milk that Johnnie Aysgarth (Cary Grant) takes to his wife, Lina (Joan Fontaine), in *Suspicion* (1941). As Johnnie carries the glass up the stairs of their home, it glows with an alarming light. This moment reflects and communicates Lina's suspicion that the glass of milk contains poison. As in other Hitchcock films, a commonplace food product becomes the site of anxiety and a means for questioning everyday assumptions; it suggests that one never knows if the straightforward offer of a glass of milk is a sign of affection or malice. The image of Johnnie ascending the stairs with the ominously glowing glass of milk is one of the most iconic in Hitchcock's cinema, and the indelible nature of this image signifies the large role that contradictory feelings and beliefs about food play in his films.

The ambivalent portrayal of food in his films has been linked to Hitchcock's own admitted difficulties with food. On one hand, Hitchcock spoke publicly about how much he adored food (Spoto 516); on the other, according to biographer Patrick McGilligan, the director would be devastated by news articles that mentioned his weight (205). Like Spoto (516), Robin Wood speculates that Hitchcock's confused relationship with food stemmed from his fear of sexuality. According to Wood, Hitchcock's habit of overeating was spurred by an unconscious urge to make himself sexually unattractive; at the same time, however, Hitchcock "longed to be attractive to women and experienced agonies of frustration over his fatness" (Wood, *Hitchcock's* 343). This cycle, familiar to many people, suggests that Hitchcock's films—and Hitchcock who himself became a television star in his own right during the 1950s—are appreciated by popular and academic audiences because the films explore consumer society's emblematic food anxieties.

While the films of Spielberg, Ford, and Hitchcock, with their contradictory attitudes and feelings about food, reside fairly comfortably within the mainstream of commercial cinema, more avant-garde features like the films of Luis Buñuel represent an openly uncomfortable site of contestation. Buñuel begins his interrogation of food beliefs and behaviors with his faux documentary *Land without Bread* (1933) and continues it with films such as *Discreet Charm of the Bourgeoisie* (1972), in which he develops his scathing attack on the blithe immortality of society's respected members by following a collection of smug upper-class men and women as they fill their leisure time with plans to dine together. Despite the fact that their series of meetings never lead to completed, satisfying meals, the self-centered characters remain focused on conspicuous food consumption. Like *La Grande Bouffe, Discreet Charm of the Bourgeoisie* suggests that (food) consumption in consumer society provides no emotional or spiritual nourishment. Even eating together does not create community because the participants see meals as private experiences of sensory pleasure rather than opportunities to share food and drink.

In *The Phantom of Liberty* (1974), Buñuel uses food behavior to mount an even more pointed critique of upper-class norms and values. In a parody of upscale food etiquette, Buñuel presents a "dinner scene" in which well-dressed characters sit on toilets at the table. During the "meal," a few characters excuse themselves and then slip into a tiny room down the hall where they eat from individual trays of food that are passed to them through a small opening with a sliding door. While the characters leaf through magazines as they sit around the table on their toilet seats, one complains that he had to cut a vacation to Madrid short because the city "smelled of food." As if mocking concerns that population growth will lead to food shortages, the characters agree that an increase in excrement is the primary challenge facing society. For Buñuel, conventions surrounding food are a window into the social and material problems of consumer society. Like Hitchcock, Buñuel explores the often-overlooked implications of everyday food interactions. While Hitchcock focuses on the persistently unsettling dimensions of human interactions that involve seemingly

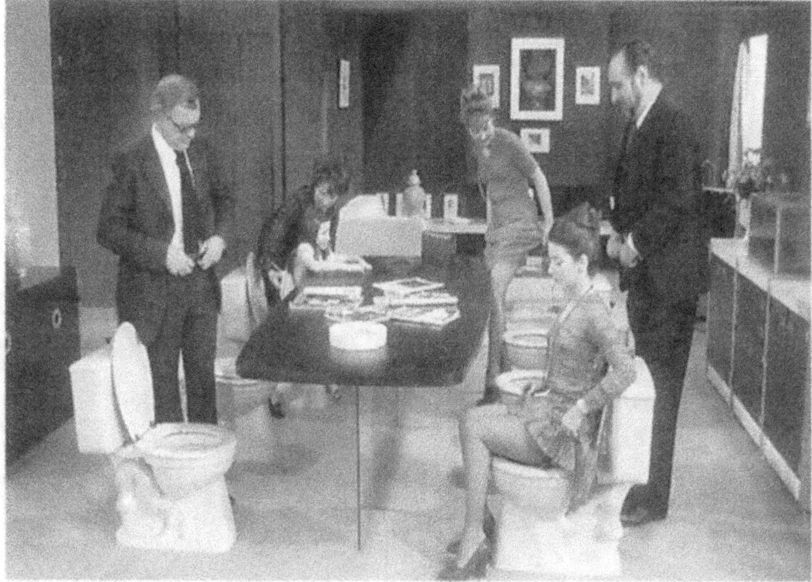

A parody of dining etiquette contributes to an ongoing critique of conventional social norms in The Phantom of Liberty *(Euro International Films, Greenwich Film Productions).*

innocuous food products and utensils, Buñuel is concerned with the ideological implications of conventional food behavior. Buñuel's depiction of foodways gives him an opportunity to express his disgust with the smug platitudes of mainstream society and his critique of a status quo that continues to foster social injustice.

Looking at selected films by Spielberg, Ford, Hitchcock, and Buñuel suggests that directors deploy foodway elements in specific and identifiable ways. Considering their films in light of the foodways paradigm reveals that these directors express their conservative or liberal politics, sentimental or cynical attitudes, and conventional or iconoclastic approaches in their representations of food and food behavior. Foodways analysis thus contributes to auteur studies by providing another means for gauging the ideological implications of directors' stylistic and thematic choices.

7

Foodways in Documentary Films

Consumer Society in a Wider Frame

Fiction films weave foodways into their representations in genre-specific ways. Directors' representations of food activities are sometimes integral to the meanings conveyed by their syntactical arrangement of narrative and mise-en-scène elements. Syntactical arrangements of foodway elements in fiction films create a wide spectrum of utopian as well as dystopian visions of food and society. However, even the many perspectives provided by food films and fiction films in various genres and auteur collections do not fully capture the full range of films' food representations. For studies of food in film, documentaries' representations of foodways warrant analysis, because despite crucial points of contact between food films and food documentaries, the nonfiction films' emphasis on the food activities that surround consumption indirectly illuminates the shared ideological viewpoints that underlie the visions of food and society presented by fiction films of various types.

Food films and food documentaries share common ground and, at the same time, offer different insights into society. On the one hand, food films and food documentaries suggest that "procuring and consuming food is fundamental to our lives, not only for survival but also as it concerns our conceptions of ourselves and our perceptions of the natural and social environments" (Jones et al., "Prologue" xii). They both stress that eating constitutes a social experience and that "there is perhaps no more fundamental act than that of sharing food, whether food and drink are distributed to strangers, offered to friends, or used as the basis of, as well as the justification for, interacting with others" (Jones et al., "Resources and Methods" 91). However, food films highlight questions of food and culture, while food documentaries tend to focus on food security. Food films place greater emphasis on eating and drinking as "an intellectual experience among us as individuals whose personal and direct impressions occur in varied social settings," whereas food documentaries often emphasize that "the act of consuming food is first and foremost a biological necessity" (Jones et al., "Prologue" xii).

By exploring the foodways arc from procurement to disposal, documentaries represent food in ways that contrast sharply with food advertising, the corporate form of nonfiction film. Whereas corporate and "mass entertainment [have] glamorized the convenience-consumption ethic" (Belasco, *Appetite* 157), documentaries emphasize the fact that agriculture binds culture to nature. Rather than ignore or mystify "the details of food production" (Belasco, *Appetite* 157), nonfiction films about foodways examine problems in and alternatives to the industrial food system. Documentaries about food show the influence of various traditions in documentary filmmaking. Those influences lead to different stylistic choices. Thus, like food films, food documentaries have stylistic and thematic variations. However, whereas food films share semantic elements but structure those elements in ways that create different visions of food and society, documentaries about foodways possess an ideological consistency, for they tend to highlight the promise of local, sustainable food production and examine the threat posed by industrial food production.

Food films and food documentaries explore the pleasures, dangers, and implications of food consumption, yet the documentaries place greater emphasis on ways that food production, consumption, and disposal impact nature and economic relationships between people. Nonfiction films about food communicate the countercuisine's view that food is not simply another product in consumer society. The films explore the countercuisine's mistrust of processed food, its delight in "improvisation, craftsmanship, [and] ethnic and regional cooking," and its support for organic farming and a "decentralized infrastructure" for food production and distribution (Belasco, *Appetite* 4). Documentaries about foodways place consumer society in a larger frame and propose that food is not simply an industrial product but also an aesthetic and cultural object that reflects the values of individuals and of societies as a whole.

Like food films, food documentaries represent responses to the food wars of the 1970s. As Carole Counihan and Penny Van Esterik note, food studies, food films, food documentaries, and the "food movements that promote organic, local, fairly traded, slow food" all reflect the growing interest in and anxieties about food that arose in the 1970s (2). Concerns about food in industrialized consumer society explain the rise of food films and food documentaries. Emerging together in the 1970s and 1980s, food-focused fiction and documentary films reflect consumers' sense that the food industry's expanding line of convenient products could destroy the personal and cultural identities that food labor and cuisine choices had conferred in earlier periods. Like food films, food documentaries reflect the (counterculture) view that food matters enormously.

At the same time, whereas food in fiction films provides a window into characters and their societies, in documentaries food illuminates relationships between individuals, societies, and nature. Documentaries that explore foodways do not celebrate or challenge the pleasures of eating and drinking, but instead represent "eat-your-peas cinema that could make viewers not want to eat anything at all" (Severson "Eat Drink"). Yet food documentaries resonate with many contemporary viewers because the films capture the aspirations and anxieties of people who live with the promise and threat of industrialized food production as well as the promise and threat of slow cooking, organic food, and local sources. In today's consumer society, food might be a "frequently indulged pleasure," but it is also an "object of considerable concern and dread [because what] we eat and how we eat it together may constitute the single most important cause of disease and death" (Belasco, *Meals* vii).

By considering food films and food documentaries together and through the foodways lens, the ideological positions underlying both lines of work come into sharper focus. In both instances food functions as a window, yet in the fiction films, food exists in a social world and food behaviors illustrate characters' thoughts, feelings, values, relationships, and social status. By comparison, in food documentaries, food exists at the intersection of nature and culture. Foodways choices and behaviors reveal individuals' and societies' relationship with nature and one another. Nonfiction films often represent the dominant industrial food system as a threat to health, community stability, and the environment, and thus focus more directly on problems of social inequality, resource crises, and systemic abuses of institutional power. Stepping outside the bubble of consumer society, food documentaries remind audiences that agriculture is a part of nature and culture. The films give weight to all aspects of food, from production to disposal. They illuminate the politics of food in film by indirectly revealing that even food films tend to elide activities outside the realm of preparation, presentation, and consumption. Thus, food films and food documentaries together supply a more complete picture of food in film than offered by one or the other.

Documentaries and the Sustainable Food Movement

Despite the presence of best-selling books on food's place in the larger scheme of things and news reports about tainted beef, spinach, and peanut butter, widely distributed films continue to highlight the easy pleasures of food consumption. In response, documentaries now explore the labor behind and health issues surrounding food production, distribution, and disposal. As Robert Kenner explains, the production team for *Food, Inc.* discovered that food production and consumption are intimately tied to the environment, worker and animal abuse, health care, and even First Amendment provisions. They found that the film belonged to "a growing movement . . . like the civil rights movement" because it was about people's right to "speak freely" and have a voice in food policies ("DocuDays Q & A: 'Food, Inc.'").

Concerned with activities surrounding food consumption, food documentaries do not focus on the joys that might result from skilled preparation of gorgeous ingredients that appear magically in glossy kitchens. Instead, as perceived problems in the industrial food system continue to be ignored by most movies, and with enthusiasm about sustainable agriculture on the rise, a cycle of films that started as isolated productions gathered into a wave of documentaries that identify various causes for problems in the current food system. The films illustrate the humanistic values of the multifaceted food movement, which "embraces a great range of issues that have in common demands for more healthful alternatives to the current food system, as well as for more meaningful—moral, ethical, and sustainable—alternatives" (Nestle x). To refer to a movement is not overstating the case. As Kim Severson observes, the individual and collective action now taken to make sustainable agriculture a viable alternative to the current food system is seen by many farmers and the growing number of college students doing summer internships on organic farms as "the political movement of their time" (Severson "Many Summer"). The extensive research on "the enormous complexity of meals" (Meiselman 2), the far-reaching studies on "food as a window on the political" (Watson and Caldwell 1), and the many groups working to make healthy, affordable food and water possible indicate the considerable scope of what has become known as "the food movement" (Nestle x). Food documentaries contribute to that movement by depicting the wider implications of consumption in consumer society.

Drawing on a tradition of documentaries that includes Pare Lorentz's *The Plow That Broke the Plains* (1936) and Frederick Wiseman's *Meat* (1976), filmmakers in the 1980s sought to create socially and environmentally conscious documentaries about food and water. The new food documentaries were a response to several factors: increased interest in food once associated with the counterculture; escalating concerns about high-input agriculture's use of land and water resources; and growing awareness that patented seeds and government pressure to produce commodity crops has negative effects on farmers across the globe (Berry; Jackson and Jackson; Belasco, *Appetite*).

While out of step with social and political trends associated with Reagan-era America, filmmakers' desire in the 1980s to explore the shared interests of farmers and environmentalists reflects a line of American thought that goes back to Henry David Thoreau's observations in *Walden; or, Life in the Woods* (1854). The food documentaries also tapped into traditions of conservation and preservation that had led to the creation of Yellowstone National Park in 1872 and the Sierra Club in 1892. The films revealed renewed interest in work started by botanist and inventor George Washington Carver, whose research on sustainable agriculture was published regularly from 1898 to 1943. Publications like *Silent Spring* (1962) by Rachel Carson, *The Unsettling of America: Culture and Agriculture* (1977) by Wendell Berry, *The End of Nature* (1989) by Bill McKibben, and *Stolen Harvest* (2000) by Vandana Shiva continue to influence the films that express the hopes and concerns of the sustainable agriculture movement.

The new food documentaries were also inspired by J. I. Rodale's efforts to share his "belief that American agricultural practices, which relied heavily on chemical fertilizers and pesticides, were harmful" (Rudick 2). In 1947, Rodale had established the Soil and Health Foundation, later known as the Rodale Institute (Rudick 2). Based on his experience working with others involved in sustainable agriculture during the Depression, Rodale had "launched *Organic Farming and Gardening* in 1942," a magazine known today as *Organic Gardening* (Rudick 2).[1] In the years following World War II, an audience had emerged for Rodale's work and for publications like *Foxfire* (started in 1966) and *Mother Earth News* (started by John and Jane Shuttleworth in 1970). *Foxfire* featured interviews with people about traditional rural culture. It included recipes for making cheese and jelly, canning, cooking wild game, producing country hams, and more. A subsequent proliferation of publications in the 1970s touted the value of organic, home-grown food and stressed not only the physical but also the spiritual benefits of local foods grown with attention to preserving land and water resources. The publications reflected and reinforced the back-to-the-land ethos that celebrated the joy of living simply and apart from the industrialized way of life that had become more widespread since the 1950s.

Food documentaries illustrate connections between rural and urban food communities and even right- and left-leaning food advocacy groups. Accounts of hardworking farmers and hard-pressed consumers explore the foodways arc that spans food procurement and disposal. The films highlight that food is not just a commodity delivered by a high-tech industry, but that the food people eat and share with others is also a part of nature and culture. In response to food companies' claims that food and water resources are commodities, food documentaries propose that access to safe food and water is a basic human right. Food documentaries celebrate alternative methods of food procurement, distribution, and performance and thus create a vision of food that is quite different from the picture generated by the food and film industries.

The documentaries reflect the food movement's interest in building a sustainable and equitable food system. They feature exhaustive research on corporate and alternative methods of food production, distribution, and consumption. The films present this material as information that can serve as a basis for individuals, communities, and countries to make informed decisions about one of the essentials of human life. By providing information that mainstream sources do not, the films reveal that widely circulated representations do not show all aspects of foodways, but instead offer a highly selective, censored view that supports the interests of the food and film industries. The contrast between the stages of foodways covered in the documentaries and mainstream cinema's focus on the pleasure of consumption is a reminder that commercial media does not aim to provide an informative picture of the world, but one that creates repeat customers whose constant hope is to feel fulfilled by consuming more (Britton).

There is a fundamental difference between the documentaries and the productions of the mainstream media in how they convey the meaning and significance of food. While widely distributed films present food consumption as a sign of personal identity, as something to purchase and use as self-expression, the documentaries show that food belongs to the larger worlds of nature, culture, politics, and economics. Mainstream movies mask out representations of industrial agriculture because the food industry maximizes profits by directing attention to its nicely packaged end-products rather than its unseemly means of procurement and preservation. By comparison, food documentaries explore ways in which agriculture is necessarily a part of nature and community.

Today's food documentaries are a contemporary version of New Deal–era documentaries like *The Plow That Broke the Plains.* As noted in Chapter 2, Lorentz's film offered what he termed a "picturization" of studies that had determined that the agricultural, economic, and social crisis of "the dust bowl" had been caused by the "mistaken homesteading policy" of earlier administrations and a system of agriculture that served the interests of government and business but not individuals (Clement 4). *The Plow That Broke the Plains* reflected the views of farmers and policy makers interested in "the new agriculture," as it was referred to by people like Louis Bromfield, novelist, screenwriter, conservationist, and founder of Malabar Farm in Ohio.[2] Echoing the ecologically grounded views expressed in work such as Aldo Leopold's *A Sand County Almanac* (1949), the current wave of food documentaries conveys ideas central to the today's sustainable agriculture movement.[3]

Foodways Represented in Films Shaped by Documentary Traditions

Food documentaries are crafted to make a point, and so exist on a fact-fiction continuum that includes documentaries, mockumentaries, docudramas, and fiction films (Roscoe and Hight 7).[4] Their depictions of food and food behavior also reveal varying uses of strategies employed by reality television, reconstructions, and performances by documentary-auteurs.[5] However, despite their differences, they consistently echo John Grierson's interest in using films to dramatize social issues, call citizens to action, and highlight the dignity of ordinary labor.

The current wave of food documentaries also exists at the intersection of recent political and environmental documentaries. As a consequence, they often carry a sense of "uncertainty, anxiety, [and] suspicion," particularly a "suspicion of politics" (Kahana 321). For example, Deborah Koons Garcia's *The Future of Food* (2004) examines a host of political problems. The film begins by outlining threats to world food supplies that are caused by "monoculture," the name given to agricultural practices that produce high volumes of limited crop varieties. The film's second segment covers a legal battle between Monsanto and a canola farmer who resisted the company's demand that farmers purchase their patented seeds. The third touches on the health risks of genetically modified food products. The fourth covers corporate and government abuse of power; it identifies legislation crafted by food companies and legal decisions made by public officials who had been Monsanto executives. Subsequent segments make the arguments that

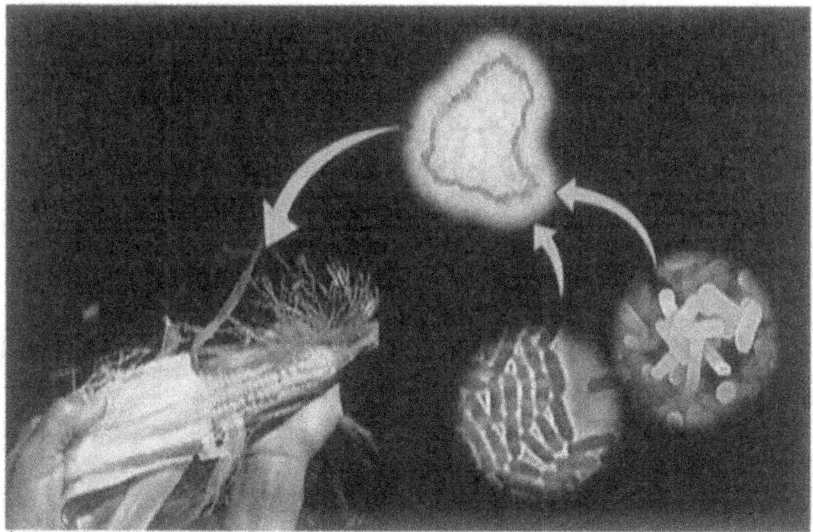

The Future of Food *(Lily Films) illustrates the role that bacteria and viruses play in the genetic engineering of commodity crops and examines the dystopian dimensions of industrial production.*

taxpayers are subsidizing the biotech industry, that the overproduction of a limited range of crops has not stopped world hunger, and that terminator technology to protect seed patents poses a serious threat to global food security. The film concludes with a long (utopian) segment on the increasing number of people involved in sustainable farming, community-supported agriculture, and farmers' markets.

Their articulated suspicion of corporate and governmental politics cause many food documentaries to share common ground with social and environmental documentaries such as *Fahrenheit 9/11* (Moore, 2004) and *An Inconvenient Truth* (Guggenheim, 2006). Their sometimes shrill tone reflects the filmmakers' determination to be heard in a public sphere so dominated by the interrelated interests of the food and film industries. For instance, to compete in a media market filled with gore, hype, and action, the *Food, Inc.* trailer uses "experts," "victims," quick cuts, dramatic music, and computer-generated images. The trailer zips through the dense set of interlocking issues covered in the film: food safety, food industry advertising and the lack of accurate labeling, laws against exposing the mechanics of the industrial food system, and a call to action. It emphasizes that consumers need to recognize that they are in a position to change the food system.

The trailer presents audiences with a David-and-Goliath story, with the industrial food system on the one side and individual farmers, food producers, and food consumers on the other. The trailer features interview clips with "underdogs": Joel Salatin, owner of Polyface Farms in Virginia; Gary Hirshberg, CEO of Stonyfield Farm yogurt; and Troy Roush, a farmer in Indiana and former vice president of the American Corn Growers Association. The latter group was established in 1987 in response to what farmers then termed "a farm crisis of a magnitude not seen since the Great Depression," which was exacerbated by the close ties between a forerunner organization, the National Corn Growers Association, and various grain processors, exporters, chemical manufacturers, and seed companies ("About the ACGA").

In contrast to *Food, Inc.*'s assertive tone, Les Blank's *Garlic Is as Good as Ten Mothers* (1980) is an easy-going account that celebrates good food, farm workers, and sustainable agriculture. It features interviews with countercuisine founder Alice Waters of Chez Panisse and documents the time in the 1970s when Berkeley, California, became a place where "health food, herbalism, folk medicine, organic growing, and gourmet cooking" came together in a way that would shape what Marion Nestle terms "the good food movement" (Sherman 105; Nestle x). The film shows workers harvesting garlic in fields around Gilroy, California. Highlighting food labor, one scene shows the words "Support the people who grow the food we eat" superimposed on a freeze-frame of a produce box marked with the emblem for the farm workers' union.

The celebratory food documentary *Terra Madre* (*Mother Earth*, Olmi, 2009), produced almost thirty years later, highlights Alice Waters in her role as vice president of Slow Food International leading the organization's bi-annual 2006 and 2008 conferences in Turin, Italy, with representatives from 150 countries in attendance. The film covers the conferences' speeches, panels, and workshops, which endorse biodiversity (as opposed to monoculture) and sustainable, responsible agricultural practices. The film pays tribute to Carlo Petrini, founder of the Slow Food Movement, and illustrates the movement's importance by showing the Svalbard Global Seed Vault that it established. Located on an island in the remote Norwegian Arctic Svalbard archipelago and housing more than 10,000 seed samples, the Seed Vault functions as insurance against global seed crises. The film also calls attention to the pleasure of local, organic food. As Waters said at the film's U.S. premiere at the 2009 Telluride Film Festival, "Our health, our wealth comes first from food [yet] I don't come to this philosophically, but to eat and to eat really well" (Waters). The film suggests that eating well and caring for the Earth's resources go together. That vision of foodways differs fundamentally with the food and film industries' emphasis on the pleasure of convenient food produced by technological wizardry.

As a film like *Terra Madre* suggests, today's food documentaries continue to explore the cultural, aesthetic, and material dimensions of food in ways marked out by Les Blank's work. Contemporary documentaries also show the influence of Frederick Wiseman. Often associated with direct cinema, Wiseman is perhaps more accurately compared to Emile de Antonio, for Wiseman's films "challenge the arbitrary, secretive, and silent power of the state" (Kahana 38). Best known for *Titicut Follies* (1967), his film about the inhumane treatment of patients at a state hospital for the criminally insane, Wiseman is at his most nuanced in his food documentary *Meat*. However, the subtle way that *Meat* conveys its message is indicative of the more than twenty films Wiseman directed, which all offer a thoughtful look at "the rigid, mechanical, insulated nature of authority in a self-contained society" (Barsam 339).

Wiseman's films expose dehumanization in every aspect of consumer society. Richard Barsam explains that the deeply troubling "process of socialization embodied by the military" in Wiseman's *Basic Training* (1971) is also illustrated by his films about "the educational institution in *High School* (1968), the court system in *Juvenile Court* (1973), and the social service system in *Welfare* (1975); the military service in *Canal Zone* (1977), *Sinai Field Mission* (1978), and *Manoeuvre* (1979); fashion models in *Model* (1980); and consumer buying habits in *The Store* (1983)" (340). Acknowledging Wiseman's deft work in those films, Barsam proposes that *Meat* is "Wiseman's masterpiece" because the film explores "themes that are deeper and more provocative than any Wiseman had previously developed" (340). In a reading that shows how the film's "images of pens, traps, holding structures, and closing doors reinforce the interpretation that [the] technology for processing animals entraps [people] as well," Barsam also explains how the film,

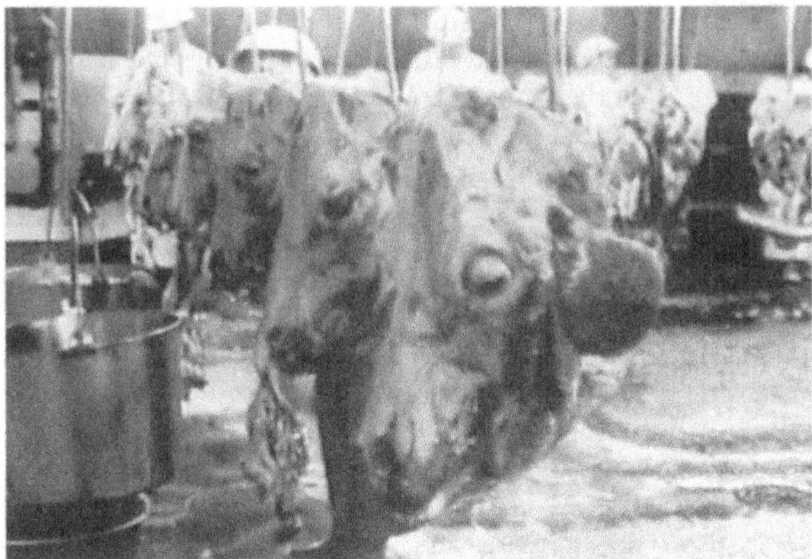

Meat *(Zipporah Films): Frederick Wiseman's film led to the subsequent wave of documentary films that examine the dehumanizing effects of the industrial food system.*

by attending to all aspects of foodways, offers insights into the modern problems of communication, self-determination, and alienation (341).

Les Blank and Frederick Wiseman directly influenced a number of contemporary food documentaries. In addition, it is evident from the comprehensive, even exhaustive analyses in many films about problems in the industrial food system that Emile de Antonio has been an important influence on recent work as well. The "master of a compilation genre that he created," de Antonio made films between 1963 and 1989 that included "the standard elements—interviews and archival footage," but that notably achieved their persuasive power through the "cumulative forcefulness" of de Antonio's editing choices (Barsam 342, 344). In films ranging from *Rush to Judgment* (1967), about problems in the Warren Commission's report on the assassination of John F. Kennedy, to *Mr. Hoover and I* (1989), which capped de Antonio's career-long interest in "the cold war and its attendants such as Nixon, McCarthy, and [F.B.I. Director J. Edgar] Hoover" (Lewis, *Emile* 230–31), de Antonio examined "the infinitely corruptible and corrupting political and ideological system that dominated America during the period he was making films" (Bruzzi 35).

Employing an approach used by Soviet filmmaker Esther Shub in the silent era, de Antonio's films demonstrated the "clear distinction [that] exists between 'newsreel' and 'documentary'" by exploring the "dialectical collision between the inherent perspective of [archival footage] and its radical re-use" (Bruzzi 27). For example, in *Point of Order* (1964), de Antonio uses newsreel footage of the Army-McCarthy hearings in which a congressional committee examined Senator Joseph McCarthy's charge that the U.S. Army had tried to "conceal evidence of espionage among Army officers" (Barsam 343). The selected footage highlights the sharp contrast between McCarthy's freewheeling, blustery attacks and the measured questions of Joseph Welch, the attorney for the Army. Cutaways to bored, distracted, and exasperated listeners make McCarthy's pronouncements seem overblown. Using similar strategies, de Antonio's film *In the Year of the Pig* (1968) draws on interviews and archival footage to craft a history of Vietnam totally at odds with the U.S. government's official position. The film's calculated mix of interviews with "those supporting the war and those working to stop it" conveys the point that "the escalation of war [in Vietnam] represented the degradation of American values" (Barsam 344). Using interviews as "a tool of historical analysis," de Antonio consistently contrasts information provided by people in personal interviews with the "official history found in newsreels and other mainstream sources of political information" (Kahana 186). That approach, where official statements are undercut by images and quiet personal integrity is contrasted with bombastic rhetoric, is used in contemporary food documentaries and in the food segments of documentaries like *The Corporation.*

With de Antonio's work modeling ways to structure material, other films from the 1970s and 1980s explore topics taken up by more recent food documentaries. For example, Les Blank's films about Cajun life in Louisiana, *Spend It All* (1972) and *Dry Wood* (1973), anticipate today's food documentaries in that they feature scenes of eating, drinking, food procurement, and food preparation. *Dry Wood* shows women slaughtering and dressing a hog, and it follows the preparation process as they make "cracklings and hogshead cheese" (Sherman 100). Blank's

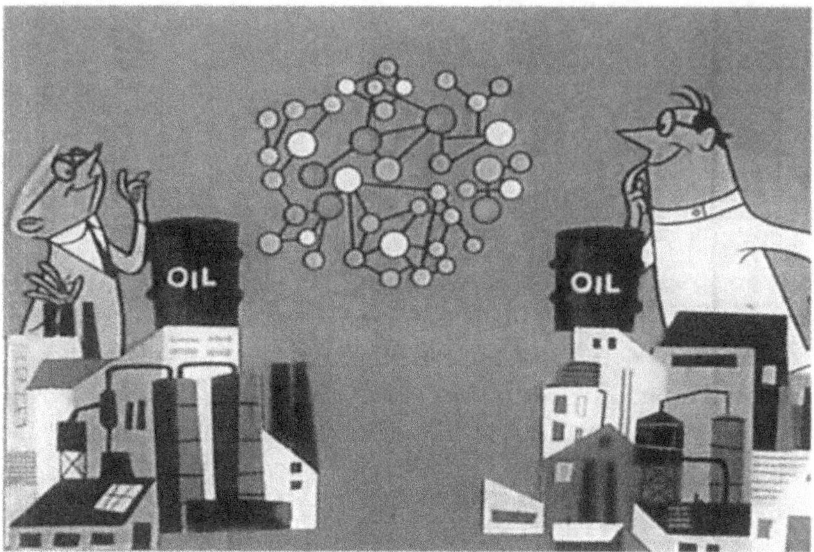

The Corporation *(Big Picture Media Corporation) cuts from this promotional film on "the wonders of science" to footage that documents the toxic effects of petrochemical engineering.*

longstanding interest in Louisiana food and culture is reflected in his 1990 film *Yum, Yum, Yum! A Taste of the Cajun and Creole Cooking of Louisiana,* which highlights "traditional foodways" and "covers the actual process of making a number of dishes" (Sherman 110).

Diet for a Small Planet (Lappé and Bullfrog Films, 1974), based on Frances Moore Lappé's 1971 book, covers material central to recent food documentaries. Its comprehensive look at the global food system shows that in the face of world hunger, meat-centered diets in wealthy nations can and should change to emphasize vegetarian meals. Robert Lang's *Fragile Harvest* (1986) examines problems in the high-tech agricultural system that promised to "end world hunger" but that now seems to benefit the "multinational chemical companies that have taken over seed companies [that] are breeding and marketing seeds to suit their agrichemical interests" ("Fragile Harvest"). *Wheat Today, What Tomorrow?* (Oldfield, 1988) features botanist David Bellamy's analysis of emerging dust bowls. These films have led to documentaries such as *My Father's Garden* (Smith, 1996), an evocative look at differing approaches to agriculture; *Beyond Organic* (de Graf, 2000), about the work of author and organic farmer Michael Ableman in Goleta, California; *Good Food* (Dworkin and Young, 2008), about sustainable farming and ranching in the Pacific Northwest; and *Tapped* (Soechtig and Lindsey, 2009), about the problems of the bottled water industry (see Appendix 3).

The rhetorical strategies drawn from Blank, Wiseman, and de Antonio have influenced today's food documentaries, part of what has been called a "golden age of documentary film production" (McEnteer xx). In fact, it is possible to see the entire documentary tradition from a new perspective, namely, one that has been concerned with foodways. With John Grierson's study of herring fisherman in *Drifters* establishing the "two major themes that characterized many of the British [documentary] films that followed: the dignity of labor and the worth of individuals" (Barsam 83–84), and with *The Plow That Broke the Plains* establishing "the direction that the American documentary film was to take until the outbreak of the Second World War" (Barsam 154), today's documentaries about food are not oddities, but best understood as integral to longstanding and abiding thematic concerns for documentary filmmakers. Grierson's film anticipates contemporary filmmakers' attention to differing modes of food production, for its "underlying theme is the shift that transforms small, independent herring fishing efforts into a large, industrial operation" (Barsam 84). Lorentz's film provides a model for later documentaries because it lays bare the effects of profiteering and government supported agribusiness. Its focus on ill-conceived food production methods links it to documentaries produced in more recent decades, when social, economic, and environmental crises created or at least amplified by government and corporate actions have again reached visible levels. The film industry's disinterest in distributing Lorentz's film prefigures current practices (discussed in Chapter 8).

Documentaries Explore Foodways to Share Information in Mediated Consumer Society

Grounded in established documentary traditions, today's food documentaries also expand the audience for writing about foodways. Subsequent to the collaboration between Lappé and Bullfrog Films (John

Hoskyns-Abrahall and Winifred Scherrer) in 1974, there are films like *Diet for a New America* (Schuman, 1991), based on the 1987 book by John Robbins. Charles Clover's book *The End of the Line* (2008) is the basis for Rupert Murray's 2009 film of the same name. Designed to raise awareness about "the greatest environmental disaster that people haven't heard about," Murray's film introduces audiences to research on fishing stocks conducted after the cod industry collapsed in Newfoundland, Canada, in 1992 ("The Film"). It provides ample evidence that continued use of industrial fishing methods to procure food will cause the collapse of fishing stocks by 2050, and argues for vastly increased marine reserves and fishing quotas that will allow stocks to recover. Further, Murray encourages consumers to eat fish from sustainable sources and to stop eating endangered species. The film includes scenes of blue-fin tuna slaughter as troubling as scenes from *The Cove* (Psihoyos, 2009), the award-winning film about the capture of dolphins sold alive or as meat.[6]

Blue Gold: World Water Wars (Bozzo, 2008) and *Water on the Table* (Marshall, 2010) are other films that raise awareness of foodways re-

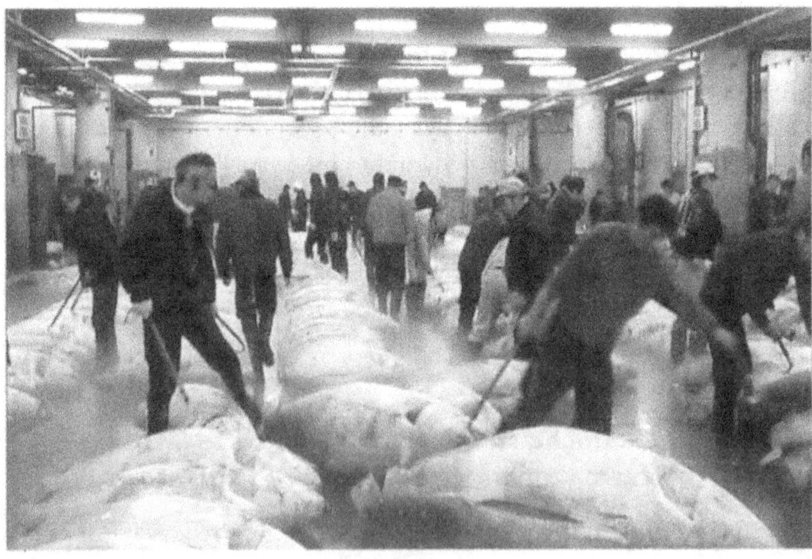

The End of the Line *(Arcane Pictures, Calm Productions, Dartmouth Films, The Fish Film): Mitsubishi has bought tons of blue fin tuna to sell at a profit when the species becomes extinct.*

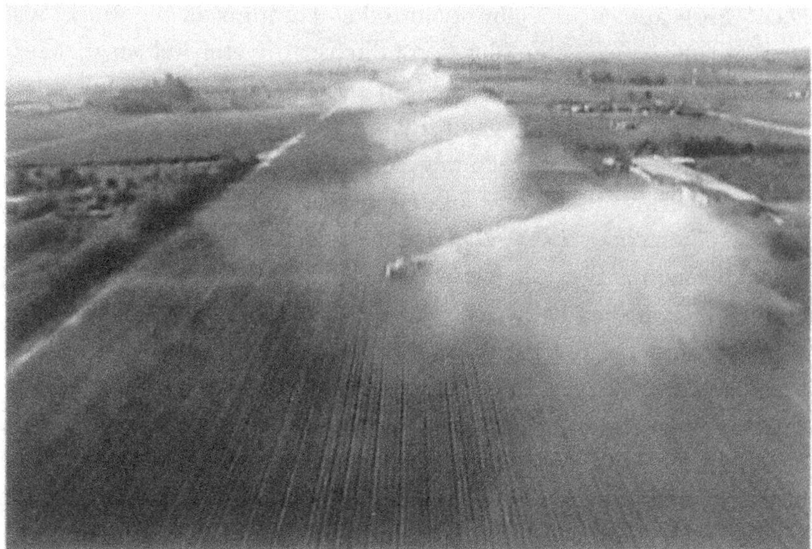

FLOW: For Love of Water *(The Group Entertainment, Steven Starr Productions) shows that people do not have adequate access to water while industrial agriculture uses massive amounts.*

search. Both films use *Blue Gold: The Battle Against Corporate Theft of the World's Water* (2002) by Maude Barlow and Tony Clarke as a primary source. Irena Salina's *FLOW: For Love of Water* (2008) has created a wider audience for Barlow and Clarke's book *Blue Gold* as well as books such as *The Holy Order of Water: Healing the Earth's Water and Ourselves* (2001) by William E. Marks, *Silenced Rivers: The Ecology and Politics of Large Dams* (1998) by Patrick McCully, and books by Peter H. Gleick that include *Water in Crisis: A Guide to the World's Fresh Water Resources* (1993) and *Bottled and Sold: The Story behind Our Obsession with Bottled Water* (2010).

FLOW examines the social, economic, and environmental issues surrounding water resources from historical and public policy perspectives.[7] Contrasting innovative use with thoughtless abuse of water resources, the film illustrates that water is a precious resource, gorgeous to behold in its pristine state. Using examples from Bolivia, China, India, Mexico, South Africa, and the United States that show egregious waste and unfettered profiteering, the film mounts a persuasive case for rethinking habits and prevailing attitudes about water resources.

FLOW gives audiences a glimpse into the operations of the World Water Council, which sets policies conducive to water industry leaders Suez, Vivendi, and Thames. The film also provides a forum for information that scientists and water rights activists think important. In the picture that emerges, it becomes clear that water is the third largest industry worldwide after oil and electricity, and that agriculture consumes 70 percent, industry 20 percent, and individuals 10 percent.

Some segments of the film show people around the globe being negatively impacted by policies shaped by corporate interests. Other segments focus on the positive results of small-scale, community-organized, sustainable water projects. The film illustrates that "many in government, academia, and industry look to new tools . . . to feed us tomorrow without any modification of our modern high-consumption values, [while] others propose low-tech alternatives organized around smaller scale, localized food systems dependent on a return to more traditional appreciation of limits" (Belasco, *Meals to Come* vii). The production team behind *FLOW* makes its position clear: the film's many case studies communicate the point that dams and other large-scale projects benefit institutions like the World Bank but leave individuals without access to clean and affordable water.

FLOW starts with an overview of the water crisis and the dangers of tap and bottled water. Describing the film's opening, one reviewer explains: "From the dubious quality of our tap water (possibly laced with rocket fuel) to the terrifyingly unpoliced contents of bottled brands (one company pumped from the vicinity of a Superfund site), the movie ruthlessly dismantles our assumptions about water safety and government oversight" (Catsoulis). Another critic notes: "Rocket fuel seems to have made its way into some American water systems, and herbicides such as Atrazine, banned in the European Union, are still in wide use over here" (Turan). Responding to the film's comprehensive account that examines problems in the current system *and* innovative solutions, another reviewer observes: "It's not all doom and gloom—low-cost, sustainable purification technologies like ultraviolet water-health [systems] run by village cooperatives can make dramatic development differences for the poorest, most vulnerable people in the world, who are able to maintain their own systems without foreign involvement" (Doctorow).

FLOW's conclusion, which shows people around the world responding to systemic abuses of power by governments and corporations, includes a call for audiences to sign a petition asking the United Nations to amend its 1948 Universal Declaration of Human Rights so that an article identifying access to clean water as a basic human right can be added to the original thirty articles in the declaration. To date, the Declaration of Human Rights has not been amended, but on 28 July 2010 the General Assembly passed a resolution "calling on States and international organizations to [use their] financial resources [and more] to provide safe, clean, accessible and affordable water and sanitation for all" (United Nations).[8]

Foodways in Documentary Films: A View of Food Anathema to Food and Film Industries

In fictional films, characters' cuisine reveals their beliefs and values. Food behavior makes characters' relationships visible. By comparison, in documentaries, food production and cleanup scenes shed light on larger social values; scenes of food processing and food disposal reveal power relations in consumer society. By showing foodways activities that lie outside the frame of consumption, food documentaries tacitly highlight the food and film industries' power to control representations in consumer society. Thus, even though a few widely distributed fiction films use foodways problems to generate visually compelling, viscerally exciting, stimulating scenarios, food documentaries have limited visibility because they offer evidence that directly challenges the vision of food promoted by commercial media and the food industry.

As films like *Chinatown* and *Rango* show, conflicts involving water issues are integrated into narratives that feature familiar elements of romance, intrigue, and adventure. Even the plots of Poverty Row westerns (those films made by less prestigious producers working outside of the studio system) once touched on water rights in characters' power struggles. Yet today, natural resources seldom function as the focus of the narrative conflict, even though exploitation and destruction of food and water resources are issues that have dramatic potential. For example, the David and Goliath battle between Nestlé and Michigan residents who filed suit against the food and water product giant has the ingredients for a Hollywood movie. As *FLOW* documents, Michigan Citizens for Water Conservation sued Nestlé because the company's use of area water was damaging the ecosystem of Mecosta County. But Nestlé claimed their use was legal because water is transient and so cannot be owned (except when sold at a 100 percent profit as Ice Mountain bottled water). Nestlé took their case to Michigan's Supreme Court and secured the right to keep pumping groundwater. A 2009 court decision allowed Nestlé to continue water extraction but, due to the efforts of local residents, at levels lower than the company wanted. Compelling as it is, this story of small-town citizens fighting an uphill battle will not be coming to a multiplex soon; it would be unwise for food and film industries to facilitate fiction or documentary work that exposes the process and effect of corporations exercising their "rights."

At the same time, the environmental movement has made today's audiences aware of food and water's importance. News reports continue to remind consumers that access to clean water is declining and that the price of safe, healthy food is increasing. With countercuisine perspectives increasingly a part of mainstream culture, what people bring to documentaries' representation of food and water is more complex than in the past. Geographical regions will have different attitudes about food and water; people living in farming or ranching regions will have views that differ from people living on the coasts; desert and temperate inhabitants will look at food and water differently. However, documentaries depict the shared concerns of the food movement and so present the crises of oceans, rivers, ranches, farmlands, towns, and cities as interrelated problems.

Food documentaries present research findings in condensed audiovisual form that involves simplification. However, films like *The End of the Line* and *The Future of Food* clearly delineate the larger implications of food consumption. Their focus on health and environmental factors are thus an annoyance to industries that profit from mass-produced consumer objects like food and film. Influenced by a tradition that includes de Antonio's documentaries about abuses of political power, today's documentaries about foodways explicitly articulate counterculture objections to the dominant food system. They disclose filmmakers' concerns about getting a hearing in a media environment shaped by corporate interests, but, like the early documentaries of John Grierson and Pare Lorentz, today's food documentaries reveal an investment in calling citizens to action.[9]

Although a film such as *Super Size Me* (Spurlock, 2004) shares common ground with reality TV shows and films by the more visible doc-auteurs, other food documentaries are comparable to the New Deal–era documentaries in their earnest call for land stewardship. Some food documentaries focus on the dehumanizing effects of the industrial food system and thus share common ground with work by Frederick Wiseman. Other films' provocative use of archival footage and exhaustive analysis of food and water systems suggests the influence of de Antonio. However, food documentaries share an interest in shattering the official story of the petrochemical era, ushered in during the mid-twentieth century with support from military suppliers and Madison Avenue marketing. In various ways, the films challenge the view that corporate-funded science and technology are the only or best approach to agriculture. Yet they consistently support methods comparable to the conservation-minded "new agriculture" approach that emerged in the 1930s.

The films' focus on the need for safe food and water and sustainable foodway practices makes them unsuitable for wide distribution, for their depictions can be construed as criticism of business and government behavior. The established policy of censoring realistic depictions of corporate mismanagement and social problems has led to the film industry's standard practice of proceeding as if people are not interested in where their food and water comes from. However, as Jonathan Rosenbaum notes, that is a form of political censorship (159). *FLOW* is one of many films assigned to the margins of the media marketplace because it shows that government and corporate mismanagement, indifference, and outright exploitation have contributed to and continue to exacerbate health, economic, and environmental crises. Given its limited audience, what is striking is that the production team behind *FLOW* would be compelled to invest their time, energy, and creative resources to grapple with the fascinating and frustrating, wondrous and abused real world illuminated by the documentary. The next chapter examines the impact that the food and film industries have on representations of food in film by exploring the industrial context that determines the type of representations that will have wide circulation.

8

The Politics Surrounding Documentaries' Depiction of Foodways

Documentaries emphasize that food belongs to culture *and* nature. As a consequence, they indirectly illuminate fiction films' focus on the cultural dimensions of foodways. Food documentaries also indirectly but vividly illustrate the politics surrounding representations of food in mainstream cinema because their production-distribution-exhibition sequence differs so greatly from the blockbusters buoyed up by fast-food brand integration. Documentaries that examine the implications of food production, consumption, and disposal have little in common with films that strategically display consumer products. Whereas convenience food co-promotion opportunities encourage film companies to invest in action blockbusters, documentaries' disturbing revelations about the industrial food system discourage media companies from participation in any phase of their production-distribution-exhibition process.

When compared to widely distributed fiction films, food documentaries' countercultural perspective becomes especially visible. However, the films present views that are often shared by people with mainstream credentials. For instance, as Mark Bittman of the *New York Times* notes, while the "oldest and most common dig against organic agriculture is that it cannot feed the world's citizens," that is "a supposition, not a fact." He points out that "increasing numbers of scientists, policy panels and experts (not hippies!) are suggesting that agricultural practices pretty close to organic—perhaps best called 'sustainable'—can feed more poor people sooner, begin to repair the damage caused by industrial production and, in the long term, become the norm" (Bittman "Sustainable"). Many established farmers also hold that view. Speaking about the 2008 global food crisis that became news even in food-abundant countries, Jim Goodman, a dairy farmer in Wisconsin, explained that the crisis should have made U.S. politicians able to see that "after all these years of pushing globalization and genetically modified seeds, that instead of feeding the world we've created a food system that leaves more people hungry. If they'd listened to the farmers instead of corporations, they would've known this was going to happen" (Nichols 6).

Yet documentaries' representation of foodways seems radical because critiques of other industries have been censored in mainstream movies for a century. The apparently radical nature of food documentaries' depictions indirectly reveals that the film industry's deep-rooted policy to work with, rather than against, other industries has had a profound effect on representations of food in film. The significant differences in the way blockbusters and food documentaries reach audiences illuminate the industrial and cultural politics that shape dominant representations of food in film. The sharply contrasting market share secured by industry-supported blockbusters and non-commercial food documentaries' sheds light on the food behaviors that have come to define consumer society.

Documentaries about foodways resonate with people interested or involved in the many campaigns that aim to create a better food future. However, because these campaigns are opposed to corporate control of food, the film industry's profit-focused distribution and exhibition practices ensure that even films with theatrical releases reach limited audiences. For instance, *The Corporation* is one of the most economically successful documentaries to detail problems in the food industry, yet the film made only $3 million at the box office.

While these figures might seem to suggest that these films were of little interest to audiences, the numbers actually illuminate the films' reception context. Today, box office winners overshadow films that are

Box Office Statistics for Selected Food Documentaries

Film and Year	Domestic (U.S. and Canada) Theatrical Gross	Box Office Ranking among Documentary Films (through 2012)	Box Office Ranking among All Films in Year of Release	Number of Theaters for Widest Release
The Corporation (2004)	$3,493,516	46	192	28
FLOW (2008)	$142,569	366	337	11
King Corn (2007)	$105,422	417	367	8
The Future of Food (2005)	$81,000	363	357	5
McLibel (2005)	$4,337	918	516	3
We Feed the World (2005)	N.A.	not in the top 1,000	not listed	limited North American release
The End of the Line (2009)	N.A.	not in the top 1,000	not listed	limited North American release

Source: BoxOfficeMojo.com

forced to use alternative means of distribution because only once in a while will exhibitors break with established agreements to show low-budget unrated documentaries.[1]

Input Costs and Ratings: Standard Practices That Function as Gatekeepers

Today's documentaries about foodways contribute to "the golden age of documentary film production" that started with films like *Roger and Me* (Moore, 1989) and *Manufacturing Consent: Noam Chomsky and the Media* (Achbar and Wintonick, 1992) and that has been sustained by the low-tech, collaborative methods used in films like *This Is What Democracy*

Looks Like (Friedberg and Rowley, 2000) (McEnteer xiv). Many observers see the mid-1990s as a significant moment for documentary cinema, noting the attention given to films such as *Hoop Dreams* (James, 1994), *Crumb* (Zwigoff, 1994), and *When We Were Kings* (Gast, 1996). Others see the mid-2000s as a time when documentaries became visible, as films such as *Bowling for Columbine* (Moore, 2002), *The Corporation, Super Size Me,* and *Fahrenheit 9/11* reached larger audiences. Highlighting developments in the mid-2000s, in March 2005 the National Association of Theatre Owners noted that documentaries released between 1990 and 2001 had grossed a respectable $174 million, but that in only three years afterward, between 2002 and 2004, documentaries had grossed $322.2 million at the domestic box office (Freeman).

Today's golden age of documentaries includes Oscar-winning films such as Alex Gibney's *Taxi to the Dark Side* (2007) and Charles Ferguson's *Inside Job* (2010). It features Errol Morris's critically acclaimed films *The Fog of War: Eleven Lessons from the Life of Robert S. McNamara* (2003) and *Standard Operating Procedure* (2008). *Tupac: Resurrection* (Lazin, 2003), *Religulous* (Charles, 2008), and *Waiting for "Superman"* (Guggenheim, 2010) reached larger audiences. The funding and distribution techniques Robert Greenwald has used for films such as *Outfoxed: Rupert Murdoch's War on Journalism* (2004), *Wal-Mart: The High Cost of Low Price* (2005), and *Rethink Afghanistan* (2009) are also a salient feature of this era's documentaries. Greenwald has received financial support from MoveOn.org and the American Civil Liberties Union. The films are shown at house parties, DVDs are sold on organizations' websites, and individual sponsors receive email updates and requests to support new productions.

Michael Moore directed four of the twenty highest-grossing documentaries: *Fahrenheit 9/11, Sicko, Bowling for Columbine,* and *Capitalism: A Love Story.* Another seven are nature or environmental films: *March of the Penguins, Earth, Chimpanzee, An Inconvenient Truth, Oceans, African Cats,* and *Winged Migration.* Other high-grossing films, like *Justin Bieber: Never Say Never, Katy Perry: Part of Me, Madonna: Truth or Dare* and *Religulous,* appealed to youth audiences. The box office figures for documentaries released after 2000 do suggest increased audience interest, but they also reflect a rise in what farmers call input costs. A little over half of the top twenty documentaries had releases that involved

Top Twenty Documentaries in Domestic Box Office Receipts (through 2012)

Film	Domestic Box Office Receipts	Number of Theaters
1. *Fahrenheit 9/11* (2004)	$119M	2,011
2. *March of the Penguins* (2005)	$77M	2,506
3. *Justin Bieber: Never Say Never* (2011)	$73M	3,118
4. *2016: Obama's America* (2012)	$33M	2,017
5. *Earth* (2009)	$32M	1,804
6. *Chimpanzee* (2012)	$29M	1,567
7. *Katy Perry: Part of Me* (2012)	$25M	2,732
8. *Sicko* (2007)	$24M	1,117
9. *An Inconvenient Truth* (2006)	$24M	587
10. *Bowling For Columbine* (2002)	$22M	248
11. *Oceans* (2010)	$19M	1,232
12. *African Cats* (2011)	$15M	1,220
13. *Madonna: Truth or Dare* (1991)	$15M	652
14. *Capitalism: A Love Story* (2009)	$14M	995
15. *Religulous* (2008)	$13M	568
16. *Winged Migration* (2003)	$12M	202
17. *Super Size Me* (2004)	$12M	230
18. *Mad Hot Ballroom* (2005)	$8M	202
19. *Hoop Dreams* (1994)	$8M	262
20. *Expelled: No Intelligence Allowed* (2008)	$8M	1,052

Source: BoxOfficeMojo.com

simultaneous screenings in more than 1,000 theaters. Advertising budgets for wide releases of Hollywood films average $64 million. In addition, in the pre-digital age, each print cost about $2,000, which meant that to supply prints for 1,000 screens there was an additional expense of about $2 million, totaling around $70 million for each wide release. While wide releases do fail, there is a distinct correlation between upfront expense and box office return: a film backed by the investment required for a wide release stands the chance of reaping big box-office figures; a film with a limited theatrical release does not.

To be successful in a theatrical release, a film also needs to be rated, and it needs the right kind of rating. As John Fithian, president and CEO of the National Association of Theatre Owners, explains, "Theatre operators generally treat unrated pictures as they would movies rated NC-17, by not allowing anyone under 18 to view those pictures" (3). In the top-twenty group, *March of the Penguins, Justin Bieber: Never Say Never, Earth, Chimpanzee, Oceans, African Cats,* and *Winged Migration* were rated G; *2016: Obama's America, Katy Perry: Part of Me, An Inconvenient Truth, Mad Hot Ballroom,* and *Expelled: No Intelligence Required* were rated PG; *Sicko, Super Size Me,* and *Hoop Dreams* were rated PG-13; and *Fahrenheit 9/11, Bowling for Columbine, Madonna: Truth or Dare, Capitalism: A Love Story,* and *Religulous* were rated R. There is no NC-17 or unrated film in the top twenty. That pattern parallels theatrical grosses in general: figures from 1995 to 2011 show that PG-13 films secure about 45 percent of the box office, G-rated films about 5 percent, PG films about 20 percent, and R-rated films about 29 percent. The remaining 1 percent covers films rated NC-17, films rated NC-17 but distributed as unrated, and films never submitted to the MPAA for rating ("Top-Grossing").

For a study of food in film, it is significant that unrated movies make up less than 1 percent of the box office, for films like *The Corporation, FLOW: For Love of Water, King Corn, The Future of Food, We Feed the World,* and *The End of the Line* were never submitted to the MPAA for rating. The DVDs for *The Corporation* and *The Future of Food* are identified as not rated, while the other films do not mention that they are unrated. This unrated status significantly affects circulation in the marketplace, for, as noted earlier, theaters "treat unrated pictures as they would movies rated NC-17, by not allowing anyone under 18 to view those pictures" (Fithian 3). Thus, makers of food documentaries forgo a wide audience in theaters.

That choice does not arise from some prohibitive cost to getting a film rated. The fees collected by the MPAA for rating films are $3,000 for films with production budgets up to $500,000; $5,000 for productions up to $5 million; $8,000 for films up to $15 million; $15,000 for films up to $40 million; $20,000 for films up to $75 million; and $25,000 for films over $75 million (Classification). Given the comparatively low costs for rating films with small budgets, other factors lead filmmakers to focus on alternative distribution channels. One of those is the food industry's threat of legal action against a film's distributor. To protect the large investment in the print and advertising campaigns required for even modest theatrical exhibition, film distributors make a pragmatic assessment: because of the food industry's clout and its willingness to litigate, filmmakers set on even a modest theatrical release must have already devoted extensive financial resources to legal counsel. As noted in Chapter 2, the legal fees during the production of *Food, Inc.* were higher than the combined cost of the legal expenses for Kenner's previous fifteen films (Golding), but because they had the financial resources, the team behind *Food, Inc.* determined that legal clearance for the documentary was a good investment. While any film released has the potential to get caught in litigation, one thing is certain: a film will not be picked up for even modest distribution unless a distributor is assured that the filmmakers' legal team has anticipated or blocked all legal challenges that might jeopardize the distributor's investment. Filmmakers who cannot give distributors that guarantee use non-theatrical distribution venues as their primary means of reaching audiences.

Food Companies' Evolving Public Relations Policies

Documentaries submitted for rating by the MPAA have circulated more successfully in the media marketplace. The top two food documentaries in box office receipts are *Super Size Me*, rated PG-13 for "language, sex and drug references, and a graphic medical procedure," and *Food, Inc.*, rated PG for "some thematic material and disturbing images." Yet even with the MPAA's seal of approval, neither film had a wide release, and their box office figures pale in comparison to industry-backed feature films.

There are about 6,000 theaters in the domestic box office market ("Statistics"). Thus, during its initial release, there were days when *Shrek 2* (Adamson, Asbury, and Vernon, 2004), the top-grossing film of 2004 ($441 million), was in more than 70 percent of North American (U.S. and Canadian) theaters (4,223 theaters). By comparison, that same year, even at its widest release, *Super Size Me* ($11 million, or a box office rank of 138 for the year) was in fewer than 4 percent of the theaters in the North American market, or 230 theaters. The story is much the same half a decade later regarding *Food, Inc.* and the highest grossing film of that year, *Avatar,* which played in over 3,400 theaters and raked in $749 million. Other top-grossing films also dominated the box office: during the opening weekend of *Avatar,* the same fifty-three films were showing in more than half the theaters in the North American market. Nine films were in more than 4,000 theaters and forty-four films were in more than 3,000. By comparison, *Food, Inc.,* which earned $4 million and ranked number 164 in box office among 2009 films, opened in eight theaters, or 0.1 percent of all the theaters in the United States and Canada; the film's widest release (155 theaters) represented about 3 percent of the theaters in North America.

Morgan Spurlock's approach in *Super Size Me* is patterned after Michael Moore's provocateur methods. The film delivers an entertaining but appalling snapshot of fast-food habits in consumer society. While obesity has doubled in the United States since 1980, every day one in four Americans eats fast food. McDonald's commands 43 percent of that business with franchises worldwide and more eating establishments in Manhattan than anywhere else in the world. Prompted by these statistics, Spurlock embarked on a one-month experiment in which he ate nothing but McDonald's food. The experiment included four rules: Spurlock had to eat only what was on the menu; he could not opt to super-size unless it was offered; he had to eat every menu item at least once during the month-long experiment; and he had to eat three meals a day. Before beginning the experiment, Spurlock consulted with doctors, a nutritionist, and an exercise cardiologist. During the month, he had his weight, cholesterol, triglycerides, blood pressure, and other bodily functions monitored. The results were shocking:

in one month Spurlock gained over 24 pounds on his 6'2", 185-pound frame.

Reiterating the dire consequences of the hundredfold increase over the past half-century in empty calorie snack and drinks, John Seabrook notes that "one study cited by federal health officials estimates that, in 2008, obesity cost the U.S. a hundred and forty-seven billion dollars in health-care charges and resulted in about three hundred thousand deaths" (56). Spurlock's film makes those statistics tangible, showing that his cholesterol increased sixty-five points; his percentage of body fat went from 11 to 18 percent; his chance of heart disease doubled; and his liver function was altered. Spurlock shows that on several occasions throughout the month, doctors advised him to stop the experiment.

Like his 2011 film *The Greatest Movie Ever Sold, Super Size Me* features an insightful analysis of advertising ploys. It also echoes Michael Moore's approach, as Spurlock makes repeated attempts throughout the film to get McDonald's spokespersons to take his calls. McDonald's, however, had learned by this time that it is financially prudent to ignore critics. In fact, the financial and critical success of *Super Size Me* is best understood in light of the twenty-year David-and-Goliath battle between transnational corporation McDonald's and individual London Greenpeace members Helen Steel and Dave Morris, who came to be known as the McLibel Two after they decided to defend themselves in a legal battle now regarded as one of the most spectacular public relations failures in corporate history.

By 2004 McDonald's had determined that litigation against whistle blowers who identified shortcomings in the company's products, management policies, and advertising approaches actually increased damaging exposure, drawing attention to the unhealthy nature of McDonald's food and its negative impact on the people who work and eat at its franchises. Marketing experts have noted that the legal action McDonald's took against Steel and Morris was ill advised because with "180 witnesses called to the stand, the company endured humiliation after humiliation as the court heard stories of food poisoning, failure to pay legal overtime, bogus recycling claims and corporate spies sent to infiltrate the ranks of London Greenpeace" ("Brand PR Failures"). While Steel and Morris's "original pamphlet [has] become a cult collector's item . . . very few people would now know about the contents of that pamphlet if McDonald's hadn't taken the matter to court" ("Brand PR Failures"). The case is the subject of John Vidal's book *McLibel: Burger Culture on Trial* (1997); there have been TV programs about the trial, including a three-hour dramatization on the BBC's Channel 4; and the trial is discussed in Naomi Klein's book *No Logo* (1999) ("Brand PR Failures").

Franny Armstrong and Ken Loach's unrated film *McLibel*, completed in 1998 and updated in 2005, takes audiences through the personal, legal, and cultural aspects of the case as it developed from 1986, when the "What's Wrong with McDonald's" leaflets were first distributed, to 2005, when the European Court of Human Rights found that the United Kingdom's libel case against gardener Helen Steel and postman Dave Morris breached their right to a fair trial and their right to freedom of speech. The film traces the downward trajectory of McDonald's public profile from 1990, when it filed its libel suit against Steel and Morris; to 1996, when the McLibel Two posted court transcripts on their "McSpotlight" website; to 1997, when the British court decision made it possible for McDonald's to claim victory even as it lost public credibility; to 2002, when McDonald's began to shut down franchises throughout the world; and finally to 2005, when McDonald's health, safety, and labor infractions were exposed again in the course of the European Court's examination of British libel laws. With the audience for *Super Size Me* already primed by the twenty-year McLibel case, McDonald's prudently determined that it would be unwise to do anything that would increase media attention to Spurlock's food documentary. The corporation's calculation was correct; the film reached theatrical audiences, but its $11 million box office was but 2 percent of *Shrek 2*'s $441 million gross.

Corporate Policies That Shape Public Taste

The vast disparity between the market share captured by *Super Size Me* and *Shrek 2* is a sign of their contrasting input costs. On any weekend, films backed by huge capital investment control the reception context. For example, *Food, Inc.* opened the same weekend as *The Taking of Pelham 1 2 3*, the R-rated Denzel Washington–John Travolta action remake (which ranked third in box office for the weekend), and *Imagine That*,

Opening Weekend Box Office for New Releases, June 12–14, 2009

Film	Weekend Gross	Number of Theaters	Box Office Rank, Opening Weekend
The Taking of Pelham 1 2 3	$23,373,102	3,074	3
Imagine That	$5,503,519	3,008	6
Moon	$136,046	8	25
Food, Inc.	$60,513	3	35
Street Dreams	$45, 816	21	38
Youssou N'Dour	$32,598	3	46
Tetro	$30,504	2	48

Source: BoxOfficeMojo.com

the PG-rated Eddie Murphy family film (ranked sixth). The other slots in the top ten that weekend were films already in wide release (*The Hangover, Up, Night at the Museum,* and *Land of the Lost,* playing in over 3,000 theaters, and *Star Trek, Terminator Salvation, Angels & Demons,* and *Drag Me to Hell,* playing in over 2,000), each fueled by massive print and advertising budgets.

Opening weekend box office figures matter. They are interpreted as an indication of a film's "predicted theatrical revenue"; opening weekend numbers are also seen as "a partial determinant" of a film's value in the television and home video markets (Drake 64). The small opening-weekend grosses for *Super Size Me* and *Food, Inc.* thus not only ensured there would be only limited additional investment by distributors during their theatrical release period; it also meant that the film's value as a commodity in ancillary markets such as DVD and broadcast and cable television would drop.

One might ask why the independent distributor for *Super Size Me,* IDP (Samuel Goldwyn and Roadside Attractions), did not invest the $70 million needed to secure a strong opening weekend and, thus, a strong afterlife in ancillary markets. And why would independent distributor Magnolia (owned by billionaires Todd Wagner and Mark

Cuban) not invest the $70 million that might have led to a big box office for *Food, Inc.*? For either company, the decision to put a film into wide release would have been a departure from their regular business plans. It is likely that the distributors did not see marketable qualities in the films, and that they imagined they would not recoup a reasonable return for their investment. The films did not feature iconic talent (compare Michael Moore in *Fahrenheit 9/11* and other films, or Justin Bieber or Katy Perry in their respective films, or TV celebrity Bill Maher in *Religulous,* or Madonna in *Madonna: Truth or Dare,* or even Al Gore in *An Inconvenient Truth*); nor did they promise the heart-warming entertainment of Disney nature films. While the reasoning behind a distributor's decision to limit investment in a film's release could be reasonable from an economic standpoint, it also amounts to censorship that is not seen as censorship, because it is "sanctioned by the 'profit principle'" (Jansen 15).

The prediction that a film distributor might make about what will attract consumers (because it is not boring or offensive to important segments of the audience) has been shaped by decades of industry practice. As we have discussed, the film industry's unpublicized censorship policies are a response to the demands of powerful constituencies, which early on understood that films depicting problems in the free market system were "more threatening [to their profits] than cinematic displays of sex and violence" (Ross 87–88). And as also noted earlier, by the mid-1920s film executives knew that they needed to control film content because local censorship boards had shown they would stop exhibition of "features or newsreels that criticized capitalists" (Ross 196). The result of the film industry's censorship activities is that today, fueled by investments based on distributors' expectations about profitable films and consumers' acquired taste for that product, the top-grossing food film is something as far from the food documentaries as possible. With a domestic box office of $206 million, an international theatrical box office of $414 million, and a DVD sales record of $189 million, that prize goes to the Disney-Pixar release *Ratatouille.*

To some degree, increasingly visible problems in the food system have led to debates about causes and solutions. However, governments, institutions like the World Bank, and the corporations in control of the global food system see mistakes, such as E. coli in Nestlé Toll House cookie dough (June 2009), as minor glitches in an industrial system that generates a huge volume of product and substantial profits for shareholders. From their perspective, more and better food will result from new technology, scientific breakthroughs, and continued unfettered operation in a free-market economic system. By comparison, critics of the corporate food system, like Lester R. Brown, founder of the Earth Policy Institute, emphasize that the industrial food system's devastating environmental effects and continued depletion of resources will lead to the end of civilization (Brown *"Could"*). Building on that perspective to articulate solutions, groups like Food First point out that in an era of "mounting agricultural surpluses," millions are already going hungry; countering the corporate proposal that increased production is the solution, they stress the need for "resource redistribution" and "a more equitable economic system" (Belasco, *Meals to Come* ix).

However, critics of the practices used by ConAgra, Vivendi, Cargill, and other food industry giants do not control the food system that consumers depend on. Moreover, critics of the food system do not have working relationships with media giants like TimeWarner, Disney, Viacom, and News Corp. As a consequence, even well-placed critics have not changed the stockholder-safe picture of food that masks out the labor and real costs of food procurement, preservation, distribution, and disposal. The illusion that consumer society food products originate in pristine meadows and amber waves of grain was sustained even by a supposedly liberal PBS program like *The News Hour with Jim Lehrer:* when its corporate sponsors were credited, viewers saw bucolic images of farmland as they heard the announcer's warm but authoritative voice explain that the program had been made possible by "ADM, supermarket to the world."

The film industry's practice of eliding the unseemly aspects of agribusiness is consistent with its profit-motivated decisions to ignore government and corporate mismanagement. In the case of food representations, the tradition is encouraged by lucrative co-promotion deals with fast-food companies. It is also bolstered by risk management policies that lead film companies to steer clear of laws that give food producers and manufacturers the right to sue whistle blowers and make it illegal to picket, boycott, or engage in any investigations that might affect the profits of a factory farm or research facility that conducts experiments on animals.

Food Documentaries Bridge the Divide between Food Producers and Consumers

Food documentaries challenge policies protecting corporate agribusiness, for they consistently emphasize that food and film companies have a stake in ensuring that farmers and consumers do not recognize their common ground. Commercial media increases the gap between food producers and consumers by giving agribusiness a forum for discrediting consumer advocates. In the absence of alternative views and information, farmers, who are in massive debt and thus beholden to their suppliers and distributors, can be persuaded that opponents of big agriculture are outside agitators bent on destroying farmers' livelihood. With most depictions of the food system coming from film companies accustomed to working with the food industry, consumers who depend on the fast food that film companies co-promote are persuaded that reliance on "cheap" food and technology is the only reasonable course of action.

By recirculating rhetoric that pits rural communities against urban dwellers, food companies silence opposition to public policies that benefit giants like Nestlé, Monsanto, and DuPont, which profit from but do not engage in the actual activity of farming, ranching, or fishing. For example, Farm Policy Facts, an umbrella group supported by sugar, corn, wheat, cotton, milk, sorghum, and rice trade associations, begins its four-part discussion of challenges to the American farmer by stating: "Nowadays, it's pretty difficult to get a mainstream news organization to pay much attention to the business of farming or the importance of the profession to the country. Big-city reporters today tend to focus on the sensational and the conflicts created by a handful of over-zealous farm opponents" ("TIME Flies: Part 1"). Trade organizations that reasonably see their interests aligning with the corporations that control seed supplies, herbicide and pesticide input products, processing plants, distribution routes, and government policy also silence opponents to the industrial food system by reactivating rhetoric from the U.S. wars in Vietnam, the Persian Gulf, and Iraq that equates objections to policy decisions with attacks on individuals. Echoing the idea that criticism of policy makers' war plans is tantamount to an attack on soldiers in the field, Farm Policy Facts tells readers that agriculture's "opponents" lead people to believe that "most farmers are raking in the big bucks," and that farmers now face even greater challenges than in the past because "a group of well-heeled vocal extremists from opposite ends of the political spectrum have turned their [sights] on America's farmers" ("TIME Flies: Part 2"; "TIME Flies: Part 4").

However, in contrast to commercial cinema, documentaries do not ignore farmers' contributions. They do not intimate that farmers are getting rich. They do not present farmers in an unsympathetic light. Instead, documentaries like *We Feed the World* and *Our Daily Bread* (*Unser täglich Brot*) aim to convey the complexities of food procurement to people who are removed from these practices. Addressing the reality that now only a small percentage of people are involved in food production, documentaries illustrate the labor of food producers and the practices that lead toward and away from actual consumption.

While food laborers are ignored by the mainstream, food documentaries demonstrate a respect for the people who work in food

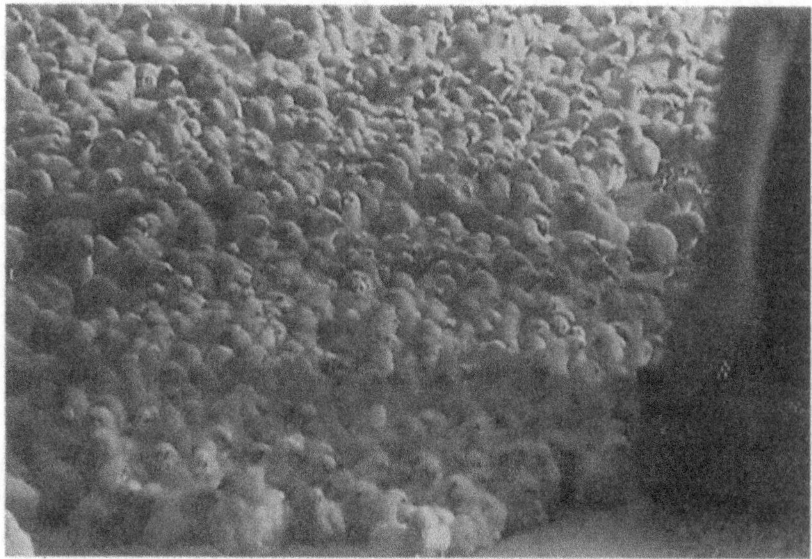

We Feed the World *(Allegro Film): By showing routine food production, the film reveals what modern consumers do not know about the industrial practices that make "cheap" food possible.*

procurement, preservation, preparation, presentation, cleanup, and disposal. *King Corn,* a 2007 release directed by Aaron Woolf, follows fellow filmmakers Ian Cheney and Curt Ellis during a year in which they plant an acre of corn on land they lease from Chuck Pyatt, who owns a farm near the small town of Greene, Iowa. Cheney and Ellis, who became friends in college in Boston, decide to embark on the adventure in Iowa after discovering that their grandfathers had both come from the Greene area. Taking a low-key approach that echoes the work of Les Blank rather than the confrontational style of Michael Moore or Morgan Spurlock, Woolf, Cheney, and Ellis establish a way for audiences who access the world through media to see the farmers in the Greene area as regular people who go quietly and efficiently about the business of food procurement and have a wry sense of humor, even though they find themselves in a largely untenable economic situation.

With capable assistance from members of the farming community, the filmmakers take care of their farm subsidy paperwork and get their acre of corn planted, sprayed (with fertilizer, insecticide, and herbicide), harvested, and delivered to the grain elevator. After discovering that their commodity crop corn is not edible, the filmmakers locate likely destinations for their acre of corn. With most of the corn used as animal feed, they visit a CAFO, a Concentrated Animal Feeding Operation; with a percentage of the corn likely destined for a corn sweetener plant, the filmmakers explore the health implications of corn syrup used as an ingredient in most of what consumers eat and drink.

The next year, Cheney and Ellis return to Greene for an auction that carries special weight because the equipment being sold belongs to Pyatt, the man who had leased the acre of land to them. Determined to keep the harvest of one acre from becoming sweetener or cattle feed, the filmmakers lease the acre again, but this time they plant grass. The film ends with a quiet scene that shows Cheney and Ellis playing baseball, one pitching and the other at bat, on the acre that is now a clearly defined field of grass set within the surrounding expanse of corn. For audiences who have seen *Field of Dreams* (Robinson, 1989), the image is reminiscent of the fictional Iowa farmer (Kevin Costner) who set out on the insane project of building a baseball diamond in his cornfield because he heard a voice say, "If you build it, they will come." *King Corn* shows that the current agricultural system is taking a toll on farmers and consumers. However, the film's final scene is a gentle invitation. By ending with an image of their own "field of dreams," the filmmakers express their hope that audiences will come with them as they explore alternatives to high-input agriculture.

While a mild-mannered statement, *King Corn* offers strong criticism of the status quo. The local Greene farmers candidly explain that they are "growing crap," and interviews with author Michael Pollan identify problems with the industrial food system's focus on commodity crops. Yet the film identifies those problems as existing within an evolving historical context. It gives audiences some sense of that context by including archival television footage of Earl Butz, the secretary of agriculture from 1971 to 1976, announcing his decision to replace New Deal farm policies with ones beneficial to large-scale commodity farming.

The film also includes an interview in which Cheney and Ellis politely ask Butz to reflect on his decisions as secretary of agriculture. Butz cites the low cost of food made possible by increased crop yields, and the filmmakers illustrate the merits of this position by looking back

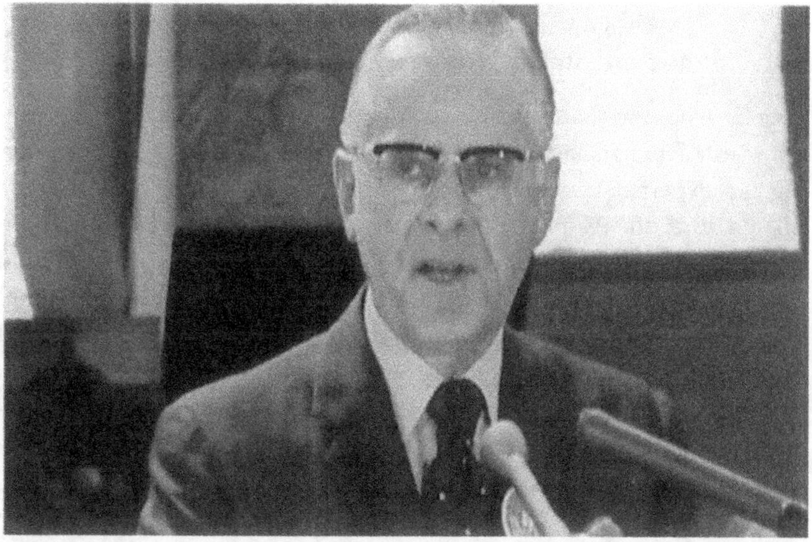

King Corn *(ITVS, Mosaic Films): Agriculture Secretary Earl Butz was known for telling farmers in the 1970s to "get big or get out" and to plant commodity crops "from fencerow to fencerow."*

at the enormous labor their grandfathers invested to produce decidedly smaller yields. At the same time, the film illustrates that Butz does not reckon with the increasing input costs for fertilizer, insecticide, and herbicide, the decreasing income from production of commodity crops, and the increased cost of seed that now has to be purchased each year because it is patented.

The filmmakers explain that in contrast to their grandfathers, today's farmers are not able to feed themselves with the crops they grow. The situation is troubling: "America no longer grows enough edible fruits and vegetables for everyone to eat our own government's recommended five servings a day" (Bittman, *Food Matters* 23). Instead, corn "accounts for 27 percent of the harvested crops in the United States" and soy accounts for another 25 percent (Bittman, *Food Matters* 25). What's more, almost all of that goes to feed livestock. With this in mind, *King Corn* takes *consumers* step by step through the stages of foodways, showing that America has allowed its heartland to become something quite different from the bucolic world of the family farm (Berry; Jackson and Jackson).

Alternative Channels of Distribution for Documentaries' Representations of Foodways

King Corn demonstrates that food documentaries can respect the workers whose labor makes it possible for consumers to eat while challenging the expertise and authority food companies claim in all matters related to food. By presenting views that do not square with those of agribusiness, the documentaries create an occasion in which food companies are compelled to invoke their "right" to discredit material that might hinder shareholder and executive profits. Moreover, food documentaries sometimes feature representations of food practices that pose public relations and legal problems even for the food industry. For example, audiences could not easily dismiss footage of piglets being "slammed up against [a] post and tossed into [a] bucket still in their death throes" in *Death on a Factory Farm* (Simon and Teale, 2009) ("Interview"). The film, which first aired on HBO on 16 March 2009, features this and other footage from an undercover investigation of the Wiles Hog Farm near Creston, Ohio. The investigation led to indictments against owner Ken Wiles and others; while the charges of animal cruelty were ultimately dismissed, the court called for an end to the practices that had led to the indictments.

Films that engage youth audiences by using appealing, computer-generated imagery and familiar images from popular culture also present public relations problems for the food industry. *The Meatrix* (Louis Fox, 2003) is the first of several animated stories. In all of them Leo (a pig) fights back against the agents of the industrial food system after Moopheus (a cow) shows him the reality behind the illusion of the "meatrix," which is "the story we tell ourselves about where our meat and animal products come from." Running less than four minutes, the exposé covers animal cruelty, antibiotic-resistant germs, massive pollution, and the demise of farming communities. Available on the Free Range website and YouTube, *The Meatrix* and its sequels aim to shatter the illusion created by the mainstream food and media industries. Videos documenting animal cruelty at slaughterhouses and factory farms are also widely available on the web, one of the preferred alternative outlets for food documentaries that do not have access to large-scale distribution.

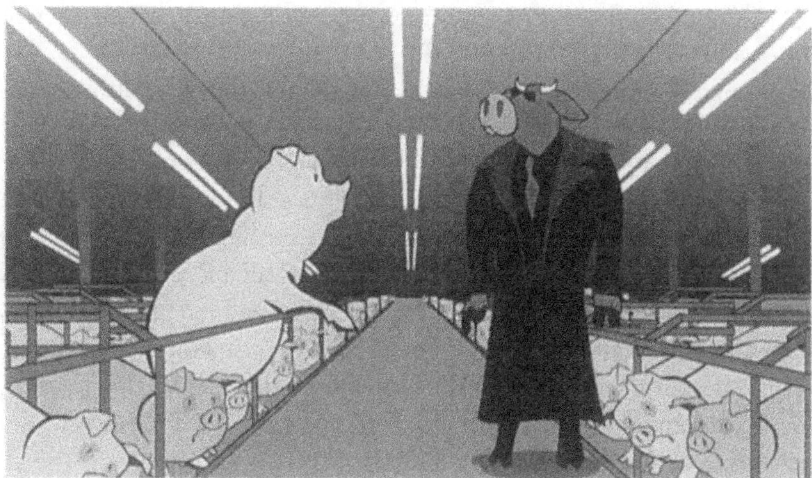

The Meatrix *(Free Range Studios, Sustainable Table): This web film has been seen by millions and is one of many Free Range pieces designed to foster support for sustainable food practices.*

In addition, documentary filmmakers develop production and distribution partnerships for their works. For instance, the team behind Shelley Rogers's 2010 film *What's "Organic" about Organic?* started a website and blog early in the production process in order to raise funds and create a buzz about their film before its release. When the film was completed, they expanded its reach through "screen and green events" with companies and organizations looking to expand interest in the organic movement ("Call for Outreach"). Federal programs and professional organizations like the University Film and Video Association provide screening opportunities for food documentaries. For example, the American Documentary Showcase, an international touring showcase organized by the U.S. Department of State's Bureau of Education and Cultural Affairs, selected *The Garden* (Kennedy, 2008) and *The New Frontier: Sustainable Ranching in the American West* (Levin and Klavner, 2010). Documentary filmmakers also generate publicity using organizations that support sustainable agriculture, healthy and nutritious food, worker and animal rights, the environment, children's safety, and people's access to clean and affordable water ("Issues"). For instance, house parties organized by Food and Water Watch let people know about *Food, Inc.* and *FLOW: For Love of Water.* Food documentaries also reach viewers involved in the network of food movements such as the Community Food Security Movement and the School Food Movement (Nestle ix).

Many documentaries are made available by Bullfrog Films, established in 1973 by John Hoskyns-Abrahall and Winifred Scherrer. Media-Rights.org is an online commons for social issue documentaries. The site, created by Katy Chevigny and Julia Pimsleur (founders of Arts Engine and Big Mouth Films), provides a venue for films about sustainable agriculture. Food documentaries are made available on DVD by the Ironweed Film Club, which distributes shorts and independent films. Documentaries about foodways are in the DVD catalog of Docurama, a distributor of "cutting-edge" documentaries since 1999. The Independent Documentary Association and the Hot Docs Film Festival also showcase documentaries about foodways.

For decades, alternative exhibition venues have made it possible for audiences to encounter representations at odds with ideological positions promoted by the commercial production-distribution-exhibition system. As Jonathan Kahana notes, filmmakers' use of Google Video, the Internet Archive, and "narrowcast" via networks of satellite-dish operators builds on the longstanding practice of showing "non-commercial" films at festivals, on public-access cable television, and in the "specialty theaters of documentary's heyday, the proverbial church basements, union halls, classrooms, student unions, co-ops, pubs, barracks, and living rooms of non-theatrical film and video distribution" (3; see 328–31). Like other non-commercial films, food documentaries may acquire their significance over time. For instance, even though *American Dream* (Kopple, 1990) gained some recognition when it received the Academy Award for Best Documentary, the film's account of union meat packers locked out by Hormel in 1985–86 might reach more viewers and acquire deeper significance as it comes to be seen as one of many documentaries on the politics of the food system. Retrospective consideration of food documentaries might also lead audiences to recognize the central role women filmmakers have played in documentaries about foodways.

Cultural Politics Surrounding Films' Representations of Foodways

Given the food and film industries' influence in the production-distribution-exhibition system, could any films change consumers' thoughts and feelings about food and the industrial food system? Can small-scale productions that examine all aspects of foodways lead consumers to think or behave in ways that are inconsistent with representations in heavily promoted films? Can films prompt mainstream consumers to see that the apparent variety in the movies that people see most of the time is like the illusion of choice offered at supermarkets and fast-food outlets? How could films that identify problems in the food system have any appeal in today's reception context? Movies without the familiar elements of sex, violence, and happy endings are oddities at best. Just as people grow up learning to speak certain languages, today consumers grow up in a media culture that leads people to search for and expect the pleasure films can provide, whether that emerges from watching something "edgy" or being satisfied by the story's outcome.

Is it possible for even a wave of related documentaries to affect people's choices when there is no public consensus about the way food and water resources should be used? The mismatch between facts and perceptions never has a simple explanation. Tangible scientific evidence documents the crisis in food and water resources, yet divergent views contest that evidence. Some futurists "are confident that the current way of producing and distributing food will take care of the future. Others see the status quo as a sure route to disaster" (Belasco, *Meals to Come* viii). Similarly, "while many in government, academia, and industry look to new tools . . . to feed us tomorrow without any modification of our modern high-consumption values, others propose low-tech alternatives organized around smaller scale, localized food systems dependent on a return to more traditional appreciation of limits" (Belasco, *Meals to Come* viii).

People's perceptions about the future of food and water are colored by their experiences, cultural identities, and economic status. Yet today perceptions are also shaped in unprecedented ways by the form and content of media culture. As Raymond Williams explains, in industrialized regions, media culture began to eclipse a culture of literacy in the mid-twentieth century. Once television became part of daily life, watching others perform was no longer an occasional experience, and people's immersion in "the flow of action and acting" led to "a need for images, for representations, of what living is . . . like, for this kind of person and that, in this situation and that" (6). With complex ideas embedded in formulaic stories and with evidentiary claims transformed into exciting struggles between opposing characters, the conventions and the technology that allowed people to care about events beyond the confines of their homes also became the basis for a systematically distorted dramatization of politics and personal consumption. While movies create connections for people who feel cut off from the outside world, the drama and the news from elsewhere is programmed by institutional powers. Mainstream media thus does not deliver material for "free-floating contemplation" but instead supplies product that most effectively enhances corporate profit (Benjamin 226).

Like other non-commercial films released in recent decades, films about foodways represent a response to the increasingly "concentrated ownership of news media, the corporatization and trivialization of the news, and the decreasing spectrum of information" (McEnteer xii). With the films' views at odds with food companies, it is doubly certain that they will be required to use alternative distribution channels, for the film industry necessarily restricts distribution of films that contain overt criticism of other industries or the free enterprise system. Hollywood publicizes its efforts to protect children from sex and violence even as it pumps out titillating sex and myriad scenes of graphic violence; its actual, ongoing policies of political censorship ensure that films like *Fast Food Nation,* with its limited release by Fox Searchlight, and *Super Size Me,* with its limited release by Samuel Goldwyn and Roadside Attractions, are the exceptions that prove the rule.

Even though censorship might not seem relevant to studies of food in film, keeping films that challenge industrial food practices out of mainstream circulation has an unquantifiable effect on consumer behavior and public policy. With tantalizing depictions of cooking and eating dominating mainstream media, personal choices and government policies will likely fail to consider what happens before food gets to the supermarket and after it leaves the restaurant table. Without well-publicized debates between World Bank administrators, who back "free-market capitalism and biotechnology," and people at Food First, who see "resource redistribution as the solution to hunger," consumers' perceptions of food, water, and environmental realities will be based on scenarios and narratives crafted by powerful institutions (Belasco, *Meals to Come,* ix). In consumer society, people make uninformed decisions about food because "food companies use every means at their disposal—legal, regulatory, and societal—to create and protect an environment that is conducive to selling their products" (Nestle 93). The film industry contributes to that environment by assigning documentaries about foodways to the margins. Food documentaries' minuscule market share is a reminder that film companies profit by co-promoting fast-food consumption. Their box office numbers provide a window into the politics of food in film.

9

Food as a Window into Personal and Cultural Politics

Food documentaries examine the material economy of food by exploring the full arc of foodways, from extraction to production to distribution to consumption and then on to disposal. Yet Hollywood sidelines film products that fail to promote the mainstream vision of food as an expendable consumer product. Their limited distribution reveals the politics that prompt profit-driven films to deliver a circumscribed picture of food that emphasizes consumption rather than labor and immediate pleasure rather than long-term consequence. By making those naturalized choices more visible, the foodways lens provides a window into American national cinema.

To illustrate how foodways analysis facilitates insights into American and other national cinemas, this final chapter briefly discusses films from several national cinemas. It also looks at two films that show how American consumer society contrasts with both traditional and alternative (food) cultures: *Mr. Saturday Night* examines the intersection of food, gender, and ethnicity; *Mysterious Skin* uses characters' interaction with consumer culture food to convey the promise and anxiety of desire, seduction, and sexuality. As with the book's other examples that reveal how foodways analysis contributes to ideological studies, these films show that personal food beliefs and behaviors are joined to cultural norms and values, and that, to varying degrees, personal food choices mirror or challenge dominant beliefs and practices.

The chapter closes by considering two essay films, *The Gleaners and I* and *How to Cook Your Life*, that communicate the countercuisine's vision that a person's relationship to food is both personal and political. That vision contrasts sharply with the consumer society ideas that food is a commodity to be purchased for personal pleasure and that personal food choices have no political importance. Yet from the 1970s forward, countercuisine proponents have emphasized that food has aesthetic, cultural, and economic dimensions. As the essay films reveal, the wide vista of activities surrounding food vividly reflects individuals' and societies' fundamental values.

Despite commercial media's mystification of everything beyond the frame of convenient food consumption, personal choices about food are political. Cultural and ideological studies of film can use that insight to examine films' representational politics. They can work with the idea that food behavior is both personal and political to explore questions surrounding identity politics and the effects of economic structures of power. Films' depictions of food are pertinent to analyses of gender and sexuality, because, as food scholars explain, "one of the most significant domains of meaning embodied in food centers on the relation between the sexes, their gender definitions, and their sexuality" (Counihan, *Anthropology* 9). Food provides a window into other aspects of identity and other structures of power because "race, class, nation, and personhood" are expressed all "through food production and food consumption" (Counihan and Van Esterik 5).

Food, Identity, and Nation

National cinemas have been considered from a range of perspectives, demonstrating the value of analyzing films in relation to countries' unique cultures and histories.[1] As Wimal Dissanayake proposes, "How a nation tells its unifying and legitimizing story to its citizens is exceedingly important in the understanding of nationhood, and, in modern times, the role of cinema in this endeavor has come to occupy a central place" (xiv). Looking at films' depictions of foodways clarifies cinema's role in that process by showing what food and food behaviors reveal about personal and cultural identities. Characters' cuisine choices and their relationships to food production, distribution, consumption, and cleanup shed light on films' "construction of national identity" (Counihan and Van Esterik 5). Food functions as a sign of personal, cultural, and national identities, so films' representations of food and food behaviors provide a window into personal and political domains.

Films' representations of food can suggest authentic national or local identity. Food also provides a means for depicting global intrusion or for revealing other facets of character and country. As Carole Counihan and Penny Van Esterik note, "The contested transformation of [local or national] cuisine," along with the prevalence of "cultural food colonialism" in industrialized countries, reflects cross-cultural contact and globalization (5). Given that environment, films' depictions of food sometimes reveal the effects of the transnational marketplace. A rise in multinational film production exists alongside increased debates about the effects of globalization and multiculturalism in a transnational, even post-national world. Essentialist notions of national cinema have evolved into more nuanced concepts in the transnational era without causing an end to national cinema studies that yield rich insights into the formal, thematic, economic, aesthetic, and cultural characteristics of a country.

Foodways analysis can unlock the traditions, social practices, and cultural politics of countries. From the ordinary to the ostentatious, the traditional to the taboo, food provides a window into a country's dominant climatic environments, accumulated historical influences, and pervasive religious principles. As Counihan points out, "Food is a product and mirror of the organization of society on both the broadest and most intimate levels, . . . a prism that absorbs and reflects a host of cultural phenomena" (*Anthropology* 6). Foodways analysis can locate shared cultural practices and identify a variety of warring, often suppressed issues. In its essence, foodways communicates culture and provides a useful means for cross-cultural analysis.

While cultures share some "beliefs and behaviors surrounding the production, distribution, and consumption of food" (Counihan, *Anthropology* 6), each national cinema reveals its unique intersection of country and culinary values and practices. Representations of food in cross-cultural remakes offer a useful window into a nation's culture and cinema. For instance, *Eat Drink Man Woman* illuminates social pressures in contemporary Taiwanese culture and the strategies its art cinema has used to reach international audiences. By comparison, the remake *Tortilla Soup* is a glossy Hollywood film about a Mexican American family in Los Angeles. This production illustrates the U.S. film industry's formulas for commercial success that involve remaking successful films and testing the waters to reach growing market segments such as the U.S. Hispanic population.

Food films with close connections to their production context illuminate their social and political environment. The propaganda film *Earth* (Dovzhenko, 1930), set in the Ukraine, gives poetic form to Soviet policies to replace private landownership with collective farming. By comparison, *Our Daily Bread* dramatizes American New Deal efforts to combine private enterprise and government support. Scenes of food preparation in commercial U.S. productions like *No Reservations* will have a very different tone and message from ones produced by Third Cinema filmmakers. Whereas shiny upscale kitchens and stories of personal fulfillment are the stylistic and thematic center of commercial food films, earthen colors and the pragmatic demands of subsistence living are integral to the understated scenes of food preparation in Haile Gerima's *Harvest: 3,000 Years* (1976).

Food documentaries often explore cultural and economic developments specific to a country or region. For example, *Bitter Seeds* (Peled, 2011) is set in India, a nation that leads the world in the number of working farmers. The introduction and dominance of Monsanto's genetically engineered cottonseeds has hurt cotton farmers because so many tend small acreage. Required to purchase seeds each year, one low-yield season means disaster for the farmers who cannot secure the loans needed to invest in the next year's crop. The dire situation has contributed to a high suicide rate. Anchored by the investigation of a young female journalist whose father committed suicide, *Bitter Seeds* describes the agrarian problems in India and the cultural norms and values that surround this tragedy.

Taking a celebratory approach, the documentary *Jiro Dreams of Sushi* (Gelb, 2011) interweaves multiple threads of Japanese culture as it profiles eighty-five-year-old Jiro Ono. Jiro has dreamed of sushi since he began his apprenticeship at age ten. He runs Sukiyabashi Jiro, a ten-seat, sushi-only restaurant at a Tokyo subway stop where a twenty-sushi meal costs about $300 and requires a month's wait for a reservation. Jiro's restaurant enjoys a three-star Michelin rating, the only establishment of its type to have that designation. After seventy years, Jiro continues to work daily to achieve the perfect sushi that he still aspires to realize.

Jiro embodies the Japanese concept of *shokunin,* an attitude and social consciousness that influences an individual to strive always to learn more in the pursuit of perfection. As Jiro explains, "You have to fall in love with your job. You must dedicate your life to mastering your skill." For his accomplishments, Japan has honored Jiro with the Meijou Award that gives him the status of Japanese national treasure. Jiro's oldest son, fifty-year-old Yoshikazu, follows in his father's footsteps, serving a lengthy apprenticeship, as do several other workers. The film includes scenes with Japanese businessmen who supply Jiro's tuna, shrimp, and other fish. They share this approach to life; one man will sell his rice only to Jiro, knowing no one else would know how to cook it properly. The film presents these perfectionists talking about their lived philosophy.

The unique facets of Japanese culture conveyed by the individuals' relationship to food in *Jiro Dreams of Sushi* are echoed in the food film *Tampopo.* Here, representations of food highlight Japan's reputation for and obsession with exceptional noodles. The film identifies this cuisine preoccupation as uniquely Japanese. It also highlights conventions of Japanese etiquette, for the Japanese practice of loudly slurping noodles to convey culinary appreciation collides with western protocols that require silent consumption. Eating protocols become a vehicle for poking fun at Japan's emphasis on social respect and knowing one's place in the hierarchy; the film highlights the nation's inflexible cultural systems in a scene that shows a company employee transgressing business and food etiquette when he fails to follow the food and drink requests of his superiors.

By comparison, food behavior in *301/302* reflects deep anxieties in South Korean society. The continuing American presence in Korea causes friction to exist over film, music, and food. Given that cultural context, the film's representations reflect local and global influences.

Discussing South Korean national cinema vis-à-vis American cinematic hegemony, David James writes, "In Korea, community and art alike have been caught between an extraordinarily rich array of the preconditions of a national culture and the ruinous negation of them. For Korea, more dramatically than anywhere else, a national cinema has been simultaneously an imperative and an impossibility" ("Preface" 11).[2]

Frances Gateward has shown that the embattled Korean film industry reflects the shifting political fortunes of "what many consider the most dynamic national cinema in the world today" (11). Seung Hyun Park explains that once "Korean filmmakers and companies realized film's value, both as an entertainment commodity and as a medium for symbolic expression," they "cultivated the cultural value of Korean cinema through diverse cinematic themes" (31). *301/302* examines the South Korean national identity conundrum. While the film uses the women's interactions with food to explore social problems that have national and pan-national dimensions, their food disorders suggest analogies with South Korean history. Like films produced in other countries, Korean films comment on historical and contemporary events in allegorical narratives. Rape, greed, unfaithfulness, and obsessive fixation are metaphors for Korea's struggle for independence from colonizers and occupiers. However, the film is not nationalistic; by making Korean dishes seem unappetizing, it presents Korean culture in a negative light.[3]

In *301/302,* the women's food disorders are direct responses to their disabling experiences with men, and so the film's critique exposes the fact that South Korea's "national subjectivity has been exclusively a male subjectivity" throughout "Korea's long history of colonial and neo-colonial domination" (Choi 14). While Korean men have been constructed as "victims of the emasculation of the Korean nation" (Choi 13), as the film suggests, that role has led them to become "complicit with the colonizer in disdaining Korean women" (Choi 17). However, whereas some representations of the new Korean nation have "reinforced the patriarchal gender ideology of male domination" (Choi 20), *301/302* shows that Korean women are put in a double bind. If they embrace the past, they can expect the same kind of treatment they received in their childhoods: cold food rather than warm meals; red meat rather than juice and fruit; isolation and sexual abuse rather than commensality, support, and acceptance. If they try to participate in modern Korea, they are shut out, for Korea's postcolonial nationalism is shaped by the narrative that Korean men are victims of foreign powers and so must subjugate Korean women. Thus, as adults, 301 and 302 remain isolated individuals, even though 301 has embraced modern American food products and 302 has replaced eating with writing.[4]

Reflecting on the disparate threads in contemporary Korean culture, Marian Lief Palley writes: "Though a nation's productive capacity may become modernized, it does not necessarily follow that its social and political values, which have evolved through the centuries, will be completely supplanted" (275). She points out that "the material culture in South Korea has modernized and been affected by Western influences, [but that] its behavioral culture maintains and embraces some Confucian traditions, and it is slow to change" (275). Recognizing the factors that are central to the *301/302* narrative, Palley explains that part of the "behavioral culture [that is slow to change] is reflected in the inequalities of women's roles" (275). Hesung Chun Koh elaborates on that point to explain that "neither the intellectuals nor the general public see [gender] equality as a desirable or necessary goal, because they see no harmful effects from the present inequality" (159).

Identified as women's domain, food preparation and presentation offer a vehicle for conveying the intersection of Korean gender and national dilemmas. Marjorie Baumgarten identifies the overriding concern with equality that pervades 301's and 302's lives; she writes, "As these two unlikely soulmates begin sharing the details of their personal histories, we begin to see how psychological transferences between food, love, sex, and violence are all part of larger feminist issues" (Baumgarten). However, for 301 and 302, translating trauma into food behaviors involves restricted options for liberation. For these frighteningly resistant women, 302's self-destruction and 301's obsessive need to perfect her cooking amount to Pyrrhic victory, for assisted suicide (302) and cannibalism (301) do not seem like choices that lead to equality or fulfillment in any cultural context.[5]

The film might suggest that the most "productive" course of action for women in contemporary Korean society is to embrace anarchic roles designed to destroy the conventions and structures of postcolonial, patriarchal Korean society. It might also express the view that in Korean society, women's lives are so circumscribed that they are forced into impractical, destructive actions. Through its dramatization of 301's and 302's deeply troubled relationship to food, the film illuminates the cultural issues that Korea wrestles with today. Analysis of the film reveals that a look at the beliefs and behaviors surrounding food can enrich studies of national cinemas and national cultures. Food can be a window into personal and national identity, for it "functions effectively as a system of communication because everywhere human beings organize their foodways into an ordered system parallel to other cultural systems" (Counihan, *Anthropology* 20).

Food, Gender, and Ethnicity

Foodways analysis can also contribute to studies of gender and ethnicity. Films' depictions of food and gender warrant inquiry, for as Carole Counihan explains: "In Western culture, women have variously used compulsive eating, obesity, fasting, or the symbolic value of food as a means of expressing themselves and coping with the problems of achieving a meaningful place in a world where they are defined as subordinate" (*Anthropology* 215). Representations of "the Jewish mother" reflect the duality of coping and self-expression that surrounds women's food labor; in Jewish culture, the home-cooked meals that mothers provide for their families are signs of their subordinate status and their importance to the family, its ancestors, and its descendants.

The stereotypical Jewish mother is "presented as an overeating, overcaring, and overbearing matriarchal figure who stuffs her children with far more than they can possibly digest" (Abrams 88). She is thus a figure who warrants subordination and even ridicule. However, because certain foods "are intimately related to Jewish identity and culture" (Abrams 88), and because family members sharing meals of Jewish food is "a key signifier of their difference from the gentile world" (Abrams 97), the Jewish mother's cooking is what unites the family and binds them to their heritage. The traditional dishes that she prepares sustain her family physically and emotionally, for she essentially feeds them their culture. Thus, she is also a figure to be revered and respected.

The Jewish mother's ambiguous status reflects contradictions in Jewish food behavior. Family meals are "an important ritual for Jewish families" (Abrams 97). However, the "dinner table also becomes the arena for articulating competing versions of Jewishness" (Abrams 98). Consequently, the Jewish mother is praised when things go well and blamed when discord occurs. Jewish dietary traditions also create an unstable status for her, for the strictures do not simply sustain Jewish cultural identity; they also keep family members from participating in multi-ethnic societies the way other groups do. Jewish cuisine establishes the regular list of "foods eaten and not eaten and the legitimate bases of their combinations" (Counihan, *Anthropology* 20). Jewish etiquette and rules of consumption determine the "meals, the arrangement and sequence of foods, people's role in preparation and serving of food, and people's placement at the table" (Counihan, *Anthropology* 20). Jewish food taboos determine that certain foods will not be eaten. Thus, sometimes and for some people, the symbolism embodied by Jewish traditions makes the Jewish mother a source of strength and comfort; at other times and for other people, she is the symbol of everything that stands between them and true fulfillment.

The foodways lens can thus illuminate the intersection of gender and ethnicity in films such as *Mr. Saturday Night*. The film creates tension in its opening moments by using scenes of food preparation, presentation, consumption, and implicit cleanup to show that the Jewish mother occupies a subordinate position and that her subordinate position reflects anxieties and resentments generated by Jewish food protocols. The opening scene's many images of traditional Jewish dishes, combined with shots of the mother's vigorous handling of meal preparation, present the mother and the food activities in a warm and positive light. However, the sound track is peppered with caustic comments that Buddy Young Jr. (Billy Crystal) makes about his mother, Jewish food, and Jewish food culture. An offscreen interview about his career as a comedian provides the occasion for Buddy's voiceover remarks about his childhood, family, and culture. Buddy's comments make it clear that he sees his mother as inferior. His vocal aversion to her cooking disturbs the pleasure of seeing the delicious dishes. However, the contrast between the mother's bountiful meal and Buddy's bitter comments suggests that his disdain for his mother, her cooking, and his relatives' embrace of Jewish cultural traditions arises from his anger, resentment, and belief that Jewish traditions are to blame for his unhappiness.

The film telegraphs food's central role in Jewish culture's gender relations by combining the opening credits with food images and Buddy's scathing comments about Jewish food behavior.[6] To begin, as the title card "A FACE Production" fades to black, the audience hears Buddy say, "My mother was trying to kill us . . . with fat." In the pause between "trying to kill us" and "with fat," a large matzah ball thuds onto the center of a wooden board. The ugly splat of the matzah ball lends support to Buddy's negative view of Jewish cooking traditions. However, as the sequence continues, it becomes clear that Buddy's view of Jewish food, rather than his mother's cooking, is the problem.[7]

The next shots show the mother dropping matzah balls into a pot of boiling water, chopping an onion, and quartering a pickled tomato. Then, shots feature stuffed derma, or kishke (beef casing stuffed with matzah, onion, and suet that is boiled and then roasted); the mother takes a small amount of stuffing in her hand and pushes it into the end of the casing. In the sixth shot, she cuts fat off a brisket (a beef or veal cut that requires slow, moist cooking). In the next shot, she stuffs dressing into a chicken. The subsequent shots show her rub salt into

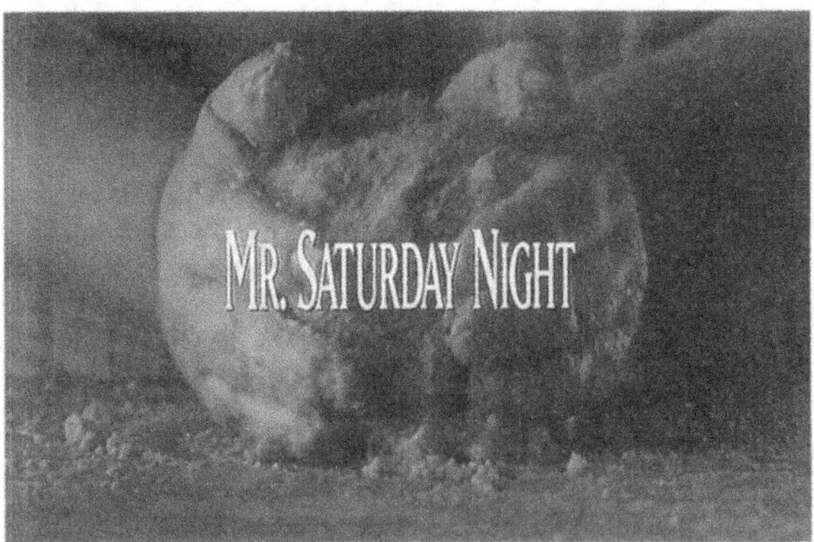

The matzah ball's splat communicates Buddy's disdain for his mother's Jewish food in Mr. Saturday Night *(Castle Rock Entertainment, Face Productions, New Line Cinema).*

the brisket; fold a stuffed cabbage leaf; grind liver; pour chicken stock onto potatoes; cook and drop seasoning onto caramelized onions; fry and flip latkes (potato pancakes); cut the brisket; slice braided bread; serve matzah balls (boiled in chicken soup) and gefilte fish (poached fish minced with matzah meal stuffed into fish skin); and ladle out cabbage leaves and cooked onions with mashed potatoes dropped on top. Over the shots of the mother's laborious food preparation and presentation, audiences listen to Buddy belittle his mother's cooking and his family's earthy food behavior.

Shot 21 of the title sequence suggests that the family members his mother has labored to feed have completed their many main course options and moved on to dessert. In a close-up, a man's hands peel the skin from an apple. Shot 22 is a close-up of tea being brewed in a small ornate cup; a man's hand reaches in, picks up the cup, and then gets a sugar cube to drop in the tea. Shot transitions then shift from straight cuts to slow dissolves that suggest the family's satiated feeling at meal's end. A series of dissolves from one tracking shot to another feature images of empty or near empty plates. At this point, in the voiceover, Buddy talks about the after-dinner entertainment he and his brother would provide for his family. The juxtaposition of image and sound suggest that while the family relaxes in the living room after dinner, the mother will be in the kitchen laboring to clean up dirty dishes, cups, pots, and pans.

The final piece of the tracking shot features a close-up of a fish skeleton. The image is ambiguous. On one hand, the fish sitting in the dish with all its flesh removed suggests that by the end of the meal the mother has been emotionally picked clean. On the other hand, the image shows that Buddy's mother has provided sustenance in accord with Jewish laws by offering the right kind of seafood, one so desirable that no morsel remains. As Nathan Abrams notes, because in Jewish culture "seafood is only kosher if it has fins and scales, all shellfish are forbidden" (Abrams 94). Moreover, in traditional Jewish foodways, the "symbolic or allegorical interpretation of the *kashrut* laws has it that fins and scales are signs of endurance and self-control" (Abrams 94). Thus, the image of the spent fish visually expresses the mother's nurturing, ethnically sensitive concern and her intrinsic strength while also metaphorically conveying Buddy's verbal shredding of her emotions through his mockery of the food she presents.

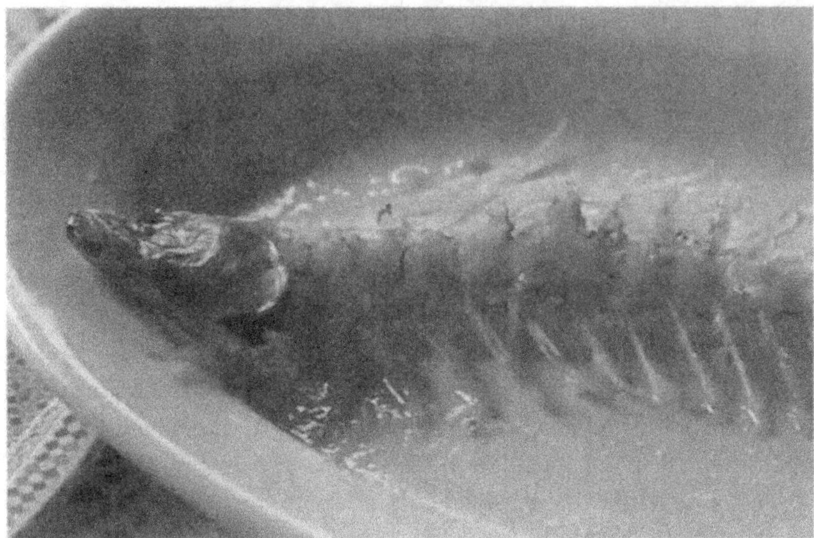

The beautifully lit fish skeleton conveys a complex message in Mr. Saturday Night *(Castle Rock Entertainment, Face Productions, New Line Cinema).*

After the image of the fish skeleton has filled the frame, the tracking shot continues a bit longer until it stops on the image of a delicate china bowl. The lace tablecloth, which has been visible in all the shots of the table, now becomes especially noticeable and so emphasizes the feminine qualities of the bowl. However, the china bowl does not hold traces of the mother's traditional cooking. Instead, it holds an ugly cigar stub. On the sound track, Buddy resorts to a juvenile fart joke about the effects of eating his mother's Jewish cooking. The unsightly cigar butt contrasts with the fragile china dish and delicate lace tablecloth just as Buddy's blatant disrespect of his mother contrasts with her earnest efforts to fulfill her duty by sustaining Jewish ethnic traditions.

The contrast between the cigar and the delicate dish and tablecloth conveys the son's complete disregard for the mother's labor and devotion to Jewish tradition. The troubling image of the cigar in the bowl reinforces the negative response that is now created by Buddy's cynical comments that denigrate his mother's efforts to prepare the traditional meal designed to sustain her family and culture. Thus, within the first few minutes of *Mr. Saturday Night*, the film establishes character as well

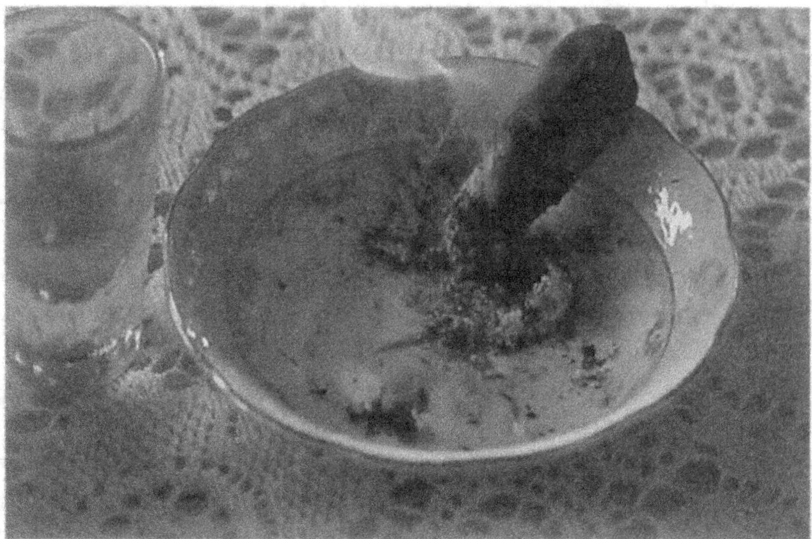

The unsightly cigar butt contrasts with the fragile china bowl and the delicate lace tablecloth in Mr. Saturday Night *(Castle Rock Entertainment, Face Productions, New Line Cinema).*

as ethnic context. Buddy's ostensibly amusing ridicule of his mother's cooking and his family's overindulgence in traditional Jewish food reveals the tensions created by Jewish dietary laws and the fact that Jewish cuisine, etiquette, and taboos can make the Jewish mother's cooking the target of resentment. Carefully designed and choreographed, the opening sequence establishes Buddy's fraught relationship with Jewish culture. At odds with the warm tone set by the bountiful meal, Buddy's mockery establishes that family members' efforts to sustain Jewish traditions can be a burden to individuals who want to assimilate. Buddy dismisses rather than appreciates the considerable labor that has gone into the creation of the meal because he sees the family's matriarch as a controlling figure who limits his opportunities. For Buddy, Jewish dietary laws do not provide a means for community and spiritual renewal, but instead symbolize the kind of restrictions that impede his path to individual success. Always chaffing against the limitations of Jewish culture and cuisine, Buddy will later try to persuade his fiancée "to part with her traditional Jewish parents" so he can treat her "to a roast pork dinner" (Abrams 92).

Throughout the opening sequence, Buddy's thoughts and feelings are clearly communicated, but his mother's are not because she is shown only from the neck down. Since the sequence does not show the mother's face, it is difficult to imagine if she would be amused or outraged by the disparaging comments Buddy makes about her cooking. The overwhelming presence of male speech contrasts with the female silence and food labor. Buddy dominates with his disrespectful comments; she works wordlessly. The contrast highlights gender inequity in Jewish culture that manifests in tensions surrounding what is often considered women's arena: meal selection. The contrast between the mocking voiceover and the partially seen woman preparing and serving food might seem to support Buddy's deep-seated misogyny. Films generally identify "the male subject . . . with mastering speech" (Silverman ix). Voiceovers often suggest "a position of superior knowledge [superimposing] itself 'on top' of the diegesis" (Silverman 48). Amy Lawrence points out that "the male disembodied narrator has historically been positioned as the authoritative 'enunciator' of his cinematic text" (169).

However, the sequence builds to the image of the ugly cigar in the delicate bowl and shows that the problem resides in Buddy rather than his mother. Thus, the contrast between the commanding male voiceover and the silent, laboring woman shows that the mother is a nurturer who tries to provide sustenance for a son who consistently wrecks his own chances for success. Rather than make a mark in the world, Buddy ends up as a has-been comedian. Over time, he finds himself slipping farther and farther from the limelight until he is reduced to entertaining at retirement homes. Flashbacks chronicle his initial performances that are warmly received by his immediate family. Subsequent professional appearances lead to modest successes, even though Buddy consistently directs aggressive, unpleasant jokes at audience members. More sad than comic, Buddy lacks self-awareness, and his need for approval overrides empathetic concern for others.

Buddy's opening "jokes" about his mother's cooking economically communicate his emotional shortcomings that unfold throughout the plot. They reveal his inadequacies rather than those of his Jewish mother because the images emphasize the enormous labor she invests in food preparation and presentation. By framing the images so that audiences never see the mother's face, the opening sequence focuses attention on the labor even more than the person laboring. As a consequence, it highlights the care and labor that women devote to nourishing and sustaining their families and cultural traditions. By combining the images of the mother's food labor with Buddy's derisive comments about her cooking, it also calls attention to the general lack of appreciation for women's work.

Since the 1970s, feminist scholars have analyzed films' representations of women. Reflecting the fact that feminist scholarship involves "a highly complex and continuously changing set of ideas" (Humm 36), analyses have increasingly focused on questions of women and food. Scholars have explored ways in which food provides a vehicle for women's self-expression in films such as *Salt of the Earth* (Biberman, 1954), *Babette's Feast,* and *Chocolate* (Counihan "Production"; McFadden). They have also shown that food illuminates women's often difficult relationship to patriarchal society in films such as *Years of Hunger, Superstar: The Karen Carpenter Story,* and *Life Is Sweet* (Joglekar; Papazian). As in the contrast between *Bagdad Cafe* and *301/302,* scholarship on films that explore women's relationship to food reveals that film's differing syntactical arrangements of foodways lead to a spectrum of representations that range from utopian to dystopian.

Food, Gender, and Sexuality

Films' use of foodways also enriches insights into gender and sexuality because the "instinctive drives for food and sex are similar, and they often take on overlapping symbolic connotations" (Counihan, *Anthropology* 9). As Carole Counihan notes, "In many cultures, particularly those with food scarcity, food gifts may be an important path to sexual liaisons" (*Anthropology* 9). Counihan also points out: "Precisely because eating and intercourse involve intimacy, they can be dangerous or threatening when carried out under adverse conditions or with untrustworthy people" (*Anthropology* 9–10). She explains that those dangers lead "all cultures [to] have rules and taboos to regulate food and sex and to define appropriate bed and table mates" (*Anthropology* 10).[8]

The links between food taboos and sexual taboos make foodways analysis a useful means for exploring representations of sexual identities and experiences that do not conform to dominate heterosexual norms. Depictions of characters' food behaviors can convey a film's perspective about dominant values in subliminal rather than overt ways. For example, in *Brokeback Mountain* (Lee, 2005), the two Thanksgiving scenes delineate the respective challenges that the guarded Ennis Del Mar (Heath Ledger) and the less secretive Jack Twist (Jake Gyllenhaal) face. In addition, the staging of food preparation and consumption reinforces the narrative's contrast between emotionally sustaining and emotionally unsatisfying relationships. Thus, preparing food over an open campfire, as Ennis and Jack do, differs markedly from the cooking done by Ennis's wife, Alma (Michelle Williams), in their cramped kitchen.

Gregg Araki's *Mysterious Skin* uses "a limited number of food items as controlling or defining metaphor(s)" to illuminate the emotional malnourishment that plagues a fast-food nation fed by snack foods and hollow imitations of home cooking (Keller 190). For Neil (Chase Ellison; later Joseph Gordon-Levitt) and Brian (George Webster; later Brady Corbet), the world is filled with little other than food treats (cookies, ice cream, pie, popcorn, pizza, and soda). For central character Neil McCormick, the conflicting connotations surrounding Froot Loops, the sugar-coated cereal marketed by Kellogg's since 1963, mirror his experience of and lingering feelings about being seduced by his baseball coach (Bill Sage) when he was eight years old.[9]

Food products and characters' food behavior illustrate the "intertwining but distinctly different" ways in which Neil and Brian deal with their shared experience of sexual abuse as eight-year-old boys. Brian exists "in a state of suspension" (Zacharek *Mysterious*), "living at home and drawing pictures of aliens in a sketch pad" because the memories of his two isolated encounters with the coach have been transformed into nightmares of alien abduction (LaSalle). By contrast, Neil not only remembers his experiences with Coach but remains deeply attached to them. Even a decade later when he is a young man working as a hustler in New York, Neil still mourns the loss he experienced when Coach left town without warning. As Neil explains to his friend Wendy (Michelle Trachtenberg), "No one ever made me feel that way before or since; I was special . . . I was his prize . . . I was his only true love." Thus, the film not only explores "the radically dissimilar ways in which trauma can be transmitted and remembered," it asks us to "contemplate the unthinkable" and consider a situation in which it is "possible for a child to 'love' a pedophile" (D. Lim).

Initially, food clarifies differences between Brian's and Neil's lives. For instance, whereas Brian's mother (Lisa Long) takes a break from watching TV with him to get a bowl of ice cream, in a parallel scene, Neil's mother (Elizabeth Shue) gets a little tipsy as she watches a game show by herself. Later, a comical scene of Brian's mother offering milk and cookies to Brian and his friend Eric (Jeffrey Licon) from the local community college is followed by a sad and slightly scary scene of Neil drinking a beer alone in a dark New York bar as he waits for a client to come along. That contrast is repeated when shots of Neil grabbing a slab of baloney for breakfast and working alone at a fast-food sandwich shop are followed by a scene in which Brian's mother offers homemade peanut butter peach pie to Brian and his older sister who is home from college for the Christmas holiday.

Alongside these differences, other references to food and the larger framework of the characters' dysfunctional meal system make the point that both boys grow up without emotional nourishment. Neil's father is not around, and his mother is focused on a series of boyfriends. Brian's father moves out a couple years after Brian is molested; Brian's self-absorbed mother seems to go through the motions of parenting. The mothers' failures to provide meaningful nourishment in scenes near the end of the film underscore those parallel family problems. As Brian races out of his house to meet Neil and so finally finds out what happened to him the summer they were eight, Brian's mother, annoyed and exasperated, reminds him that Christmas Eve dinner is at 6:00 sharp. Thus, she has no idea what's important to Brian and nothing to offer him; for her a holiday meal is a task that involves punctuality rather than meaningful enjoyment of food and family. In the next scene, Neil's mother weakly offers cookies to fill the time waiting for Neil; when Neil then enters the living room, cut and bruised from an encounter with a sadistic client in New York, it becomes painfully clear that cookies are hardly a remedy and that Neil's mother continues to provide little if any real nourishment for him. These hollow offers of food reveal that the boys were vulnerable and could be drawn in by a pedophile because the lack of commensality at home had left them emotionally undernourished.

Patterns in the characters' meal system establish other parallels between Brian's and Neil's lives. There are glimpses of commensality: Brian and Eric eat lunch together at their community college; Neil's mom and Eric get ice cream at the local Dairy Queen. However, throughout the film, characters eat alone. *Mysterious Skin* conveys the loneliness underlying Brian's embrace of alien-abduction theories in a pair of scenes that feature characters eating by themselves. Brian's visit to Avalyn (Mary Jane Rajskub), a young woman who has also been "abducted," opens with them talking on her porch as she finishes the saltine crackers that have served as her solitary lunch. In a later scene, when Brian arrives home late for dinner, his mother sets him down alone at the dinner table with a plate of plastic-looking food that is neatly divided into meat, starch, and vegetable.

The isolation and emotional starvation Neil feels as a young man, one who is still childish because he has grown up too quickly, is conveyed by the way he consumes the fast-food treat before his first trick as teenage hustler. When he's offered treats by the snack food salesman who has picked him up at a local playground, Neil grabs a package of cheese and crackers, tears it open, and then quickly shoves some crackers in his mouth. Earlier, the film had used a scene of eight-year-old Neil eating alone to depict his loneliness as a young boy. In a telling moment, Neil's mom gives him a big kiss as she leaves for a date, but her burst of affection does not mitigate the fact that Neil has to somehow sustain himself because he has been left alone, presumably again, with a dinner that consists of canned pasta and a glass of milk. Here, even the supposedly kid-friendly pasta does not nourish Neil because he is required to eat alone.

By comparison, Neil thrives on the popcorn, pizza, and soda the coach gives him on their first platonic "dates" because the food is shared and enjoyed as part of special occasions. In the Froot Loops seduction scene, Coach uses Neil's hunger for sweetness, comfort, and emotional nourishment to seduce the boy. The scene plays on audiences' conflicted associations with sugary cereals, and it uses food products' symbolism by having Neil initially choose innocent, light-colored Corn Pops, whereas Coach chooses dark-colored Cocoa Krispies. The seduction scene reveals Coach's considerable efforts and abilities to use food as a lure. His attention to detail and his skill in procuring the mass-produced food products that would most appeal to a young boy makes enticing, forbidden food seem to appear magically in his cupboard.

It was that evening when Coach started his amorous advances in the living room. However, Neil quickly gets uncomfortable. Switching tactics, Coach takes Neil into the kitchen and shows him his cupboard of junk food delights. For Neil, the treasure trove of sweet, salty, and crunchy snacks is great on its own. The treats are especially wonderful because he will get to enjoy them with the person who has ostensibly offered emotional nourishment. What makes the junk food irresistible is that Neil gets to choose a treat that is both familiar and forbidden; he selects single-serve boxes of cereal because his mother won't buy them for him.

The attractive but unhealthy food is tucked away in a cabinet. Neil chooses breakfast cereal, appropriate for a meal that starts him on a new path in life. Coach leads the way in breaking social rules when he tosses cereal in the air and then encourages Neil to follow suit. The junk-food cereal's divergent connotations communicate Neil's contradictory emotions of delight and shame. The images of the rainbow-colored

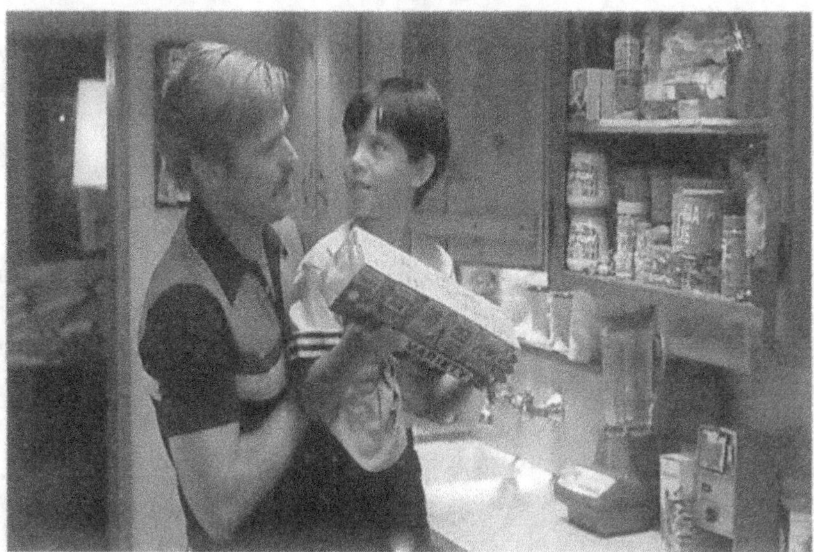

Mysterious Skin *(Desperate Pictures, Antidote Films, Fortissimo Film Sales) highlights ways that processed foods entice and then fail children in a fast-food society without commensality.*

cereal sailing through the air, cascading on the boy's face and scattering across the floor, give vivid expression to the complexities of desire in terms available to an eight-year-old boy.

The seduction scene reveals the degree to which value is encoded in certain objects: Coach's cupboard simply needs to contain the treasured objects to preserve their attraction. The scene echoes others throughout the film, for again there is no time spent on food preparation because in the world of *Mysterious Skin* food is a commodity that promises but consistently fails to provide emotional nourishment. As in other scenes, there is no attention to food preparation or presentation. The Froot Loops scene carries that to an extreme, with Coach setting aside the milk and dispensing completely with bowls and utensils. With sugary cereal as the aphrodisiac, the overturning of table manners leads the characters to dispense with cleanup as well. Thus, the scene compares Neil's seduction to a familiar junk-food experience, where people rip open the package to get to the treats and give no attention to preparation, presentation, etiquette, or cleanup. As this and other scenes with sweets and snacks make clear, Araki's film is not a celebration or condemnation of pleasure. Instead, it is a wistful look at the politics of seduction in fast-food society and the way young people's longing, elation, dismay, and regret arise from a world shaped by adults' limitations and self-interests.

Food imagery and characters' food choices and behavior convey Araki's measured commentary on power and pleasure in consumer society. Given the emotionally and nutritionally impoverished meal system depicted in the film, mass-marketed comfort food would facilitate Neil's seduction, whose summer of love and abuse begins when he gets to choose the meal, select forbidden food, and then dispense entirely with eating protocols after Coach ushers in the experience by impishly pouring Froot Loops on his own head. *Mysterious Skin* thus uses foodways to explore people's inchoate desires and to present a sharp critique of fast-food consumer society's missing commensality and failure to supply physical or emotional nourishment.

The Personal and Political Dimensions of Food

Films' representation of familiar food products, ethnic cooking traditions, and radical food choices illuminates personal and cultural dilemmas surrounding sexuality, gender, ethnicity, and national identity. Foodways analysis can open up discussions about the intersecting factors regarding the what, when, where, how, and why of people's food choices, activities, and visions of food's relationship to nature and society. A supplement to existing ideological approaches, foodways analysis can contribute to work that examines the meaning and politics of personal and cultural beliefs, values, and practices.

The foodways paradigm, which maps out the aesthetic, cultural, and economic dimensions of activities that range from food procurement to food disposal, points out well-defined factors to consider when doing ideological studies. It draws attention to the personal and political dimension of food practices. Implicitly drawing on that paradigm and giving voice to the countercultural view that food choice signifies intersections between personal and societal realms, filmmakers such as Agnes Varda and Doris Dörrie have created film essays that comment on individuals' contrasting relationships to food in industrialized societies. Their films underscore that some people are acutely aware of food's connections to nature, culture, and society whereas most consumers, dependent on "information" provided by the food and film industries, know nothing about the labor or economic and environmental externalities that consumer society tends to "disappear."

Varda's *The Gleaners and I* and Dörrie's *How to Cook Your Life* are, to different degrees, performative documentaries that acknowledge the presence of the filmmaker and "the construction and artificiality of even the non-fiction film" (Bruzzi 186). Each film bears "the signature of the maker" and manifests a folkloristic vision that sees "film as individual creation and a form of communication" (Jones ix). The two essay films share an important connection with the work by Frederick Wiseman, for despite the quiet, whimsical quality of each film, they both belong to the hard-hitting "observational tradition" because they stress the need for "institutional change" (Bruzzi 205).

Varda's film considers gleaning traditions in France, whereas Dörrie's film explores Buddhist cooking traditions used in monasteries around the world. Yet both contrast meaningful "traditions of networks and individuals" with the many alienating experiences that result from living in "industrialized societies" (Jones x). The films document "expressive or symbolic behavior [that is] learned, taught, displayed, or utilized in" people's interactions surrounding food procurement, preparation, consumption, and disposal (Jones x). By showing alternatives to the food behaviors fostered by consumer society, the films give credence to the core elements of the countercuisine perspective: the "consumerist component" that encourages people to avoid fast and processed food; the "therapeutic component" that invites people to explore "improvisation, craftsmanship," and slow cooking; and a production/distribution component that values cooperative methods that enhance community and counter consumer society's "pattern of waste" (Belasco, *Appetite* 4, 58).

Initially inspired by canonical impressionist paintings of peasants gleaning grain left in fields after the harvest, *The Gleaners and I* documents Varda's encounters with various types of gleaners in France. The folkloristic film gives time and attention to the gleaners' "personal experiences, motivations, and interactions with others" (Jones xi). Varda notes the contrast between the paintings' romanticized images of rural life and the pragmatic outlook of today's urban gleaners who dumpster-dive or pick through food left behind at farmers' markets. Varda examines the cultural conflict represented, on the one side, by supermarkets that douse their trash bins with bleach to discourage dumpster diving and, on the other, the many people who glean as a matter of necessity or ethics.

Varda's search for gleaners leads her to meet a variety of people who recognize the value of salvaging food that has been discarded by others. In her research on gleaners, she discovers hidden aspects of the industrial food system. For example, Varda learns that in France alone tons of potatoes are wasted each year because the ones that are too small, too large, or too oddly shaped to fit commercial standards are trucked back to the countryside and dumped in open fields to rot.

Befitting the "mother" of the French New Wave, Varda links the practice of gleaning food with other types of gleaning (Quart 136). She describes herself as a gleaner of images. She notes that psychoanalysts are gleaners of dream images, and she explains that anyone who searches to discover facts, ideas, and points of view is a gleaner. Varda visits artists who create sculptures using everyday items discarded by others. Fancifully bringing filmmaking and food gleaning together, Varda visits the estate that once belonged to Étienne-Jules Marey, inventor of the first instrument able to capture a series of images. She

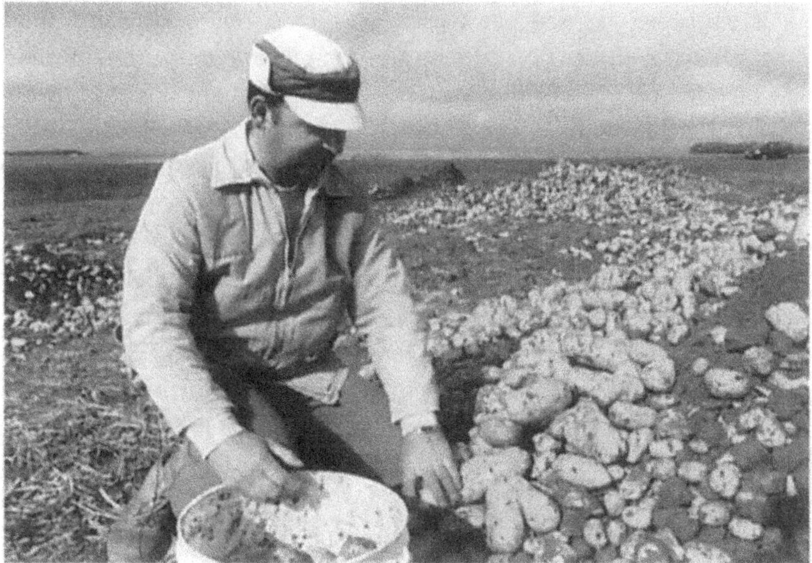

The Gleaners and I *(Ciné Tamaris) reflects on the personal choices of gleaners who explore options outside of modern consumer culture and the industrial food system.*

discovers that the estate not only has wonderful light, but that its current owners permit gleaning in its fields.

How to Cook Your Life is another example of a film about people's relationship to food that offers the occasion for "personal, sometimes poetic, statements" (Jones x). As in *The Gleaners and I,* Dörrie shows alternative methods of food procurement. One scene features a woman who gleans fruit from trees on residential streets. Other scenes show people taking the time to reflect on what they cook and what they eat. Interviews emphasize that food behaviors reflect individuals' values and influence their quality of life. In tone, structure, and content, the film reveals that Dörrie is well acquainted with the precepts of Zen Buddhism: "Best known in Germany for her 1985 hit comedy 'Men,' [Dörrie] is herself a practicing Zen Buddhist. She [had] turned to the Japanese philosophy [in 1992] when her husband Helge Weindler, who was the cameraman on 'Men,' was diagnosed with terminal cancer" (Beier). The film is thus a document of her very personal relationship to food and the lessons one can learn from cooking and eating with awareness.

In the same way that Varda creates a window into alternative food practices through her portraits of gleaners, Dörrie makes countercuisine beliefs and behaviors legible through its portrait of Buddhist monk Edward Espe Brown, who became known for his cookbooks *The Tassajara Bread Book* (1970), *Tassajara Cooking* (1973), and *The Tassajara Recipe Book* (1985). Through interviews with Brown and others involved with cooking at the San Francisco Zen Center and elsewhere, the film documents ways that food figures into their "personal experiences, motivations, and interactions with others" (Jones xi). The film shows that in contrast to the vision of food that dominates fast-food consumer society, from the Buddhist perspective cooking can nurture the soul as much as the body. Structuring segments of the film in ways that recall de Antonio's montage technique, *How to Cook Your Life* mixes images of fast-food products and meals supplied by short-order cooks with scenes that explore the rewards of fresh ingredients, thoughtful food preparation, and slow cooking. The film shows people treating food with a respect and level of awareness that contrasts sharply with how consumers approach convenience food. To emphasize the attention that food and food preparation warrants, Brown quotes his teacher Suzuki Roshi: "When you wash the rice, wash the rice. When you cut the carrots, cut the carrots. When you stir the soup, stir the soup."

The Gleaners and I and *How to Cook Your Life* give credence to countercuisine beliefs and behaviors. Both "folkloristic films isolate from the continuum of human experience examples of . . . traditional symbolic behavior in order to call attention to them as historical artifacts, describable phenomena, elements of culture, and aspects of human behavior" (Jones xi). The films' look at people who think carefully about food and its connection to people, society, and nature makes that alternative perspective tangible. By concentrating on personal food choices that contrast sharply with ones that dominate fast-food consumer society, the films document human behavior that lies outside the frame presented by commercial media. The films not only call attention to the wide vista of foodways components; they also show that there are alternatives to food behaviors fostered by the commercial food and film industries.

Ideological studies and work in film and political economy have shown the need to examine the effect that global power and Holly-

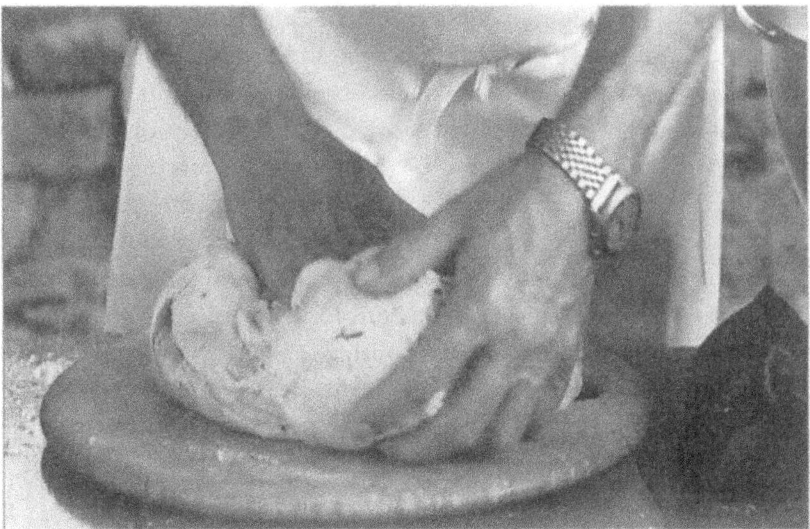

How to Cook Your Life *(Megaherz TV Fernsehproduktion GmbH) is a reminder that people's relationship to food reveals how they see themselves and the world.*

wood formulas have on representations. Analyses of the cultural politics of film have demonstrated the value of looking closely at films' representations of race, gender, class, and sexuality. By drawing on scholarship that has shown how food behaviors are markers of cultural identity, studies of food in film can contribute to ideological and material studies of film. As Anne Bower points out, "A focus on food gives us startling new insights into a wide variety of films" (10).

Reinvigorating the documentation of foodways first undertaken in the 1930s by New Deal folklorists, in the 1960s Don Yoder, Warren Roberts, and Henry Glassie highlighted the need to study "the beliefs, aesthetics, economics, and politics involved in food behaviors" (Long 144). Today, it is possible to see the value of examining "the beliefs, aesthetics, economics, and politics" of food behaviors represented in films of all types, especially in light of the economics and politics that determine what aspects of food are presented in cinema. The varied food films and food documentaries that have become more visible since the 1980s invite audiences to examine the contrast between "the beliefs, aesthetics, economics, and politics" that drive the mainstream food system which delivers consumer products and those underlying the alternative food system comprising backyard gardens, community-supported agriculture, and rooftop fruit and vegetable production in urban settings. Timothy Newman has observed "that embedded in the different modes of food production are different conceptions and framings of the self and 'the human'" (Newman). Research on the food industry, and "the medical, political, and environmental costs of our modern feast [and people's] conflicted feelings about food," has led Warren Belasco to propose, "There is nothing more basic than food" (*Food: The Key Concepts* i). Food's central role in personal identity, social interactions, and humans' relationship to their environment makes looking at food in film important.

Appendix 1

Insights from Food Stylist Ann Schulz

In well-crafted films, directors, aided by skilled craftspeople, endeavor to make every detail enhance the production's thematic and stylistic effect. In this enterprise, food stylists are the individuals responsible for creating the desired look for food on the set. Their work testifies to the exceptional cultural and symbolic significance of food in social interaction, and to the ways that directors employ food to enhance thematic objectives. As a food stylist for over three decades and one who has worked with many A-list directors, Ann Schulz provides a privileged glimpse into that behind-the-scenes work. Her experiences translating directors' ideas about food into visually effective objects confirm that components of foodways should be as meticulously evaluated as other facets of art direction, such as costuming, set design, makeup, and hair. Schulz's revealing insider descriptions validate the importance of attending to food procurement, preservation, preparation, presentation, consumption, performance, and cleanup as it appears or is elided in films.

Schulz has worked as a food stylist in New York, Atlanta, Los Angeles, Minneapolis, and St. Louis. Her credits include movies and television programs, from *Hook* (1991) and *Mr. Saturday Night* (1992) to *Bugsy* (1991) and *Chaplin* (1992), from *The Young and the Restless* to *Columbo*, from *L.A. Law* to *The Trials of Rosie O'Neill*. In three far-ranging interviews over several hours, she discussed the many facets of food activities and the ways each detail reveals and/or reinforces character, hinders or propels plot, and establishes and influences ambience.

As all cooks know, once a menu is set, procurement and preparation demand significant organizational expertise and time investment. Though films rarely if ever depict meal preparation in a realistic manner, the food stylist invests considerable energy and skilled planning during preproduction to ensure that the onscreen presentation of food efficiently and effectively transmits the director's desired impressions. For cinematic food stylists, the difficulty of the enterprise is multiplied by having to anticipate repeated takes (almost always at the director's, not the food stylist's, request), last-minute changes, and even improvisation. The food requested for any scene reveals the connotations the director hopes to evoke, often subconsciously, in the viewer. It is the food stylist's job to realize that vision and follow the director's specifications to transmit those ideas.

Steven Spielberg and *Hook* (1991)

Providing unique insight into the off-camera planning and intentions for the food in *Hook*, Schulz clarified the food stylist's contributions with examples that illustrate the demanding work behind the scenes and the deceptively effortless presentation within the film. As in most filmic representations, the actual labor expended by food stylists, from procurement and preparation to presentation and cleanup, is invisible. For example, in the food fight between the Lost Boys and Peter in *Hook*, the elaborate, colorful, plentiful food eschews any hint that labor might be required to produce the bounty. While audiences would not expect to see the considerable behind-the-scenes efforts of the production crew, having a privileged insight into their contributions enhances awareness of the aspects of foodways that often remain invisible in films.

As with most scenes, retakes pose significant challenges, and, as part of the food stylist team for *Hook*, Schulz had to respond on site and quickly execute the food design. She recalled one scene that required a fantasy drink "to hold on the upper lip as it does in milk advertisements. I was told that if a character was drinking a strawberry banana milkshake, it had to have sufficient thickness so that when he takes the glass away, hints of the shake hang on his upper lip. So I used dream whip in the milk to thicken it; quadruple Dream Whip added 4:1 to milk gives the thickness needed and is still food safe. And food safety is the primary, crucial concern. I have to ask, 'How long has the food been on the set and waiting for the scene?' We can't have an actor get a case of food poisoning, and with the turkey used on *Hook*, this became a central concern."

Actors also have to be coached on how to eat or pretend to eat the food: "Robin Williams was very smart because he'd put the milkshake up to his lips and pretend to, but not really, drink it. He did the same thing with the turkey leg when he'd feign biting into it, chewing and swallowing. Of course, this also poses huge continuity problems, which the prop master should supervise. However, the food stylist has to watch drink levels and match them from one take to the next. The same holds true for matching meat with the same size steaks, size and arrangement of potatoes, and even the same number of broccoli spears. Similarly, if you never have a complete omelet, the food stylist has to repeat that perfectly, as I've had to do on one film. Someone will notice as in *E.T.* and comment that Drew Barrymore's hamburger shrinks and grows and shrinks and grows again. It can be distracting, so the food stylist has to monitor consistency for all the takes."

Food stylists must also respond on a moment's notice to changes the director requests. On *Hook*, Schulz had plenty of whipped cream, but Spielberg wanted to change some colors so they would read better on film: "The director might want it darker or see that yellow doesn't read well so let's put green there. In addition, some colors read well from a distance but others will blend together in medium or close-up shots, and the food stylist needs to know this. The director of photography never talked with me, but someone in the hierarchy might weigh in. In the rare case that we're shooting in black and white, the food stylist also has to know how shades of gray photograph and that may be as subtle as how the green of parsley registers versus the green of broccoli. Most people don't have to think about this, but the food stylist needs to know exactly how the food will appear once it reaches the screen."

Schulz explained that food stylists must also translate abstract ideas to tangible, real food. When Spielberg wanted to know if Schulz could create a more kid-like appearance in the pies, she concocted several samples. The preferred pies had brightly colored whipped cream, and, once approved, she had to prepare twenty pies in order to hold several in reserve for retakes of the food-fight scene. Resetting for repeated takes with food requires extensive cleanup, redressing the set, changing wardrobe, and repairing makeup. In the Lost Boys–Peter food fight, a huge crew had to clean and reset as quickly as possible to avoid cost overruns.

While every aspect of the food choices contributes to the shooting of the scene, only what registers on camera matters. Schulz did not have to bake the pies since they would only be thrown, but she did have to factor in their weight so they could be thrown easily. In addition, Schulz often spent part of her weekends recreating the food needed for the next week's takes because the production crew, committed to avoiding waste as much as possible, donated edible food to firehouses on Fridays (some production companies now contribute to food banks). But even this seemingly simple procedure isn't so simple: if the food has been invented just for the film or is to be included in a promotion, then no food can be released before it is available in the commercial retail market.

Billy Crystal and *Mr. Saturday Night* (1992)

As the lead food stylist for *Mr. Saturday Night*, Schulz worked closely with Billy Crystal, who as director (as well as star) devoted meticulous attention to every nuance of the food displayed in the film, well aware that food conveys explicit information and elicits subliminal associations. In the film, food not only evokes specific memories for the lead character, Buddy Young Jr., but also establishes historical context and pinpoints cultural and family traditions. The appearance of specific dishes, fruits, and vegetables were also designed to trigger intense, very precise associations for the viewer.

In the director's commentary on the DVD, Crystal discusses the film's opening series of shots: "I decided mom's food was a big character in the movie and that she was also important to the boys, so I got her to cook and we made all this great food." He insisted that food itself become a character that, in the opening and in significant narrative moments afterward, transmits important impressions about the family and their heritage. For the first shot of the film, Crystal gave Schulz precise directions concerning the food items and their visual presentation. He specified that in the first and subsequent shots, Buddy's mother should appear in a medium close-up from the waist to the shoulders in front of a cutting board, and that she should drop and then knead the matzah ball. As Schulz recalled, "Crystal used a stand-in for the opening credit sequence because he wanted plump arms that would jiggle as the mother plopped the matzah ball onto the board. The arms should suggest those of a mother, not of a typical arm model with smoothly sculpted, thin arms. This body double had to know how to roll a cabbage leaf so it looks like she's done it a thousand times and knows exactly what she's doing. This should come through in her efficient actions. For retakes, the actor's hand had to be wet, the set had to be fogged, and the soft, golden light reset. Every minute detail must communicate the desired effect."

Subsequent shots in the opening sequence include the stunning shot of the fish skeleton, one of Schulz's all-time favorite food shots. Audiences see only the bones as the camera travels left to right moving along the skeleton from head to tail. Crystal's choice of soft-focus lighting and filters creating yellow-gold tones complemented by a white plate immediately communicates its 1940s milieu, especially in contrast to the cleaner, starker lighting characteristically used for the film's more contemporary scenes. Moreover, because the close-up fills the screen, Crystal conveys, even if subconsciously for the viewer, the contrasts between this more idyllic event and the less pleasant ones that take place during the succeeding decades in Buddy's life.

The friction that characterizes Buddy's persona is intensified by the tension between what audiences see onscreen and what they hear in voiceover, because Buddy's narration so clearly clashes with the appealing, well-designed food images. Crystal here telegraphs Buddy's most serious failing, his acerbic humor, a flaw that will cause his personal and professional downfall. Those around him, especially his family, provide physical and emotional sustenance, metaphorically visualized in the nourishing food, which contrasts with the sarcasm of Buddy's comments. Crystal communicates the story visually through careful culinary art direction: while Buddy, in the guise of humor, insults those around him, a lovely meal has been prepared and consumed. Crystal emphasizes the idea that food is important to this family in the image of the fish skeleton with nary a morsel of flesh left on its bones. The family has had a satisfying meal with every ounce savored.

Notwithstanding Crystal's attention to food presentation, Schulz notes that food stylists, and some viewers, have far greater knowledge of food than do many directors. Thus directors would do well to heed their food stylists' advice with regard to the details. As a case in point, the opening sequence in *Mr. Saturday Night* communicates unintended information for those attuned to food preparation. The woman whose hands are featured in the opening credit sequence actually lacks expertise in manipulating the ingredients, Schulz noted: "There's too much matzo meal on her hands and she shows a lack of grace in shaping the matzah ball. Her massaging the matzah ball shows she's a non-food person; she's squeezing it like a loaf of bread, a non-specific massage for a specific food item."

Similarly, in the second shot of the brisket, "The model should just pat the salt into the meat on the top and bottom, patting, not massaging it as she does here. . . . We might not notice that the cabbage is almost too young for this; however, we will probably appreciate that the cabbage on the left catches the light beautifully, enhancing the ambience of the scene." In the shot of the potatoes, "the various colors of yellow and the old potato masher establish the time period. The golden warm tone purposefully indicates an older feel." And as the scene moves through the meal preparation, "the cooked brisket looks appetizing, with the carving fork and salt shaker catching the light." But in the shot of the braided egg bread, Schulz explained that "this is the wrong knife for the bread, the challah, and the hand shouldn't be squashing it as the person cuts it."

Because a film's first moments must transport the audience into an imaginary world, the smallest detail matters enormously to an astute viewer. A director wants to convince the viewer to surrender to the willing suspension of disbelief in the opening scene, to embrace the cinematic world. In the opening scene of *Mr. Saturday Night*, the mistakes in the preparation of traditional Jewish dishes compromise authenticity, creating dissonance and distraction for knowledgeable audience members. Gaining the culturally knowledgeable viewer's involvement can be an uphill battle if too many errors occur.

Despite the mistakes in the opening sequence, food enthusiasts will welcome, even applaud, the film's depiction and appreciation of traditional Jewish fare. The lovely lighting and the fact that the mother is hands-on in preparing the meal will gain further admiration from people interested in cooking. As Schulz noted, "Crystal, who knows that all of this accumulates to produce a significant impact, telegraphs the care given to this meal by using different colored plates for every course, suggesting the mother pulled everything out of the family's dish huts. Crystal also insisted on a lace tablecloth, clearly visible in several shots, and a wooden table underneath to enhance the traditional appeal." The beautiful tablecloth could easily be regarded as an heirloom, a treasure someone crocheted, thus further enhancing the meal's appeal and alienating the viewer from Buddy because his voiceover shows that he is an unappreciative son. Anyone interested in food would realize that this opening sequence telegraphs profound truths about the character and the film's themes.

Food is important in other scenes in the movie as well, though not always as thematically resonant as in the opening. For a scene in the Friar's Club when a young agent (Helen Hunt) meets with Buddy, the actors wanted to have edible food (omelets) for rehearsals as well as takes. This presented one challenge for Schulz, but in addition Hunt and Crystal wanted specific ingredients so they could enjoy the omelets and thus enhance the reality of the scene. Schulz had to prepare a dozen omelets and have sufficient ingredients on hand for another half-dozen, all ready for warming in the microwave for multiple takes. And, she noted, "The food stylist must always pay attention to minutiae. The same amount of tomato had to be showing in every one of the omelets for each take."

Locations in which food appears even as a backdrop also communicate, sometimes metaphorically. For example, as Schulz explained, at the dinner theater where Buddy meets Elaine (Julie Warner), his future wife, the intercutting between the backstage and kitchen scenes present the parallel, behind-the-scenes preparations: "Simultaneously the kitchen staff prepares ingredients for a finished dish as Buddy gets ready with his makeup and attire. Both the dish and Buddy will be presented as one of the courses, and the parallel activity reinforces the anticipation through glimpses into the unfinished, usually unobserved work that goes into a 'course.'" By revealing parallels between food preparation and other types of labor, the film suggests that Buddy's problems are both personal and cultural, for they harken back to his making a joke of the love and labor behind his Jewish mother's cooking. Every detail conveys meaning as *Mr. Saturday Night* validates the importance of and contributions made by food.

Additional Observations

Elaborating on the implicit information embedded in dining events, Schulz explained that "the point in a meal that the scene enters may say a lot about serious conversation, which usually takes place later in a meal." When family and friends begin a meal, they are usually not yet engaged in deep conversation. That comes later, once formalities and connections have been reestablished as the event unfolds: "And so expectations vary without our thinking about it once we observe the layout and point of entry in food scenes." A food stylist's input can be enormously valuable in shaping these points of entry.

Other cinematic concerns dictate food choices as well, as they did for director Barry Levinson's *Bugsy*. Color and sound should complement the energy and mood desired. Schulz noted that in the prison dinner scene in *Bugsy*, Annette Bening had "wanted poached chicken breasts and celery slices so she could eat them on camera, but the color palate ruled against this. Onscreen, the visual effect of such pale-colored food would be weak, lacking, as it would not be for vibrant color." So, while we see Bening drink from a champagne glass and eat a few bites of food, we never actually see what is on her plate. In fact, we only catch a glimpse of the meat on Warren Beatty's plate when he abruptly covers it with the silver-warming dome he had lifted from the plate a few seconds earlier. And in the second jail scene, from an audio and visual perspective, Bugsy chomping angrily on a carrot effectively conveys his irritation.

Schulz noted that a moment similar to Bugsy's frustrated eating of a carrot occurs in *Terms of Endearment* (Brooks, 1983): "While making a snack for her children, Emma Horton [Debra Winger] becomes exasperated as she talks with her mother Aurora [Shirley MacLaine] on the phone. As a great ad-lib, Winger crunched a lettuce leaf rudely into the telephone, getting her emotional state across visually and aurally." Returning to *Bugsy*, Schulz explained how the food reveals character and situation in the scene where Bugsy is killed: "Traditional, stereotypical mobster food was requested. A certain pasta had to be recreated with peas and tomato sauce, the latter perhaps a precursor of the blood to come."

The food stylist must be alert to a myriad of technical and period details. In preproduction meetings, Schulz might meet with the art director to learn about the scenes involving food. It might well be her responsibility, and would certainly enhance her role, to know about the food and service ware of the story's time period. On several occasions, after the art director or coordinator has told Schulz what a scene required, she has had to tell them, "No, that's not what these characters would eat or how they would eat it." This could be as specific as what types of meat would be found on the grill or what kind of platters would be on the tables. As Schulz explained, she has been required to know about stemware and select "a red wine goblet versus a white wine goblet since different wines require a specific shape for the glass. Also garnishes are telltale signs that date a scene and give a period feel whether intentional or not. The same is true with plates and trends in plates. There's been an era of white plates, clear plates, black plates, marble plates, geometrically shaped plates and patterned plates. The set dresser might know some of this, so I often work with that person."

Food choices that reflect cultural and geographic differences impart authenticity when used accurately: "Potato salad on the West Coast will be totally different from potato salad on the East Coast, and food stylists have to know this and take it into consideration. . . . Potato salad, for one example, in the forties is very different from the trendy eighties and nineties. The stylist has to remain consistent with the timeline."

Schulz is equally adept at evaluating how food functions in films that she is not working on, where she is simply a viewer. She knows better than most that a character may telegraph a change of heart or attitude through food choices: "In *Mermaids* [Benjamin, 1990], Mrs. Flax's [Cher] approach to mothering is symbolized by the kinds of food she feeds her daughters Charlotte [Winona Ryder] and Kate [Christina Ricci]." In the opening scene, as the daughters sit in front of the television, Mrs. Flax (as she is consistently called) serves them "cheese ball pick me ups accompanied by miniature franks and, for dessert, marshmallow kabobs." Mrs. Flax's primary cookbook is *Fun Finger Foods* and, as her daughter Charlotte says in voiceover narration, "Anything more is too big a commitment." Mrs. Flax takes the appetizer approach to food; she's fine with fruit and marshmallows on a skewer or meatballs and vegetables. For her, both the main course and dessert merit their own shish kabob, so disjointed is her approach to creating dinner.

As Schulz pointed out, "When they're eating breakfast, Mrs. Flax's family exhibits an on-the-fly approach. While they're all in the kitchen, each exists in her own world, each having made individual breakfasts. One literally sits on the countertop; each takes care of her own needs. But once Mrs. Flax's love interest develops, a more traditional perspective and concomitant food choices prevail. After Mrs. Flax and Lou spend a romantic afternoon in bed, she goes to the kitchen and brings back Coke and pretzels, instant identifiers of the era. But Lou Landsky's [Bob Hoskins] approach is to have everyone sit down together with chicken, carrots, and a more nourishing dinner. He treats food as a cohesive force. Mrs. Flax bristles, thinking he's trying to rein her in through food, wanting a more serious commitment." She certainly understands, as the attentive viewer does, that food can communicate intent.

In an important subplot, after Charlotte jeopardizes her younger sister Kate, their mother's frustration, aggravation, and fright are channeled into her hacking apart the Rice Krispies treats she made earlier. Food again reflects an emotional state and signals the time period. Schulz summarized the point of the food choices: "This encapsulates the character as much as what car they drive, and you don't need much dialogue to say a lot. The food they eat and the restaurant they choose are as important as the clothes they wear." Food manufacturers also know more than the average customer about the purposes food serves. As Schulz explained, "Companies that sell crunchy food take readings of the amount of crunch delivered by their product knowing that crunch alleviates consumers' frustration and aggression level. Consumers approach such foods to satisfy an emotional need as much as a consumption need. A creamy pudding or nursery kind of food that is soothing satisfies different feelings and expresses a different mood from potato chips. So, within a film, the food chosen to tell the story expresses subtle or not-so-subtle subliminal emphasis."

Food stylists have to use creativity to respond to some of the more unusual requests: "In *Toys* [Levinson, 1992] Alsatia Zevo [Joan Cusack] has to eat a vitamin sandwich to indicate her neurosis. So, I used things like Sweet Tarts so she could eat it. That kind of sandwich tells you about her personality. As in *Hook*, the childlike food reinforces the playful, fun qualities of the film. This even extended to the deviled egg on a tray that the server made dance. The secret to this was putting a magnet inside the deviled egg and the server moving another magnet under the tray so the egg danced."

The food stylist must know a lot of tricks of the trade, such as how to make food look appealing or repulsive in order to create the correct emotional mood: "In *Naked Gun 33 1/3: The Final Insult* [Segal, 1994], Lt. Frank Drebin [Leslie Nielsen] had to have three kinds of edible dirt, taking into consideration the granularity, because he escapes in one scene by eating dirt. We used cake that I crumbled, chocolate and coffee and cornmeal to break up the color, and flecks of oatmeal to look like rocks in extreme close-ups." Since Schulz has worked in still photography for years, she knows that "to enhance a lettuce leaf, we position light to come through it to suggest freshness and aliveness. This is symbolic of health and vibrancy. Similarly, glazed fruits lit from behind enhance their appetite appeal, as will spritzing fruits with glycerin and using corn syrup to keep the shiny look. Otherwise, with many takes, the fruit may dry out too quickly. On peaches, rubbing some oil or Vaseline on the skin will bring up the color to make them look riper, while grapes need to have a fine dusting to confirm freshness, as do blueberries. But for the best dewy quality, a spray bottle with a mixture of corn syrup and glycerin works best."

Food communicates volumes quickly and efficiently: "Rocky [Sylvester Stallone] drinking an egg in a glass shouts macho attitudes, while making a pâté of dog food, as Barbara Rose [Kathleen Turner] does in *War of the Roses,* is using food as a weapon." Who eats, what they eat, how they eat it, when they eat it, and with whom, this familiar and pervasive part of people's lives works as a powerful element contributing to every film in which food appears. Once sensitized to this, audiences become aware of how evocative and important food is. As with other craftspeople, food stylists' labor-intensive contribution to storytelling in film is rarely understood or acknowledged, not because people are not interested, but because they seldom are aware of what food stylists such as Ann Schulz actually do and the role food plays in film.

Appendix 2

Selected Fiction Films Featuring Foodways

Unlike the filmographies in *Food, Film and Culture* by James Keller and *Food in the Movies* by Steve Zimmerman and Ken Weiss, the lists below place greater emphasis on the roles that food, drink, and water play in character interactions and the narrative as a whole.

Utopian/Dystopian Visions in Prestige Films

301/302 (Cheol-su Park, 1995)
Alambrista! (Robert M. Young, 1977)
Alice Doesn't Live Here Anymore (Martin Scorsese, 1974)
American Psycho (Mary Harron, 2000)
Antonia's Line (Marleen Gorris, 1995)
Au Petit Margeury (Laurent Bénégul, 1995)
Autumn Moon (Clara Law, 1992)
Babette's Feast (Gabriel Axel, 1988)
Bagdad Cafe (Percy Adlon, 1988)
Belle Epoch (Fernando Trueba, 1992)
Big Night (Campbell Scott and Stanley Tucci, 1996)
The Blue Diner (Jan Egleson, 2001)
Bolivia (Adrián Caetano, 2001)

The Bread, My Sweet (Melissa Martin, 2001)
Burn! (*Queimada*, Gillo Pontecorvo, 1969)
La Cena (Ettore Scola, 1998)
Charlie and the Chocolate Factory (Tim Burton, 2005)
A Chef in Love (Nana Dzhordzhadze, 1996)
Chinatown (Roman Polanski, 1974)
The Chinese Feast (Hark Tsui, 1995)
Chocolat (Lasse Hallström, 2000)
Cloudy with a Chance of Meatballs (Phil Lord and Chris Miller, 2009)
The Cook, the Thief, His Wife, and Her Lover (Peter Greenaway, 1989)
A Corner in Wheat (D.W. Griffith, 1909)
Country (Richard Pearce, 1984)
Couscous (*La Graine Et Le Mulet*, Abdel Kechiche, 2007)
Delicatessen (Marc Caro and Jean-Pierre Jeunet, 1991)
Dinner at Eight (George Cukor, 1933)
Dinner Rush (Bob Giraldi, 2000)
The Discrete Charm of the Bourgeoisie (Luis Buñuel, 1972)
Distant Thunder (*Asani Sanket*, Satyajit Ray, 1973)
Do the Right Thing (Spike Lee, 1989)
Dona Flora and Her Two Husbands (Bruno Barreto, 1976)
Earth (Aleksandr Dovzhenko, 1930)
Eat Drink Man Woman (Ang Lee, 1994)
Eat Pray Love (Ryan Murphy, 2010)
Eat Your Heart Out (Felix O. Adlon, 1997)
Eating (Henry Jaglom, 1990)
Everyday People (Jim McKay, 2004)
Fast Food Nation (Richard Linklater, 2006)
A Feast at Midnight (Justin Hardy, 1995)
Felicia's Journey (Atom Egoyan, 1999)
Festen (*The Celebration*, Thomas Vinterberg, 1998)
Flakes (Michael Lehmann, 2007)
Frankie and Johnny (Garry Marshall, 1991)
Fried Green Tomatoes (Jon Avnet, 1991)
The God of Cookery (Stephen Chow and Lik-Chi Lee, 1996)
The Gods Must Be Crazy (Jamie Uys, 1980)
La Grande Bouffe (*The Big Feast, Blow Out,* Marco Ferreri, 1973)
The Green Butchers (Anders Thomas Jensen, 2003)
Heavy (James Mangold, 1995)

Home for the Holidays (Jodie Foster, 1995)
Hook (Steven Spielberg, 1991)
Hotel Splendide (Terence Gross, 2000)
How Tasty Was My Little Frenchman (Nelson Pereira dos Santos, 1971)
Intermission (John Crowley, 2003)
It Happened One Night (Frank Capra, 1934)
Jamón, jamón (Bigas Luna, 1992)
The Joy Luck Club (Wayne Wang, 1993)
Julie and Julia (Nora Ephron, 2009)
Killer of Sheep (Charles Burnett, 1979)
Kitchen Stories (Bent Hamer, 2003)
The Last Supper (Stacy Title, 1995)
Life Is Sweet (Mike Leigh, 1990)
Like Water for Chocolate (Alfonso Arau, 1992)
Long Live the Lady! (*Lunga Vita Alla Signora,* Ermanno Olmi, 1987)
Love's Kitchen (James Hacking, 2011)
The Lumnitzer Sisters (Péter Bascó, 2006)
Magic Kitchen (Chi-Ngai Lee, 2004)
Mambo Café (Reuben Gonzales, 2000)
The Man Who Fell to Earth (Nicholas Roeg, 1976)
The Milagro Beanfield War (Robert Redford, 1988)
Mildred Pierce (Michael Curtiz, 1945)
Mostly Martha (*Bella Martha,* Sandra Nettelbeck, 2001)
Mr. Saturday Night (Billy Crystal, 1992)
Mysterious Skin (Gregg Araki, 2004)
Mystic Pizza (Donald Petrie, 1988)
No Reservations (Scott Hicks, 2007)
One, Two, Three (Billy Wilder, 1961)
Our Daily Bread (King Vidor, 1934)
Pieces of April (Peter Hedges, 2003)
Pulp Fiction (Quentin Tarantino, 1994)
Raise the Red Lantern (Zhang Yimou, 1992)
The Ramen Girl (Robert Allan Ackerman, 2008)
Rango (Gore Verbinski, 2011)
Ratatouille (Brad Bird and Jan Pinkava, 2007)
The Recipe (Anna Lee, 2010)
Red Sorghum (Yimou Zhang, 1987)
Repo Man (Alex Cox, 1984)

The River (Mark Rydell, 1984)
The Road (John Hillcoat, 2009)
The Road to Wellville (Alan Parker, 1994)
Scotland, PA (Billy Morrissette, 2001)
Sideways (Alexander Payne, 2004)
The Silence of the Lambs (Jonathan Demme, 1991)
Simply Irresistible (Mark Tarlov, 1999)
Soul Food (George Tillman Jr., 1997)
Soul Kitchen (Fatih Akin, 2009) J
Soylent Green (Richard Fleischer, 1973)
Spanglish (James L. Brooks, 2004)
Struggle (Ruth Mader, 2003)
Sugar Cane Alley (Euzhan Palcy, 1983)
Superstar: The Karen Carpenter Story (Todd Haynes, 1988)
Tampopo (Jûzô Itami, 1985)
Taxidermia (György Pálfi, 2006)
A Thousand Acres (Jocelyn Moorhouse, 1997)
Today's Special (David Kaplan, 2009)
Tortilla Soup (María Ripoll, 2001)
The Van (Stephen Frears, 1996)
Vegetarian (Woo-Seong Lim, 2009)
Volver (Pedro Almodóvar, 2006)
Waiting (Rob McKittrick, 2005)
Waitress (Adrienne Shelley, 2007)
Walkabout (Nicholas Roeg, 1971)
WALL-E (Stanton, 2008)
The Wedding Banquet (Ang Lee, 1993)
What's Cooking (Gurinder Chadha, 2000)
Who Is Killing the Great Chefs of Europe? (Ted Kotcheff, 1978)
Willy Wonka and the Chocolate Factory (Mel Stuart, 1971)
Woman on Top (Fina Torres, 2000)
Years of Hunger (Jutta Brückner, 1980)

Dystopian Visions in Exploitation Films

Anthropophagus (Aristide Massaccesi [Joe D'Amato], 1980)
Attack of the Killer Tomatoes (John De Bello, 1978)

Bad Taste (Peter Jackson, 1987)
Blood Diner (Jackie Kong, 1987)
Blood Feast (Herschell Gordon Lewis, 1963)
Cannibal Ferox (Umberto Lenzi, 1981)
Cannibal Holocaust (Ruggero Deodato, 1980)
Cannibal Women in the Avocado Jungle of Death (J. F. Lawton, 1989)
Cannibal! The Musical (Trey Parker, 1993)
Death Line (Gary Sherman, 1973)
Death Row Diner (B. Dennis Wood, 1988)
Deep River Savages (Umberto Lenzi, 1972)
Deranged (Jeff Gillen and Alan Ormsby, 1974)
Eaten Alive! (Umberto Lenzi, 1980)
Eating Raoul (Paul Bartel, 1982)
Emanuelle and the Last Cannibals (Aristide Massaccesi, 1977)
Flesh Eating Mothers (James Aviles Martin, 1989)
Frightmare (Peter Walker, 1974)
The Hills Have Eyes (Wes Craven, 1977)
Last Cannibal World (Ruggero Deodato, 1977)
Little Shop of Horrors (Roger Corman, 1960)
The Mad Butcher (Guido Zurli, 1971)
Motel Hell (Kevin Connor, 1980)
Mountain of the Cannibal God (Sergio Martino, 1978)
Night of the Living Dead (George A. Romero, 1968)
Ravenous (Antonia Bird, 1999)
Slaughterhouse (Rick Roessler, 1987)
The Texas Chain Saw Massacre (Tobe Hooper, 1974)
The Texas Chainsaw Massacre 2 (Tobe Hooper, 1986)
Three on a Meathook (William Girdler, 1973)
Trouble Every Day (Claire Denis, 2001)
Zombie Holocaust (Marino Girolami, 1979)

Utopian/Dystopian Visions in Selected Scenes

The Age of Innocence (Martin Scorsese, 1993)
Annie Hall (Woody Allen, 1977)
As Good as It Gets (James L. Brooks, 1997)
Battle of the Century (Clyde Bruckman, 1927)

Battleship Potemkin (Sergei Eisenstein, 1925)
Bedevil (Tracey Moffatt, 1993)
The Bicycle Thieves (Vittorio De Sica, 1948)
Bread and Chocolate (Franco Brusati, 1973)
Bugsy (Barry Levinson, 1991)
Chicken and Duck Talk (Clifton Ko, 1988)
Citizen Kane (Orson Welles, 1941)
Days of Heaven (Terrence Malick, 1978)
Dirty Shame (John Waters, 2004)
Five Easy Pieces (Bob Rafelson, 1970)
Freaks (Tod Browning, 1932)
Frenzy (Alfred Hitchcock, 1972)
The Godfather (Francis Ford Coppola, 1972)
Gold Rush (Charles Chaplin, 1925)
Goodfellas (Martin Scorsese, 1990)
The Graduate (Mike Nichols, 1967)
Grand Illusion (Jean Renoir, 1937)
The Grapes of Wrath (John Ford, 1940)
Harvest: 3000 Years (Haile Gerima, 1976)
The Hours (Stephen Daldry, 2002)
Jeanne Dielman, 23 Quai du Commerce, 1080 Bruxelles (Chantal Akerman, 1975)
The King of Comedy (Martin Scorsese, 1983)
The Last Laugh (F. W. Murnau, 1924)
M.A.S.H. (Robert Altman, 1970)
Mermaids (Richard Benjamin, 1990)
Modern Times (Charles Chaplin, 1936)
Nine ½ Weeks (Adrian Lyne, 1986)
Notorious (Alfred Hitchcock, 1946)
Phantom of Liberty (Luis Buñuel, 1974)
Picnic at Hanging Rock (Peter Weir, 1975)
Public Enemy (William A. Wellman, 1931)
Salò, or The 120 Days of Sodom (Pier Paolo Pasolini, 1975)
The Scent of Green Papaya (Tran Anh Hung, 1993)
Strawberry and Chocolate (Tomas Gutiérrez Alea and Juan Carlos Tabío, 1994)
Tess (Roman Polanski, 1979)

Tom Jones (Tony Richardson, 1963)
Vertical Ray of the Sun (Tran Anh Hung, 2000)
Weekend (Jean-Luc Godard, 1967)
White Heat (Raoul Walsh, 1949)
Women in Love (Ken Russell, 1969)

Appendix 3

Selected Food Documentaries

Information about these and other food documentaries can be found on the films' official websites, the Internet Movie Database, and websites for organizations such as Bullfrog Films, Ironweed Films, Collective Eye, Arts Engine/Media That Matters, and the Fair Trade Resource Network.

All in This Tea (Les Blank and Gina Leibrecht, 2009)
American Dream (Barbara Kopple, 1990)
Asparagus! Stalking the American Life (Anne de Mare and Kirsten Kelly, 2009)
Beyond Organic (John de Graaf, 2000)
Big River (Curt Ellis, 2009)
Big Spuds, Little Spuds (Christoph Corves and Delia Castiñeira, 1999)
The Bitter Aftertaste (Philip Thompson, 2006)
Bitter Seeds (Micha X. Peled, 2011)
Black Gold (Mark Francis and Nick Francis, 2005)
Blue Gold: World Water Wars (Sam Bozzo, 2008)
Born of the Sun (Bertram Verhaag, 2007)
The Botany of Desire (Michael Schwarz and Edward Gray, 2009)
Broken Limbs: Apples, Agriculture, and the New American Farmer (Jamie Howell and Guy Evans, 2004)

Buyer Be Fair: The Promise of Product Certification (John de Graaf, 2006)
Circle of Plenty (Bette Jean Bullert and John de Graaf, 1987)
The Close to Nature Garden (Rodale Publishing; with Masanobu Fukuoka, 1982)
The Corporation (Mark Achbar and Jennifer Abbott, 2003)
Cultivating Change (David Springbett and Heather MacAndrew, 2001)
Darwin's Nightmare (Hubert Sauper, 2004)
Death on a Factory Farm (Tom Simon and Sarah Teale, 2009)
Deconstructing Supper (Marianne Kaplan, 2002)
Diet for a New America (Ed Schuman, 1991)
Diet for a Small Planet (Bullfrog Films producer; with Francis Moore Lappé, 1974)
Dirt! The Movie (Bill Benenson and Gene Rosow, 2010)
Dry Wood (Les Blank, 1973)
Empty Seas, Empty Nets (Steve Cowen, 2003)
The End of the Line (Rupert Murrary, 2009)
Farmageddon (Kristin Canty, 2011)
Farming for the Future (Matthew Kraus, 2005)
Farming the Seas (Steve Cowan and Barry Schienberg, 2004)
Field of Genes (Janet Thomson, 1998)
FLOW: For Love of Water (Irena Salina, 2008)
Food (David Springbett and Heather MacAndrew, 2000)
Food Beware: The French Organic Revolution (Jean-Paul Jaud, 2008)
Food Fight (Chris Taylor, 2008)
Food for Thought (Robert Dean and Roger Bingham, 1990)
Food, Inc. (Robert Kenner, 2009)
Food Matters (James Colquhoun and Laurentine Ten Bosch, 2008)
Forks over Knives (Lee Fulkerson, 2011)
Fragile Harvest (Robert Lang, 1985); short version, *Seeds* (Robert Lang, 1987)
Frankensteer (Marrin Canell and Ted Remerowski, 2006)
Fresh (Ana Sofia Joanes, 2009)
The Future of Food (Deborah Koons Garcia, 2004)
Garden Song (Jim Mulligan and John de Graaf; with Alan Chadwick, 1981)
The Garden (Scott Hamilton, 2008)
Garlic Is as Good as Ten Mothers (Les Blank, 1980)

The Gleaners and I (Agnes Varda, 2000)
Global Gardener (Julian Russell and Tony Gailey, 1996)
Good Food (Mark Dworkin and Melissa Young, 2008)
Grains of Change (Carolyn Barnwell, 2006)
The Greenhorns (Severine von Tscharner Fleming, 2010)
The Greening of Cuba (Jaime Kibben, 2005)
Grow! (Christine Masterson and Owen Masterson, 2011)
A Growing Season (Robert Waldeck and Paul Eichhorn, 2008)
Harvest of Fear (Jon Palfreman, 2001)
Hidden Korea (Jan Thompson, 2000)
Hot Potatoes (John de Graaf, 2002)
How to Cook Your Life (Doris Dörrie, 2008)
How to Make Sorghum Molasses (Carl Fleischhauer, 1971)
Ingredients (Robert Bates, 2009)
Jiro Dreams of Sushi (David Gelb, 2011)
King Corn (Aaron Woolf, 2007)
Life and Debt (Stephanie Black, 2001)
Life Running Out of Control (Bertram Verhaag, 2005)
McLibel (Franny Armstrong and Ken Loach, 2005)
Meat (Frederick Wiseman, 1976)
The Meatrix (Free Range Studios, 2003)
Meatrix II: Revolting (Free Range Studios, 2003)
Meatrix II ½ (Free Range Studios, 2006)
My Father's Garden (Miranda Smith, 1996)
Net Loss: The Storm over Salmon Farming (Mark Dworkin and Melissa Young, 2003)
The New Frontier (H.P. McClure, 1934)
The New Frontier (Melinda Levin, 2010)
Not for Sale (Mark Dworkin and Melissa Young, 2002)
One Man, One Cow, One Planet (Thomas Burstyn, 2007)
Our Daily Bread (Nikolaus Geyrhalter, 2005)
Pastriology (Alexis Krasilovsky, 2013)
Percy Schmeiser: David versus Monsanto (Bertram Verhaag, 2009)
The Plow That Broke the Plains (Pare Lorentz, 1936)
The Price of Sugar (Bill Haney, 2007)
Queen of the Sun: What Are the Bees Telling Us? (Taggart Siegel, 2010)
The Real Dirt on Farmer John (Taggart Siegel, 2006)

Red Gold (Ben Knight and Travis Rummel, 2008)
Ripe for Change (Emiko Omori and Jed Riffe, 2006)
Risky Business (Mark Dworkin and Melissa Young, 1996)
Running Dry (Jim Thebaut, 2005)
Seeds of Plenty, Seeds of Sorrow (Manjira Datta, 1994)
Soul Food Junkies (Byron Hurt, 2012)
Sowing for Need or Sowing for Greed? (Judith Bourque and Peter Gunnarson, 1990)
Spend It All (Les Blank, 1972)
Step Up to the Plate (*Entre les Bras,* Paul Lacoste, 2012)
The Story of Bottled Water (Annie Leonard, 2010)
Super Size Me (Morgan Spurlock, 2004)
Tapped (Stephanie Soechtig and Jason Lindsey, 2009)
Terra Madre (*Mother Earth,* Ermanno Olmi, 2009)
Valley at the Crossroads (John Doxey and George Spies, 2002)
Water on the Table (Liz Marshall; with Maude Barlow, 2011)
We Feed the World (Erwin Wagenhofer, 2005)
Weather the Storm (Charles Menzies and Jennifer Rasleigh, 2008)
What's on Your Plate? (Catherine Gund, 2009)
What's Organic about Organic? (Shelley Rogers, 2010)
Wheat Today, What Tomorrow? (Barrie Oldfield, 1998)
The World According to Monsanto (Marie-Monique Robin, 2008)
Yum, Yum, Yum! A Taste of the Cajun and Creole Cooking of Louisiana (Les Blank, 1990)

Appendix 4

Selected Work in Food and Cultural Studies

Journals with research essays on foodways include *Food and Foodways: Explorations in the History and Culture of Human Nourishment*; *Food, Culture & Society: An International Journal of Multidisciplinary Research*; and *Gastronomica: The Journal of Food and Culture.*

Albala, Ken. *Three World Cuisines: Italian, Mexican, Chinese*. Landham, Md.: Alta Mira, 2012. Print.

Albala, Ken, and Trudy Eden, eds. *Food and Faith in Christian Culture.* New York: Columbia UP, 2011. Print.

Allen, Gary, and Ken Albala, eds. *The Business of Food: Encyclopedia of the Food and Drink Industries.* Westport, Conn.: Greenwood, 2007. Print.

Anderson, Eugene N. *Everyone Eats: Understanding Food and Culture.* New York: New York UP, 2005. Print.

Arens, William. *The Man-Eating Myth: Anthropology and Anthropophagy.* New York: Oxford UP, 1979. Print.

Ashley, Bob, Joanne Hollows, Steve Jones, and Ben Taylor. *Food and Cultural Studies*. New York: Routledge, 2004. Print.

Astyk, Sharon, and Aaron Newton. *A Nation of Farmers: Defeating the Food Crisis on American Soil.* Gabriola Island, B.C.: New Society, 2009. Print.

Atkins, Peter, and Ian Bowler. *Food in Society: Economy, Culture, Geography*. New York: Arnold/Hodder Educational, 2001. Print.

Avakian, Arlene Voski, and Barbara Haber, eds. *From Betty Crocker to Feminist Food Studies: Critical Perspectives on Women and Food*. Amherst: U of Massachusetts P, 2005. Print.

Barlow, Maude, and Tony Clarke. *Blue Gold: The Fight to Stop the Corporate Theft of the World's Water*. New York: New Press, 2002. Print.

Barndt, Deborah. *Tangled Routes: Women, Work, and Globalization on the Tomato Trail*. Lanham, Md.: Rowman & Littlefield, 2002. Print.

Belasco, Warren J. *Appetite for Change: How the Counterculture Took on the Food Industry, 1966–1988*. New York: Pantheon, 1989. Print.

Belasco, Warren. *Food: The Key Concepts*. New York: Berg, 2008. Print.

Belasco, Warren. *Meals to Come: A History of the Future of Food*. Berkeley: U of California P, 2006. Print.

Belasco, Warren, and Philip Scranton, eds. *Food Nations: Selling Taste in Consumer Societies*. New York: Routledge, 2002. Print.

Bell, David, and Gill Valentine. *Consuming Geographies: We Are Where We Eat*. New York: Routledge, 1997. Print.

Bentley, Amy. *Eating for Victory: Food Rationing and the Politics of Domesticity*. Champaign: U of Illinois P, 1998. Print.

Berris, David, and David Sutton, eds. *The Restaurants Book: Ethnographies of Where We Eat*. New York: Berg, 2007.

Berry, Wendell. *The Unsettling of America: Culture and Agriculture*. San Francisco: Sierra Club, 1996. Print.

Bittman, Mark. *Food Matters: A Guide to Conscious Eating*. New York: Simon & Schuster, 2009. Print.

Bourdain, Anthony. *Kitchen Confidential: Adventures in the Culinary Underbelly*. Rev. ed. New York: Ecco, 2007. Print.

Bromfield, Louis. *Malabar Farm*. Rev. ed. Wooster, OH: Wooster Press, 1999. Print.

Brown, Lester R. *Full Planet, Empty Plates: The New Geopolitics of Food Scarcity*. New York: Norton, 2012. Print.

Brown, Lester R. *Outgrowing the Earth: The Food Security Challenge in an Age of Falling Water Tables and Rising Temperatures*. New York: Earthscan, 2005. Print.

Brown, Linda Keller, and Kay Mussell, eds. *Ethnic and Regional Foodways in the United States: The Performance of Group Identity*. Knoxville: U of Tennessee P, 1984. Print.

Brownell, Kelly D., and Mark S. Gold, eds. *Food and Addiction: A Comprehensive Handbook*. New York: Oxford UP, 2012. Print.

Brownell, Kelly D., and Katherine Battle Horgen. *Food Fight: The Inside Story of the Food Industry, America's Obesity Crisis, and What We Can Do about It*. New York: McGraw-Hill, 2004. Print.

Bruegel, Martin. *Farm, Shop, Landing: The Rise of a Market Society in the Hudson Valley, 1780–1860*. Durham, N.C.: Duke UP, 2002. Print.

Bryant, Carol A., Kathleen M. Dewalt, Anita Courtney, and Jeffrey Schwartz. *The Cultural Feast: An Introduction to Food and Society*. 2nd ed. Belmont: Thomson/Wadsworth, 2003. Print.

Civitello, Linda. *Cuisine and Culture: A History of Food and People*. 3rd ed. Hoboken: Wiley, 2011. Print.

Clover, Charles. *The End of the Line: How Overfishing is Changing the World and What We Eat*. Rev. ed. Berkeley: U of California P, 2008. Print.

Coleman, Leo, ed. *Food: Ethnographic Encounters*. New York: Berg, 2012.

Cooper, Ann, and Lisa M. Holmes. *Bitter Harvest: A Chef's Perspective on the Hidden Danger in the Foods We Eat and What You Can Do about It*. New York: Routledge, 2000. Print.

Counihan, Carole M. *The Anthropology of Food and Body: Gender, Meaning, and Power*. New York: Routledge, 1999. Print.

Counihan, Carole, ed. *Food in the USA: A Reader*. New York: Routledge, 2002. Print.

Counihan, Carole, and Penny Van Esterik, eds. *Food and Culture: A Reader*. 2nd ed. New York: Routledge, 2008. Print.

Coveney, John. *Food, Morals and Meaning: The Pleasures and Anxiety of Eating*. 2nd ed. New York: Routledge, 2006. Print.

Davidson, Alan, et al. *The Oxford Companion to Food*. 2nd ed. New York: Oxford UP, 2006. Print.

Davidson, Osha Gray. *Broken Heartland: The Rise of America's Rural Ghetto*. Rev. ed. Iowa City: U of Iowa P, 1996.

Denker, Joel. *The World on a Plate: A Tour through the History of America's Ethnic Cuisine*. New York: Bison, 2007. Print.

Erdkamp, Paul. *The Grain Market in the Roman Empire: A Social, Political and Economic Study*. New York: Cambridge UP, 2005. Print.

Fernando-Armesto, Felipe. *Near a Thousand Tables: A History of Food*. New York: Free Press, 2002. Print.

Fiddes, Nick. *Meat: A Natural Symbol*. New York: Routledge, 1992. Print.

Freedman, Paul, ed. *Food: The History of Taste*. Berkeley: U of California P, 2007. Print.

Fromartz, Samuel. *Organic, Inc.: Natural Foods and How They Grew*. New York: Harcourt, 2007. Print.

Fuller, Gordon W. *Food, Consumers, and the Food Industry: Catastrophe or Opportunity?* Boca Raton, Fla.: CRC, 2001. Print.

Fuller, Gordon W. *New Food Product Development: From Concept to Marketplace*. 3rd ed. Boca Raton, Fla.: CRC, 2011. Print.

Gabaccia, Donna R. *We Are What We Eat: Ethnic Food and The Making of Americans*. Cambridge, Mass.: Harvard UP, 2000. Print.

Gleick, Peter H. *Bottled and Sold: The Story behind Our Obsession with Bottled Water*. Washington, D.C.: Island, 2011.

Gleick, Peter H. *Water in Crisis: A Guide to the World's Fresh Water Resources*. New York: Oxford UP, 1993.

Gottlieb, Robert, and Anupama Joshi. *Food Justice*. Cambridge, Mass.: MIT Press, 2010. Print.

Grace, Eric S. *Biotechnology Unzipped: Promises and Realities*. 2nd ed. Washington, D.C.: Joseph Henry, 2006. Print.

Griffiths, Sian, and Jennifer Wallace, eds. *Consuming Passions: Food in the Age of Anxiety*. Manchester: Manchester UP, 1998. Print.

Gussow, Joan Dye. *Chicken Little, Tomato Sauce and Agriculture: Who Will Produce Tomorrow's Food?* Lowell, Mass.: Bootstrap, 1991. Print.

Gussow, Joan Dye. *The Feeding Web: Issues in Nutritional Ecology*. Boulder, Colo.: Bull, 1978. Print.

Hauck-Lawson, Amy, and Jonathan Deutsch, eds. *Gastropolis: Food and New York City*. New York: Columbia UP, 2009. Print.

Holt-Giménez, Eric, and Raj Patel. *Food Rebellions: Crisis and the Hunger for Justice*. Oakland: Food First, 2009. Print.

Inglis, David, and Debra Gimlin, eds. *The Globalization of Food*. New York: Berg, 2010. Print.

Inness, Sherrie A., ed. *Cooking Lessons: The Politics of Gender and Food*. Lanham, Md.: Rowman & Littlefield, 2001. Print.

Inness, Sherrie A. *Dinner Roles: American Women and Culinary Culture*. Iowa City: U of Iowa P, 2001. Print.

Inness, Sherrie A., ed. *Kitchen Culture in America: Popular Representations of Food, Gender, and Race*. Philadelphia: U of Pennsylvania P, 2000. Print.

Inness, Sherrie A. *Secret Ingredients: Race, Gender, and Class at the Dinner Table*. New York: Palgrave Macmillan, 2005. Print.

Jackson, Dana L., and Laura L. Jackson, eds. *The Farm as Natural Habitat: Reconnecting Food Systems with Ecosystems*. Washington, D.C.: Island, 2002. Print.

Jones, Michael Owen, Bruce Giuliano, and Roberta Krell, eds. *Foodways and Eating Habits: Directions for Research*. Los Angeles: California Folklore Society, 1983. Print.

Katz, Solomon H., ed. *Encyclopedia of Food and Culture*. Vol. 1–3. New York: Scribner/Thomson Gale, 2002. Print.

Kimbrell, Andrew, ed. *The Fatal Harvest Reader: The Tragedy of Industrial Agriculture*. Washington, D.C.: Island, 2002. Print.

Kiple, Kenneth F. *A Moveable Feast: Ten Millennia of Food Globalization*. New York: Cambridge UP, 2007.

Kiple, Kenneth F., and Kriemhild Coneè Ornelas, eds. *The Cambridge World History of Food*. Vol. 1–2. New York: Cambridge UP, 2000. Print.

Kittler, Pamela Goyan, and Kathryn P. Sucher. *Food and Culture*. 3rd ed. New York: Wadsworth, 2001. Print.

Kneafsey, Moya, et al. *Reconnecting Consumers, Producers and Food*. New York: Berg, 2008. Print.

Knechtel, John, ed. *Food*. Cambridge, Mass.: MIT Press, 2007. Print.

Kümin, Beat. *Drinking Matters: Public Houses and Social Exchange in Early Modern Central Europe*. New York: Palgrave Macmillan, 2007. Print.

Lappé, Francis Moore. *Diet for a Small Planet*. New York: Ballantine, 1991. Print.

Lappé, Francis Moore, and Anna Lappé. *Hope's Edge: The Next Diet for a Small Planet*. New York: Jeremy P. Tarcher/Putnam, 2003. Print.

Lawrence, Felicity. *Eat Your Heart Out: Who Really Decides What Ends Up on Your Plate?* New York: Penguin, 2008. Print.

Levenstein, Harvey. *Paradox of Plenty: A Social History of Eating in Modern America*. Rev. ed. Berkeley: U of California P, 2003. Print.

Levenstein, Harvey A. *Revolution at the Table: The Transformation of the American Diet*. Berkeley: U of California P, 2003. Print.

Lien, Marianne E., and Brigitte Nerlich, eds. *The Politics of Food*. New York: Berg, 2004. Print.

Long, Lucy M., ed. *Culinary Tourism*. Lexington: UP of Kentucky, 2010. Print.

Lyman, Howard F. *Mad Cowboy: Plain Truth from the Cattle Rancher Who Won't Eat Meat*. New York: Scribner, 2001. Print.

Lyson, Thomas A. *Civic Agriculture: Reconnecting Farm, Food, and Community*. Medford, Mass.: Tufts UP, 2004. Print.

Macbeth, Helen M., and Jeremy MacClancy, eds. *Researching Food Habits: Methods and Problems*. New York: Berghahn, 2004. Print.

Magdoff, Fred, John Bellamy Foster, and Frederick H. Buttel, eds. *Hungry for Profit: The Agribusiness Threat to Farmers, Food, and the Environment*. New York: Monthly Review, 2000. Print.

Marks, William E. *The Holy Order of Water: Healing the Earth's Waters and Ourselves*. Rev. ed. Great Barrington, Mass.: Bell Pond Book, 2001. Print.

Martin, A. Lynn. *Alcohol, Violence, and Disorder in Traditional Europe*. Kirksville, Mo.: Truman State UP, 2009. Print.

Mather, Robin. *A Garden of Unearthly Delights: Bioengineering and the Future of Food*. New York: Plume, 1996. Print.

Mauer, Donna, and Jeffrey Sobal, eds. *Interpreting Weight: The Social Management of Fatness and Thinness*. Piscataway, N.J.: Aldine Transaction, 1999. Print.

Mauer, Donna, and Jeffrey Sobal, eds. *Weighty Issues: Fatness and Thinness as Social Problems*. Piscataway, N.J.: Aldine Transaction, 1999. Print.

McCully, Patrick. *Silenced Rivers: The Ecology and Politics of Large Dams*. Rev. ed. London: Zed, 2001. Print.

McKibben, Bill. *The End of Nature*. Rev. ed. New York: Random House, 2006. Print.

McMillan, Tracie. *The American Way of Eating: Undercover at Walmart, Applebee's, Farm Fields and the Dinner Table*. New York: Scribner, 2012.

Meiselman, Herbert L., ed. *Dimensions of the Meal: The Science, Culture, Business, and Art of Eating*. Gaithersburg, Md.: Aspen, 2000. Print.

Miller, Jeff, and Jonathan Deutsch. *Food Studies: An Introduction to Research Methods*. New York: Berg, 2009. Print.

Mintz, Sidney W. *Sweetness and Power: The Place of Sugar in Modern History*. New York: Penguin, 1986. Print.

Mintz, Sidney W. *Tasting Food, Tasting Freedom*. Boston: Beacon, 1997. Print.

Montanari, Massimo. *Food Is Culture*. Trans. Albert Sonnenfeld. New York: Columbia UP, 2006. Print.

Nabhan, Gary Paul. *Desert Terroir: Exploring the Unique Flavors and Sundry Places of the Borderlands*. Austin: U of Texas P, 2012. Print.

Nabhan, Gary Paul. *Where Our Food Comes From: Retracing Nikolay Vavilov's Quest to End Famine*. Washington, D.C.: Island, 2011. Print.

Nabhan, Gary Paul. *Why Some Like It Hot: Food, Genes, and Cultural Diversity*. Washington, D.C.: Island, 2006, Print.

Nestle, Marion. *Food Politics: How the Food Industry Influences Nutrition and Health*. Rev. ed. Berkeley: U of California P, 2007. Print.

Nestle, Marion. *Safe Food: The Politics of Food Safety*. Rev. ed. Berkeley: U of California P, 2010. Print.

Nestle, Marion. *What to Eat*. New York: North Point, 2007. Print.

Nuetzenadel, Alexander, and Frank Trentmann, eds. *Food and Globalization: Consumption, Markets and Politics in the Modern World*. New York: Berg, 2008. Print.

Parasecoli, Fabio. *Bite Me: Food in Popular Culture*. New York: Berg, 2008. Print.

Parasecoli, Fabio, and Peter Scholliers, eds. *A Cultural History of Food*. Vol. 1–6. New York: Berg, 2012. Print.

Patel, Raj. *Stuffed and Starved: Markets, Power and the Hidden Battle for the World Food System*. Rev. ed. London: Melville House, 2012. Print.

Pawlick, Thomas F. *The End of Food: How the Food Industry Is Destroying Our Food Supply—And What We Can Do about It*. Fort Lee, N.J.: Barricade, 2006. Print.

Petrini, Carlo. *Slow Food Nation*. New York: Rizzoli Ex Libris, 2007. Print.

Petrini, Carlo. *Terra Madre: Forging a New Global Network of Sustainable Food Communities*. Trans. John Irving. White River Junction, Vt.: Chelsea Green, 2010. Print.

Pollan, Michael. *In Defense of Food: An Eater's Manifesto*. New York: Penguin, 2009. Print.

Pollan, Michael. *The Omnivore's Dilemma: A Natural History of Four Meals*. New York: Penguin, 2007. Print.

Potter, Will. *Green Is the New Red: An Insider's Account of a Social Movement under Siege*. San Francisco: City Lights, 2011. Print.

Rampton, Sheldon, and John Stauber. *Mad Cow U.S.A.* Monroe, Me.: Common Courage, 2002. Print.

Ray, Krishnendu. *The Migrant's Table: Meals and Memories in Bengali-American Households*. Philadelphia: Temple UP, 2004.

Roberts, Paul. *The End of Food*. New York: Houghton Mifflin, 2008. Print.

Rousseau, Signe, ed. *Food Media: Celebrity Chefs and the Politics of Everyday Interference*. New York: Berg, 2012. Print.

Rubin, Lawrence C., ed. *Food for Thought: Essays on Eating and Culture*. Jefferson, N.C.: McFarland, 2008. Print.

Schanbacher, William D. *The Politics of Food: The Global Conflict between Food Security and Food Sovereignty*. Santa Barbara, Calif.: Praeger, 2010. Print.

Schlosser, Eric. *Fast Food Nation: The Dark Side of the All-American Meal*. New York: Harper Perennial, 2005. Print.

Shiva, Vandana. *Earth Democracy: Justice, Sustainability, and Peace*. Cambridge, Mass.: South End, 2005. Print.

Shiva, Vandana. *Stolen Harvest: The Hijacking of the Global Food Supply*. Cambridge, Mass.: South End, 2000. Print.

Shiva, Vandana. *The Violence of Green Revolution: Third World Agriculture, Ecology and Politics*. London: Zed, 1992. Print.

Shiva, Vandana. *Water Wars: Privatization, Pollution, and Profit*. Cambridge, Mass.: South End, 2002. Print.

Short, Frances. *Kitchen Secrets: The Meaning of Cooking in Everyday Life*. New York: Berg, 2006. Print.

Shortridge, Barbara G., and James R. Shortridge, eds. *The Taste of American Place: A Reader on Regional and Ethnic Foods*. Lanham, Md.: Rowman & Littlefield, 1999. Print.

Simon, Michele. *Appetite for Profit: How the Food Industry Undermines Our Health and How to Fight Back*. New York: Nation, 2006. Print.

Singer, Peter, and Jim Mason. *The Ethics of What We Eat: Why Our Food Choices Matter*. Emmaus, Pa.: Rodale, 2007. Print.

Smith, Andrew F. *Eating History: Thirty Turning Points in the Making of American Cuisine*. New York: Columbia UP, 2011. Print.

Smith, Andrew F., ed. *The Oxford Companion to American Food and Drink*. New York: Oxford UP, 2009. Print.

Smith, Andrew F., ed. *The Oxford Encyclopedia of Food and Drink in America*. 2 vols. 2nd ed. New York: Oxford UP, 2012. Print.

Smith, Andrew F. *Popped Culture: A Social History of Popcorn in America*. Washington, D.C.: Smithsonian Institution, 2001. Print.

Smith, Jeffrey M. *Seeds of Deception: Exposing Industry and Government Lies about the Safety of the Genetically Engineered Foods You're Eating*. Fairfield, Ia.: Yes, 2003. Print.

Spang, Rebecca L. *The Invention of the Restaurant: Paris and Modern Gastronomic Culture*. Cambridge, Mass.: Harvard UP, 2000. Print.

Tannahill, Reay. *Food in History*. Rev. ed. New York: Broadway, 1995. Print.

Thursby, Jacqueline S. *Foodways and Folklore: A Handbook*. Westport, Conn.: Greenwood, 2008. Print.

Trubek, Amy B. *The Taste of Place: A Cultural Journey into Terroir*. Berkeley: U of California P, 2009. Print.

Visser, Margaret. *The Rituals of Dinner: The Origins, Evolution, Eccentricities, and Meaning of Table Manners*. 2nd ed. Toronto: HarperCollins Canada, 2008. Print.

Warde, Alan. *Consumption, Food, and Taste: Culinary Antimonies and Commodity Culture*. Thousand Oaks, Calif.: Sage, 1997. Print.

Warde, Alan, and Lydia Martens. *Eating Out: Social Differentiation, Consumption and Pleasure*. New York: Cambridge UP, 2000. Print.

Watson, James L., ed. *Golden Arches East: McDonald's in East Asia*. 2nd ed. Stanford, Calif.: Stanford UP, 2006. Print.

Watson, James L., and Melissa L. Caldwell, eds. *The Cultural Politics of Food and Eating: A Reader*. Malden, Mass.: Blackwell, 2005. Print.

Wilk, Richard. *Home Cooking in the Global Village: Caribbean Food from Buccaneers to Ecotourists*. New York: Berg, 2006. Print.

Williams-Forson, Psyche A. *Building Houses Out of Chicken Legs: Black Women, Food, and Power*. Chapel Hill: U of North Carolina P, 2006. Print.

Williams-Forson, Psyche, and Carole Counihan, eds. *Taking Food Public: Redefining Foodways in a Changing World*. New York: Routledge, 2011. Print.

Wilson, David, and Angus Kress Gillespie, eds. *Rooted in America: Foodlore of Popular Fruits and Vegetables*. Knoxville: U of Tennessee P, 1999. Print.

Wilson, Thomas M., ed. *Drinking Cultures: Alcohol and Identity*. London: Berg, 2005. Print.

Witt, Doris. *Black Hunger: Soul Food and America*. Minneapolis: U of Minnesota P, 2004. Print.

Wrangham, Richard. *Catching Fire: How Cooking Made Us Human*. New York: Basic, 2010. Print.

Yoder, Don. "Food Cookery." *Folklore and Folklife: An Introduction*. Ed. Richard M. Dorson. Chicago: U of Chicago P, 1972. 325–50. Print.

NOTES

Introduction

1. The campaigns within the social movement that Nestle discusses include the Good Food Movement, which calls for "local, organic, or humanely raised food produced by family farms"; the Farm-to-Community Movement, which "aims to connect farmers to local communities"; the Community Food Security Movement, which works "to provide fresh, locally produced food to low-income urban and rural communities that bear the highest burden of health problems associated with poor diets"; the Stop-Marketing-Foods-to-Kids Movement, which uncovers "the harmful effects of marketing junk food to children"; and the School Food Movement, which advocates for healthier meals in schools (Nestle x).

2. The case studies in Chapter 5 are also framed to illustrate developments in film history and audience reception. The Brazilian film *How Tasty Was My Little Frenchman* highlights perspectives offered by the international post-colonial movement known as Third Cinema. The film's critical success in the United States provides a glimpse into the era's cosmopolitan taste in movies. That reception context differs from the increased critical and commercial attention invested in exploitation cinema from the late 1970s to the present. To explore those changing tastes in film, the chapter briefly looks at *Cannibal Holocaust*, one of cinema's most infamous cannibal films. This film illuminates trends in Italian cinema that made it possible for Italian films to compete with big-budget Hollywood productions and, at the same time, allowed exploitation filmmakers to mount critiques of economic and cultural imperialism. Touching on questions of taste, national cinema, and political economy, a close look at Hooper's original *The Texas Chain Saw Massacre* film shows how the film's representations of food reflect filmmaking in an industrial climate that requires political statements to be allegorical.

Chapter 2

1. Other American films that feature water in a prominent way include *Our Daily Bread, Wild River* (Kazan, 1960), *The River* (Rydell, 1984), *A River Runs through It* (Redford, 1992), *The River Wild* (Hanson, 1994), *Northfork* (Michael Polish, 2003), and *Into the Wild* (Penn, 2007). Works by director John Sayles, along with films such as *The China Syndrome* (Bridges, 1979) and *Michael Clayton* (Gilroy, 2007), show that political subjects can be at the center of interesting film narratives.

2. The film was made possible in part through financing secured by Jeff Skoll, head of Participant Media, which has backed feature films such as *Syriana* (Gaghan, 2005) and *Good Night, and Good Luck* (Clooney, 2005) and documentaries such as *An Inconvenient Truth* (Guggenheim, 2005), *Standard Operating Procedure* (Morris, 2008), and *The Cove* (Psihoyos, 2009). Skoll was president of eBay from 1996 to 1998. In sharp contrast to his successor, Meg Whitman, as president of eBay Skoll helped to create the eBay Foundation; when he left the company in 1998 he took his $2 billion profit and set up Participant Media.

3. Linklater is known for films like *Slacker* (1991) and *A Scanner Darkly* (2006). *Fast Food Nation* features Greg Kinnear as the fast-food executive and stars Catalina Sandino Moreno, star of *Maria Full of Grace* (Marston, 2004), and Wilmar Valderrama, known for playing "Fez" in *That 70s Show,* as migrant workers trying to make a living. Other threads of the story feature brief but memorable roles played by Bruce Willis, Kris Kristofferson, Ethan Hawke, Paul Dano, and Avril Lavigne.

4. The establishment of the MPPC was quickly followed by rival trade associations such as the Independent Film Protection Association, which became the National Independent Moving Picture Alliance, and the Motion Picture Distributing and Sales Company, which split into the Mutual Film-Supply Company and the Universal Film Manufacturing Company.

5. After major strikes by the International Alliance of Theatrical and Stage Employees (IA) in 1918 and 1919, as well as other strikes against theater owners by "projectionists, musicians, and attendants" and the IA's newfound control of "motion picture machine operators, stage hands, carpenters, plasterers, electricians, painters, grips, and other studio workers," eleven studios retaliated in 1921 by issuing "a drastic set of wage cuts" (Ross 132).

6. That same consolidation of anti-union power marked the transition in 1945 from the MPPDA to the MPAA, the Motion Picture Association of America. In response to strikes by the Conference of Studio Unions (CSU) in 1945, the studios locked out workers and refused to negotiate, claiming that the labor dispute had arisen from jurisdictional conflicts between rival unions. With members of the Screen Actors Guild opting to cross picket lines and IA

members taking positions formerly held by CSU workers, the studios were not adversely affected by the strikes. The *Hollywood Reporter* published articles suggesting that the strikes were caused by communist agitators. In 1945, the California Fact Finding Committee on Un-American Activities held hearings to air allegations that Herb Sorrell, head of the CSU, was a communist. In 1945, the efforts of the anti-union Motion Picture Alliance for the Preservation of American Ideals were rewarded when the House Un-American Activities Committee (HUAC) opened its investigation of communist activity in Hollywood. As in the 1920s, executives crushed labor demands through coordinated efforts behind the scenes, but portrayed their public actions as moral responses to ethical misconduct, in this case membership in the Communist Party. Film executives were friendly witnesses at the HUAC hearings, and they produced the 1947 Waldorf Statement, which prohibited employment of known communists. The MPAA gained power by blacklisting employees on the grounds of their communist affiliation. That power translated into the MPAA's new effectiveness in regulating film content. For studies on the reduced number of social problem films and political censorship under the Code and Rating Administration (1968–77) and the Classification and Rating Administration (1977–present), see Maltby 471–90; Vasey, "Beyond" 105, 112; Black 247–87; Lewis, *Hollywood* 181–87, 289, 298; and Baron "Sayles."

7. NAMPI, the MPPDA, and the MPAA have functioned essentially as fronts for the film industry's labor-management associations, the MPPA, the AMPP, and today's AMPTP (the Alliance of Motion Picture and Television Producers).

8. Lorentz was born Leonard MacTaggert Lorentz. He began using his father's name, Pare, when he started publishing essays (*FDR's Moviemaker* 5). After working as a film critic, Lorentz produced government films until 1947, when he was tacitly blacklisted by Republicans and Hollywood executives (*FDR's Moviemaker* 232). For scholarship on Lorentz, see Barsam 397n16 and 398n30.

9. The claims that U.S. agricultural practices were driven by profiteering during wartime and that government and business involvement in unsustainable agricultural practices had caused hardship and suffering for individual Americans challenged the "rights" of corporations to have limited liability for the consequences of externalizing their costs. These are rights that have been increasingly invoked ever since the 1890s, when the Fourteenth Amendment was first used, not to protect the rights of disenfranchised African Americans, but instead as the basis for businesses to secure the freedoms enjoyed by private citizens (Hartmann; Achbar and Abbott).

10. Between 1926 and 1941, Lorentz's commentaries on the film industry appeared in *Judge, New York Evening Journal, Vanity Fair, Town and Country,* and *McCall's.* Acknowledging that his articles did not sit well with Wall Street,

the Republican Party, or the Hollywood establishment, Lorentz dedicated the volume of his collected writings on film to the editors who had "risked their own security by refusing to allow their business offices to have [him] censored or fired" (*Lorentz on Film*, v; see 37, 79–81).

11. Morris L. Ernst was known for his involvement "in several famous literary censorship fights, including his successful effort to have James Joyce's *Ulysses* allowed through U.S. Customs" (Lorentz, *FDR's Moviemaker* 20). He co-authored *To the Pure: A Study in Obscenity and the Censor* (1928) and *The Censor Marches On* (1940) and authored *The First Freedom* (1946).

12. Lorentz does not mince words about partisan politics. For example, in passing he refers to President Warren Harding being "put into the White House by a typical Ohio gang" of Republicans (*FDR's Moviemaker* 112). Lorentz followed this critique of the coordinated Hollywood and Republican Party establishment with a book of photos and accompanying text on "protests, breadlines, farm riots, [and] dust storms" (Barnouw 114).

13. Hearst had already fired Lorentz before, when his negative review of *Svengali* (Mayo, 1931) appeared in Hearst's *New York Evening Journal* at the same time the film's lead (John Barrymore) and screenwriters (Ben Hecht and Charles MacArthur) were "house guests at [Hearst's] San Simeon" estate (*FDR's Filmmaker* 26).

14. At the time, the total number of movie theaters was somewhere between 14,000 and 20,000, with more than half of box office receipts generated at the theaters owned by the studios (see Clement 2; Barnouw 118; *Public Relations* 12–13; *Lorentz on Film* 20).

15. Disney campaigned against *The River* being nominated for an Academy Award despite the fact that (a) Lorentz's articles consistently praised Disney for his innovation and (b) whenever Lorentz previewed *The River*, he had shown a copy of the cartoon "that introduced Pluto, the dog, to the world"; Disney had asked Lorentz for help in that he was "locked out" of many cities "because he would not agree to the terms of the big chain theatre companies" owned by the major studios (*FDR's Moviemaker* 57).

The factors that blocked the distribution of Lorentz's films parallel challenges to the distribution of Robert Flaherty's film *The Land* (1942). *The Land* carries echoes of the Lorentz films, for it examines the ways in which decades of unchecked cotton production had left vast areas of farmland exhausted and many people without a means to survive. The film's critique of conventional farming and its support for farming methods shaped by conservation practices also anticipates the views expressed in many of today's food documentaries. *The Land* was the last film produced by the short-lived U.S. Film Service, which was eliminated by congressional Republicans who argued that the agency was a waste of money, that the administration was using Film Service films in a "propaganda campaign," and that the Film Service was unconstitutional because it usurped states' rights to deliver education (Kahana 120). Congressional Republicans also voiced film executives' objection that the U.S. government was competing unfairly with Hollywood because the Film Service produced films with "high production values, famous talent, relatively large budgets," and epic narratives that critics described as "poetic and magnificent" (Kahana 119, 121). An annoyance to New Deal opponents, *The Land* had a prestige premiere at the Museum of Modern Art in early 1942 and was then permanently denied release. The government explained that with the United States involved in World War II following the attack on Pearl Harbor in December 1941, the film's grim view of American agriculture might "aid the enemies' propaganda campaigns" (Starr 3).

16. While the newsreels attracted audiences because of their showmanship, the *Motion Picture Herald* owned by censorship advocate Martin Quigley objected to the Academy Award the newsreels received, warning that the exhibition of nonfiction film meant the destruction of "the public's escape from the bitter realities, the anguishes, and the turmoil of life" (Barnouw 122). Hollywood embraced Quigley's position, for even though Lorentz's films had helped to create a situation where public "interest in documentary films dealing with contemporary problems exceeded the number of films being made," the studios had "little or no interest in producing nonfiction films" until they began to make films for the U.S. Office of War Information during World War II (Barsam 157).

During World War I, Hollywood produced films according to the dictates of the Committee on Public Information, established by Woodrow Wilson to "sell the war to the American public" (Ross 123). Hollywood's cooperation with the U.S. government during World War II was not only lucrative; it also demonstrated the film industry's loyalty after hearings were convened to air Washington's view that films such as *Blockade* (Dieterle, 1938) were an indication that Hollywood moguls harbored communist sympathies and were guilty of what U.S. government officials termed "premature anti-fascism" (sympathy with the communists who were fighting the fascist regime in Spain before the outbreak of World War II).

17. The MPAA companies are related to corporate entities such as General Electric, Comcast, News Corp., and Viacom. Since Jack Valenti's retirement, the MPAA has been in a period of transition. For example, while it had been working with a $20 million budget, in 2008 the studios reduced its funding to $2.7 million and then to $1.9 million in 2009 (Becker). Public relations remain the focus of the MPAA, whereas the updated AMPP, now known as AMPTP, still handles "internal" affairs. For instance, it represents MPAA companies in labor negotiations. Close coordination continues between these two wings of the organization, with the MPAA and the AMPTP both located at 15301 Ventura Boulevard, Building E, Sherman Oaks, California ("MPAA:

Contact Us"; "AMPTP: Contact Us"). The MPAA "is also the parent organization of the MPA (Motion Picture Association)," which had been "known as the MPEA (Motion Picture Export Association) [and] established in 1946 as a legal cartel under the provisions of the Webb-Pomerane Export Trade Act" (Scott). In 1994, the MPEA became the MPA to "more accurately reflect the global nature of audiovisual entertainment in today's international marketplace" ("Associated Organizations"). As Allen Scott notes, with MPA offices around the globe, the American film industry "carries out its basic mission of promoting Hollywood motion pictures, protecting intellectual property rights, and asserting the goals of the industry generally in foreign markets" (Scott).

18. Members of the Akin, Gump, Strauss, Hauer & Feld, LLP lobbying firm include former FCC commissioner Kathleen Abernathy; former Speaker of the U.S. House Tom Foley; Ruth Harkin, the wife of Iowa senator Tom Harkin; Vernon Jordan, prominent advisor to President Bill Clinton; Ken Mehlman, former chair of the Republican National Committee; James Rogers, CEO of Duke Energy; Robert Strauss, former U.S. Ambassador to Russia and chairman of the Democratic National Committee; and Tommy Thompson, former governor of Wisconsin and secretary of the U.S. Department of Health and Human Services.

19. Louisiana was the first state to pass a food disparagement law in 1991. "Based on a model developed by the American Feed Industry Association," state legislatures also passed food disparagement laws in Idaho (1992); Colorado, Georgia, Mississippi, and South Dakota (1994); Florida, Oklahoma, and Texas (1995); Alabama, Arizona, and Ohio (1996); and North Dakota (1997) (Holt; see Rampton and Stauber *Mad Cow* 17–24, 137–45). Food disparagement laws have been proposed but not passed in many other states; the most recent bill, sponsored by the Ventura County, California, Agricultural Association, was written in 2007 by Assemblywoman Audra Strickland (R-Moorpark).

20. We would like to thank Beckett Warren very much for letting us know about the various versions of the Animal Enterprise Protection/Terrorism Act and for directing us to Will Potter's blog, "Green Is the New Red." Justin Philpot, who let us know about Potter's book of the same title, made it much easier to cite the body of information Potter has been collecting over the years.

21. In 2009, Marie Mason was sentenced to twenty-one years in prison for a 1999 ELF attack on a genetic-engineering research facility at Michigan State University (see Potter 229). In 2009, four animal-rights activists in California were indicted under the 2006 Animal Enterprise Terrorism Act, which makes real or perceived economic loss to animal-enterprise business or affiliated companies a criminal act of domestic terrorism. The case was dismissed in 2010, but that same year William Viehl and Alex Hall "were convicted in

connection with the August 2008 release of three hundred mink from a South Jordan fur farm" (Potter 233). In February 2011, Scott DeMuth was sentenced under the 1992 law for his role in an animal-rights action in Minnesota in 2006 ("Activist Scott DeMuth").

Chapter 3

1. The film was based on a screenplay co-authored by director Percy Adlon, producer Eleanor Adlon, and screenwriter Christopher Doherty; Percy and Eleanor Adlon's son, Felix, is the writer-director of the 1997 food film *Eat Your Heart Out*. While *Bagdad Cafe* was Adlon's first English-language film, he had been a director in German TV and film since 1970. *Bagdad Cafe* was the basis for the CBS television series of the same name, which ran for a season and a half beginning in 1990, starring Whoopi Goldberg as Brenda, Jean Stapleton as Jasmin, and James Gammon as Rudi. For additional analysis of *Bagdad Cafe,* see Baron 2003.

2. The film also contrasts Brenda and Jasmin with Debbie (Christine Kaufman), the thin, white, listless tattoo artist who lives at the Bagdad Motel.

3. In her study of hunger, malnutrition, and poverty in contemporary America, Janet Fitchen points out that for poor Americans, human behaviors that involve "some items, such as coffee, are more social than dietary" (395). She notes that during her field research on Americans living in poverty, she was offered a cup of coffee "almost every time [she] entered a home" (395).

4. Intrigued by Jasmin's Bavarian costume and exotic taste in coffee, a bit later in the scene Rudi makes another attempt at flirtation. This time, the failed attempt also offers an amusing parody of Hollywood seduction scenes. Played like a bad imitation of a Hollywood movie where the man "casually" strikes up conversation with the women he desires, Jack Palance languidly floats over to and then around Marianne Sägebrecht, who now sits rigidly at the counter, anxiously twisting the strap of her handbag. Grinning with excitement and delight, he asks if she plans to stay a while, and then breathlessly introduces himself as "Rudi Cox from Hollywood, tinseltown, the movies." Preoccupied, Sägebrecht remains largely unresponsive, and so the actors' performances not only underscore the silliness of Rudi's name and ideas about seduction, they amplify the contrast established earlier between the shy German tourist and the swaggering movie cowboy who cannot drink the strong coffee Jasmin enjoys.

5. The film's early references to cannibalism show that in environments marked by incomplete socialization, racial prejudice can create deep divisions. Yet by tracing the women's journey from suspicion to friendship through scenes of cleanup and other women's work, the film also points to connections that transcend that divide. Near the end of the film, Adlon

presents us with a comical twist that perhaps ties the imagery of cannibalism (or dismemberment) and cleanup together. During one of their magic acts at the diner, Brenda gives the crowd a big grin as she places a wash bucket from the kitchen under the arm of a woman who is set to be sawed in half by Jasmin. The moment seems to suggest that even their feelings of being isolated, cut off, and half a person have, by the end of the film, become something the women know how to make jokes about. Grounded securely in life experiences in which wash buckets are a constant, Jasmin and Brenda know how to handle those feelings because they have found ways to sustain connections across a world divided by racial prejudice.

6. Jasmin's metamorphosis causes and is caused by Rudi's and Brenda's transformations. Costuming and props illustrate Rudi's journey from tinseltown oddball to Jasmin's considerate friend and adoring suitor. At the outset, his snakeskin boots and garish satin shirts make Rudi appear to be little more than a braggart in a TV western. As useless as his rifle that has a hair trigger that cannot be repaired, early on Rudi tries to catch Jasmin's attention by waving to her with a little green flower stalk that hangs limply in his hand. The prop echoes the idea suggested by Rudi's interaction with Jasmin and the Rosenheim coffee thermos, namely, that he starts off as a character that cannot even mimic conventional seduction scenes. By the end of the film, however, visual elements show that Rudi has moved far beyond the limitations of convention. For during the scene in which Rudi proposes to Jasmin, Rudi clasps Jasmin's pink-feathered slippers softly to his chest. As he speaks, he holds them out gently to her, who stands quietly as he sits and then kneels before her. The picture of lanky Jack Palance gently grasping the pink slippers as he makes his proposal of marriage leaves no doubt that Rudi has journeyed a long distance from the domain of cardboard movie tough guy.

Tracing a line of symbolism that parallels the clichéd movie props that reveal Rudi's changing identity and the foodstuffs that will symbolize Jasmin's transformation, the film conveys Brenda's transformation from shrew to gracious hostess through the changing physical condition of the diner. When the film opens, Brenda's relationships are not working and in fact have turned to garbage: her diner's coffee machine is broken and rusty tin cans litter the ground outside the diner. Yet as the film ends, Brenda has mended her relationships and even built new ones. CCH Pounder (Brenda) is radiant as she entertains the family members and guests who now sit together as they fill the diner to capacity. Bright colors in the characters' costumes show that the Bagdad Cafe is brimming with physical and emotional nourishment.

7. The scenes also go beyond the modernist treatment of the scene, for they also leave out the machine featured in *Persimmon* (1964), Robert Rauschenberg's modernist version of Rubens's painting *Venus at the Mirror,* which stands in for the black slave in Rubens's painting.

8. For some, the squash might also be a symbol that conveys and comments on dominant culture's ambivalence about women's sexuality. The green winter squash is related to the much larger common pumpkin (cucurbita pepo), a member of the gourd family and the same genus (cucurbita) as many varieties of squash. That connection might mean that the squash can serve to hint at associations often linked to pumpkins and women, for like pumpkins, women have been defined in contradictory terms, their sexuality equated to "the intemperate energy of a wild thing and the comforting strength" of a docile, domesticated fruit (Tuleja 143).

9. Future studies could examine distinctions between the representational strategies in *Bagdad Cafe*'s painting sequence and those central to established traditions in painting. For example, comparison between Adlon's film and Édouard Manet's "Le Déjeuner sur l'herbe" (1863) would illustrate that in contrast to Manet's work, Adlon's images of the female nude are not meant to shock or scandalize and that the food is not an afterthought in the image. Comparisons between Adlon's film and impressionist still lifes by artists such as Claude Monet, Paul Cezanne, or Paul Gauguin would help to show that in *Bagdad Cafe* images of food are not experiments in line or color but instead are designed to carry symbolic meaning. Claude Monet's "Still Life with Melon" (1872), Paul Cézanne's "Ginger Pot with Pomegranate and Pears" (1890–93), and Paul Gauguin's "Still Life with Tahitian Oranges" (1892) could be comparative examples to consider.

To better understand the use of allegory in Jasmin's portraits, it could prove useful to study seventeenth-century Flemish still lifes and mythological paintings. Here one might consider seventeenth-century still lifes by Jan de Heem, Willem Kalf, and the Spanish artist Van der Hamen. In works by these artists, still life elements can be found in portraiture and paintings of mythological subjects, as in Van der Hamen's "Pomona and Vertumnus" (1626). It would be important to remember that in Adlon's film, Rudi's artistic rendering is clearly *not* "better than the original" (Johnston 26). In contrast to exquisite Flemish paintings that created "a competition between the representation and the objects" (Johnston 26), Rudi's painting are in a primitive folk art style that provides a comic commentary on the amateur painter's attempts to express his devotion to Jasmin.

Chapter 4

1. For a more thorough discussion of the gender and national cinema aspects of *301/302*, see Chapter 9.

2. Park's twelfth feature film won the 1995 Grand Bell Award for Best Film in Korea. An official selection of both the 1996 Sundance Film Festival and the 1996 Berlin International Film Festival, and the South Korean

nominee for a foreign film Academy Award, *301/302* carries impressive endorsements merited by its daring content and unique style. Though the Motion Picture Arts and Sciences Academy did not select *301/302* to compete in the foreign film category, South Korea submitted it as its official nominee. Kee notes that *301/302* was the first internationally distributed South Korean film and received positive critical reviews both domestically and internationally. Nevertheless, "the film was unsuccessful at the local box office when it was released in April 1995, earning roughly 350 million won (approximately $391,000 as of 1 December 1995)" (Kee 464n2).

3. While dogs have been and are eaten in some Asian countries, to cook a dog treated as a family pet is universally considered a transgressive and unacceptable act.

4. South Korean writer/director Woo-Seong Lim's *Vegetarian* (2009), screened at Sundance, dramatizes the repulsion meat causes a young housewife who clashes with her meat-eating husband. A study of food, its attractive qualities as well as its rich symbolism, in South Korean society would be another fruitful subject for inquiry.

5. For more discussion on the distorted shots and body as well as narrative fragmentation, see Papazian.

6. Not unexpectedly, these problems occur more often in industrialized countries (Daniels). The U.S. statistics on eating disorders long ago reached staggering proportions, signaling the complicated interrelationships among emotional, psychological, and physical aspects. Five to ten million women and one million men struggle with eating disorders (Weber). But while women exhibit more symptoms of anorexia and bulimia than men do, both genders explain that food is not the issue. In effect, control of food is a baseline attempt to exert power over their lives. For the anorexic, "the daily routine of self-denial is a form of self-assertion" (Gidday). However, the effects of starvation on the mind as well as the body include depression and escalating isolation. Individuals increasingly shut themselves off from interaction with others, eroding self-esteem. And before long, the eating disorder controls daily routines, disrupts all normal life patterns, and threatens any already precarious stability. The opposite side of the coin is the grotesquely obese patients who eat uncontrollably. Recent estimates define five million Americans as morbidly obese, that is, an average man who is one hundred or more pounds overweight (see Gawande).

7. Publications include *Food, Culture & Society; Food and Foodways;* and *Gastronomica.* See also Levi-Strauss for a landmark discussion of cultural context.

8. In the year 2000, the average American woman was 5'4" and weighed 140 pounds. The average model was 5'11" and weighed 117 pounds (Weber). It is estimated that three of every one hundred women will develop an eating disorder.

Chapter 5

1. The varied and cyclical pattern of cannibal films relates to the films' differing production contexts. For example, the financial success of Lewis's *Blood Feast* reflects specific circumstances in the American film industry. In the mid-1960s a new market for blood and gore emerged because Hollywood's financially expedient system of self-regulation would not be updated until the rating system was put in effect in 1968. At the same time, it became safe and thus lucrative to show movies that did not conform to the Production Code because the 1964 Supreme Court decision in Jacobellis v. Ohio weakened the power of local censorship organizations. That decision made it possible for low-budget gore films like *Blood Feast* to screen in neighborhood and drive-in theaters without risking cost-prohibitive local interference. As films like *Black Tavern* (Yip, 1972), *Dragon Inn* (Lee, 1992), and *The Beheaded 1000* (Ting, 1993) reveal, circumscribed references to cannibalism also appear in Hong Kong and Taiwanese films designed for the international market for action and spectacle that emerged in the 1970s.

2. Italian exploitation filmmaker Umberto Lenzi is apparently skeptical of Arens's position. His 1981 film *Cannibal Ferox,* considered by many to be the most brutal of the cannibal cycle (see Parkinson), features Lorraine De Selle as Gloria Davis, a Ph.D. candidate who journeys, with her brother and a friend, to the South American rainforest for research. Davis's Ph.D. thesis sounds similar to Arens's book, as she argues that cannibalism is a myth made up by racist imperialists. The title of her thesis, "Cannibalism: End of a Myth," recalls the title of Arens's book. However, Davis learns that cannibalism is very real as flesh-eating savages beset her and her friends in the jungle. The only survivor of the bloody ordeal, Gloria escapes and returns to New York City to receive her doctorate. During the ceremony, she exhibits only a blank stare, as if she is ashamed of herself for lacking the courage to admit that her thesis is false and that cannibalism is real. Lenzi's film thus insists on the existence of cannibalism and the hypocrisy of those who say differently.

3. Beckett Warren brought this film to our attention. His insights into cannibalism and cannibal films also played a central role in the ideas discussed throughout the chapter.

4. See Arens 22–31 for various problems with the logic of Staden's account; for example, he could not communicate with a Frenchman but seems to have been "particularly adept at recounting verbatim the Indian dialogue on the very first day of his captivity, as they discussed among themselves how, when and where they would eat Staden" (25).

5. The country has also been treated as a colony by first-world financial institutions that entice the country to borrow money and then wreak havoc with Brazil's ability to devote resources to its citizens.

Chapter 6

1. Food's importance extends well beyond Italian American associations, as *Bonnie and Clyde* (Penn, 1967) proves. Shortly after Bonnie (Faye Dunaway) flees her dull life with the thrillingly dangerous Clyde (Warren Beatty), they eat at a diner, one of the few times they sit in public for a meal. The meal creates conflict rather than connection, for it prompts Clyde to tell Bonnie she should change her hair; noticing the waitress's hairstyle, Clyde decides that both women have unattractive curls by their ears. This and subsequent food scenes (eating in the car, collecting carryout from another diner) depict the gangsters as unglamorous, inarticulate, and impotent.

Gangster films use food to critique the all-consuming nature of capitalism. However, many gangster films do not offer a progressive view of women. Before and after the infamous grapefruit and boiling coffee assaults, gangster films have contrasted mothers who provide delicious meals with molls who cannot cook; they establish the dichotomy between the good, nurturing mother and the disreputable girlfriend through the female characters' food activities.

2. Schulz worked as a food stylist on *Bugsy*. See Appendix 1 for a description of the food stylist's contributions and responsibilities. Schulz notes that Bugsy's lack of table manners conveys his coarse persona. She notes that near the film's conclusion, a more formal dinner at the Brown Derby features appetizing food that no one eats. In the scene where Bugsy is killed, the food again emphasizes the character and the situation. As Schulz points out, "Traditional, stereotypical mobster food was requested. A certain pasta had to be recreated with peas and tomato sauce, the latter perhaps a precursor of the blood to come" (Schulz).

3. The two food-fight scenes feature the film's most explicit use of food, yet other scenes of food also convey characters' personalities. For example, the first time food figures prominently in a scene, Smee reveals his grotesque appetites and unfettered indulgence. Alone in Hook's cabin, Smee gobbles down turkey drumsticks that he grabs from tables piled with food. Here the food and the food behavior are both slightly repulsive.

Chapter 7

1. Rudick notes, "Rodale, one of the oldest and most successful niche publishers, came about not because readers were clamoring for information, but because of the personal philosophy of the company's founder, J. I. Rodale" (1). After the explosion of niche magazines in the 1990s (e.g., 700 new magazines in 1992), Rodale Press "began developing new magazines and acquiring ones such as *Bicycling, Mountain Bike, Runner's World, Back Packer*, and

Scuba Diving" (Rudick 2). Rodale now publishes ten health, fitness, and lifestyle magazines.

2. Filmmakers interested in sustainable agriculture have been inspired by Bromfield's books such as *Pleasant Valley* (1945) and *Malabar Farm* (1948). Bromfield, who wrote a number of best-selling novels, adapted his novel *The Rains Came* for the 1939 film of the same name, which starred Tyrone Power and Myrna Loy. The film won an Oscar for special effects and was nominated for best art direction, black/white cinematography, editing, musical score, and sound recording. YouTube has various infomercials about Malabar Farms.

3. Jeremy L. Korr and Christine Broussard provide a concise recommended reading list in their essay "Challenges in the Interdisciplinary Teaching of Food and Foodways" in *Food, Culture & Society*. The list includes publications by Anthony Bourdian, Lester Brown, Eric Grace, Howard Lyman, Eric Schlosser, and Margaret Visser.

4. At one end of the fact-fiction continuum are documentaries, which themselves have a wide range of form and content. A step away from "nonfiction" documentaries are faux documentaries or mockumentaries, such as *David Holzman's Diary* (McBride, 1967), *This Is Spinal Tap* (Reiner, 1984), the HBO mini-series *Tanner 88* (Altman, 1988), and *Man Bites Dog* (Belvaux, Bonzel, and Poelvoorde, 1992), which have documentary form but fictional content. Moving further along the continuum, one next finds docudramas, which have dramatic or fictional form but documentary content. These films range from work such as *The War Game* (Watkins, 1965) and *The Battle of Algiers* (Pontecorvo, 1966) to *Schindler's List* (Spielberg, 1993) and *Fair Game* (Liman, 2010), the latter starring Naomi Watts as Valerie Plame and Sean Penn as her husband, Joe Wilson. Finally, at the far end are films with fictional form and fictional content. Like fiction films, documentaries feature music, narrative design, and performances by subjects and filmmakers.

5. Reality TV shows like *Big Brother* are a form of observational cinema in a controlled artificial environment; the first such show aired in the Netherlands in 1999 and soon after became a media sensation in England, the United States, and across the globe. Formatted reality TV shows like *Wife Swap* (first aired in the United Kingdom in 2003), which have appeared in both the United States and Europe, are instances of observational cinema that place people in contrived, real-world situations. Cooking competitions are also reality TV fare. *Iron Chef* began in Japan in 1992 and is now a worldwide phenomenon, with versions airing in Australia, England, Israel, and the United States. In addition, there are documentaries such as *The Thin Blue Line* (Morris, 1988) and *Touching the Void* (Macdonald, 2003) that include reconstructions of previous or possible events. There are also films that feature the performances of doc-auteurs such as Michael Moore and British director Nick Broomfield, best known in the United States for his documentaries about serial killer Aileen

Wuornos (1993 and 2003) and his celebrity profiles that include *Heidi Fleiss: Hollywood Madam* (1995), *Kurt & Courtney* (1998), and *Biggie and Tupac* (2002).

6. The dynamics of media culture make it difficult to determine the specific effects that representations have on individuals' thoughts, beliefs, and actions. However, the massive audience study on *The End of the Line* shows the degree to which food documentaries have an effect on public perceptions. The eighteen-month "Social Impact Evaluation" conducted by the Channel 4 BRITDOC Foundation between May 2009 and January 2011 concluded that the film "did appear to create a tipping point in corporate policy" (4).

7. *FLOW* was nominated for the Grand Jury Prize at the 2008 Sundance Film Festival, was named Best Documentary at the Vail Film Festival and the U.N. Association Film Festival, and won the International Jury Prize at the Mumbai International Film Festival. Irena Salina acted in French theater before coming to New York, where she studied with Charles Laughton at the Actors Studio. The niece of French actor Philippe Noiret, she has worked in various capacities on film production and appeared in *King of New York* (Ferrara, 1990).

8. The proposed Article 31 would read: "Everyone has the right to clean and accessible water, adequate for the health and well-being of the individual and family, and no one shall be deprived of such access or quality of water due to individual economic circumstance." The U.S. Geological Survey provides valuable information on water resources; see www.USGS.gov.

9. In one way or another, the various food documentaries produced in the last two decades reckon with the realities of the industrial farm, which depends on war technologies being repurposed rather than decommissioned. The discoveries that led to the use of nitrogen bombs in World War I served as the basis for today's nitrogen-based fertilizers; nerve gas used in World War II became the basis for insecticides; and chemical companies have produced defoliants that later helped them to develop both weed killers and genetically modified seeds for commodity crops that can withstand such products (examples include Monsanto's role in creating Agent Orange and its current herbicide Roundup).

Chapter 8

1. A few unrated horror films have also been shown in theaters. AMC theaters showed *Hatchet II* (Green, 2010) in the top twenty markets in the United States. *I Spit on Your Grave* (Monroe, 2010) was released unrated.

Chapter 9

1. See, for example, S. Lim; Grant, *Film Genre* 102–8; Crofts "Reconceptualizing"; Crofts "Concepts"; and Higson, who argues for inclusion of

"the activity of national audiences and the conditions under which they make sense of and use the films they watch" to construct their cultural identity (36). In their analysis of national cinema and imperialism, Ella Shohat and Robert Stam point out that as the West demonized and patronized the non-West, "cinema, as the world's storyteller *par excellence,* was ideally suited to relay the projected narratives of nations and empires" (101). For studies that illustrate how foodways analysis increases insights into films' production and reception contexts, see Barnard; Fried.

2. See also James, "Im Kwon-Taek" 14–31. In 1985, the South Korean film industry was energized by the lifting of restrictive regulations. As if in response to the loosening of years of control, directors produced strong, confrontational fare. Even through the mid-nineties economic downturn, established and new talent continued to produce daring work while routine action films shared the screen. The trend continued with, for example, writer/director Ki-Duk Kim's *The Isle* (2000) stunning audiences at the 2001 Sundance Festival with its graphic and intense violence and arresting style. Writer/director Kwak Kyung-taek's *Friend* (a.k.a. *Those Were the Days,* 2001) and writer/director Kim Sung-Soo's *The Warrior* (*Musa,* 2001) were among the South Korean films at the 2001 Cannes International Film Festival; *Screen International,* among others, subsequently devoted several articles to the dynamic South Korean film industry. In South Korea, the government supports the film industry with a law requiring that at least 40 percent of all screen time in theaters be reserved for domestic films. Even with that quota, *301/302* would not have been guaranteed a screening because of its challenging style and confrontational content.

3. Other directors' efforts to visualize cinematic feminist alternatives received attention around the time of *301/302*'s release. These include Oh Byong-chul's *Go Alone Like a Rhino's Horn* (1995) and Lee Min-yong's *A Dog-Day Afternoon* (1995). In the melodramatic *Go Alone Like a Rhino's Horn,* one of the three female protagonists, Kyong-hye, commits suicide after agonizing over her husband's affairs and her own retaliatory affair. The character's success as a television announcer fails to provide fulfillment, and the other two thirtyish women in the story also find the dreams of marriage wanting. In other words, fulfillment as defined by mainstream (patriarchal) Korean society leads to women's unhappiness. By contrast, in *A Dog-Day Afternoon* ten women accidentally beat an abusive husband to death and lead feminist supporters in their arguments of self-defense. Female audience members at screenings have burst into spontaneous applause and cheers "when the three heroines cracked jokes about their husbands' incompetence and sexual clumsiness" (Hye-son 28). *Go Alone's* writer Kong Ji-young noted, "In Korean movies, women have always been depicted to fit men's tastes, but *Go Alone* has no such characters. Here, the women are unyielding and self-reliant" (Hye-son 28). She maintains that not economic but "mental independence is more important" for women

to find contentment and happiness (Hye-son 28). See Gateward, Frances, ed. *Seoul Searching.*

4. The South Korean film industry has employed its leverage to "re-masculinize Korean Cinema," as Kyung Hyun Kim argues. Finding the trope of masculinity embedded in South Korean films over the last twenty-five years, Kim sees films produced since 1980 as reflections of anxiety about male self-definition, a topic familiar in its various applications to the American films that reflect a response to the women's movement in the United States. However, it is useful to move beyond the modernity-tradition binary and stereotypical gender struggles that offer grim options for contemporary women. As Park's film suggests, "the sexualized feminine Other" has not been silent as economic and sociocultural changes increased (Choi 15). By confronting stereotypical expectations, *301/302* asks audiences to acknowledge changes in the Korean social landscape. As Hesung Chun Koh points out, Korean writers in the late twentieth century have carefully examined "male dominance and female subordination" (159). However, responses to those imbalances of power have also taken less rational form. As Koh notes, "Manifestations of Korean's women's emotional conflicts can best be seen in cases of hysterical neurosis" (160). Statistics show that 75.6 percent of such cases between 1958 and 1973 were women, a consequence of the pressure for Korean women to have a son, the emphasis on patriarchal and patrilineal principles, and the prejudice against women for child custody. Through dysfunctional behavior, the women known as 301 and 302 defy stereotypical entrapment, perhaps even to claim, as Joan Kee argues, "sites of independence" through the articulation of their hysteria (449). In her detailed explication of the film, she contends that "by developing a language of hysteria . . . the female protagonists evade patriarchally defined scripts" (450).

5. The characters' choices—preferable to capitulation to patriarchal definition with its concomitant surrender of agency and self, more viable than the erasure of desire—offer only compromised alternative space. But the film indicates that it could not be otherwise. This is perhaps the film's most honest and painful, but crucial, message. It speaks directly and compellingly to the contemporary woman for whom economic and emotional self-reliance exists as an attractive and perhaps the only acceptable choice. Teresa de Lauretis concluded in the 1980s that "women *must either* consent *or* be seduced into consenting to femininity" (134). Then, as now, for the United States and South Korea, de Lauretis defines the pan-national project explored in the film: "The real difficulty, but also the most exciting, original project of feminist theory remains precisely this—how to theorize that experience, which is at once social and personal, and how to construct the female subject from that political and intellectual rage" (166).

Chul-Soo Park's *301/302* participates in the small but important body of films imagining this unaccommodating female subject located in a specific national moment. More often, despite the increasingly visible, if struggling, independent woman in Korean films, "Recent cinematic examples of independent women never succeed in dislodging the woman from an ultimate dependency on men for validation. This failure is a fundamental one that circumvents the aspirations of many contemporary Korean films for being credible narratives of female independence" (Kee 450). While feminism has found supporters in contemporary South Korea (over forty organizations have some affiliation with the women's movement), and while South Korea has succeeded in many facets of modernization, as noted earlier "its behavioral culture maintains and embraces some Confucian traditions, and it is slow to change" (Palley 275).

In the 1990s, failure to adhere to the tenets of filial piety and self-sacrifice led to criticisms of modern Korean women "as confused and misled by the charges brought about by modernization-cum-westernization" (Lee 69). Those criticisms reflected the country's continued adherence to the crucial and central concept of *han*, the fundamental concept conveying the trauma of Korean history. As "the essential national experience, *han* is constituted from sentiments of loss and rage at the severance of wholeness and continuity between self and history. . . . and—inevitably in a strict Confucian patriarchy—especially of women" (James, "Im Kwon-Taek" 19). The national cultural concept of *han* identifies feelings of oppression and the resentment caused by injustices against which the individual has little recourse. By extension, an individual may seek revenge to alleviate the painful grief caused by the unjust situation, and this applies metaphorically in *301/302*. Neither woman feels whole; 302 in particular embodies symbolic and enervating starvation. 301 attempts to coax and then to force 302 to rejuvenated health with irresistible culinary offerings. However, neither woman can find satisfaction as their encounters, instead of healing, produce further resentment, anger, and trauma.

6. In *Mr. Saturday Night*, the opening shots are as follows:

1. Matzah balls being shaped 0:01–0:12 (12 seconds)
2. Matzah balls being dropped into pot of boiling water 0:13–0:18
3. Knife cutting onion 0:19–0:20
4. Knife quartering pickled tomato 0:22–0:27
5. Hand stuffing sausage 0:28–0:35
6. Brisket: hand cutting fat off 0:36–0:39
7. Hand stuffing chicken 0:40–0:45
8. Hand rubbing salt into brisket 0:46–0:48
9. Cabbage being folded and held with toothpick 0:49–0:53
10. Liver being ground 0:54–1:00
11. Potatoes being cooked 1:01–1:04
12. Onions cooking, caramelizing, and being seasoned 1:05–1:08
13. Pancakes (latkes) being cooked, turned 1:09–1:14
14. Brisket cooked and served 1:15–1:18

15. Bread being cut 1:19–1:24
16. Matzah balls are served 1:25–1:27
17. Fish being served, picked at with fork 1:28–1:30
18. Ladling sauce / cabbage 1:31–1:36
19. Onions served 1:37–1:39
20. Mashed potatoes plopped on top of full plate 1:40–1:41
21. Apple being peeled by male hands 1:42–1:44
22. Tea being poured, sugar cube picked up 1:45–1:51
23. Three dissolves at the end of the meal as the camera tracks across nearly empty plates 1:52–2:25

7. Director Billy Crystal told food stylist Ann Schulz that he wanted the matzah ball to splat onto the board to reinforce the sardonic comments and rob the image of a more idyllic cooking setting. Crystal reiterates this in his commentary on the DVD—that he wanted to start the film with a "splat." For more on Crystal's on-set directions to Schulz, see Appendix 1.

8. Studies that explore taboo violations have considered films such as *Suddenly, Last Summer* (Mankiewicz, 1959), *The Cook, the Thief, His Wife, and Her Lover,* and *The Silence of the Lambs.* See Ohi; Johnston; Staiger.

9. With its attention to characters who are young, alienated, and products of an American society filled with junk food, media, and empty distraction (Levy 467, 485), *Mysterious Skin* has thematic connections with other works directed by Gregg Araki, whose 1992 film *The Living End* made him an important contributor to American independent and New Queer Cinema (Biskind, *Down and Dirty* 21, 117; Levy 264, 467; King 227). Yet there are profound distinctions in approach. *Mysterious Skin* is distinguished by its understated design and the actors' remarkable performances, whereas Araki's better-known trilogy of films, *Totally Fucked Up* (1993), *The Doom Generation* (1995), and *Nowhere* (1997), features an "aesthetic of excess" that revels in "garish, overstylized images . . . bombastic acting . . . trashy ephemera [and] parody" (King 235–36). Thus, while Araki's films in the nineties explored the "*nihilism* of alienated youth" and aimed to shock mainstream audiences with "steamy sex, macabre violence, absurdist humor, boisterous music, and flamboyant art design" (Levy 485; emphasis added), *Mysterious Skin* might be difficult to watch but has no connection to exploitation cinema. Instead, it has been seen as "a meditation on the necessity of making your way past, or through, [things that prevent] you from being a thinking, feeling person" (Zacharek *Mysterious*). Despite its unflinching emotional realism, there is no graphic sex in the film; and despite its weighty subject, "the film has a weird buoyancy" (Zacharek *Mysterious*). When it was released, a reviewer commented that *Mysterious Skin* "is at once the most harrowing and, strangely, the most touching film I have seen about child abuse" (Ebert).

Mysterious Skin is also a film that shows "it's possible to talk about pedophilia—indeed, to condemn it—without resorting to the histrionics of Fox News," largely because Scott Heim's novel provided the blueprint for the scenario and the reflective tone of the film (D. Lim). Araki's adaptation thus "watches with care and attention as its characters grow in the direction that childhood pointed them" (Ebert). The film's pensive mood also arises from audiences' alignment with the main characters that is created by their voiceover narration and the point-of-view shots in moments of emotional intensity. Viewers thus see and understand the childhood experiences as they appear when the characters look back on them. *Mysterious Skin* also brings viewers into the main characters' subjective experience and highlights that "young people interpret experiences in the terms they have available to them" by presenting Neil and Brian surrounded by mundane but telling details—such as the food in their respective lives, which is perhaps distinguished by the empty promises of nourishment offered by the boys' mothers and the contrasting supply of enticing and at least temporarily satisfying food that Neil enjoyed with his coach during the summer he was eight years old (Ebert).

WORKS CITED

"2011 Kellogg Company: Financial Highlights." *Kellogg's*. N.d. Web. 8 July 2012.

"About the ACGA." *American Corn Growers Association*. N.d. Web. 21 July 2012.

Abrams, Nathan. "'I'll Have Whatever She's Having': Jews, Food, and Film." *Reel Food: Essays on Food and Film*. Ed. Anne L. Bower. New York: Routledge, 2004. 87–100. Print.

Achbar, Mark, and Jennifer Abbott. *The Corporation*. Big Picture Media. 2003. Film.

"Activist Scott DeMuth Taken into Custody for 6-Month Jail Term." *Fight Back News*. 17 February 2011. Web. 8 July 2012.

Alpers, Svetlana. *The Making of Rubens*. New Haven, Conn.: Yale UP, 1996. Print.

Altman, Rick. "A Semantic/Syntactic Approach to Film Genre." *Film Genre Reader III*. Ed. Barry Keith Grant. Austin: U of Texas P, 2003. 27–41. Print.

Amato, Rebecca, and Rahul Hamid. "The Business of Dinner: An Interview with Robert Kenner." *Cineaste* 34:3 (Summer 2009): 38–41. Print.

"The Amazing Spider-Man—Partners." *The Amazing Spider-Man*. Sony. N.d. Web. 12 July 2012.

"AMPTP: Contact Us." *Alliance of Motion Picture and Television Producers*. N.d. Web. 14 July 2012.

Ansen, David. "*Bagdad Cafe*." *Newsweek* (25 April 1988): 62. Print.

"Appeals Court Upholds Oprah Decision." *Oklahoma City Journal Record*. 10 February 2000. Web. 14 July 2012.

Arens, William. *The Man-Eating Myth: Anthropology and Anthropophagy*. New York: Oxford UP, 1979. Print.

"Associated Organizations." *Motion Picture Association–Canada*. N.d. Web. 14 July 2012.

Barnard, Timothy P. "Chickens, Cakes, and Kitchens: Food and Modernity in Malay Films of the 1950s and 1960." *Reel Food: Essays on Food and Film*. Ed. Anne L. Bower. New York: Routledge, 2004, 75–85. Print.

Barnes, Brooks, and Michael Cieply. "Motion Picture Industry Group Names Ex-Senator Dodd as Its New Chief." *New York Times*. 1 March 2011. Web. 8 July 2012.

Barnouw, Erik. *Documentary: A History of Non-Fiction Film.* 2nd rev. ed. New York: Oxford UP, 1993. Print.

Baron, Cynthia. "Food and Gender in *Bagdad Cafe.*" *Food and Foodways* 11:1 (2003): 49–74. Print.

Baron, Cynthia. "Sayles between the Systems: Bucking 'Industry Policy' and Indie Apolitical Chic." *Sayles Talk: New Perspectives on Independent Filmmaker John Sayles.* Ed. Diane Carson and Heidi Kenaga. Detroit: Wayne State UP, 2006. 16–50. Print.

Barsam, Richard M. *Nonfiction Film: A Critical History.* Rev. ed. Bloomington: Indiana UP, 1992. Print.

Baumgarten, Marjorie. *"301/302."* *Austin Chronicle.* 11 October 1996. Web. 28 June 2012.

Becker, Amanda. "Motion Picture Association of America Struggles to Choose a New Leader." *Washington Post.* 17 January 2011. Web. 8 July 2012.

Bederman, David J. "What Are Agricultural Disparagement Statutes?" *ProCon.* N.d. Web. 8 July 2012.

Beier, Lars-Olav. "Spiegel Interview with Director Doris Dörrie: 'Death Can Make People Feel Very Alive.'" *Spiegel Online.* 2 June 2008. Web. 19 July 2012.

Belasco, Warren J. *Appetite for Change: How the Counterculture Took on the Food Industry, 1966–1988.* New York: Pantheon, 1989. Print.

Belasco, Warren J. *Food: The Key Concepts.* New York: Berg, 2008. Print.

Belasco, Warren J. "Food Matters: Perspectives on an Emerging Field." *Food Nations: Selling Taste in Consumer Societies.* Ed. Warren Belasco and Philip Scranton. New York: Routledge, 2002. 2–23. Print.

Belasco, Warren J. *Meals to Come: A History of the Future of Food.* Berkeley: U of California P, 2006. Print.

Benjamin, Walter. "The Work of Art in the Age of Mechanical Reproduction." *Illuminations.* Ed. Hannah Arendt. New York: Schocken, 1968. 217–67. Print.

Berger, John. *Ways of Seeing.* London: British Broadcasting Corporation and Penguin Books, 1972. Print.

Berglund, Jeff. *Cannibal Fictions: American Explorations of Colonialism, Race, Gender, and Sexuality.* Madison: U of Wisconsin P, 2006. Print.

Bernard, Mark. "Selling the Splat Pack: The DVD Revolution and the American Horror Film." Ph.D. diss. Bowling Green State University, 2010. Print.

Berry, Wendell. *The Unsettling of America: Culture and Agriculture.* San Francisco: Sierra Club Books, 1996. Print.

Birnbaum, Jeffrey H. "Glickman Succeeds Valenti at MPAA." *Washington Post.* 2 July 2004. Web. 8 July 2012.

Biskind, Peter. *Down and Dirty Pictures: Miramax, Sundance, and the Rise of Independent Film.* New York: Simon & Schuster, 2004. Print.

Biskind, Peter. *Easy Riders, Raging Bulls: How the Sex-Drugs-and Rock 'n' Roll Generation Saved Hollywood.* New York: Simon & Schuster, 1999. Print.

Bittman, Mark. *Food Matters: A Guide to Conscious Eating.* New York: Simon & Schuster, 2009. Print.

Bittman, Mark. "Sustainable Farming Can Feed the World?" *New York Times.* 8 March 2011. Web. 23 July 2012.

Black, Gregory D. *Hollywood Censored: Morality Codes, Catholics, and the Movies.* New York: Cambridge UP, 1994. Print.

Boliek, Brooks. "Dialogue: Dan Glickman." *Hollywood Reporter.* 1 September 2004. Web. 8 July 2012.

Bower, Anne L. "Watching Food: The Production of Food, Film, and Values." *Reel Food: Essays on Food and Film.* Ed. Anne L. Bower. New York: Routledge, 2004. 1–13. Print.

"Brand PR Failures: McDonald's–the McLibel Trial." *Brand Failures—and Lessons Learned!* 3 December 2006. Web. 19 July 2012.

BRITDOC. "The End of the Line: A Social Impact Evaluation." *BRITDOC.* N.d. Web. 22 July 2012.

Britton, Andrew. "Blissing Out: The Politics of Reaganite Entertainment." *Britton on Film: The Complete Film Criticism of Andrew Britton.* Ed. Barry Keith Grant. Detroit: Wayne State UP, 2009. 97–154. Print.

Brown, Lester R. "Could Food Shortages Bring Down Civilization?" *Scientific American.* 22 April 2009. Web. 13 July 2009.

Brown, Lester R. *Plan B 3.0: Mobilizing to Save Civilization.* New York: Norton, 2008. Print.

Brown, Linda Keller, and Kay Mussell. "Introduction." *Ethnic and Regional Foodways in the United States: The Performance of Group Identity.* Knoxville: U of Tennessee P, 1984. 3–15. Print.

Browne, Nick. "The Spectator-in-the-Text: The Rhetoric of *Stagecoach.*" *Film Quarterly* 29:2 (1975–1976): 26–38. Print.

Bruzzi, Stella. *New Documentary.* 2nd ed. New York: Routledge, 2006. Print.

"Call for Outreach Partners." *What's "Organic" about Organic?* N.d. Web. 21 July 2012.

Casten, Liane. "The Media Can Legally Lie." *Censored 2006: The Top 25 Censored Stories.* Ed. Peter Phillips and Project Censored. New York: Seven Stories, 2006. 164–66. Print.

Catsoulis, Jeannette. "'FLOW: For Love of Water.'" *New York Times.* 12 September 2008. Web. 21 July 2012.

Cheyfitz, Eric. *The Poetics of Imperialism: Translation and Colonization from The Tempest to Tarzan.* Philadelphia: U of Pennsylvania P, 1997. Print.

Choi, Chungmoo. "Nationalism and Construction of Gender in Korea." *Dangerous Women: Gender and Korean Nationalism.* Ed. Elaine H. Kim and Chungmoo Choi. New York: Routledge, 1998. 9–32. Print.

Clark, Josh. "How Cannibalism Works." *How Stuff Works*. N.d. Web. 19 July 2012.

Classification and Rating Administration. "Agreement to Submit Motion Picture for Rating." *CARA*. 1 January 2012. Web. 17 March 2013.

Clement, Oliver. "*The Plow That Broke the Plains* 1936 and *The River* 1937." DVD liner notes. Franklin, Tenn.: Naxos Rights International, 2007. Print.

Cochran, Daniel E. "State Agricultural Disparagement Statutes: Suing Chicken Little." *Third Year Paper*. Harvard Law School. N.d. Web. 8 July 2012.

"Coke Lore: Coke in the Movies." *The Coca-Cola Company*. N.d. Web. 28 June 2012.

Conklin, Beth. *Consuming Grief: Compassionate Cannibalism in an Amazonian Society*. Austin: U of Texas P, 2001. Print.

Cook, David A. *A History of Narrative Film*. 4th ed. New York: Norton, 2004. Print.

"Corbis Acquires Norm Marshall Group." *NMA Group News*. Norm Marshall & Associates. 10 January 2011. Web. 8 July 2012.

Counihan, Carole M. *The Anthropology of Food and Body: Gender, Meaning, and Power*. New York: Routledge, 1999. Print.

Counihan, Carole M. "Production, Reproduction, Food, and Women in Herbert Biberman's *Salt of the Earth* and Lourdes Portillo and Nina Serrano's *After the Earthquake*." *Reel Food: Essays on Food and Film*. Ed. Anne L. Bower. New York: Routledge, 2004. 167–80. Print.

Counihan, Carole, and Penny Van Esterik. "Introduction to the Second Edition." *Food and Culture: A Reader*. Ed. Carole Counihan and Penny Van Esterik. 2nd ed. New York: Routledge, 2008. 1–13. Print.

Crisp, Arthur H. "Anorexia Nervosa as Flight from Growth: Assessment and Treatment Based on the Model." *Handbook of Treatment for Eating Disorders*. Ed. David M. Garner and Paul E. Garfinkel. 2nd ed. New York: Guilford Press, 1997. Print.

Crofts, Stephen. "Concepts of National Cinema." *The Oxford Guide to Film Studies*. Ed. John Hill and Pamela Church Gibson. New York: Oxford UP, 1998. 285–94. Print.

Crofts, Stephen. "Reconceptualizing National Cinema/s." *Quarterly Review of Film and Video* 14:3 (1993): 49–67. Print.

Crystal, Billy. "Director's Commentary." *Mr. Saturday Night*. Santa Monica, Calif.: MGM/UA Home Entertainment, 2002. DVD.

Daniels, Anna. *Anorexia and Bulimia*. Hunt Valley, Md.: Time-Life Medical Video, 1996. VHS.

De Cordova, Richard. "Genre and Performance: An Overview." *Star Texts: Image and Performance in Film and Television*. Ed. Jeremy G. Butler. Detroit: Wayne State UP, 1991. 115–24. Print.

De Lauretis, Teresa. *Alice Doesn't: Feminism, Semiotics, Cinema*. Bloomington: Indiana UP, 1984. Print.

Denby, David. "Anxiety Tests: 'The Hurt Locker' and 'Food, Inc.'" *New Yorker* (29 June 2009): 84–85. Print.

Denning, Michael. *The Cultural Front: The Laboring of American Culture in the Twentieth Century.* New York: Verso, 1996. Print.

De Schutter, Olivier. "Summary: Report Submitted by the Special Rapporteur on the Right to Food." United Nations General Assembly. Human Rights Council. 20 December 2010. Print.

Dissanayake, Wimal. "Introduction: Nationhood, History, and Cinema: Reflections on the Asian Scene." *Colonialism and Nationalism in Asian Cinema.* Ed. Wimal Dissanayake. Bloomington: Indiana UP, 1994. ix–xxix. Print.

Doctorow, Cory. "'FLOW: For Love of Water.'" *Boingboing.* 7 April 2008. Web. 21 July 2012.

"DocuDays Q & A: 'Food Inc.'" *International Documentary Association.* 2010. Web. 23 July 2012.

Drake, Phillip. "Distribution and Marketing in Contemporary Hollywood." *The Contemporary Hollywood Film Industry.* Ed. Paul McDonald and Janet Wasko. Malden, Mass.: Blackwell, 2008. 63–82. Print.

Durand, Adam, and Nathan Runkle. *Fowl Play Movie.* Mercy for Animals. N.d. Web. 8 July 2012.

Ebert, Roger. "*Mysterious Skin.*" *Chicago Sun-Times.* 2 June 2005. Web. 29 July 2012.

"Eco-Farming Can Double Food Production in 10 Years, Says New UN Report." United Nations, Office of the High Commissioner for Human Rights. 8 March 2011. Print.

Edelstein, David. "*Bagdad Cafe.*" *Village Voice* (3 May 1988): 64. Print.

Egan, Timothy. "Apple Growers Bruised and Bitter after Alar Scare." *New York Times.* 9 July 1991. Web. 8 July 2012.

Elliott, Stuart. "Advertising's Big Four: It's Their World Now." *New York Times.* 31 March 2002. Web. 8 July 2012.

Elsaesser, Thomas. "Tales of Sound and Fury." *Monogram* 4 (1972): 2–15. Print.

Epstein, Rebecca L. "Appetite for Destruction: Gangster Food and Genre Convention in Quentin Tarantino's *Pulp Fiction.*" *Reel Food: Essays on Food and Film.* Ed. Anne L. Bower. New York: Routledge, 2004. 195–208. Print.

Ernst, Morris L., with Pare Lorentz. *Censored: The Private Life of the Movies.* New York: Cape & Smith, 1930. Print.

Fallon, Patricia, and Stephen A. Wonderlich. "Sexual Abuse and Other Forms of Trauma." *Handbook of Treatment for Eating Disorders.* Ed. David M. Garner and Paul E. Garfinkel. 2nd ed. New York: Guilford Press, 1997. Print.

"The Film." *The End of the Line.* N.d. Web. 21 July 2012.

Fitchen, Janet M. "Hunger, Malnutrition, and Poverty in the Contemporary United States." *Food and Culture: A Reader.* Ed. Carole Counihan and Penny van Esterik. New York: Routledge, 1997. 384–401. Print.

Fithian, John. "Comments by John Fithian: President and CEO, National Association of Theatre Owners." *NATO.* 13 March 2007. Web. 17 March 2013.

Flynn, Dan. "'Veggie Libel Laws' Still on Books." *Food Safety News.* 8 November 2009. Web. 17 March 2013.

"Food, Inc. Movie." *Monsanto.* N.d. Web. 12 July 2012.

"'Food, Inc.' Offers Troubling View of U.S. Food Industry." *Boston Herald.* 8 June 2009. Web. 8 July 2012.

"Fragile Harvest." *Bullfrog Films.* N.d. Web. 21 July 2012.

Freeman, Alma. "Get Real." *In Focus: A Publication of the National Association of Theatre Owners.* March 2005. Web. 19 July 2012.

Fried, Ellen J. "Food, Sex, and Power at the Dining Room Table in Zhang Yimou's *Raise the Red Lantern.*" *Reel Food: Essays on Food and Film.* Ed. Anne L. Bower. New York: Routledge, 2004, 129–46. Print.

Friedman, Lauren F. "Can You Stomach It? Filmmaker Examines Our 'Broken' Food Production System." *Philadelphia Daily News.* 15 June 2009. Web. 12 July 2012.

"Fruit Growers Pull Commercials to Protest Report by CBS on Alar." *New York Times.* 7 May 1989. Web. 12 July 2012.

Garcia, Jason. "Disney Sees Record Profit Amid Gains at Theme Parks, TV Channels." *Orlando Sentinel.* 10 November 2011. Web. 12 July 2012.

Gateward, Frances. "Introduction." *Seoul Searching: Culture and Identity in Contemporary Korean Cinema.* Ed. Frances Gateward. Albany: State U of New York P, 2007. 1–12. Print.

Gawande, Atul. "The Man Who Couldn't Stop Eating." *New Yorker* (9 July 2001): 74–75. Print.

Gianos, Phillip L. *Politics and Politicians in American Film.* Westport, Conn.: Praeger, 1998. Print.

Gidday, Katherine. *The Famine Within.* Los Angeles: Direct Cinema, 1990. Film.

"Glossary." *Brand Channel.* N.d. Web. 12 July 2012.

Golding, Shira. "Change: It's What's for Dinner: 'Food, Inc.' Takes on Agribusiness." *International Documentary Association.* 27 April 2010. Web. 12 July 2012.

Goldstein, Patrick. "'Avatar' Arouses Conservatives' Ire." *Los Angeles Times.* 5 January 2010. Web. 12 July 2012.

Grant, Barry Keith. *Film Genre: From Iconography to Ideology.* London: Wallflower, 2007. Print.

Grant, Barry Keith. "Introduction: Spokes in the Wheels." *John Ford's* Stagecoach. Ed. Barry Keith Grant. New York: Cambridge UP, 2003. 1–19. Print.

Greven, David. "Engorged with Desire: The Films of Alfred Hitchcock and the Gendered Politics of Eating." *Reel Food: Essays on Food and Film.* Ed. Anne L. Bower. New York: Routledge, 2004. 297–310. Print.

Harrington, Luke. "Food, Inc." *Movie Zeal.* 9 August 2009. Web. 12 July 2012.

Hartl, John. "Food Obsessions Simmer in South Korean Mystery." *Seattle Times*. 1 March 1996. Web. 10 July 2012.

Hartmann, Thom. *Unequal Protection: The Rise of Corporate Dominance and Theft of Human Rights*. New York: Rodale Books, 2004. Print.

Higson, Andrew. "The Concept of National Cinema." *Screen* 30:4 (1989): 36–47. Print.

Holm, D. K. "*Spellbound*: The Criterion Collection–Review." *DVD Journal*. N.d. Web. 1 January 2013.

Holt, Tom. "Could Lawsuits Be the Cure for Junk Science?" *American Council on Science and Health*. American Council on Science and Health, 1 April 1995. Web. 12 July 2012.

Hulme, Peter. "Introduction: The Cannibal Scene." *Cannibalism and the Colonial World*. Ed. Francis Barker, Peter Hulme, and Margaret Iversen. New York: Cambridge UP, 1998. 1–38. Print.

Humm, Maggie. *Feminism and Film*. Bloomington: Indiana UP, 1997. Print.

Hutchings, Peter. *The Horror Film*. Harlow, England: Pearson Longman, 2004. Print.

Hye-son, Shin. "Feminism Gaining Ground in New Novels and Movies." *Newsweek* (11 November 1995): 27–29. Print.

"Interview with Sarah Teale and Tom Simon." *Death on a Factory Farm*. Home Box Office. N.d. Web. 21 July 2012.

"Issues: The McLibel Trial." *McSpotlight*. N.d. Web. 21 July 2012.

Jackson, Dana L., and Laura L. Jackson. "Introduction." *The Farm as Natural Habitat: Reconnecting Food Systems with Ecosystems*. Ed. Dana L. Jackson and Laura L. Jackson. Washington, D.C.: Island Press, 2002. 1–10. Print.

Jacobs, Lea. "Industry Self-Regulation and the Problem of Textual Determination." *Controlling Hollywood: Censorship and Regulation in the Studio Era*. Ed. Matthew Bernstein. New Brunswick, N.J.: Rutgers UP, 1999. 87–101. Print.

James, David E. "Im Kwon-Taek: Korean National Cinema and Buddhism." *Film Quarterly* 54:3 (Spring 2001): 14–31. Print.

James, David E. "Preface." *Im Kwon-Taek: The Making of a Korean National Cinema*. Ed. David E. James and Kyung Hyun Kim. Detroit: Wayne State UP, 2002. 9–18. Print.

Jansen, Sue Curry. *Censorship: The Knot That Binds Power and Knowledge*. New York: Oxford UP, 1988. Print.

Joglekar, Yogini. "Images of Consumption in Jutta Brückner's *Years of Hunger*." *Reel Food: Essays on Food and Film*. Ed. Anne L. Bower. New York: Routledge, 2004. 181–92. Print.

Johnson, Randal, and Robert Stam, eds. *Brazilian Cinema*. Expanded ed. New York: Columbia UP, 1995. Print.

Johnston, Ruth D. "The Staging of the Bourgeois Imaginary in *The Cook, the Thief, His Wife, and Her Lover*." *Cinema Journal* 41:2 (2002): 19–40. Print.

Jones, Michael Owen. "Foreword." *Documenting Ourselves: Film, Video, and Culture* by Sharon R. Sherman. Lexington: UP of Kentucky, 1998. ix–xii. Print.

Jones, Michael Owen, Bruce Giuliano, and Roberta Krell. "Prologue." *Foodways and Eating Habits: Directions for Research.* Ed. Michael Owen Jones, Bruce Giuliano, and Roberta Krell. Los Angeles: California Folklore Society, 1983. vii–xii. Print.

Jones, Michael Owen, Bruce Giuliano, and Roberta Krell. "Resources and Methods." *Foodways and Eating Habits: Directions for Research.* Ed. Michael Owen Jones, Bruce Giuliano, and Roberta Krell. Los Angeles: California Folklore Society, 1983. 91–93. Print.

Jones, Michael Owen, Bruce Giuliano, and Roberta Krell. "The Sensory Domain." *Foodways and Eating Habits: Directions for Research.* Ed. Michael Owen Jones, Bruce Giuliano, and Roberta Krell. Los Angeles: California Folklore Society, 1983. 1–3. Print.

Kahana, Jonathan. *Intelligence Work: The Politics of American Documentary.* New York: Columbia UP, 2008. Print.

Kearney, Christine. "Film Aims to Expose Dangers in the U.S. Food Industry." *Reuters.* 9 June 2009. Web. 12 July 2012.

Kee, Joan. "Claiming Sites of Independence: Articulating Hysteria in Pak Ch'ol-su's *301/302.*" *positions* 9:2 (2001): 449–66. Print.

Keller, James R. *Food, Film and Culture: A Genre Study.* Jefferson, N.C.: McFarland, 2006. Print.

Kim, Kyung Hyun. *The Remasculinization of Korean Cinema.* Durham, N.C.: Duke UP, 2004. Print.

King, Geoff. *American Independent Cinema.* Bloomington: Indiana UP, 2005. Print.

Kittler, Pamela Goyan, and Kathryn P. Sucher. *Food and Culture.* 3rd ed. New York: Wadsworth. 2001. Print.

Koh, Hesung Chun. "Korean Women, Conflict, and Change: An Approach to Development Planning." *Korean Women: View from the Inner Room.* Ed. Laurel Kendell and Mark Peterson. New Haven, Conn.: East Rock Press, 1983. 159–74. Print.

Korr, Jeremy L., and Christine Broussard. "Challenges in the Interdisciplinary Teaching of Food and Foodways." *Food, Culture & Society: An International Journal of Multidisciplinary Research* 7:2 (Fall 2004): 147–59. Print.

LaSalle, Nick. "Pedophile's Acts Beget Long Arc of Suffering." *San Francisco Chronicle.* 27 May 2005. Web. 27 July 2012.

Lawrence, Amy. *Echo and Narcissus: Women's Voices in Classical Hollywood Cinema.* Berkeley: U of California P, 1991. Print.

"Leading Brand Appearances This Year: Product Placement in #1 Movies." *Brand Channel.* N.d. Web. 6 July 2012.

Lee, June J.H. "Discourses of Illness, Meanings of Modernity: A Gendered Construction of Songinbyong." *Under Construction: The Gendering of Mo-*

dernity, Class, and Consumption in the Republic of Korea. Ed. Laurel Kendall. Honolulu: U of Hawai'i P, 2002. 55–78. Print.

Lepore, Jill. *The Name of War: King Philip's War and the Origins of American Identity.* New York: Vintage, 1999. Print.

Levi-Strauss, Claude. *The Raw and the Cooked.* Trans. John and Doreen Weightman. New York: Harper & Row, 1969. Print.

Levy, Emanuel. *Cinema of Outsiders: The Rise of American Independent Film.* New York: New York UP, 1999. Print.

Lewis, Jon. *Hollywood v. Hardcore: How the Struggle Over Censorship Saved the Modern Film Industry.* New York: New York UP, 2002. Print.

Lewis, Randolph. *Emile de Antonio: Radical Filmmaker in Cold War America.* Madison: U of Wisconsin P, 2000. Print.

Lim, Dennis. "The Lost Boys." *Village Voice* (26 April 2005). Web. 27 July 2012.

Lim, Song Hwee. "Is the Trans in Transnational the Trans in Transgender?" *New Cinemas: Journal of Contemporary Film* 5:1 (2007): 38–52. Print.

Lockwood, Yvonne R. "Ethnic Foodways in Greater Cleveland." *Key Ingredients: Ohio by Food.* Columbus: Ohio Humanities Council, 2008. Print.

Long, Lucy. "Holiday Meals: Rituals of Family Tradition." *Dimensions of the Meal: Science, Culture, Business, and Art of Eating.* Ed. Herbert L. Meiselman. Gaithersburg, Md.: Aspen, 2000. 143–59. Print.

López, Kimberle S. *Latin American Novels of the Conquest: Reinventing the New World.* Columbia: U of Missouri P, 2002. Print.

Lorentz, Pare. *FDR's Moviemaker: Memoirs and Scripts.* Reno: U of Nevada P, 1992. Print.

Lorentz, Pare. *Lorentz on Film: Movies 1926–1941.* Norman: U of Oklahoma P, 1986. Print.

Malek, Alia. "Gitmo in the Heartland." *Nation.* 28 March 2011. Web. 12 July 2012.

Maltby, Richard. *Hollywood Cinema.* 2nd ed. Oxford: Blackwell, 2003. Print.

Manning, Jason. "Farm Aid." *The Eighties Club.* Tripod. N.d. Web. 12 July 2012.

Martinetti, Anne, and François Rivière. *La sauce était presque parfaite: 80 recettes d'après Alfred Hitchcock.* Paris: Cahier du Cinéma, 2008. Print.

"Mcdonald's Corp." *Business Week.* Bloomberg. N.d. Web. 12 July 2012.

McEnteer, James. *Shooting the Truth: The Rise of American Political Documentaries.* Westport, Conn.: Praeger, 2006. Print.

McFadden, Margaret H. "Gendering the Feast: Women, Spirituality, and Grace in Three Food Films." *Reel Food: Essays on Food and Film.* Ed. Anne L. Bower. New York: Routledge, 2004. 117–28. Print.

McGilligan, Patrick. *Alfred Hitchcock: A Life in Darkness and Light.* New York: Regan, 2003. Print.

Meehan, Eileen R. "Ancillary Markets—Television: From Challenge to Safe Haven." *The Contemporary Hollywood Film Industry.* Ed. Paul McDonald and Janet Wasko. Malden, Mass.: Blackwell, 2008. 106–19. Print.

Meiselman, Herbert L. "Introduction." *Dimensions of the Meal: The Science, Culture, Business, and Art of Eating.* Ed. Herbert L. Meiselman. Gaithersburg, Md.: Aspen Publishers, 2000. 1–4. Print.

Mintz, Sidney W. "Food and Diaspora." *Food, Culture & Society* 11:4 (2008): 510–21. Print.

Mintz, Sidney W. "Food and Eating: Some Persisting Questions." *Food Nations: Selling Taste in Consumer Societies.* Ed. Warren Belasco and Philip Scranton. New York: Routledge, 2002. 24–32. Print.

Mintz, Sidney W. *Tasting Food, Tasting Freedom.* Boston: Beacon, 1996. Print.

"MPAA: Contact Us." *Motion Picture Association of America.* N.d. Web. 14 July 2012.

Nestle, Marion. *Food Politics: How the Food Industry Influences Nutrition and Health.* Rev. ed. Berkeley: U of California P, 2007. Print.

Newitz, Annalee. *Pretend We're Dead: Capitalist Monsters in American Pop Culture.* Durham, N.C.: Duke UP, 2006. Print.

Newman, Tim. "Monday, October 26, 2009." *Food Culture Politics.* Blogspot. 26 October 2009. Web. 29 July 2012.

Nichols, John. "Don't Blame Farmers for Food Crisis." *Progressive Populist* (15 June 2008): 6. Print.

Ohi, Kevin. "Devouring Creation: Cannibalism, Sodomy, and the Scene of Analysis in *Suddenly Last Summer.*" *Cinema Journal* 38:3 (1999): 27–49. Print.

Orgeron, Devin Anthony, and Marsha Gabrielle Orgeron. "Eating Their Words: Consuming Class a la Chaplin and Keaton." *College Literature* 28:1 (Winter 2001): 84–104. Print.

Osborne, Lawrence. "Does Man Eat Man? The Cannibalism Controversy." *Lingua Franca* (April/May 1997): 28–38. Print.

Palley, Marian Lief. "Feminism in a Confucian Society: The Women's Movement in Korea." *Dangerous Women: Gender and Korean Nationalism.* Ed. Elaine H. Kim and Chungmoo Choi. New York: Routledge, 1998. Print.

Papazian, Gretchen. "Anorexia Envisioned: Mike Leigh's *Life Is Sweet,* Chul-Soo Park's *301/302,* and Todd Haynes's *Superstar.*" *Reel Food: Essays on Food and Film.* Ed. Anne L. Bower. New York: Routledge, 2004. 147–66. Print.

Park, Seung Hyun. "Korean Cinema after Liberation: Production, Identity, and Regulatory Trends." *Seoul Searching: Culture and Identity in Contemporary Korean Cinema.* Albany: State U of New York P, 2007. 15–35. Print.

Parkinson, Andrew. "Review: *Cannibal Ferox.*" *Eaten Alive! Italian Cannibal and Zombie Movies.* Ed. Jay Slater. London: Plexus, 2006. 161–63. Print.

Patel, Raj. *Stuffed and Starved: The Hidden Battle for the World Food System.* Brooklyn: Melville House Publishing, 2007. Print.

Peña, Richard. "*How Tasty Was My Little Frenchman.*" *Brazilian Cinema.* Expanded ed. Ed. Randal Johnson and Robert Stam. New York: Columbia UP, 1995. 191–99. Print.

"*People v. Durand.*" *NYCourts.* New York State Unified Court System. 5 June 2009. Web. 14 July 2012.

Petersen, Melody. "Farmers' Right to Sue Grows, Raising Debate on Food Safety." *New York Times.* 1 June 1999. Web. 12 July 2012.

Potter, Will. *Green Is the New Red: An Insider's Account of a Social Movement under Siege.* San Francisco: City Lights, 2011. Print.

The Public Relations of the Motion Picture Industry. New York: Department of Research and Education, Federal Council of the Churches of Christ in America. 1931. Print.

Quart, Barbara Koenig. *Women Directors: The Emergence of a New Cinema.* New York: Praeger, 1988. Print.

Rabben, Linda. *Brazil's Indians and the Onslaught of Civilization: The Yanomami and the Kayapó.* Seattle: U of Washington P, 2004. Print.

Rampton, Sheldon, and John Stauber. *Mad Cow U.S.A.* Monroe, Me.: Common Courage, 1997. Print.

Rampton, Sheldon, and John Stauber. "One Hundred Percent All Beef Baloney: Lessons from the Oprah Trial." *PR Watch.* Center for Media and Democracy. N.d. Web. 12 July 2012.

"Region 7 Concentrated Animal Feeding Operations (CAFOs)." *United States Environmental Protection Agency.* N.d. Web. 27 December 2012.

Reinholtz, Eric L. "Supper, Slapstick, and Social Class: Dinner as Machine in the Silent Films of Buster Keaton." *Reel Food: Essays on Food and Film.* Ed. Anne L. Bower. New York: Routledge, 2004. 267–80. Print.

Rocha, Glauber. "An Esthetic of Hunger." *Brazilian Cinema.* Expanded ed. Ed. Randal Johnson and Robert Stam. New York: Columbia UP, 1995. 69–71. Print.

Roscoe, Jane, and Craig Hight. *Faking It: Mock-Documentary and the Subversion of Factuality.* Manchester: Manchester UP, 2001. Print.

Rosenbaum, Jonathan. *Movie Wars: How Hollywood and the Media Conspire to Limit What Films We Can See.* Chicago: A Cappella Books, 2000. Print.

Rosenbaum, Jonathan. "Multinational Pest Control: Does American Cinema Still Exist?" *Film and Nationalism.* Ed. Alan Williams. New Brunswick, N.J.: Rutgers UP, 2002. 217–29. Print.

Ross, Steven J. *Working Class Hollywood: Silent Film and the Shaping of Class in America.* Princeton: Princeton UP, 1998. Print.

Rozzi, Fernando Ramirez, et al. "Cutmarked Human Remains Bearing Neandertal Features and Modern Human Remains Associated with the Aurignacian at Les Rois." *Journal of Anthropological Sciences* 87 (2009): 153–85. Print.

Ruby, Jay. "Out of Sync: The Cinema of Tim Asch." *Visual Anthropology Review* 11:1 (Spring 1995): 19–35. Print.

Rudick, Marilynne. "Targeting an Audience." *The Unfettered Press.* Ed. Hedley Burrell. Washington, D.C.: United States Information Agency, 1994. Web. 20 July 2012.

Sadlier, Darlene J. *Nelson Pereira dos Santos.* Chicago: U of Illinois P, 2003. Print.

Safe Food Inc. N.d. Web. 12 July 2012.

Santos, Marlisa. "'Leave the Gun; Take the Cannoli': Food and Family in the Modern American Mafia Film." *Reel Food: Essays on Food and Film.* Ed. Anne L. Bower. New York: Routledge, 2004. 209–18. Print.

Sauer, Abram. "Brandsploitation: A New Genre in Film." *Brand Channel.* 27 September 2004. Web. 12 July 2012.

Schatz, Thomas. *Hollywood Genres: Formulas, Filmmaking and the Studio System.* New York: Random House, 1981. Print.

Schulz, Ann. Interview by Diane E. Carson. 22 and 24 July 2009. Personal notes.

"Scientist: Cannibal Humans Ate Neanderthals into Extinction." *Fox News.* 19 May 2009. Web. 19 July 2012.

Scott, Allen J. "Hollywood in the Era of Globalization." *Yale Global Online.* Yale Center for the Study of Globalization. 29 November 2002. Web. 14 July 2012.

Seabrook, John. "Snacks for a Fat Planet." *New Yorker* (16 May 2011): 54–71. Print.

Severson, Kim. "Eat, Drink, Think, Change." *New York Times.* 7 June 2009. Web. 26 June 2009.

Severson, Kim. "Many Summer Internships Are Going Organic." *New York Times.* 24 May 2009. Web. 21 July 2012.

Sherman, Sharon R. *Documenting Ourselves: Film, Video, and Culture.* Lexington: UP of Kentucky, 1998. Print.

Shohat, Ella, and Robert Stam. *Unthinking Eurocentrism: Multiculturalism and the Media.* London: Routledge, 1994. Print.

Sieglhor, Ulrike. "New German Cinema." *The Oxford Guide to Film Studies.* Ed. John Hill and Pamela Church Gibson. New York: Oxford UP, 1988. 466–70. Print.

Silverman, Kaja. *The Acoustic Mirror: The Female Voice in Psychoanalysis and Cinema.* Bloomington: Indiana UP, 1988. Print.

Smelik, Anneke. *And the Mirror Cracked: Feminist Cinema and Film Theory.* New York: Palgrave, 1998. Print.

Sobo, Elisa J. "The Sweetness of Fat." *Food and Culture: A Reader.* Ed. Carole Counihan and Penny van Esterik. New York: Routledge, 1997. 256–71. Print.

"Spoiling for a Food Fight: Filmmaker Robert Kenner Discusses His Documentary 'Food, Inc.'" *Washington Post.* 14 June 2009. Web. 12 July 2012.

Spoto, Donald. *The Dark Side of Genius: The Life of Alfred Hitchcock.* New York: Da Capo, 1999. Print.

Spurlock, Morgan. *The Greatest Movie Ever Sold.* Sony Pictures Classics, 2011. Film.

Staiger, Janet. "Taboos and Totems: Cultural Meanings of *The Silence of the Lambs*." *Feminist Film Theory: A Reader.* Ed. Sue Thornton. New York: New York UP, 1999. 210–23. Print.

Stam, Robert. *Tropical Multiculturalism: A Comparative History of Race in Brazilian Cinema and Culture.* Durham, N.C.: Duke UP, 1997. Print.

Starr, Cecile. "*The Land.*" *Film Reference.* Adavmeg. N.d. Web. 12 July 2012.

"Statistics." *NATO Online.* National Association of Theatre Owners. N.d. Web. 19 July 2012.

Sterritt, David. "*Bagdad Cafe.*" *Christian Science Monitor* (24 June 1988): 22. Print.

Straus, Tamara. "'Food, Inc.': Documentary on Your Dinner." *San Francisco Chronicle.* 11 June 2009. Web. 12 July 2012.

Taylor, Greg. *Artists in the Audience: Cults, Camp, and American Film Criticism.* Princeton, N.J.: Princeton UP, 1999. Print.

Thomas, Kevin. "*301–302:* Dark, Witty, Delicious." *Los Angeles Times.* 3 May 1996. Web. 8 July 2001.

Thursby, Jacqueline S. *Foodways and Folklore: A Handbook.* Westport, Conn.: Greenwood, 2008. Print.

Tierney, Patrick. *Darkness in Eldorado: How Scientists and Journalists Devastated the Amazon.* New York: Norton, 2000. Print.

"TIME Flies Part 1." *Farm Policy Facts.* 1 June 2009. Web. 21 July 2012.

"TIME Flies Part 2." *Farm Policy Facts.* 2 June 2009. Web. 21 July 2012.

"TIME Flies Part 4." *Farm Policy Facts.* 7 June 2009. Web. 21 July 2012.

Toor, Amar. "Sony Posts $350 Million Loss in Q2 Earnings Report, Forecasts Full-Year Loss." *Engaget.* AOL Tech. 2 November 2011. Web. 12 July 2012.

"Top-Grossing MPAA Ratings 1995–2012." *The Numbers.* Nash Information Services. N.d. Web. 19 July 2012.

Tuleja, Tad. "Pumpkins." *Rooted in America: Foodlore of Popular Fruits and Vegetables.* Ed. David Scofield Wilson and Angus Kress Gillespie. Knoxville: U of Tennessee P, 1999. 142–65. Print.

Turan, Kenneth. "'FLOW: For Love of Water.'" *Los Angeles Times.* 12 September 2008. Web. 21 July 2012.

Turano, Rebecca. "Agricultural Disparagement Statutes: An Overview." *Penn State University.* N.d. Web. 12 July 2012.

Turner, Cristy G., and Jacqueline A. Turner. *Man Corn: Cannibalism and Violence in the Prehistoric American Southwest.* Salt Lake City: U of Utah P, 2011. Print.

Tzioumakis, Yannis. *American Independent Cinema: An Introduction.* New Brunswick, N.J.: Rutgers UP, 2006. Print.

United Nations. "General Assembly Adopts Resolution Recognizing Access to Clean Water, Sanitation as Human Right." *United Nations.* 28 July 2010. Web. 21 July 2012.

Vasey, Ruth. "Beyond Sex and Violence: 'Industry Policy' and the Regulation of Hollywood Movies, 1922–1939." *Controlling Hollywood: Censorship and Regulation in the Studio Era*. Ed. Matthew Bernstein. New Brunswick, N.J.: Rutgers UP, 1999. 102–29. Print.

Vasey, Ruth. *The World according to Hollywood, 1918–1939*. Madison: U of Wisconsin P, 1997. Print.

Walters, Barry. "Gluttony vs. Regurgitation." *San Francisco Examiner*. 3 May 1996. Web. 29 June 2012.

Wasko, Janet. *How Hollywood Works*. Thousand Oaks, Calif.: Sage, 2003. Print.

Waters, Alice. "Remarks at *Terra madre* Premiere, Telluride Film Festival." Notes by Diane E. Carson. Telluride, Colo., 5 September 2009. Personal notes.

Watson, James L., and Melissa L. Caldwell. "Introduction." *The Cultural Politics of Food and Eating: A Reader*. New York: Blackwell Publishing, 2005. 1–10. Print.

Watson, Kelly. "Discovering Cannibalism: The *Scenario* in *How Tasty Was My Little Frenchman*." Presentation delivered at Bowling Green State University, Bowling Green, Ohio. 23 February 2008.

Weber, Amy S. *Eating Disorders: The Inner Voice*. Cambridge: Cambridge Educational Videos, Cambridge Research Group, 2000. Film.

Weiner, Mark. "Consumer Culture and Participatory Democracy: The Story of Coca-Cola during World War II." *Food in the USA: A Reader*. Ed. Carole M. Counihan. New York: Routledge, 2002. 123–42. Print.

White, Michael. "John Ford and the Cinematic Meal." White City Cinema. WordPress. 30 June 2011. Web. 1 January 2013.

Williams, Raymond. *Raymond Williams on Television*. Ed. Alan O'Connor. New York: Routledge, 1989. Print.

Wilson, Ken. "Foreword." *Where Our Food Comes From: Retracing Nikolay Vavilov's Quest to End Famine* by Gary Paul Nabhan. Washington, D.C.: Island Press, 2009. xi–xxiii. Print.

Wood, Robin. *Hitchcock's Films Revisited*. Rev. ed. New York: Columbia UP, 2002. Print.

Wood, Robin. *Hollywood from Vietnam to Reagan . . . and Beyond*. New York: Columbia UP, 2003. Print.

Yoder, Don. "Folk Cookery." *Folklore and Folklife: An Introduction*. Chicago: U of Chicago P, 1972. 325–50. Print.

Young, Theodore Robert. "You Are What You Eat: *Tropicalismo* and *How Tasty Was My Little Frenchman*." *A Twice-Told Tale: Reinventing the Encounter in Iberian/Iberian American Literature and Film*. Ed. Santiago Juan-Navarro and Theodore Robert Young. Newark: U of Delaware P, 2001. Print.

Zacharek, Stephanie. "*Munich.*" *Salon.* 23 December 2005. Web. 1 January 2013.

Zacharek, Stephanie. "*Mysterious Skin.*" *Salon.* 17 June 2005. Web. 27 July 2012.

Zimmerman, Steve, and Ken Weiss. *Food in the Movies.* Jefferson, N.C.: McFarland, 2005. Print.

INDEX

www.ingramcontent.com/pod-product-compliance
Lightning Source LLC
LaVergne TN
LVHW020431080826
844660LV00034B/1385

* 9 7 8 0 8 1 4 3 3 4 3 1 7 *